Peculiar

Uncertain

Two Egg

Peculiar, Uncertain & Two Egg

The Unusual Origins of More Than 3,000
American Place Names

Don Blevins

CUMBERLAND HOUSE
NASHVILLE, TENNESSEE

Published by Cumberland House Publishing, Inc., 431 Harding Industrial Drive, Nashville, TN 37211

Cover design: Unlikely Suburban Design
Cover art: Dan Brawner
Text design: Mary Sanford

Library of Congress Cataloging-in-Publication Data
Blevins, Don, 1933–
    Peculiar, Uncertain, and Two Egg : the unusual origins of more than
3,000 American place names / Don Blevins.
        p. cm.
    ISBN 1-58182-094-1 (alk. paper)
        1. Names, Geographical--United States. 2. Cities and towns--
United States. 3. United States--History, Local. I. Title.

E155 .B57 2000
917'.001'4--dc21

                                                          00-027923

Printed in the United States of America
1 2 3 4 5 6 7—05 04 03 02 01 00

Contents

Preface

Several years ago, while searching through the U.S. Postal Service tome called the *ZIP Code Directory* for an address, I noticed place names that defied logic as community monikers. I addressed the letter at hand, put it in the mail, and set the ZIP code book aside.

What had attracted my attention never left my thoughts, though. Some time later I picked up the directory and scanned several of those names. Out of curiosity I sent letters to the postmasters of selected ZIP codes. Answers to those few queries were the beginning of what has become an ongoing research of American communities with unusual names.

While some of the replies I received explained that the ZIP codes questioned were located at shopping malls, resorts, and other special entities, many were actual place names. The latter responses whetted my appetite to find out more: What brought about these unusual names? What events were in play at the moment to bring about such community monikers?

The next step in my research was scanning state maps in my trusty encyclopedia. As encyclopedias are understandably limited by space, the number of sites gleaned from this source was not satisfactory. I wrote to the travel agencies of each state and secured maps from those offices. After delving over each map, I had a long list of names on which to follow up. I contacted hundreds of city halls, seeking answers. Sometimes the search was successful, other times it wasn't.

On occasion, city authorities were unable to help. Sometimes they didn't have the information, but steered me to sources that might: local unofficial historians, other offices, etc. When those founts of information ran dry, my next inquiries led me to county seats. From there I went to local libraries, historical societies, state historical and record centers, federal agencies and offices, museums, chambers of commerce, and any other sources that emerged. I sometimes tried the postmasters again, but I found that the problem with querying postmasters is that many of the communities were too small to have post offices.

One of my final recourses was other books that had been published on this same subject. There were a few, but none that concentrated solely on unusual community names. Although I wanted my book to be as fresh and untainted by other commercial publications as possible, I believe this is a normal and understandable route to follow. There were times I used county and family publications with some success, but these usually were published for historical and personal reasons, rather than commercial.

With only the rarest of exceptions, my queries were answered with courtesy and true interest, sometimes with humor, but always with encouragement. People sent family histories, newspaper clippings, personal letters, and if someone to whom I had been referred didn't have an answer, they would often send me to someone who did. To those people and entities listed in the sources section at the end of this book, I owe a deep and profound appreciation. Without them, my research would have been even more difficult and time consuming, or in many cases virtually impossible.

In compiling the data for this book, I tried as much as possible to use certain constants. For example, I might show a place as being a city, a town, or simply a village or hamlet. The community status was less important in this instance than its origin. Also, I placed no criteria on population. A spot might have one resident or one million. That, too, was less important than the name. When there are such enticing monikers as Monkeys Eyebrow and Hanging Dog, Zigzag and Uncertain, the population and community status become irrelevant. Nothing, Arizona, when I found it, had only four residents.

While gathering data on hundreds of community names, I learned that odd titles were not restricted to any particular section of the country. Unusual names were spread out from coast to coast, border to border. I did notice, however, that the Upper New England states had fewer fanciful town names as a rule than other sections of the United States. Without delving into demographic philosophies, I attributed this fact to there simply being fewer towns in those states. While there are several unique tags (Woodtick and Bingo, to name a couple), such are few and far between.

The sparseness of these towns aside, I believe the early Puritan influence might have limited the designation of frivolous and nonsensical place names. Also, this being the oldest region of the country, many settlers brought names from their homelands and placed them on what would one day become American soil. As people moved south and west, away from Puritan persuasion, and where greater immigrant influences occurred, happenstance, events, and plain old folly began playing key roles in the christening of community names. Regardless of cause and effect, the names were assigned to communities for reasons that were sound, or reasonably so, at the time.

This book covers communities in forty-nine of America's fifty states. Hawaii is not included. If there is a paradise on earth, the Aloha State is it. Understandably, though, towns with names like Numila, Poipu, and Kaaawa, while beautiful and melodious, do not fit into the theme of the contents of this book.

The maps included for each state show only the approximate locations of the communities listed. It would be impossible to denote the exact spot on a state map where some of these sites are situated. Shortage of space and exact designation within a county are two reasons why such preciseness is out of the question. Another handicap is that some states simply have too many communities to adequately place on the state map.

When I first become serious about publishing a collection of unusual American community names, I had in mind a book that would be read and enjoyed, used in trivia games, and put in the car and perused while traveling or on vacation. I hope it will become a useful geographical tool, a lure from the monotonous interstate onto the back roads of America.

There are many, many communities out there for which I was unable to secure the source of their names. The data included in this book for the sites listed is the most reliable I could muster. Possibly there are other explanations for a particular name origin, or other towns I wasn't able to include because I couldn't find enough information for them. I would appreciate hearing from anyone having such information. Please write to me in care of Cumberland House Publishing, 431 Harding Industrial Drive, Nashville, Tennessee 37211.

In the meantime, read the book for its history and enjoy the inventive and tenacious American spirit that is demonstrated in many of these interesting names. Most of all, realize that what is contained in this book is a part of our heritage, a legacy passed on to us by our pioneering ancestors. It is one of the threads that make up the tapestry of what we call the United States.

Don Blevins
San Marcos, Texas

Alabama

THE HEART OF DIXIE

N

Normal
Lily Flagg   Paint Rock

Red Bay   Taint Much   Chigger Hill
                                           Red Apple   Fyffe
                                           Hustleville

Brilliant   Battle Ground   Scant City
                                          Arab   Gallant
                                               Ball Play

                                        Remlap

                                                    Rabbit Town

Blowhorn   Warrior
                    Banner

Reform   Coaling
Coal Fire
Lumbbub   Alabaster

                                Fixico
                                                    Standing Rock

                                          Cowpens

                                       Ourtown
                                                     Bottle
                              Eclectic
Intercourse   La Place
                                       Warrior Stand
             Alfalfa   Creek Stand
             Octagon   Srata   Brickyard
             Half Acre Awin
                     Sunny South   Trickem   Three Notch
                                              Suspension
Fail   Lower Peach Tree   Blues Old Stand
                        Pine Apple   Smut Eye
     Tattlersville   Coy
                   Corduroy   Shackleville   Pronto   Boot Hill
                                    Burnout
                                    Black Rock
                    Burnt Corn
                    Scratch Ankle
Bigbee   Rocky Head   Screamer
Vinegar Bend   Bermuda   Ino   Graball

                              Loadago

             Canoe   Wing   Florala

Whistler
Magazine
Seven Hills

ALABASTER: Shelby County. This city could have been named for the lime produced in the area; however, there are questions about this origin. For many years the site was covered with a fine, powdery white dust, apparently from the lime pits, that gave it the appearance of alabaster.

ALFALFA: Marengo County. This small town had at least two previous monikers, Van Doren and Eddins Station, but is called Alafalfa for the type of hay cultivated there.

ARAB: Marshall County. The names of many American communities came about through errors in transcription. Such is the case with Arab. Originally named for Arad Thompson, son of a prominent settler, the handle was inadvertently changed to Arab when the post office designation was approved.

AWIN: Wilcox County. As with Arab, this community tag also came about through a postal official's goof. The Post Office Department asked a Mr. Williams, the site's first postmaster, to submit a name for the village. Williams asked several residents for suggestions and recorded their responses. From this record, the people selected a name. Williams noted "A win" by the favored choice before he forwarded the list to postal officials. Mistaking the annotation as the name selected, the town was recorded as Awin, by which it is still known to this day.

BALL PLAY: Etowah County. The community designation comes from the fact that in early days Indians played a form of ball similar to lacrosse.

BANNER: Jefferson County. The town was so christened because it was considered the most successful (banner) coal mining site of the Pratt Consolidated Coal Company, producing more than two thousand tons of coal daily.

BATTLE GROUND: Cullman County. Relates to a Civil War battle that took place here in 1863 between the Confederate forces of General Nathan B. Forrest, and the Union soldiers under command of Colonel Abel Streight.

BERMUDA: Conecuh County. Refers to a new hybrid of grass, known as "Bermuda," which was tested on a nearby five-acre tract of land.

BIGBEE: Washington County. This is a shortened form of the Tombigbee River, for which the town was christened.

BLACK ROCK: Crenshaw County. Ed Turner moved into this area in 1856 and later donated land for the Primitive Baptist Church. He supposedly tagged the small village for a large black rock he discovered on the site.

4

BLOWHORN: Lamar County. Little of this hamlet remains, but it acquired its moniker from the fact that it used to attract avid fox-hunters, who would "blow their horns" to signal the dogs.

BLUES OLD STAND: Bullock County. Salutes former store owner Mr. Blue.

BOOT HILL: Barbour County. This is a new village, name-wise. As the story goes, some time back a Coca-Cola salesman came through and asked a local merchant if he could display a sign advertising his product, along with an indication of the village name. The merchant agreed, but at the time advised the salesman that the spot had no name. The salesman suggested the merchant christen the locale. The storekeeper, being an avid fan of the television series *Gunsmoke,* liked the name Boot Hill, for the cemetery shown in the long-running western.

BOTTLE: Lee County. This odd label comes from the fact that there was once a large sign here, used as an advertisement, in the shape of a cola bottle.

BRICKYARD: Russell County. The site where bricks were once made from clay taken from the Chattahoochee River.

BRILLIANT: Marion County. To avoid the term "diamond," a common nickname for coal, residents chose this title for their mining community.

BURNOUT: Crenshaw County. This little village was established long before the Civil War, and was at the time known as Host, the exact origin of that name unknown. Burnout is said to come from one of two sources, each with a common basis. The origin could relate to the time slaves rebelled against their masters and burned down homes and farm buildings, or from the simple fact that several homes once burned at some particular time.

BURNT CORN: Monroe County. When settlers moved to this location, they found large quantities of burned Indian corn (maize). Whether the corn was burned to prevent settlers from using it, or was part of an Indian ritual, is unknown.

CANOE: Escambia County. Local sources contend this small hamlet was named by Andrew J. Hall in the mid-1860s, and that he took the name from Canoe Creek. The stream had been tagged earlier by Indians, probably because that was their mode of transportation.

CHIGGER HILL: DeKalb County. In the summer of 1918, a revival took place here and the site was chosen for a church. Trying to decide on a name for the church, the attendees were constantly annoyed by a horde of chiggers. This served as inspiration for the name of the holy place, which was later adopted by the community.

COAL FIRE: Pickens County. In early days, some travelers heading west stopped at this site and since it was a cold, wintry night, built a fire. One of the men commented that that was the "coldest fire" he had ever warmed by. From this comment came the name of the community, with "cold" being changed to "coal," for whatever reason.

COALING: Tuscaloosa County. Site first known as Clements Depot. The first coal mine opened here in 1876, and the name depicts a coal mining operation.

CORDUROY: Monroe County. So named because when heavy rains hit the area, logs had to be placed on roads to make them passable. The logs gave the roads a "corduroy" look.

COWPENS: Tallapoosa County. Tradition has it that this town received its name from the cattle pens erected here in early days on the road between Goldville and Alexander City.

COY: Wilcox County. Family name.

CREEK STAND: Macon County. Almost certain to refer to a Creek Indian village once located here. However, some believe the title came about because this is where the Creeks took a stand against military forces of the United States during the War of 1812.

ECLECTIC: Elmore County. The community was dubbed with this unusual name by M. L. Fielder. It seems Fielder had attended school "up North," and had taken an "eclectic" course of study. He felt the name represented his home well, being as the little community reflected everything that was "best."

FAIL: Choctaw County. Named in 1836 for Alfred Fail, a settler.

FIXICO: Coosa County. Honors an Indian chief.

FLORALA: Covington County. Formerly known as Lake City and Lake View. Renamed Florala in June 1891 due to its location one mile north of the Florida state line.

FYFFE: DeKalb County. A citizen by the name of Ayes is said to have given the community its designation, intending it to be for the musical instrument, but with a unique spelling.

GALLANT: Etowah County. Named for John Gallant, a settler.

GRABALL: Henry County. Originally known as Harts Cross Roads, then as Hudspeths Cross Roads. Tradition as to the current name goes back to the time when a store sold whiskey and served as a gathering place for gamblers of all types. It seems that on one occasion, during a cockfight, law enforcement officials decided to pay spectators a surprise visit. Confusion abounded and one gambler yelled, "Grab all the stakes and run!" Ever since that memorable event, the village has been known as Graball.

HALF ACRE: Marengo County. As lore has it, a survey of the state was conducted many years ago, with two parties starting in the northern and southern sections at the same time. When the surveyors later met they discovered, to their dismay, that they had made an error of one-half acre. They called the error Hell's Half Acre. Later, when a community was established on the spot, the residents dropped the first word of the name.

HUSTLEVILLE: Marshall County. Christened for the industry and drive of the community's inhabitants.

INO: Coffee County. When this little spot had reached substantial size and warranted a name, residents gathered to select one. A resident kept interrupting, "I know what we should call it! I know!" While his remarks were ignored, his expression wasn't. When no one else could come up with an acceptable name, the individual's "I know" became Ino.

INTERCOURSE: Sumter County. Some residents call this spot Siloan, for the Siloan Baptist Church. Others refer to it as Sandtuck, for the sandy soil hereabout. But the name it officially goes by came about because of its location at an important crossroads, which served as a connecting point for several rural communities. In other words, this spot was the center for "intercourse"—communications and trade among the people.

LA PLACE: Macon County. By tradition, this handle was given when an early settler chose the spot as his new home, expressing in words, "This is the place."

LILY FLAGG: Madison County. Pays tribute to a Jersey cow owned by General Samuel H. Moore. The cow broke the world's record at the Columbia Exposition in Chicago in 1892, for the most butter produced.

LOANAGO: Covington County. First settled in 1819, the hamlet acquired its designation from the early practice of wagons that would stop in front of the local store and post office and "load and go" with their merchandise and mail.

LOWER PEACH TREE: Wilcox County. History states that this label was derived from the peach orchard maintained by a United States agent named Hawkins. Two bushels of peach stones were shipped to the agent in 1800 for distribution to Indians in hopes they would plant the stones and market the fruit from the trees. There was, according to tradition, also an Upper Peach Tree, the citizens of which changed the name to Clifton. An attempt was made to change the name of Lower Peach Tree to Stabler, but citizens rebelled in such outrage that the idea was quickly dropped.

LUMBBUB: Pickens County. The community took its name from a creek that, in turn, acquired its name from the Choctaw Indians.

The word means "warm," and apparently expresses characteristics of the water.

MAGAZINE: Mobile County. So named because the site served as an ammunition storage area (magazine) for Confederate troops during the Civil War. There is a rather interesting history behind this predominantly black community. Two years before the outbreak of the Civil War, a slave ship from the Gold Coast (now Ghana) of Africa, destined for a nearby slave market, landed near here, but only eight slaves survived the dreadful trip. Those eight escaped from the ship, made their way to this site, and established a colony. Today's residents are, for the most part, descendants of those original eight.

NORMAL: Madison County. This is the site of the post office for the Alabama State Normal School.

OCTAGON: Marengo County. There was once an eight-sided temple here known as Bethlehem Church. The community was named for the odd-shaped structure.

OURTOWN: Tallapoosa County. This community was founded in 1913, and by tradition the name came about when several investors gathered to select a label for the site. A member of the group, John S. Jones, supposedly stood up and gave a vibrant speech about, ". . . not your town! Not my town! But it is our town!"

PAINT ROCK: Jackson County. Originally known as Camden, the handle was changed in 1876, for Paint Rock River. The stream was given its name by Cherokee Indians and was so christened due to a large variegated rock that hung out over the river.

PINE APPLE: Wilcox County. There are several versions as to the origin of this unique name. One is that the pineapple is a symbol of friendliness; ergo, residents applied it to their settlement. Another source says that a northern visitor to the community crowned the name from the numerous pine burrs in the vicinity that resembled pineapples. Yet another tradition exists that a settler once had an apple cider mill located in a grove of pine trees; thus, the name. The most accepted version is simply that a resident returned from a trip, and brought with him a pineapple. Since this was the first time citizens of the community had ever seen the delicious fruit, they decided to name their town Pine Apple. While Pine Apple certainly qualifies for the unusual name category, the former designation of the small site is just as intriguing: Skillet Lid.

PRONTO: Pike County. Originally known as Clay Hill. The present name supposedly came about when the agent for the Alabama Midland Railroad, upon being asked when the train was due, always responded, "It will be here, pronto."

RABBIT TOWN: Calhoun County. First christened Egypt, the current title has nothing to do with the animal, instead honoring Rabbit, an Indian who once owned property in the vicinity.

RED APPLE: Marshall County. Named for an apple orchard that John Oulan had here in the 1880s.

RED BAY: Franklin County. First called Vincents Cross Roads, it was renamed in 1903, for the bay flower that grew along Big Bear Creek.

REFORM: Pickens County. In 1819, the year Alabama was admitted to the Union, there existed on this spot a small settlement recognized for its lack of law and order. Among the group of wild frontiersmen appeared one Lorenzo Dow, a Methodist missionary with grand ideas about saving the soul of this den of iniquity. The settlers were not receptive to his preaching, however, and he soon decided to ply his talents elsewhere. As Dow dejectedly rode away from the community, one resident asked if he could suggest a name for their home. Looking around disgustedly, the minister roared, "Reform!" and rode off. There is no record that Dow ever returned, but the name stuck.

REMLAP: Blount County. The Palmers were early settlers in this region. The head of the clan was Solomon Palmer, who settled in Red Valley. One son, Perry, resettled in Jefferson County and established Palmer's Station, now known as Palmer. Another son, James, moved to this location and set up a village. Since Palmer had already been used as a place name, James simply reversed the spelling of the name and came up with Remlap.

ROCKY HEAD: Dale County. This village was first situated on the crest of a rocky hill, three miles south. The town was moved shortly after the Civil War and named for the natural formation of its former site.

SCANT CITY: Marshall County. Some say this village acquired its name from Governor "Big Jim" Folsom, who referred to the locale as "scant a city," with *scant* being defined as "very small." But the general belief is that the moniker goes back farther than the former governor, to the prohibition era. Bootleggers hereabout purchased barrels of whiskey from moonshiners and divided their cache into thousands of twelve-ounce bottles, commonly known as "scant pints." It is from this illegal trade in booze that many opine the name for the community evolved.

SCRATCH ANKLE: Monroe County. There are at least two versions as to how this community was left with its picturesque label. One origin has it that it comes from Scratch Ankle School. The school took its name from the fact that it was located on the side of a hill, and when it rained, animals gathered under the open end of the building. Being an old country structure, the floors were not sealed and large cracks were plainly visible between the boards. Consequently, fleas and other small pests on the animals escaped and entered the building through the floor, causing the children sitting at their desks to spend a lot of time "scratching their ankles." The second version contends that horses and cows were penned near the railroad tracks and when logging crews passed by, they noticed that the people were always "scratching their ankles" because of the bites from the fleas and flies swarming around the animals.

9

SCREAMER: Henry County. At least two versions exist for the origin of this name. One has it that in early days, Indians gathered here for their annual "corn dance." As festivities progressed, they became intoxicated to such an extent that they would "scream," the noise being heard for miles. The second tenet is that residents waiting for daily steamboats spent their time in a tavern. When the boat arrived at the dock, the boatman would "scream" for passengers to come to the landing.

SEVEN HILLS: Mobile County. More than likely the hamlet tag describes the surrounding terrain, although some believe the name came from the "seven hills of Rome."

SHACKLEVILLE: Butler County. This spot was once the location of a convict labor camp. The community designation came from the time convicts were "shackled" when they worked in fields or on roads.

SMUT EYE: Bullock County. Few community names are more unusual than this. One rendering is that in early days, a blacksmith by the name of Pope had a shop here. The comment was often made that "you get smut in your eyes when you pass Pope's shop." Some contend the village name came from the fact that the blacksmith himself was always covered with smut, from the smoke blown hither and yon by the bellows, and that most of the time all that could be seen of Pope were his eyes. The tradition that makes one raise an eyebrow revolves around the origin coming from a similar settlement in Coffee County. The settlement was dominated by a sawmill, the employees of which worked their hard six-day week, then went to town on Saturday night to whoop it up. Fights and black eyes were so common that the entire community was termed "Smut Eye."

STANDING ROCK: Chambers County. Indian lore is at the root of this town name. In the nineteenth century, when Indians were rounded up and headed west along the infamous "Trail of Tears," some local Indians were involved in the resettlement. Before departing, they supposedly placed this rock on the site and warned residents that if the rock was ever moved, they (the Indians) would return to haunt the community.

STRATA: Montgomery County. This is a term referring to layers of sedimentary rock. The town is located adjacent to Strata Ridge, from which it acquired its title.

SUNNY SOUTH: Wilcox County. In the early 1800s, people in this region of the state were dependent upon Alabama River steamboats for their chief means of transportation. One of the steamboats was called *The Sunny South*. An accident caused the boat to explode near the landing at Lower Peach Tree. A member of the crew later organized a school there and named it the Sunny South School, in commemoration of the boat. In 1888, when the Mobile and Birmingham Railroad came through here, Miss C. O. Carmichael donated land for the depot. She was given the honor of christening the new village and chose Sunny South.

SUSPENSION: Bullock County. This little village dates back to before 1855. The Girard Railroad Company, later known as the Mobile and Girard Railroad Company, initiated construction of the community but ran out of money before the project could be completed. The town was named for the fact that the operation had to be "suspended" until the company could sell more bonds.

TAINT MUCH: Marshall County. As chronicled, a man by the name of Kluxie Mann purchased some land here and, after looking around, expressed the sentiment that the land "'Tain't much, but hit's mine."

TATTLERSVILLE: Clarke County. As stories go, early residents of this site were not very well liked by neighbors, having bad reputations as rumor-mongers and "tattlers."

THREE NOTCH: Bullock County. History states that this name was derived from Three Notch Road, with "Road" being dropped in 1921. In 1823, General Andrew Jackson supervised the building of a road in the area and soldiers marked the right of way through the dense forest by cutting "three notches" on the larger trees.

TRICKEM: Lowndes County. This is a case where the name has no relation to the spelling. Some time back, three area communities sought a site for Mount Giliard Church, and this spot was selected. The three-community church was often referred to as the "Tri-Com" church, which was eventually corrupted into Trickem.

VINEGAR BEND: Washington County. Legend has it that a large sawmill once operated on the site of what is now Vinegar Bend. The company owning the mill strictly forbade bringing liquor to or drinking on the premises. Not to be outdone, moonshiners smuggled in alcoholic spirits, thus satisfying the workers as well as earning a nice profit for themselves. Risk was involved, but it was minimal. Whenever a person carrying a jar was questioned by a company guard, the response most often given was that the receptacle contained vinegar. So frequently was this answer given that the place became known as Vinegar Bend.

WARRIOR: Jefferson County. Taken from the name of a river in Alabama, which is also known as the Black Warrior. The stream is just as renowned by its Indian name, Tuscaloosa.

WARRIOR STAND: Macon County. This community name came about from the time an Indian village existed here, and that the Indians took a "stand" against military forces during the Creek War, 1813–1814.

WHISTLER: Mobile County. No artistry involved in this title, having come from the fact that a train engineer blew his whistle every day as he passed a group of surveyors working the area.

WING: Covington County. Salutes Mr. Wing, manager of the Simpson Lumber Company, once located here.

Alaska

The Last Frontier

Candle

Mary's Igloo

Rampart

Poorman
Creek

Chicken

Dime Landing

Dot Lake

Holy Cross

Red Devil
Sleetmute

Nightmute

Eek

Goodnews Bay

Salt
Chuck

False Pass

N

CANDLE: Named for Candle Creek, which derived its tag from a highly combustible shrub growing along its banks. Candle, once a gold mining community of 20,000 inhabitants, is today populated by less than three dozen people.

CHICKEN: One source for this community name states that it came from a creek, where miners found gold nuggets the size of chicken feed. Another basis for the moniker is that early miners spied a number of unusual-looking birds hereabout that resembled the grouse. The miners had a hard time pronouncing the bird's name (ptarmigan), so they simply called it "chicken."

DIME LANDING: Refers to Dime Creek, which acquired its title from early miners because each pan of diggings produced barely a "dime's worth of gold."

DOT LAKE: Named for the body of water, which was apparently a reference to its small size.

EEK: This label brings to mind scenes from some early comic strip or old movie of a woman standing on a chair screaming at a mouse. But in Alaska, rodents play no part in Eek. An earlier Russian mission site, the name comes from the Eskimo word *eet*, meaning "the two eyes." A nearby stream has the same name, but significance of the term is unknown.

FALSE PASS: This is an early English moniker for Isanotski Strait, and was so named because the strait was thought impassable at the northern end, which was a "false" concept.

GOODNEWS: This is a translation of the Russian name given the bay in 1818. The reason for the name is not known, but it apparently stems from the receipt of welcome news. To validate the appropriateness of its designation, platinum was discovered in the area in 1927.

HOLY CROSS: Originally called Koserefski, a Russian name, it was changed to Holy Cross in 1912, in recognition of a Jesuit mission located at the site since 1886.

MARYS IGLOO: In 1900, gold prospectors traversed the Kuzitrin River by steamboat and landed at a small Eskimo village at the end of the boat's run. Further water travel had to be done by barge or other flat-bottomed boats. An Eskimo woman in the little village always had her door open to weary and hungry travelers, and any time of the day or night food and coffee were available. Miners started referring to the settlement as Mary's house, or igloo, the Eskimo name for shelter.

NIGHTMUTE: The first syllable has been variously recorded as nicht, nigh, and nigt. *Mute* is an Eskimo word meaning "people." It would appear the word means "night people," but there is no valid substantiation for this.

POORMAN CREEK: A family name.

RAMPART: Another gold rush city. Rampart was established in 1896 and two years later had a population of 1,500, but today has only about fifty residents. Founders of the community christened it for the high-banked (rampart-like) canyon of the nearby Yukon River.

RED DEVIL: Remembers the Red Devil Mercury Mine.

SALT CHUCK: This is an Indian term and means "salt water." It was tagged for its location on Kasaan Bay.

SLEETMUTE: Contrary to general first impressions, the name of the village has nothing to do with silent, frozen drops of water. The title translates to "whetstone people," but its origin is unknown.

Arizona
THE GRAND CANYON STATE

AJO: Pima County. Pronounced "ah-ho," this is Spanish for "garlic." The city received its tag from the mountains. Until fairly recently, it was assumed the mountains were christened for the ajo lily, which actually tastes like onion. However, a more recent and generally accepted version is that the name is from the Indian *au'-auho*, which means "paint." The mountains were named by the Spanish because in early times Papago Indians mined colored ore here, which they used as pigment in their paints.

ALI AK SHIN: Pima County. This is a translation from the Papago language and means "little mouth wash." Appropriately described, the village is located at the small mouth of a wash (a ravine or ground indentation eroded by water).

ALLAH: Maricopa County. A man named Brill owned a ranch that he called Garden of Allah, because it seemed descriptive of a novel popular at the time by that name. When a railroad station was established on the ranch, it took the name Allah.

AMERICAN FLAG: Pinal County. In the late 1870s, Isaac Lorraine started a mining operation in the area. Apparently in a patriotic mood, he named it the American Flag Mine. Within three years a sufficient number of people had moved into the vicinity to warrant a post office, which, when established, took the name of the mine.

BIG BUG: Yavapai County. In 1863, the first miners entered this area and came face-to-face with a horde of large, dark brown, beetle-like bugs, about the size of walnuts. They named a nearby creek Big Bug, in honor of their hosts. Later, a mining community was established near the stream and was also called Big Bug. From information available, the invasion of civilization didn't scare off the bugs; they are still plentiful in the area.

BLACK DIAMOND: Cochise County. This post office was named for the black silver ore found at the nearby Black Diamond Mine. The town took the same title.

BLUE: Greenlee County. This settlement was originally known as Whittum. The local postmaster, desiring more recognition for the community, circulated a petition to have the name changed to Blue, for the Blue River. He surmised that everyone knew where the Blue River was, while outside of the local gentry, Whittum was virtually a nonentity.

BULLHEAD CITY: Mohave County. Relates to a rock formation called Bullhead Rock, which now is almost entirely covered by the waters of the backed-up Davis Dam.

BUMBLE BEE: Yavapai County. This town is now all but abandoned. When prospectors came onto the site in 1863, they found a large supply of honey in a bumblebee nest situated in the cliffs along a creek. When they attempted to retrieve the sweet nectar, the bees reacted as they always do. The nearby stream served as a temporary refuse and the prospectors labeled the water Bumble Bee Creek. Later, when a post office was established, it took the name Bumble Bee.

CANE BEDS: Mohave County. Three years after the end of the Civil War, a colony of Mormons moved into this area and named their settlement Cane Beds, for the wide expanse of wild cane growing here. The former title by which the area was known is much more intriguing: Virgin Bottom.

CAREFREE: Maricopa County. Remembers the Carefree Development Corporation, developer of the community.

CHLORIDE: Mohave County. Relates to the type of silver ore found in the region.

CHRISTMAS: Gila County. In 1902, George Chittenden, with political influence, petitioned Congress to change the boundaries of the territorial lands of the San Carlos Indian Reservation, which would allow certain land to be opened for the mining of copper. When the bill came up for a vote, it was passed, and Chittenden received the news on Christmas Day, which also happened to be his birthday. When a community and a post office were set up in the area, they were named for Chittenden's lucky day.

CONGRESS: Yavapai County. For the Congress Mine.

CONSTELLATION: Yavapai County. For the Constellation Mine.

CORK: Graham County. An Irishman christened this community for his former home, County Cork.

CORNFIELD: Apache County. An appropriate and descriptive name, since Navajo Indians produce large corn crops here.

CORNVILLE: Yavapai County. Unlike the preceding community of Cornfield, this settlement name is neither appropriate nor descriptive. As a community grew on this site, residents requested it be named Coaneville, for the pioneering Coane family. Somewhere along the line an error arose, because the approved name returned by the Post Office Department was Cornville.

DOUBLE ADOBE: Cochise County. So named because in the vicinity was located a two-room adobe building with eighteen-inch walls with gun openings.

DRAGOON: Cochise County. For the mountains. The mountains acquired their moniker from the fact that the 3rd U.S. Cavalry, known as the Dragoons, was once stationed here. The Dragoons were so called because their prime weapon was a carbine rather than the saber and revolver carried by most cavalry troops.

EASTER: Maricopa County. For the Easter Mine, which was discovered on Easter Sunday.

GRASSHOPPER: Navajo County. The general theory of this name origin is that it came about from early stockmen for the horde of grasshoppers found in the area. Another contention is that the name is from that of Naz-chug-gee, an Apache woman who had a hip ailment. The translation of her name supposedly meant "the home of the woman who hops like a grasshopper."

HAPPY JACK: Coconino County. A Forest Service camp in the area was named by the supervisor for his previous station, Happy Jack, Montana. A summer logging settlement grew up across the road from the camp and took the same name.

INSPIRATION: Gila County. For the Inspiration Mine. There are two versions as to the origin of the mine's tag. One story goes that the owners, short on capital, had an "inspiration" to borrow additional funds from a bank to continue working the mine. The other source believes one of the owners was a spiritualist and had a "vision" of the mine.

KOFA: Yuma County. Took its name from the King of Arizona Mining Company.

MANY FARMS: Apache County. This is an Anglicized translation of an Indian phrase, appropriately applied. Navajos cultivate hundreds of acres hereabout.

MOCCASIN: Mohave County. The origin of this community moniker goes back to early days when an Indian, wandering through the area, came across a spring and refreshed himself. The earth around the spring was soft, and later, when a white man appeared on the scene, he spotted the moccasin prints left by the Indian and named the stream Moccasin Spring. When a settlement was established here, it took the name as well.

OCAPOS: Maricopa County. A unique origin for a name in that it was formed by reversing the first two letters of each word in "Southern Pacific Company."

ORACLE: Pinal County. The naming of the community holds no religious connotation. It relates to a ship, *The Oracle*, owned by the Oracle Mine.

PAN: Yavapai County. From sources available, this was a short title for a railroad switch, and the village was named for its location near such a switch.

PICA: Yavapai County. The original title of this small Santa Fe Railroad station was Picacho. There was, at the time, a station on the Southern Pacific line with the same name. Because of this there were frequent mix-ups in freight shipments. To rectify the situation, officials of the two lines tossed a coin to see which station would change its name. Santa Fe lost and by dropping the last three letters of Picacho, came up with the name Pica.

PICK EM UP: Cochise County. This is one of those communities of which the names are almost too fanciful to be believed. From available sources, the story goes that a tinhorn gambler, Johnny O'Rourke, commonly known as Johnny-Behind-the Deuce due to his affinity for that particular card, killed a miner in a fit of rage. This took place in Charleston. Friends of the slain miner attempted to take the law into their own hands, their ultimate aim being to hang the gambler. The Charleston constable, intent on upholding his responsibility, took his prisoner and sneaked out of town, heading for the sheriff's office in Tombstone. The irate miners, discovering what had taken place, mounted their horses and wagons and gave chase. Between the two communities of Charleston and Tombstone was a place called the First Chance Saloon, so named because it was the first place for a drink on the road between the two towns. As the constable and his prisoner neared the saloon, the lawman knew his horse was too tired to make the trip to his destination at a gait fast enough to stay ahead of the pursuing mob. As chance would have it, the owner of the saloon, Jack McCann, was a racer of horses and happened to have a racing mare at his place of business. McCann intended to run the horse at the nearby Watervale Track. Upon seeing the horse, the constable called to McCann, telling him to "pick 'em up," apparently meaning to mount his horse. McCann complied and he and Johnny-Behind-the-Deuce raced into Tombstone ahead of the miners. The sheriff took control of the prisoner and then faced down the mob with a shotgun. O'Rourke had a short-lived reprieve. In time, a small settlement grew up around McCann's First Chance Saloon and when it came time to christen it, the constable's call to McCann had already become a part of local folklore. The name Pick Em Up was adopted.

PLANET: Yuma County. From the Planet Mine. The Planet, discovered in 1864, was the first copper mine in Arizona to be worked by Americans.

PLENTY: Apache County. Originally known as Floy, being named for Floy Greer. Confusion grew in mail delivery between Floy and Eloy, which was located in Pinal County. The settlers, mostly from Texas, had never cared for the name Floy, and when a change was requested, they were readily agreeable. The name Plenty was agreed upon because the settlers felt the area was "plentiful" for everyone.

POLARIS: Yuma County. This post office was so named because it was located at the North Star Mine. Sources have it that the mine was discovered through reference to the North Star (Polaris). The little hamlet took the mine's name.

ROLL: Yuma County. Honors John H. Roll, merchant.

SALOME: Yuma County. The origin of this name was due to a bit of whimsy. In 1904, Charles H. Pratt set about establishing a settlement where he believed the railroad was going to run. His prognostication was short about a mile and the settlement had to be moved to its present location. In this venture with Pratt were two brothers, Ernest and Dick Wick Hall. After the settlement was relocated, Mrs. Grace Salome Pratt decided to walk over the area. Taking off her shoes she soon discovered that the sand burned her feet. Dick Hall, something of a wit, came up with the slogan, "Salome, where she danced!" Thus, the name for the community.

SAWMILL: Apache County. A descriptive name because the Navajos operated their own sawmill here, using lumber cut on their reservation.

SHOW LOW: Navajo County. The origin of this community name, while fanciful, is entirely believable, especially considering the love of gambling that prevailed on our early western frontier. Corydon E. Cooley established his home on a creek in Navajo County in 1874. Over a period of time he improved on the original construction and soon had a home of comfort and cleanliness, a rarity in the wilds of the Southwest of the time. Cooley had a partner in various ventures, a man named Marion Clark. Friction arose between the two and Clark eventually decided that dissolution of the partnership was the only remedy. The two men elected to play a game of seven-up to see which one would move. As the last hand was dealt, Cooley needed only one point to win. Clark, placing his hand over the cards, is said to have commented that if Cooley would show low, Cooley would win the game. With that, Cooley turned over his cards, revealing a "show low" hand. Clark, the loser, moved upstream and established a ranch at Pinetop. Because of the card game, the aforementioned stream was named Show Low, and as a community grew up around Cooley's original site it, too, assumed the name.

SIGNAL: Mohave County. For the Signal Mine.

SILVER KING: Pinal County. A mine was discovered in Pinal County in March 1875. The find was so rich and held such promise for fortune that the owners believed they had found the king of mines; thus, the name. An onrush of anxious prospectors followed the discovery, and the community that emerged took the tag, Silver King.

SILVERBELL: Pima County. For the Silverbell Mine.

SNAKETOWN: Pinal County. This is a Papago village and the name is a translation of the Pima word *sku-kaik*, meaning "many rattlesnakes."

SNOWFLAKE: Navajo County. The origin of this name is both unique and coincidental. In July 1878, William J. Flake bought some land from James Stinson. A month or so later, twelve families, the members of which were in dire straits, arrived at Flake's ranch and the benevolent man gave them shelter. Shortly thereafter, Erastus Snow arrived at a nearby ranch with a group of followers. At this time there were enough people to constitute a community, and Flake's land was selected as the townsite. The people named their settlement Snow Flake, in honor of the two founders. With the passage of time the spelling became one word.

SURPRISE: Maricopa County. Originally settled in 1937 by two families totaling eight people. Flora Statler, one of those settlers, is credited with naming the settlement, because she said she would be "surprised" if the place ever became a town. The present population of the community is near the 4,000 mark.

TIGER: Pinal County. For a nearby mine.

TINTOWN: Cochise County. There is little of this town remaining, but at one time it resounded with the sounds and smells of Old Mexico. In 1904, Mexicans working the Bisbee mines were anxious to align themselves where they could talk and be festive in their cultural ways. They gathered tin cans and oil drums and flattened them. Then, with discarded scrap lumber they erected shanties, built close together and housing as many as two or three families to a shelter. Here, they danced, sang, and celebrated without interruption. The community name came about quite naturally from the shelters.

TOMBSTONE: Cochise County. For a mine. The mine tag was not self-imposed, being so designated because area residents believed warring Apaches would make the mine a "tombstone" for the miners.

TORTILLA FLAT: Mohave County. In Spanish *tortilla* means "omelet" or "pancake," an apt description of a mesa, a flat-topped hill. A Mexican settlement existed here in the 1880s on a mesa north of what is now New Virginia. The Mexicans apparently kept pretty much to themselves, growing watermelons, making adobe, and reveling in the festivities so unique and enticing south of the border. Because of its shape, the settlement acquired the name Tortilla Flat.

TOTAL WRECK: Pima County. An almost unbelievable name for a community. In 1877, John Dillon uncovered the first silver mine in the Empire Mountains. The area discovered by Dillon was around a large ledge of rocks, the hillside of which was thick with quartz. The quartz had broken loose in several places and tumbled down onto and over the ledge. Dillon, not having a paper of ownership to the area, went to the nearest settlement to secure the document. When asked the name of the location, he described the ledge and scattered rocks, stating that the place looked like a "total wreck." Ergo, the Total Wreck Mine was christened. When a small community grew up around the mine, it took the same name.

TWO GUNS: Coconino County. This trading post was established in the 1950s, and was named strictly as a lure to tourists. It has no connection with any event out of the Old West.

WHY: Pima County. This unusual name was selected by early settlers because people were always asking "why" anyone would want to live here.

WIKIEUP: Mohave County. This is a term frequently given to brush shelters built by Indians of the Southwest, especially Apaches. When the town was of sufficient size to warrant organization, two names for the site were proposed. The Post Office Department refused to accept either Sandy or Owen, probably because of duplication. As fate would have it, there happened to be an Indian tepee situated at a nearby spring and the townspeople proposed the name Wikieup, which was accepted by postal officials.

Arkansas
The Land of Opportunity

AIRBASE: Jackson County. Appropriately named, having been the site of a military airfield during World War II.

APT: Craighead County. Community name came about in 1882, when citizens were discussing a label for their newly established settlement. One resident made the offhanded comment, "I suppose they will be apt to name the place." Other residents caught the word *apt* and thought that was as good a name as any for their hometown.

BAND MILL: Izard County. So tagged because there once existed on this site a sawmill, which used a band saw in its operation. People began calling the place Band Mill, and the name stuck.

BEN GAY: Sharp County. The community was christened for Benjamin Gay, an early resident who raised peacocks.

BEN HUR: Newton County. For the popular novel, written by Lew Wallace and published in 1880.

BIRDEYE: Cross County. For Birdeye Church, which acquired its designation because it was situated on a hill and had a bird's-eye view of the surrounding area.

BIRDSONG: Mississippi County. A family name.

BLACKFOOT: Phillips County. For the Indian tribe.

BLOCKADE HILL: Woodruff County. For the battle that was fought on this site during the Civil War.

BLUE BALL: Scott County. When this settlement was first a post office, a name had to be selected. One of the residents, staring at a distant mountain, commented that it looked like a blue ball.

BLUE EYE: Carroll County. This small community, divided by the Arkansas-Missouri state line, received its moniker from the fact that Elbert Butler, instrumental in having a post office established here, had blue eyes.

BOARD CAMP: Polk County. In very early days, a migrating family stopped at a creek near what is today Board Camp. Some members of the family were ill, so they decided to stay there until the unfortunates recouped. The father cut down some trees and carefully stripped and hewed the timber into boards, with which he erected a cabin. Practically all cabins in the area were constructed of rough logs. After several months, the family moved westward, leaving the cabin standing. Hunters began using the shelter, and the site became known as "the place of the board camp." Silver was later discovered in the vicinity, and the community took the name Silver Center. When diggings played out and the mine was shut down, residents decided to return to the previous name, Board Camp.

BOAT RUN: Poinsett County. This was the site of a logging camp and was so named because everything from mail to supplies had to be brought in by boat.

BOX SPRINGS: Benton County. From the family name of Box, connected to a nearby stream.

BRIGHT FUTURE: St. Francis County. A commendatory name.

BRIGHT STAR: Miller County. One night, two men were traveling on horseback through this area when one of them noticed an exceptionally bright star in the sky. Sharing the discovery with his companion, the man commented that it was the brightest star he had ever seen. At the time, the two were approaching the hamlet of Stuckeyville. They were unaware of the community name and referred to it as the place where they had seen the bright star. In time, Stuckeyville changed its title to Bright Star.

BUGSCUFFLE: Greene County. Also known as Mount Union. The name Bugscuffle came about years ago when a revival was being held at a local church. The minister, while his religious fervor could not be questioned, lacked the oratory skill to hold the attention of his audience. The menfolk knew this and always hung back while their wives went into the church. One particular night, the men were talking outside the church when they noticed two tumblebugs struggling (scuffling) over ownership of a small ball of manure. The encounter captivated the men, and they set about placing bets on which bug would win. The scuffle lasted so long that the church service was over before the men realized it. The wives, exiting the building, discovered what had deterred their husbands and were livid with anger. However, from that incident came the little hamlet's name.

BULL TOWN: Woodruff County. For Jerry Bull, a settler.

BULLFROG VALLEY: Pope County. For an Indian, Chief Bullfrog.

CALAMINE: Sharp County. Relates to a calamine ore operation that once existed here.

CALICO ROCK: Logan County. Refers to a variegated rock situated on a nearby bluff.

CALICO ROCK: Izard County. For picturesque, colored cliffs near the town.

CHALK: Van Buren County. Family name.

CHECKS CORNER: Benton County. For a local family, whose home probably rested on the corner of a roadway.

CHIMES: Van Buren County. Chosen simply because it was a pretty name.

COIN: Carroll County. Exact origin of this hamlet name is unknown, although it is almost certain to have been selected with William

Hope Harvey in mind. Harvey was an advocate of silver, rather than gold, as the standard for the American monetary system. This is why he was given the nickname "Coin." Harvey even moved to Chicago around 1891 and began publishing a weekly magazine, *Coin*. Whether this community's name was taken from Harvey's nickname or the magazine is up for grabs. There is supposition that the name has another origin, from the fact that a coin was flipped to decide on a handle for the settlement.

COLT: St. Francis County. This community name came about through chance. An early settler was a man named Williams, and the construction engineer for the railroad was named Colt. When a tag for the little village was needed, these two men wanted it named for the other. Williams said they should flip a coin to decide on a name, and Colt won.

CORD: Independence County. Honors Rev. J. W. McCord, a Presbyterian minister.

COTTON PLANT: Woodruff County. William Lynch migrated here from Mississippi in 1846 and built a home and store. Lynch brought some cottonseeds with him, a few of which were accidentally spilled near the store. In time, the seeds took root and produced several healthy plants. People in the area began referring to Lynch's place of business as the "Cotton Plant Store," which eventually evolved into the town name.

COW MOUND: Woodruff County. Long ago, a man named George lived on a mound located here. A favorite saying of the time by men going fishing was, "We'll have to go by Cow Mound George's place."

COZAHOME: Searcy County. Originally called Pleasant Ridge. When George Rhoades established a store and post office, he renamed it Cozahome, because he thought he had such a "cozy home."

DELIGHT: Pike County. Christened by William H. Kirkham, who donated land for the town, because "This is such a delightful place to live, we shall call the town Delight."

DEMOCRAT: St. Francis County. The original name of this community was Turnipseed, for the abundance of turnips grown in the area. Shortly after the Civil War, Republican carpetbaggers moved into the state and took over the government. This made the Republicans a hated faction in Arkansas, as well as in the rest of the South. In covert defiance, this community changed its name to Democrat, getting the change approved through dictatorial state officials by claiming that it was a brand-new brand of turnips. Yankee officials, unfamiliar with turnips, unknowingly sanctioned the new name and even went so far as to have a Yankee-owned restaurant in Little Rock, the state capital, serve "Democrat turnips" on the menu.

DIAMOND: Pope County. After the first post office was established here, it was discovered that the mail route was in the shape of a diamond. This, plus the fact that Arkansas has the only diamond mine in the United States, made the name a natural.

DOGPATCH: Newton County. Originally known as Marble City, for a nearby marble quarry, a block of which is a memorial in the Washington Monument in our nation's capital. The town, which was once a thriving settlement, became practically a ghost town and was owned by a single individual. In 1966, a group of businessmen purchased the land, made arrangements with Al Capp, the cartoonist, to use his "Dogpatch" names, and established the recreation park known today as "Dogpatch, USA." It has been in operation since 1968.

DOLLARWAY: Jefferson County. Community refers to a road by the same name, built in 1912–1913, which connected Pine Bluff with Little Rock. The road took its name from the fact that it cost a dollar a square yard to build.

ELEVEN POINT: Randolph County. Apparently named for the Eleven Point River, which probably acquired its name from the fact that it was formed by eleven springs.

EVENING SHADE: Sharp County. Settled by Captain James Thompson in the early 1800s, a village soon grew up around the mill Thompson built. He decided to petition for a post office and was informed that the settlement had no name. Thompson, looking up at the pine trees surrounding his mill, which were so tall they cut off sunlight earlier than any other area around, said, "Evening Shade." The community gained prominence when Burt Reynolds and Marilu Henner starred in a television sitcom by the same name.

EVENING STAR: Greene County. Community designation is believed to have come from an early day Methodist church.

EVENING STAR: Searcy County. For a mine in operation during World War I.

FAKES CHAPEL: Woodruff County. Around 1885, Mrs. G. B. Fakes donated an acre of land on which was built a Methodist church and a cemetery. The place later took the name Fakes Chapel, for the woman and the church.

FAREWELL: Carroll County. Citizens met to select a name for their community. Time passed, but no agreement could be reached. One resident, tired of the whole affair, said, "It's getting late. I'm leaving. Farewell to you!" After the man left, someone suggested naming the village Farewell, and this was accepted.

FIFTY SIX: Stone County. Took its tag from the number of the local school district.

FIGURE FIVE: Crawford County. Named for the "figure 5" carved into a tree by early surveyors, probably as a mile marker.

FORTY FOUR: Izard County. In 1928, area residents petitioned for a post office. A name was needed for the facility, and a man in the village simply counted the number of names on the petition, came up with forty-four, and chose that.

FRISBEE: Lawrence County. Family name.

GOBBLER: Carroll County. Community so tagged because this used to be a favorite hunting spot for wild turkeys.

GOOBERTOWN: Craighead County. This community was settled by former Georgia natives, who planted a large crop of peanuts (goobers); hence, the name.

GRAPHIC: Crawford County. Hamlet remembers the *Van Buren Graphic,* a local newspaper founded in the late 1800s by J. J. Warren.

GREASY CORNER: St. Francis County. From his daughter-in-law comes word that Bunn McCollum, founder of the settlement and apparently something of a joker, named the place Greasy Corner, "just to be different."

GREASY VALLEY: Van Buren County. This hamlet name came from the fact that so many hogs were grown in the area, or from an incident when a farmer hauling barrels of hog lard overturned his wagon here.

HARNESS: Stone County. Family name.

HASTY: Newton County. The first settlers in this small community named it Gun Tavern (or Agee). Later, when a gristmill and a sawmill were built here, the area quickly grew in population and was called Hasty Ridge. When the post office was established, the name became Hasty.

HEART: Fulton County. Named for its location in the center (heart) of several settlements.

HOG EYE: Washington County. Also known as Moffett. There are two versions as to how this small village acquired its name. The first has it that a band of gypsies stopped at a saloon here. One of them played a fiddle and took requests from the patrons in exchange for money or drinks. A favorite tune of the time was a song called "Hawk Eye." One of the customers had overindulged in the spirits and when he requested the gypsy play the tune, "Hog Eye" instead of "Hawk Eye" came out. Thinking this name funnier than the original, the other customers not only changed the name of the song, but also adopted Hog Eye as the hamlet moniker. The

34

second version, closely paralleling the former, concerns a traveling tippler who arrived at the saloon in desperate need of a drink, but sorely lacking in funds. Before the bartender would serve him, he asked to see the color of the man's money. Instead of replying, the man removed a violin from the case he was carrying and broke out with the tune "Hog Eye." Apparently blessed with talent, the man was plied with drink and became a town character for several years thereafter. In time, he moved on to greener pastures, but left the little village with its popular name.

HOG SCALD HOLLOW: Carroll County. With the passage of time, water flowing through the hollow caused large rocks to become pitted. During the Civil War, soldiers camped in the area, blocked off the rocks, filled the pits with hot water, and scalded pigs to remove the skins. Ergo, the community name.

HON: Scott County. For Jackson Hon.

INK: Polk County. When residents applied for a post office, they erred and filled out the form in pencil. Washington officials returned the application, instructing them to "fill it out in ink." They did, and that also gave inspiration for the community name.

JUMBO: Izard County. It is believed residents wanted the community named for "Jimbo" Smith, but the Post Office Department made a mistake in recording the name.

LIGHT: Greene County. For Benjamin Light.

LIGNITE: Saline County. More than likely named for a type of coal mined here.

LITTLE FLOCK: Benton County. For an early church.

LITTLE RED: White County. For the Little Red River.

LONE SASSAFRAS: Drew County. Appropriately named for a solitary sassafras tree found here by early settlers.

LOST CORNER: Pope County. First called Okay, the local post office had to change its name because of duplication. George Napier, postmaster, suggested the name Lost Corner, because of the community's "lost location amid forest and mountains."

MANY ISLANDS: Fulton County. Appropriately named, for the many islands in the area.

MARKED TREE: Poinsett County. Community designation derived from a large oak tree with an M carved in it. Speculation is the M was put there by a gang of thieves from Jackson, Tennessee, known as the Murrell Gang. The tree was marked as a guide. In early days, when this section of the country was heavily forested, the mode of travel was by water, and to get from the St. Francis River to the Little River meant an additional fifteen miles by canoe. At the point now known as Marked Tree, however, the distance was only one-quarter mile by land. To shorten travel time, boatmen would debark here and drag their canoes across the short stretch to the Little River landing. The marked tree let water travelers know the place to traverse.

MORNING STAR: Garland County. For a church. The house of worship received its name when one service lasted through the night, not being completed until the morning star was visible in the sky.

MORNING STAR: Searcy County. In the beginning the small settlement situated here was called Trickem; later, Loafer's Glory. The people, not liking the connotation of the latter, changed the name to Morning Star, probably in a commendatory vein.

MOZART: Stone County. Village was not named for the famous Austrian composer, but is still musically connected, for a resident who played the violin.

NATURAL STEPS: Pulaski County. Refers to a 300-foot-long bluff that descends to the banks of the Arkansas River by stages; thus, the name Natural Steps.

NO NAME STATION: Sharp County. A Mr. Bowman once owned a combination store and service station on the main highway here. People traveling through would ask the name of the place, to which he always replied, "It don't have a name." In time, it became known as No Name Station.

OIL TROUGH: Independence County. The village received its moniker from early days, when hunters rendered oil from bears and stored it in troughs made of hollowed-out tree trunks.

OLD JOE: Baxter County. Originally known as Naked Joe, for a treeless hill, postal authorities refused to accept that as an official name, so it was changed to Old Joe.

OZONE: Johnson County. Christened by Mrs. Delia McCracken, wife of an early settler, because of the clear, clean air and healthy atmosphere.

PEE DEE: Van Buren County. Either named for the Indian tribe, or carried over from names of locales in Scotland or Ireland.

PEEL: Marion County. Formerly called Need More; renamed to honor Sam Peel, early postmaster and store owner.

PONTOON: Conway County. Relates to an old pontoon bridge that once spanned nearby Pettijean River.

POP CITY: Woodruff County. So tagged because a local store sold a large amount of soda pop.

PROCESS CITY: Sevier County. Hamlet was named for a treating (processing) plant built here by the Dierks Company, which treated wooden posts.

PULLTIGHT: Woodruff County. As legend has it, this hamlet received its name long ago from an incident involving two women who started arguing, then proceeded to fighting. Since a woman's retort in such situations is often the pulling of hair, each did her best to scalp the other. A crowd soon gathered to watch the scuffle and calls from onlookers to "pull tight," referring to the hair pulling, were boisterous and encouraging. Ergo, the community name.

PUMPKIN BEND: Woodruff County. For the many large pumpkins grown near a bend in the road.

PUSH: Sharp County. Also known as Nelsonville. In early days, there were two stores in the area, situated about two miles apart. A traveling salesman referred to one store as Push, the other as Pull. The latter went broke, the former survived, and the community became known as Push.

RAGTOWN: Monroe County. As the local story goes, Joel Lindley passed through here around 1903 and named the village Ragtown, for the ragged clothes hanging across fences.

RALLY HILL: Boone County. According to available sources, the first settlers in this area were from Raleigh, North Carolina, and called the place New Raleigh. Later, it became simply Raleigh. A school was built on a hill, and the site soon acquired the name Raleigh Hill. Local usage, in time, changed the pronunciation to Rally Hill.

REPUBLICAN: Faulkner County. The small settlement was first known as Cash Springs. When residents petitioned for a post office, it was denied because another Cash Springs already existed. Dejected, the townspeople shrewdly petitioned again, this time suggesting the name Republican. Since a Republican administration was in power in Washington, the request was quickly approved.

ROMANCE: White County. Folklore has it that this village was so named because a teacher noticed a lot of courting going on and commented that it was a "romantic" place.

RULE: Carroll County. When a post office was established here in July 1884, the new postmaster, Alfred Webb, was asked to select a name. Looking through an arithmetic book, he spied the word *rule,* giving him inspiration for the office, and later the community, name.

SADDLE: Fulton County. Refers to a saddle repair shop that was the biggest business in town at the time a name was chosen.

SKUNK HOLLOW: Faulkner County. Labeled for the large number of skunks that made this area their home.

SMACKOVER: Union County. While this is certainly a humorous name, its origin has a French root, with no comedy intended. *Smackover* is an abbreviated form of the French *sumac-couvert,* meaning "covered with sumac or shumate bushes," and is apparently descriptive of the area.

STAMPS: Lafayette County. For James H. Stamps, a settler.

STAR OF THE WEST: Pike County. This community, located on the shores of Lake Greeson, was given this attractive name by land developers.

STORY: Montgomery County. A family name.

SUCCESS: Clay County. Once known as Bridgeport, the name was changed to Success around 1902, when the St. Louis–San Francisco Railroad built a line through here. Apparently Success was chosen in anticipation of growth expected with the coming of the railroad.

SUPPLY: Randolph County. It is believed the community received its label because it was a Confederate supply depot during the Civil War.

SWEET HOME: Pulaski County. This small community was settled by former slaves following the Civil War. In time, a church was erected, which residents called Home Sweet Home. The community took its name from the chapel.

THE PENITENTIARY: Woodruff County. Hamlet received its unusual moniker because it is situated among a dense growth of trees, making it extremely difficult to get in and out of the place.

THREE BROTHERS: Baxter County. Relates to Three Brothers Mountain. The mountains are similar in size and shape; thus, the name.

THREE SISTERS: Garland County. Community name evolved the same as that of Three Brothers; or it was christened to complement the community of Three Brothers.

TOAD SUCK: Faulkner County. Remembers a local saloon. Legend has it that river men used to patronize the saloon and "suck" on bottles of moonshine until their stomachs were swollen. Indians said that after these drinking bouts, the men looked like "toads."

TOMAHAWK: Searcy County. Village was so named because of Indian artifacts, including tomahawks, found in the area by white settlers.

TOMATO: Mississippi County. A discussion was being held in a store to decide on a name for the settlement. Several names had been suggested, but none agreed upon, when a small girl walked in and asked for a can of tomatoes. One of the residents, overhearing the girl, suggested the name Tomato.

TREAT: Pope County. Honors "Uncle" Polk Treat, a settler.

TULIP: Dallas County. Named for Tulip Ridge, which was tagged for Tulipe, an early French hunter who roamed the vicinity.

TURKEY SCRATCH: Lee County. This was once a heavily wooded area with no turkeys. Three settlers moved in, bringing with them several of the fowls. They turned the birds loose, and in time the spot became referred to as the place where "turkeys scratch." Accepting the name, one of the men erected a sign that marked the community as Turkey Scratch.

TWIST: Cross County. Family name.

UMPIRE: Howard County. According to tradition, a picnic was held on this spot in early days by the neighboring towns of Bethel and Galena. They wanted to play a game of baseball, but none of them knew anything about the sport. One of the picnickers, Billy Faulkner, from nearby Mena, was familiar with the rules and agreed to serve as umpire. When a community was eventually established here, it took the name from that event.

WAGER: Benton County. Honors Eugene Wager. Tradition has it that Wager was born in France, and at age fifteen stowed away on a ship headed for the New World. In time, he made his way to Arkansas and opened a mill here.

WAVE: Dallas County. Originally known as Waverly. Postal officials requested the name be changed because of duplication. By dropping "rly," the present name was adopted.

WILD CHERRY: Fulton County. Following the Civil War, annual revival meetings were held here because of the availability of good, clear springwater. Several wild cherry trees grew near one spring, which eventually became known as Wild Cherry Spring. Later, when a community grew up here, it took the name of the spring.

WOLF PEN: Carroll County. This tiny village's name dates back to the time when residents were having problems with wolves. The wild animals were attacking livestock as well as game, and settlers actively hunted the preying predators. Apparently, "wolf pens" were erected to trap the animals. There is another story about the name origin. Residents were having a feast when a pair of strangers appeared. The natives had ominous feelings about the two horsemen and did not invite them to supper. The men were told they could go to the nearby valley where they would find a "wolf pen." The locals advised the men they would be traveling at their own risk. The two strangers were never seen or heard of again.

YELLVILLE: Marion County. Honors Archibald Yell, onetime governor of Arkansas.

ZINC: Boone County. For a local zinc mine.

California

The Golden State

ACADEMY: Fresno County. So named because the Methodist-Episcopal Church South established an academy, or secondary school, on this site in 1974   41

ANGELS CAMP: Calaveras County. George or Henry Angel started mining at a nearby creek in June 1848. The community was incorporated as Angels in 1912, but popular usage prefers the name Angels Camp.

ARMADA: Riverside County. In Spanish the word means "fleet" or "squadron," and normally relates to the sea. In this instance, the moniker was chosen for its pleasing and inviting sound.

ASSOCIATED: Contra Costa County. The name was applied to the post office in 1913, when the Tidewater Associated Oil Company built the town.

AZUSA: Los Angeles County. There are two versions as to the origin of this name. One, the town was laid out in 1887 and christened for the Azusa land grant on which it is located. *Azusa*, by this source, is an Indian derivation for "skunk." Another source states that *Azusa* is an acronym for "Everything from A to Z in the USA."

BEN HUR: Mariposa County. This is one of the few location names of which the origin is certain. The California locale was named by the townspeople around 1890 for the hero in Lew Wallace's novel *Ben Hur.*

BIJOU: El Dorado County. This is a French word meaning "gem" or "jewel." It was applied to this resort in 1880, probably for publicity purposes. Bijou was once a popular name for movie theaters.

BLUE NOSE: Siskiyou County. Named for the Blue Nose gold mine. The mine was started by Nova Scotians who were referred to, by some, as "Blue Noses."

BOULEVARD: San Diego County. So named because the town is situated on Highway 80, known as the boulevard to the Imperial Valley.

BURNT RANCH: Trinity County. So titled because, in 1849, Canadian miners burned down an Indian rancheria. The reason for their action is unknown.

CALICO: San Bernardino County. Today only a ghost-town tourist attraction, this site thrived for a quarter of a century, beginning in 1881, as a silver mining town. Its name came from either the multihued (calico) mountains in the background, or because early settlers considered the small community "as purty as a gal's calico skirt."

CATHEDRAL CITY: Riverside County. For the canyon, so tagged for rock formations within its walls.

CHALLENGE: Yuba County. Remembers the Challenge Lumber Company.

CHINESE CAMP: Tuolumne County. The community received its name because it was the site of a Chinese settlement during gold rush days.

COARSEGOLD: Madera County. Said to have been so named because yellow ore was found here during gold rush days in nugget (coarse) form instead of dust.

COOL: El Dorado County. An old placer mining camp of the 1850s. Supposedly designated for the weather; however, sources claim this does not apply during summer months.

DESERT CENTER: Riverside County. A descriptive name, owing to the community's location.

DEVILS DEN: Kern County. Relates to a volcanic formation.

DIABLO: Contra Costa County. Spanish for "devil." This residential community name is said to have derived from Indian lore; they believed the devil lived in this high spot in the San Francisco Bay area.

FAIR PLAY: El Dorado County. According to tradition, the name arose from an incident in which an appeal for fair play forestalled a fight between two miners.

FAWNSKIN: San Bernardino County. For the meadow, which derived its name from the skins of deer stretched on trees by a hunting party and allowed to remain there for a number of years.

FIDDLETOWN: Amador County. There are two versions as to the origin of this community name. One side asserts that when miners migrated to California gold fields from Missouri, they brought their fiddles and took turns playing. It was not uncommon to see a miner panning a stream while his partner played music. Another version counters this by claiming that a family first settled at this site and named it Violin City, because four members of the family played the violin.

FIVE POINTS: Fresno County. So named because five roads converge at this point.

FREEDOM: Santa Cruz County. This community was originally known as Whiskey Hill, no doubt from the fact that in 1852, there were eleven saloons striving to quench the thirst of the people. About forty years later, in either 1892 or 1893, an enterprising saloonkeeper had a huge sign put across the front of his place of business. The sign displayed two American flags, and on it was emblazoned in large letters, "THE FLAG OF FREEDOM." It wasn't long before the place became known as Freedom, a name that was eventually applied to the town.

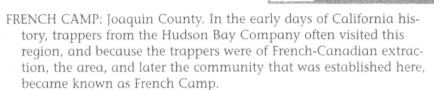

FRENCH CAMP: Joaquin County. In the early days of California history, trappers from the Hudson Bay Company often visited this region, and because the trappers were of French-Canadian extraction, the area, and later the community that was established here, became known as French Camp.   43

GAS POINT: Shasta County. Supposedly the name was given because old prospectors gathered here to "gas and spin yarns."

GIANT: Contra Costa County. When the Giant Powder Company of Wilmington, Delaware, built a plant here in 1880, the surrounding community took the title Giant. "Giant powder" was an early name for dynamite.

GOLD RUN: Nevada County. Christened for a stream where some of the richest and most famous diggings known in California were found.

GOLDTREE: San Luis Obispo County. Americanization of the surname of Morris Goldbaum, who settled here in the 1890s. "Tree" in German is *baum*.

GOODYEARS BAR: Sierra County. A man by the name of Goodyear settled this community. That fact, along with a bend in the north fork of the Yuba River that formed a bar, gave the settlement its name.

GREENSPOT: San Bernardino County. In the early 1900s, the Cram family traveled through the San Bernardino Valley, finally stopping at the upper end. They gave the site its present name, saying it was the only "green spot" they had seen since entering the valley.

GRIZZLY FLATS: El Dorado County. The town honors the bear, which was once in abundance in this area.

HALFMOON BAY: San Mateo County. The first small settlement on the bay was appropriately named Spanish Town. Later, the Coast Survey christened the bay for its shape. The town took the bay's name in the late 1860s or early 1870s.

HAPPY CAMP: Siskiyou County. Jack Titus named the camp because his partner, upon finally arriving here, exclaimed that it was the "happiest" day of his life.

HARDSCRABBLE: Siskiyou County. This once famous mining town was named by two former residents of Hardscrabble, Wisconsin. "Hardscrabble" was a common term in early America, being associated with places where the battle for daily bread and existence was hard.

HAT CREEK: Siskiyou County. For the creek, so named simply because a man lost his hat there around 1852.

HAYFORK: Trinity County. In the middle of the nineteenth century, this region was known as Hayfields because it was the largest farming section in Trinity County. Later, the name Hayfork was applied to a branch of the Trinity River and the town assumed the same name.

HOLY CITY: Santa Clara County. Founded and named in 1920 by W. E. Riker as a religious community for people of the "white" race. It was to be a place where solutions could be found for the economic, racial, and spiritual problems of the world.

IGO: Shasta County. One claim is that this moniker was suggested in 1868 by Charles Hoffman when he heard the small son of George McPherson say, "Daddy, I go, I go," whenever the latter left for the mines. Another assertion, one not so appealing but apparently somewhat common for the day, and backed by students of etymology, associates Igo with nearby Ono. The submission is that Igo acquired its name when a Chinese man was driven from his mine by other prospectors. The Chinese man said, "I go." Later, when Americans tried to drive the same man from his new claim, the Chinese man's expression was, "Oh, no!"

INGOT: Shasta County. Named for the foundry where metals were melted down and shaped into ingots for easy shipping.

JOSHUA TREE: San Bernardino County. Named for its situation as the gateway to the Joshua Tree National Monument.

LIKELY: Modoc County. Originally named South Fork. In 1878, citizens were informed by the postal officials that they would have to change the name of their settlement because it was a duplicate of an older community name. The settlers submitted three names for consideration; each was rejected because the name existed elsewhere. Exasperated, residents met again and one of them exclaimed that "it was not likely they would ever get a name." The word *likely* was jumped on by other members of the community, and the name was accepted by postal officials.

LOG CABIN: Yuba County. So named in 1927 when a post office was established in a log cabin.

LONG BARN: Tuolumne County. Remembers a long, narrow barn erected on the site in the late 1850s; the barn housed cattle and sheep.

LOOKOUT: Modoc County. As the story goes, the settlement was labeled around 1860 for a nearby hill. It is said that the Pit River Indians placed a lookout on the hill when the Modocs were on wife-stealing expeditions.

LOST HILLS: Kern County. Named for a nearby range of hills. The hills were so tagged because they are set apart from other rises in the area, therefore, looking lost.

MAD RIVER: Humboldt County. For the river, which acquired its designation in 1840 when Josiah Gregg, an explorer, "went mad" on its bank.

MINERAL KING: Tulare County. Originally called Buelah, the name was changed when a mining district was organized and proclaimed "the king of mineral districts."

MODESTO: Stanislau County. It was intended to name the railroad station for William G. Ralston, one of Central Pacific's directors and the most colorful of San Francisco's financiers. Ralston modestly declined, whereupon the name was changed to a derivation of the Spanish word meaning "modest." Another version, with a theme much the same, states that the founders of the small settlement were too modest to name it in honor of themselves, instead choosing a Spanish form of "modest."

NICE: Lake County. Communities in this region were established by developers beginning in the 1920s. One of the first settlements near what is now Nice honors Lucerne, for the city in Switzerland. To complement Lucerne, this village was named for the French Riviera town of Nice (pronounced "neese").

NUT TREE: Solano County. In 1858–1859, Sally Fox, niece of Josiah Allison, made a long and dangerous wagon trip from Iowa to California. In Arizona, she picked up several walnuts near the Gila River and carried them to her destination. In the spring of 1860, Allison planted one of the walnuts on the roadside that bordered his ranch. A century later, trees that grew from the nuts of that original tree line the roads in the Sacramento Valley neighborhood. The name for the small settlement came about when, in July 1921, Josiah Allison's granddaughter set up a fruit stand beneath the original walnut tree and placed a sign nearby denoting the site as Nut Tree.

OCCIDENTAL: Sonoma County. The town name came about from either a Methodist church, which was built here in 1876 or, since the name means "western," and the town is located near the Pacific Ocean, possibly it was derived from that source.

ONO: Shasta County. See Igo, above. Another version is that this moniker was suggested by the Reverend William S. Kidder in 1883 and relates to a town mentioned in the Bible (1 Chronicles 8:12).

OREGON HOUSE: Yuba County. Settlement named by gold prospectors traveling from or through Oregon.

PARAMOUNT: Los Angeles County. The cities of Hynes and Clearwater merged in 1948. Frank Zamboni, president of the local Kiwanis Club, suggested the new name because the main street was Paramount Boulevard, labeled for the motion picture company.

PEANUT: Trinity County. In 1898, a small settlement was located around a general store operated by a man named Cuff. The settlers decided to petition for a post office and name it for Cuff's wife. When the petition was carried to A. L. Paulsen, postmaster at nearby Weaverville, he suggested the name Peanut, because it would be unique and because he was very fond of goobers, and happened to be eating them at the time. The settlers agreed to list Peanut as a second choice. Apparently agreeing to the uniqueness of the name, postal officials approved the designation on January 20, 1900.

PROJECT CITY: Shasta County. Community was built as part of the Central Valley Project.

RAILROAD FLAT: Calaveras County. So christened because a short track conveyed carriers with gold ore and waste to and from vicinity mines.

RAISIN: Fresno County. Honors the chief product of the area.

RED TOP: Madera County. This appellation was chosen by Ray Flanagan, ranch owner, supposedly because his wife and daughter had red hair.

RESCUE: El Dorado County. For the Rescue Mine.

ROADS END: Tulare County. For its location at the end of the road running from Kernville.

ROUGH AND READY: Nevada County. Probably one of America's most unique city names, yet one with a simple, but historical, background. General Zachary Taylor, a hero of the Mexican-American War, and later president of the United States, earned the nickname "Rough and Ready" from the men serving under him. In 1849, Captain A. A. Townsend, who had served with Taylor, founded this village and named it in honor of his former commander.

SAMOA: Humboldt County. Originally known as Brownsville, but changed to its present designation in 1849. It was in that year that a group of Eureka, California, businessmen formed the Samoa Land and Improvement Company. The Pacific Island name was adopted for no reason other than that there was a crisis in Samoa at the time that was making newspaper headlines. However, in some opinions, Humboldt Bay resembles Samoa's fabled inlet, Pago Pago.

SHINGLETOWN: Shasta County. So designated because this was once a thriving center for making shingles and shakes for buildings.

STARVOUT: Siskiyou County. This was a word used as much as the word *hardscrabble* in early mining days. It expressed the miners' concern that their grub might give out and they would be forced to hunt or forage for food. Any such diversion would, of course, distract from their main interest—gold.

TARZANA: Los Angeles County. When Edgar Rice Burroughs bought the Otis estate in 1917, he bestowed upon it the name derived from his famous fictional character, Tarzan. Later, when a town grew up around the estate, it took a derivation of that name.

TEA BAR: Siskiyou County. Derived from the name of a former Karak Indian village, Ti'i.

THERMAL: Riverside County. So named because of the extreme heat in the nearby Salton Sea basin.

TOLLHOUSE: Fresno County. In early days, a private road led to the Saver and Thorpe mine. At the present site of Tollhouse, a collection point was established to collect tolls from stagecoaches traveling the road. The county took over the road later, but the name Tollhouse remains.

TOMALES: Marin County. The community takes the Spanish version of the Tamal Indians.

TURN: Imperial County. When the Southern Pacific line from Calipatria to Sandia was built in 1923–1924, this name was given to the station because the tracks made a sharp turn at this point.

WEED: Siskiyou County. Honors Abner Weed.

WHISKEYTOWN: Siskiyou County. Took its handle from Whiskey Creek. The stream was so christened after a mule train carrying a load of whiskey in kegs broke down near the creek. The kegs fell into the water and floated away. Residents of the hamlet wanted to name their home Whiskeytown, but the federal government wouldn't stand for it. The community went under an assortment of ordinary names until, finally, after much pressure and many demands, in 1952 the government bowed to the citizens' desire.

WISHON: Madera County. Remembers Albert Wishon, who was instrumental in getting public utilities into this area.

YOU BET: Nevada County. According to tradition, a discussion was taking place in a saloon in 1857 over a name for the community. Lazarus Beard, the saloonkeeper, was providing free drinks during the discussion and one participant, anxious to keep the free booze flowing, jokingly proposed "You Bet" as a suitable name. The expression, a favorite with the saloon owner, immediately caught on, and much to the chagrin of the man making the suggestion, the name was accepted and the free drinks ceased.

ZZYZX: San Bernardino County. This community, situated on the banks of Soda Lake, was established by a con artist on land that wasn't even his. In 1944, Curtis Springer, who some contend was the last of the great "snake oil" peddlers, exercised squatters' rights on 12,800 acres of Mojave Desert land belonging to the federal government. Thereon he built a hotel, health spa, castle, radio station, and several other buildings. For the next thirty years Springer used his radio station to broadcast religious messages and hawk his "cure-all" medicinal products. Finally, in 1974, Springer was sent to prison by federal authorities for violation of food and drug laws, as well as unauthorized use of federal land. Springer's enterprises were seized by the Bureau of Land Management. Today, Zzyzx houses the California State University system's Desert Studies Center. As for Springer, he died in Las Vegas in 1984 at age ninety.

Colorado
THE CENTENNIAL STATE

Surbeam Great Divide Redfeather Lake Ione Crook
Pagoda Home
Dinosaur Dacono
Teds Place Rustic
Haybro The Forks
Axial Severance Log Lane Village Last Chance
Steamboat Springs Hygiene Brush
Superior Heartstron
Hideaway Park
Boulder
Blackhawk
Rifle Silt Basalt Frisco Empire Federal Heights J
Sunlight Silver Plume Deer Trail
Parachute Dotsero Tiger Golden Buick
Antlers
Snowmass Climax Tiny Town Punkin Center
Cameo
Skyway Monument
Fairplay Abe Lincoln Wild Horse
Tincup Divide Black Forest
Cripple Creek
North Pole Firstview
Security
Paradox
Sinbad Bonanza New Deal Sugar City
Nucla Powderhorn
Egnar Slick Rock Focus Swallows Hasty
Sawpit Silver Cliff Rye
Telluride
Mutual
Red Wing Toonerville
Yellow Jacket Mayday
Model
Gem Village Romeo Stonewall
Marvel Chromo Rugby

ABE LINCOLN: Teller County. For the Great Emancipator.

ANTLERS: Garfield County. Named by Henry A. Butters, its founder, for the Antlers Hotel in Colorado Springs.

AXIAL: Moffat County. There are two completely unrelated stories as to how this town acquired its moniker. One report is that when Major J. W. Powell completed a geological survey of the area, he wrote in his report that this particular spot seemed to form the "axis" for the rise in the surrounding mountains. The second story follows the belief that Axial is derived from the Indian word meaning "soft water." There is a basis for this assumption, since there are three softwater springs in the vicinity.

BASALT: Eagle County. For Basalt Peak, which is a lava formation.

BLACK FOREST: El Paso County. For a lush stand of ponderosa pine trees.

BLACKHAWK: Gilpin County. In descending order, the town took its name from the Blackhawk Mining Company, which took its title from the trademark of some machinery, which was christened for the Blackhawk Indians.

BONANZA: Saguache County. The discovery of gold here was thought to be a "bonanza" strike. While the village name stuck, the gold didn't, and much of the population went elsewhere after 1882.

BOULDER: Boulder County. From early day gold mining in the area, the vicinity is heavily populated with "rocks"; thus, the name.

BRUSH: Morgan County. Honors Jared L. Brush, a cattleman.

BUICK: Elbert County. Originally known as Godfrey. The current name salutes the pioneering Beuck family. This moniker was difficult to pronounce, so the spelling was changed to Buick.

CAMEO: Mesa County. For a cliff formation that overlooks the town.

CHROMO: Archuleta County. Community name taken from the Greek word for "color," and received its tag from the many colored rocks in the area.

CLIMAX: Lake County. Took its name from the fact that the town has the distinction of having the highest situated depot on the railroad line.

CRIPPLE CREEK: Teller County. First known as Fremont; the town label was changed for that of a stream. The creek acquired its name because so many cattle were crippled while crossing it.

CROOK: Logan County. Remembers General George Crook, who played a major role in the capture of the Apache chief Geronimo.

DACONO: Weld County. A coal mine was opened here in early days by C. L. Baum. Later, a small settlement grew up in the vicinity of the mine. Baum derived the village name from the first two letters of his wife's name, Daisy, and the first two letters of the names of two of her friends, Cora Van Voorhies and Nona Brooks.

DEER TRAIL: Arapahoe County. For its location on a path deer once used on their way to Bijou Creek.

DINOSAUR: Moffat County. Originally known as Artesia, residents changed the name in 1965 to draw tourists flocking to nearby Dinosaur National Monument.

DIVIDE: Teller County. For its location between the drainage basin of Fountain Creek and the South Platte River.

DOTSERO: Eagle County. There are several versions for the origin of this community name. From legend, it is the name of a Ute Indian chief's daughter. Another source states it is a Ute word meaning "something new," and refers to a nearby extinct volcano. The most valid claim is that this was the site of the beginning of the 1885 regional survey. As such, the site was marked .0 (dot zero), which in time evolved to Dotsero.

EGNAR: San Miguel County. Citizens of this village wanted to name it Range. When advised that the name was already in use, they simply reversed the spelling.

EMPIRE: Clear Creek County. Four men founded this settlement and christened it with the nickname of their former home state, New York.

FAIRPLAY: Park County. Originally called Park City, then Tarryall City. A group of miners, having been unsuccessful at previous diggings, moved to this area along the South Platte River, where they found extremely rich deposits of gold ore. Because of their good fortune, they named their new settlement Fairplay.

FEDERAL HEIGHTS: Adams County. For its location on Federal Boulevard, north of Denver.

FIRSTVIEW: Cheyenne County. Appropriately named, since it is from this locale that travelers from the east are rewarded with the "first view" of Pikes Peak and the Front Range of the Rocky Mountains.

FOCUS: Custer County. Christened for the focus of its vista: Wet Mountain Valley and the Sangre de Cristo Range.

FRISCO: Summit County. Named for, but using the shortened form of, the city by the bay.

GEM VILLAGE: La Plata County. Founded by Frank Morse, a dealer in gems and minerals. It is a colony for artists and has become a mecca for "rock hounds" and workers in semiprecious stones.

GOLDEN: Jefferson County. Two versions exist as to the birth of this city name. Some contend it was named for Tom Golden, who is given credit for first discovering gold in Clear Creek. Others say it took its handle from the ore that was panned in the creek. There are those who vow it was named for nearby Golden Gate Canyon.

GREAT DIVIDE: Moffat County. Believed to have been named for a weekly publication called the *Great Divide*, which the *Denver Post* published for about four years (1914–1918).

HASTY: Bent County. Honors W. A. Hasty, who settled the site in 1907.

HAYBRO: Routt County. Salutes the Hayden brothers, coal operators.

HEARTSTRONG: Yuma County. In late 1908 or early 1909, Richard J. Gilmore migrated to Colorado from Wisconsin, settling in the vicinity of the present site of Heartstrong. In time a post office was established and given the name Happyville. The little community prospered, and the popularity of the oncoming "horseless carriage" caused an even greater growth. In 1920, a disagreement arose among some of the businessmen, and descendants and relatives of the elder Gilmore up and moved their buildings and garages two miles west. Once settled and operational, application was made for a post office at the new settlement. It was granted and given the name Heartstrong. Some old-timers in the area claim the name was "headstrong" due to the circumstances causing the relocation. The depression of the thirties, coupled with the building of a major highway some miles from the vicinity, doomed both towns. Today, little remains of Heartstrong.

HIDEAWAY PARK: Grand County. Once known as Vasquez, later as Little Chicago. It is believed that Mack Kortz, local dance hall owner, suggested the village name for its hidden location among a grove of pine trees.

HOME: Larimer County. John R. Brown suggested the settlement be christened Mountain Home. When advised there were too many Mountain Homes already, he simply dropped "Mountain."

HYGIENE: Boulder County. A most unusual name for a town. This site was originally known as Pella, but was changed to Hygiene late in the nineteenth century, taking the name from a church and sanatorium established by Perry White and known as Hygiene Home.

IONE: Weld County. Union Pacific Railroad officials queried of W. A. Davis as to who owned the land in the vicinity. He replied, in effect, "I'm the one." Thus, inspiration for the newly established community's name.

JOES: Yuma County. Among the early settlers of this community were three men whose first names were Joe. The village adopted the name Three Joes, which eventually became Joes.

54

LAST CHANCE: Washington County. A small settlement established early in this century by Essa Harburt and Archie Chapman. These two men set up a service area for early automobiles and advertised their operation as the last chance for gas, oil, water, and the like for many miles in any direction.

LOG LANE VILLAGE: Morgan County. This site was originally intended as a source of alcoholic spirits to quench the thirst of soldiers from nearby Fort Morgan, which had no other liquor outlet. The plan changed, however, with the birth of a community. The city fathers, for either aesthetic, profit or unique reasons, decreed that all structures erected within the village limits must either be built or faced with logs. Hence, the name. This building ordinance was rescinded in the mid-1960s.

MARVEL: La Plata County. For Marvel Midget, a cooperative flour mill.

MAYDAY: La Plata County. This is usually an expression meaning danger or help needed; however, the community was named for the Mayday Mine.

MODEL: Las Animas County. Originally known as Poso, Spanish for "dry hole," and apparently descriptive of the area. Later it was called Roby. In 1920, the name was changed to its current designation when the town inaugurated its own irrigation system and redesigned the town site plats. These changes were intended to make the community a model town.

MONUMENT: El Paso County. For a rock formation.

MUTUAL: Huerfano County. Refers to a mine, which was "mutually" operated by several individuals.

NEW DEAL: Fremont County. This town was created when a gold strike hit the area, and was named in 1933 for President Franklin Roosevelt's plan to help the nation out of the Great Depression.

NORTH POLE: El Paso County. This children's entertainment center is almost a carbon copy of the same fairyland built in Upstate New York in 1949. Catering to youngsters, the original attraction was designed by a Walt Disney artist, using expressions and comments by a small girl as to how she thought Santa Claus's home and workshop looked.

NUCLA: Montrose County. The Colorado Co-Operate Company organized this town in 1904 as a socialistic farm colony. C. E. Williams suggested this name—a corruption of "nucleus" (center)—because he thought the town would be the center of a large communal expansion.

PAGODA: Routt County. This Asiatic name was derived from Pagoda Peak, so named because it resembles an Oriental-style temple.

PARACHUTE: Garfield County. For the creek. The stream acquired its name because, as viewed from a distance, a parachute design is formed by the east, west, and middle forks of the creek.

PARADOX: Montrose County. Takes its name from either Paradox Creek or Paradox Valley. The valley was so named because the Dolores River cuts through the walls of the valley at right (paradoxical) angles.

POWDERHORN: Gunnison County. One explanation is that the Cebolla Valley in which the town lies resembles a large powder horn. Another version is that a powder horn was found in a stream by the first white men to enter the valley.

PUNKIN CENTER: Lincoln County. This is a derivation of "pumpkin," and salutes a local farmer who grew large pumpkins. One of the town's earlier names was Prairie Dream.

RED WING: Huerfano County. Music was in the air when this site was named. As several residents were discussing a possible name for their home, a Mexican happened by, whistling the tune of a popular song. It caught the ears of the citizens, the name was submitted to the postal department, and the community of Red Wing came to be.

REDFEATHER LAKE: Larimer County. A resort town founded by a man named Princell, and christened for Chief Redfeather, a Cherokee Indian.

RIFLE: Garfield County. For the creek. The stream was so named when, in 1880, a unit of soldiers was placing mileposts between the Colorado and White Rivers and one of the soldiers, having left his rifle by the creek, was forced to return and retrieve it. Whether his search was successful or not is unknown, but because of his forgetfulness, the stream was so christened and, eventually, so was the town.

ROMEO: Conejos County. First called Sunflower. Citizens wanted the community named for an early settler, Romero. There were other settlements by that name, so the "r" was dropped and the name Romeo adopted.

RUBGY: Las Animas County. An Englishman owned mines in the vicinity and named his mining camp for a city in England.

RUSTIC: Larimer County. Remembers the Rustic Hotel, built by S. B. Stewart. Old-timers termed a stay in the mountains as "rusticating," or getting away from it all. Among the "rusticators" to this area are said to have been Teddy Roosevelt and Ulysses S. Grant.

RYE: Pueblo County. The most plausible origin of this hamlet label is that the town site was located in a field of rye. A more colorful version exists. It seems the postmaster suggested the name Table

Mountain, but it was rejected for being too long. He then submitted Old Rye (a whiskey), but "Old" was deleted.

SAWPIT: San Miguel County. For the Sawpit Mine.

SECURITY: El Paso County. Community established by American Builders and the name was probably chosen because of its appeal to the public.

SEVERANCE: Weld County. Honors Dave Severance, a property owner.

SILT: Garfield County. Designated by the Denver and Rio Grand Western Railroad for the soil in the region.

SILVER CLIFF: Custer County. This community, incorporated in 1879, took its handle from the rich silver ore discovered in a nearby cliff.

SILVER PLUME: Clear Creek County. There are a couple of versions as to the origin of this community name. The first is that Stephen Decatur, an early Colorado pioneer, gave the site its name. Why he selected this particular moniker, if he did, is not known. The second rendition is that the settlement was named for politician James G. Blaine, who was known as the "Plumed Knight." Both Blaine and Decatur were men with illustrious careers. The former was twice nominated by his party as a presidential candidate, he was a member of Congress, and served as secretary of state. Decatur, gallant pacesetter of naval tradition, is probably best known for one of the most famous pledges in history: "Our country! In her intercourse with foreign nations may she always be in the right; but our country, right or wrong."

SINBAD: Montrose County. For the character Sinbad the Sailor, because of its remoteness and inaccessibility, places to which Sinbad ventured.

SKYWAY: Mesa County. This summer resort, at an altitude of 10,000 feet, was named for Skyway Drive, which tops Grand Mesa Mountain.

SLICK ROCK: San Miguel County. Originally called Snyders Camp, the present name comes from smooth and fracture-free sandstone found in the area.

SNOWMASS: Pitkin County. For the mountain; with the mountain name probably being descriptive.

STEAMBOAT SPRINGS: Routt County. The town was christened for a spring that was destroyed in 1908 during construction of the Moffat Railroad. The spring emitted an odd huffing and puffing sound, similar to steamboats.

STONEWALL: Las Animas County. James Stoner homesteaded in this area. There was an unusual rock formation on his ranch, and the place became known as Stoner's Wall. In time, a post office was established and given the name Stonewall, which the village later adopted.

SUGAR CITY: Crowley County. For the National Sugar Company.

SUNBEAM: Moffat County. A farmer by the name of N. C. Bonives suggested the name because he thought the sun shone brighter at this point than anywhere else in the valley.

SUNLIGHT: Garfield County. This mining town was originally christened Sunshine, a common name for early, dreary mining towns. Because of its lack of uniqueness, the citizens changed the name to Sunlight in 1897.

SUPERIOR: Boulder County. For Superior, Wisconsin.

SWALLOWS: Pueblo County. Tagged for the abundance of birds that nested in cliffs along the Arkansas River.

TEDS PLACE: Larimer County. Established by Edward "Ted" Herring when he returned from World War I. It is situated at the entrance to Poudre Canyon.

TELLURIDE: San Miguel County. Originally called Columbia; name was changed for the tellurium ore found in the area.

THE FORKS: Larimer County. The first construction here was a hotel for area lumberjacks. The site was also a way station for the stagecoach traveling between Denver and Laramie. The town acquired its name for its location on Highway 287, where it "forked" toward Livermore.

TIGER: Summit County. For the Royal Tiger Mines Company.

TINCUP: Gunnison County. Community probably received its unique name from early mining days, when saloons served drinks in tin cups. Another version is that the place acquired its moniker when a prospector, thinking the area contained gold, carried a sample of dirt to his camp in a tin cup. His suspicion proved accurate.

TINY TOWN: Jefferson County. Several years back, George Turner built an elaborate miniature city on this site along the banks of Turkey Creek. The buildings and other structures in this astonishing work averaged just three feet in height. A resort village eventually grew up around the midget-sized city and took the name Tiny Town. There is a similar miniature village at Maduradam, The Netherlands.

TOONERVILLE: Bent County. Tired of the original humdrum name of Red Rock, residents of this little community looked around for a new, unique designation for their town. It was speculated at the time that before long there might be a streetcar joyously clanging its way through the streets. A popular cartoon strip and movie comedy series of the time was "Toonerville Folks," created by Fontaine Fox. A small streetcar usually played a major role in seg-

ments of "Toonerville," so citizens adopted the name for their community.

58 WILD HORSE: Cheyenne County. For a nearby creek that served as a watering hole for bands of wild horses.

YELLOW JACKET: Montezuma County. Appropriately named for a nearby canyon that had walls covered with yellow jacket nests.

Connecticut
THE CONSTITUTION STATE

BANTAM: Litchfield County. Believed to be a corruption of the Indian word *peantum,* meaning "he prays," or "praying." *Peantum* was a word used when referring to a Christian Indian.

INDIAN NECK: New Haven County. An old Indian settlement dating back to the late seventeenth century. The first white colony was located across the river from an Indian village, which was on a peninsula. Apparently, the whites named the site for the occupants and the shape of the peninsula.

MYSTIC: New London County. In today's terminology, a mystic delves into the occult. This small community contains no mystery. Its moniker is a translation of the Mohegan Indian word *missituck,* which means "great tidal river," and was first applied to a stream, then to Mystic, Old Mystic, Mystic Bridge, etc.

TARIFFVILLE: Hartford County. Believed to relate to a carpet factory once located here that was blessed with a protective "tariff."

VOLUNTOWN: New London County. The community was so labeled because the land was granted to settlers who were "volunteers" in King Philip's War.

WOODTICK: New Haven County. There are two versions on the origin of this name. One, that it is translated from the Indian word *wudtuckgun,* meaning "a piece of wood" or "wood for burning." The more flavorful version is that the name came about when a man working a field, and evidently perspiring heavily, removed his coat and laid it aside. That evening, when he started to put the coat on, he found it full of small insects known as wood ticks.

Delaware

THE FIRST STATE

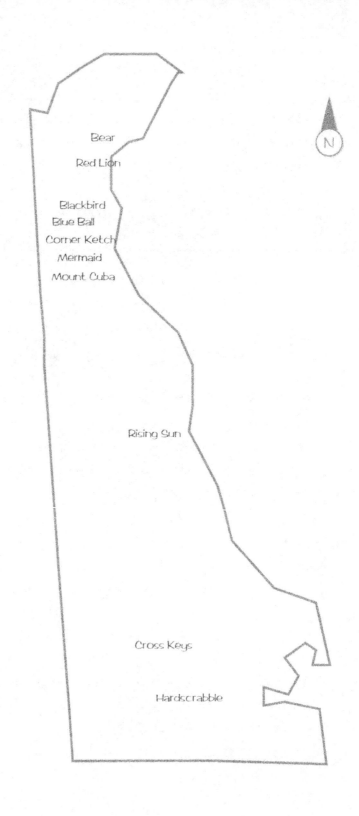

Bear

Red Lion

Blackbird
Blue Ball
Corner Ketch
Mermaid
Mount Cuba

Rising Sun

Cross Keys

Hardscrabble

N

BEAR: New Castle County. For the Bear Tavern.

BLACKBIRD: New Castle County. This is an old community and lore has it that it was founded by the notorious pirate Blackbeard. As time passed, townspeople became self-conscious about the name. They wanted to change it, yet leave some vestige of the original designation. As fate would have it, the site was a favorite roosting spot for blackbirds. This coincidence led to the renaming of the community, without completely erasing its former kinship.

BLUE BALL: New Castle County. For the Blue Ball Tavern.

CORNER KETCH: New Castle County. In early days, there was a tavern on this site that was a magnet for the rowdier elements of the area. The place gained such notoriety that strangers were warned, "They'll ketch you at the corner," referring to the tavern.

CROSS KEYS: Sussex County. Remembers an early inn that displayed "crossed keys" on its sign.

HARDSCRABBLE: Sussex County. This is a predominantly black community and is descriptive of the hard life the residents have led.

MERMAID: New Castle County. For the Mermaid Tavern, erected here in 1740.

MOUNT CUBA: New Castle County. In 1730, Cornelius Hollehan built an estate here and called it Cuba Rock. The village that grew up later adopted its current name from the estate and the hill on which it was situated.

RED LION: New Castle County. For the Red Lion Tavern.

RISING SUN: Kent County. Originally known as Five Points, for its location where five roads intersected. The community was renamed for the Rising Sun Tavern.

Florida

THE SUNSHINE STATE

ALADDIN CITY: Dade County. Part of the boom that hit Florida in the mid-1920s, this town developed so fast it was like magic. Hence, the name, which refers to the boy with the magic lamp.   69

ALLIANCE: Jackson County. Like so many towns christened at the time, this one took the name of the Farmers Alliance Organization, a semipotent political association of the 1890s.

AMERICAN BEACH: Nassau County. Established in the 1930s by employees of the Afro-American Life Insurance Company as a public beach for blacks, who were, at the time, barred from the state's other beaches. The name is a patriotic one, symbolizing a feeling that would emerge two decades later.

BALM: Hillsborough County. It is believed that the community was christened for its balmy weather.

BEAR HEAD: Walton County. According to folklore, the village was tagged for its location at the head of Bear Creek.

CANTONMENT: Escambia County. So named because this was the encampment site for General Andrew Jackson and his troops in 1814, during their expedition against Spain. This area again served Jackson in 1821, while awaiting the transfer of Florida Territory from Spain to the United States.

CAPTIVA: Lee County. This ancient site, first touched by Ponce de Leon when he was searching for the fabled "fountain of youth," has a pair of renditions for the origin of its name. It's possible the island derived its name from the fact that the pirate Gasparilla kept a harem of women captive here. The more accepted explanation for the name is that Juan Ortiz, a Spanish sailor, was lured ashore and taken prisoner by Indians. His life was saved by an Indian woman, and he eventually returned to his own people. The place, in early days, carried the name *Boca Cautiva*, which is Spanish for "pass of the captive."

CELEBRATION: Orange County. Built by Walt Disney, Inc., as a modern, environmentally sound community. The moniker was chosen to "put residents in a positive frame of mind from the outset."

CENTURY: Escambia County. Relates to an event, the construction of a timber mill here the first month of the twentieth century. Its former name was much more enticing: Teaspoon.

CHOSEN: Palm Beach County. This name was selected by members of the Church of the Brethren because they considered it to be the chosen place.

CHRISTMAS: Orange County. Honors a no longer existing fort, with construction being completed on the site on Christmas Day, 1835. The U.S. Army used the fort in its campaign against the Seminole Indians. While the town may no longer have a fort, its popularity is tremendous, especially during December of each year when people from all over America send cards and letters to the small community to have them postmarked "Christmas, Florida."

COCOA: Brevard County. There are conflicting origins for this town's name. One source claims it comes from the cocoa plum so abundant in the area. The more traditional minded assert that when a name for the settlement was being considered, an elderly woman happened to spy the label on a box of Baker's Cocoa and suggested the name.

CORAL GABLES: Dade County. So named because the first houses built here had gables decorated with coral rock.

CORKSCREW: Collier County. For Corkscrew Creek, which obtained its tag for its winding and twisting course.

CREELS: Franklin County. A creel is a basket in which those who are lucky put their daily catch of fish. In this instance, though, the city honors a Mr. Creel, early owner of a turpentine and navel business in nearby Eastpoint.

DOCTOR PHILIPS: Orange County. For a Doctor Phillips, reportedly the largest citrus fruit grower in the state.

DOCTORS INLET: Clay County. Information on the origin of this name is sketchy. The community is situated on a body of water known as Doctors Inlet. Lore has it that a doctor, who had his home on the lake, slipped into the water and drowned. This is apparently the traditional version of the name origin for the lake, with the settlement later taking the same title.

DOGTOWN: Gadsden County. Designated for its early history as a site where dogs were pitted against each other in what some people term "sport."

DOUBLESINK: Levy County. Relates to natural sinks (hollows) located near here.

FIDELIS: Santa Rosa County. The community is believed to have acquired its name from the Fidelis Methodist Church, established here many years ago.

FORT LONESOME: Hillsborough County. The only agreement on the origin of this name is that there never was a fort here. One source states that the community was named by Mrs. Davis Stanland, storekeeper, because the land was flat for miles around and completely devoid of any other population. The second version is that the site was labeled by a National Guard unit stationed here in 1929 to prevent the spread up the peninsula of the Mediterranean fruit fly.

FROSTPROOF: Polk County. An appropriate name applied to the site
by early cowboys who moved their cattle into this region during
winter months.

GOLDEN GATE: Collier County. This community was developed by
the Gulf-American Corporation in the mid-1960s. It was established on what at one time was a swamp and given its name by
the developers.

GOLF: Palm Beach County. Founded in 1950 by the same links
enthusiasts that founded Golf, Illinois.

GREENHEAD: Washington County. Long ago, this was a favorite
camping spot for people traveling to Panama City. Nearby was a
spring, around which the grass always stayed green; thus, the
name Greenhead was applied to the locale and then to the community.

GULF BREEZE: Santa Rosa County. So named because it is swept by
soft breezes flowing inward from either Pensacola Bay or the Gulf
of Mexico.

HACIENDA VILLAGE: Broward County. Originally called Hacienda
Flores, to reflect an aura of homes and flowers. When the city was
incorporated in 1950, "Flores" was replaced by "Village."

INDIALANTIC: Brevard County. Another town born during Florida's
boom of the '20s. A contest was held to select a name for the site.
Mrs. G. F. Duren submitted the winning entry with the geographical name, depicting the community's location between the Indian
River and the Atlantic Ocean.

INTERCESSION CITY: Osceola County. First called Inter-Ocean City,
this boomtown failed during the depression. A religious sect, the
Household of Faith, came here from Point Pleasant, West Virginia,
in the 1930s and purchased the property, with the aim of establishing a Bible school. In accordance with their faith, and to give the
site a religious orientation, they named their new home
Intercession (Prayer) City.

JUPITER: Palm Beach County. This site was originally called Jobe or
Jove (pronounced "Hoe-bay") by Indians. When English mapmak-
ers cataloged their maps, they marked the site as Jupiter. This mistake, nevertheless, was inspiration for naming nearby settlements
Juno, Mars, and Venus.

LONGBOAT KEY: Manatee County. Christened by Hernando de Soto
in July 1539, because a longboat lost by one of his crewmen was
found on this jut (key) of land.

MARATHON: Monroe County. From a local source, when a railroad
was being constructed here in earlier years, the laborers were urged
to work faster. Some of them were heard to complain, "What is

this, a marathon?" Later, when a community was established here, it took the name Marathon.

MEDLEY: Dade County. Dual inspiration served for this handle. First, because the name was pretty and, second, for Sylvester Medley, an early settler.

NICEVILLE: Okaloosa County. The people thought it was a "nice" place to live.

NORUM: Washington County. Tradition states that this community acquired its name because citizens kept it dry (free of alcoholic beverages).

OSPREY: Sarasota County. Relates to the hawk-like bird found here by settlers.

PAISLEY: Lake County. For Paisley, Scotland.

PANACEA: Wakulla County. For nearby springs, believed to have "all-curing" powers.

PENNEY FARMS: Clay County. This community, founded by chain store mogul J. C. Penney, was established for retired ministers and their wives. It was a tribute to his father, who was a minister.

PERKY: Monroe County. Honors Ritter Clyde Perky, who purchased the site in 1925.

PICNIC: Hillsborough County. This settlement was once known, unofficially, as Hurrah, because of its location on Hurrah Creek. It used to be a favorite spot for picnics and other family outings and, in time, this brought on the changing of the name to Picnic.

POSTAL COLONY: Lake County. The settlement was established in 1923 by retired postal clerks; thus, appropriately named.

ROMEO, JULIETTE: Marion County. Juliette, spelled differently from Shakespeare's famous work, is located just over seven miles from Romeo. Like the bard's famous tragedy, these two cities reportedly had a boy-girl situation, with disagreeing families, and the love affair also had a sad ending.

SAWDUST: Gadsden County. For an early sawmill.

SOPCHOPPY: Wakulla County. Supposedly derived its name from the Seminole language, and pertains to the red oak tree.

SUNRISE: Broward County. The developers of this community pulled a boner when they first set up the village as a retirement center. When organized, the community was called Sunset. Developers soon learned that retirees had no liking for a name that reminded them of their waning years. In 1961, the name was changed to Sunrise Golf Village; then, in 1971, it was incorporated as Sunrise.

TAINTSVILLE: Seminole County. A geographical situation brought about this rather comical name. Between the two cities of Oviedo and Chuluta, there sat a nameless little settlement referred to as "a

spot" between the two aforementioned towns. A delegate to the
county commissioners wanted a name for his home. The delegate
also informed them that his settlement "'tain't in Oviedo and
'tain't in Chuluta." Hence, inspiration for the name.

TANGERINE: Orange County. For the citrus fruit.

TWO EGG: Jackson County. Few locations have a more unique name
than this small panhandle community. There are two versions as
to the origin of the label. One states that two brothers opened a
store on the site and their first customer asked for "two eggs." The
second rendition is that a small child walked into the store, placed
two eggs on the counter, and said, "Mammy says give her one egg's
worth of bladder snuff, and one egg's worth of ball potash."

YANKEETOWN: Levy County. Originally settled by the Knotts family
in 1923, the community went by that name. The Knotts and their
followers were from the North, however, and native residents
referred to the place as Yankeetown. When the city was incorporated in 1925, the latter name was officially recorded.

Georgia

THE EMPIRE STATE OF THE SOUTH

AERIAL: Habersham County. Appropriately named for its location among high mountains.

AIRLINE: Hart County. A popular railroad name for a straight or direct route. This community was tagged for the Piedmont Airline Railroad.

ALLIANCE: Jasper County. For the Farmers Alliance, a rural organization with some political clout in the 1890s.

ARABI: Crisp County. Relates to R. A. Bedgood, sawmill operator. Bedgood received supplies and equipment for his mill by horse and wagon, and the crates and cartons were addressed to "RAB," his initials. As the community grew in size and a post office was established, residents added the A and I to Bedgood's initials and thus christened the town. Why those particular letters were selected remains a mystery.

ARCADE: Jackson County. For a community school housed in an arcade-like building.

ARCH: Forsyth County. For a Cherokee Indian linguist, whose tribal name was K'tsi, which was, in time, corrupted into Arch.

ASBESTOS: White County. Refers to the mineral that was mined in the vicinity.

BALL GROUND: Cherokee County. Apparently so tagged because Indians here once played a game of ball similar to lacrosse. This was their favorite sport and was attended by much ceremony and ritual.

BAREFOOT (BEARFOOT): Towns County. The name of this little hamlet either refers to a bear track or a place where residents had to go without shoes.

BENEVOLENCE: Randolph County. In 1840, members of the Primitive Baptist Church split over the issue of establishing missions. Those in favor of such an undertaking withdrew and set up their religious meetings in the community schoolhouse. Later that year, Thomas Coram donated five acres of land for a church and cemetery. The congregation thought this such a "benevolent" gesture that they named their new church Benevolence; the community name followed.

BETWEEN: Walton County. For its geographical position between the cities of Monroe and Loganville.

BOX SPRINGS: Talbot County. The town has nothing to do with sleeping paraphernalia, having been so named when, in 1853, railroad workers "boxed" a spring near the track to supply water for locomotives.

BUCKHEAD: Morgan County. A hunting party killed a large deer and hung its head on a tree near here; thus, the name.

BUCKHORN: Harralson County. Isaac E. Cobb once killed a deer and hung its horns in front of his house. As an adjacent community emerged, residents took the site's name from Cobb's decoration.

BUGABOO ISLAND: Ware County. "Bugaboo" is an often expressed term even today and usually has a negative meaning. This location was named in early days when a hunter became frightened by noises he heard but couldn't explain. It's assumed the hunter never told his friends that the terrible noise was only caused by the wind making two trees rub together. Anyway, the "strange noise" legend accounts for the name of the place.

BURNT FORT: Charlton County. By tradition, a fort, once located here, was destroyed by fire.

CABBAGETOWN: Fulton County. One version asserts that the origin of this community name came about when a produce cart over-turned, spilling its contents. Another source claims the name stems from the odor of cabbage coming from the kitchens in this mostly blue-collar suburb of Atlanta.

CALVARY: Grady County. Settled in the early 1800s by staunch Baptists who migrated from North Carolina; the town's name reflects their religious leanings.

CEMENT: Bartow County. For a cement plant that once operated here.

CENTER POST: Walker County. A designation derived during early days because it was the midway (center) point on the mail route between Bronco and Trion.

CHINA HILL: Telfair County. For the abundance of chinaberry trees growing on a nearby hill.

CLIMAX: Decatur County. Two explanations for this community name. One, it is from the Greek *klimax*, which means "the order of plants and animals in their natural environment," and the town was named for the South Georgia Agricultural and Experimental Studies. The second theory is that the site was so named because it is the highest point on the main railway line between the Chattahoochee River and Savannah. At least one source challenges this latter contention, pointing out that there are one or two other cities located at higher elevations on the same line.

COUNCIL: Clinch County. Family name.

CRABAPPLE: Fulton County. For a log cabin school built around 1874 near a malformed crab apple tree.

DAMES FERRY: Monroe County. The community was so designated from the fact that George and John Dame operated a ferry across the Ocmulgee River in the early 1800s. The ferry was still in use at the turn of the century.

DASHBOARD: Carroll County. There are few settlements in the United States with a more unusual moniker than this one. Cecil Spruell was proudly showing off his new buggy to the townspeople. There happened to be a mule nearby owned by a man named Slick Chambers. As Spruell drove past in his shiny vehicle, the mule lashed out with his feet and kicked in the dashboard.

DEEPSTEP: Washington County. There are two versions—one legend, one supposedly fact—for the origin of this name. Lore claims that an Indian once stepped into a large hole here and exclaimed, "Ugh. Deep step." Fact has it that Gus Avant, the first postmaster, suggested the name, taking it from nearby Deeptstep Creek. The stream supposedly acquired its handle because the banks near the present town site were so steep that people wanting to cross over had to go downstream where the banks were less steep.

DEWY ROSE: Elbert County. In the early 1800s, a community was established on this site and was called Willis Crossing. When a post office was set up, the postmaster wanted a more unique name and one that would not be easily confused with any other. Early one morning, his young daughter went out into the yard where dew covered the ground. Entranced by the glistening picture before her, she ran back into the house and excitedly exclaimed, "Daddy, come outside and look at the dewy roses!" Thus was born the town's name.

DOCTORTOWN: Wayne County. So tagged because the town was established on the site of an old Indian medicine village.

DOUBLE RUN: Wilcox County. Some believe this name was derived from the fact that "two" creeks "run" parallel to each other near this site. The second rendition leans to the theory that the name emerged from the intersecting lines of two railroads that once ran through the area.

DUE WEST: Cobb County. Apparently labeled for its location five miles due west of Marietta.

ENIGMA: Berrien County. An appropriate name, an enigma (riddle) in itself, since no one seems to know where the name came from, or why.

ENTERPRISE: Morgan County. Remembers the Enterprise Compress Company of Augusta, producers of cottonseed oil.

EXCELSIOR: Candler County. For an early school located here, which was named to personify "excellence" in academics.

EXPERIMENT: Spalding County. For the Georgia Agricultural Experiment Station, which was moved to this site in 1899.

FENDER: Tift County. For the Frank Fender Turpentine Works.

FLINTSTONE: Walker County. No cartoon character this, having been named for the flint stone used by Cherokee Indians for arrowheads and other weapons and tools, and found in abundance around here.

FREEDMAN: Liberty County. Both the community and the county are well named. At the end of the Civil War, a plantation owner deeded part of his estate to his former slaves. The settlement established on this land became known as Freedman.

GARDI: Wayne County. For nearby Gardi Swamp. The swamp was so named because the thickets were so dense, people had to "guard" their "eyes" when they traveled through it.

GOAT TOWN: Washington County. So tagged because an early store owner had a large herd of goats.

GOOD HOPE: Walton County. Relates to a futuristic and optimistic feeling settlers had for their community.

GRATIS: Walton County. Stunned residents christened their community when they learned that the opening of a post office would not cost them any money. Townspeople originally wanted to call the place Free, but the Post Office Department felt Gratis was more suitable.

GREENS CUT: Burke County. Refers to a railroad "cut" (right of way) running through the Moses P. Green plantation.

GUESS: Henry County. For Sequayah, the Cherokee Indian whose English name was George Guess.

HALFWAY: Lumpkin County. So named because when traveling by wagon, this locale was situated halfway between Gainesville and Dahlonega.

HEMP: Fannin County. For Tal-danigi-ski, a Cherokee chief whom whites referred to as "Hemp-carrier," because he dealt in fabrics.

HENTOWN: Early County. So named because J. D. Kilpatrick raised thousands of chickens around here.

HOPEFUL: Mitchell County. Tagged by early settlers because of its optimistic connotation.

HOPEULIKIT: Bulloch County. A last-ditch effort by the townspeople to secure a name for their community. After many suggestions were rejected by postal authorities, Hopeulikit was, in effect, a final plea by the residents.

IDEAL: Macon County. By some accounts, this name came about when railroad officials, seeking a good spot for a stop, came upon this site. One of the officials supposedly commented that the site was ideal. Others believe the town was named for its ideal location for future prosperity: plenty of water, good land, and near the railroad.

JET: Carroll County. Jet is a type of coal and was discovered in this region. Jet is dark and has a fine grain; it is easily polished and in early days was often used for buttons and costume jewelry.

JEWTOWN: Glynn County. Named for a Mr. Levinson, who once owned a store here. The storekeeper wanted to have the community called Levinsonston, but many locals insisted on calling the place Jewtown, and the name stuck.

JOLLY: Pike County. First called Travelers Rest, a railroad employee suggested the new name because of the good nature and humor of the residents.

JOT EM DOWN STORE: Pierce County. This hamlet was given the comic handle by an early store owner.

KITE: Johnson County. Salutes Shaderick Kight, who donated land for the townsite. It was he who simplified the spelling of his name for convenience.

LAVENDER: Floyd County. Honors George Lavender, settler and trading post owner.

LICKLOG: Lumpkin County. An early county seat of Lumpkin County, livestock used to be driven through this area. Logs were hollowed and filled with salt for the animals to lick.

MAXIM: Lincoln County. Community's name has a religious connection, the book of Proverbs, which contains "maxims," or sayings of truth and wisdom.

MAYDAY: Echols County. This is a term in modern usage that usually refers to a call for help. To this small Georgia settlement, however, it was on a day in May, in the late 1800s, that the railroad made its first run through the town.

METTER: Candler County. While on the surface this name may not have romantic inclinations, the root does. The community is said to have been named by a railroad official for his wife, because he "met her" here.

MYSTIC: Irwin County. Christened by a Mr. Tift for Mystic, Connecticut.

NAMELESS: Laurens County. The townspeople submitted several hundred names as possible choices for their hamlet. None of them were suitable to postal officials, so the decision was made that the community would be Nameless.

NEEDMORE: Echols County. So named because residents complained to a local store owner that they "need more" merchandise to buy.

NEWBORN: Newton County. A Methodist evangelist, Sam P. Jones, once delivered a moving sermon to the inhabitants of this community. His words were so stirring that residents decided to rename the town, assigning it a name that would reflect their "rebirth" of religion.

NEW ENGLAND: Dade County. In 1889, a group of northeastern promoters established this community in hopes of making it the future industrial capital of the South. While their hopes failed, the geographical designation of New England remains.

NICKAJACK: Cobb County. Legendary teachings state that this community received its name from Jack, an old resident black, who area Indians called "Nicko" instead of Negro.

PANTHERVILLE: DeKalb County. Tradition has it that the name came about from an event occurring around 1830, when a Mr. and Mrs. Johnson and their children were chased by a panther. There are those who believe, however, the name comes from that of an old Cherokee Indian clan.

PERCALE: Monroe County. A new community established as recently as 1966, it is the location of a Bibb Manufacturing Company plant, which makes percale bed linen.

PIONEER VILLAGE: Ware County. This is a village set up by Okefenokee Swamp Park to demonstrate to visitors how swampers in the pioneer days lived.

PLOWSHARES: Carroll County. Following the tragedy of the Civil War, this community desired a name that would hopefully remind people that peace was more desirable than war. Residents took the name from the Bible: ". . . and they shall beat their swords into plowshares . . ." (Isaiah 2:4).

POETRY: Chattooga County. Another new community, this one established in 1973 by Anne C. Otwell, who wanted to create a colony of poets. Poetry was once known as Tulip.

PULLTIGHT: Decatur/Grady counties. On the county line. This community was given its name partly through comical inclination and partly because it denotes a "poor mouthing" attitude.

RABBIT HILL: Bryan County. Christened during early settlement days when rabbits were the mainstay of inhabitants' diet.

RACEPOND: Charlton County. For Race Pond. The water was so named when, during the Civil War, Confederate soldiers, resting between battles, raced horses around the pond for sport and relaxation.

RECOVERY: Decatur County. Originally called Fort Recovery, this was the site where, during the First Seminole Indian War, wounded soldiers were sent to recover. A hospital was located here at the time.

RED CLAY: Whitfield County. Descriptive in name.

REDBUD: Garden County. So tagged for the presence of a small ornamental tree known as a redbud. The community was first called Crane Eater.

REGISTER: Bulloch County. For Franklin Pierce Register, who founded the town in 1894.

RELEE: Coffee County. For the Confederate general Robert E. Lee.

REMUS: Paulding County. For the "Uncle Remus" character created by Joel Chandler Harris.

REPUBLICAN: McDuffie County. Named in a less political vein, more for the idea of representative government.

RISING FAWN: Dade County. Romantics believe the town received its name from a lovely Indian princess named Rising Fawn, who lived in the area. More realistic minds associate the moniker with an Indian chief.

ROCK FACE: Whitfield County. For a nearby rock formation that resembles a face.

ROCKMART: Polk County. Slate deposits that have received world recognition were discovered here in 1849. The community name is a modification of the words "Rock Market."

ROOSTERVILLE: Heard County. So named because of nearby farms, from which there seemed to be heard a steady crowing of roosters.

ROYAL LODGE: Harris County. Established in 1973 by wealthy land developer John B. Amos. The settlement took its name from a lodge once situated on the site, and from the proposed English village format of the community.

SALE CITY: Mitchell County. For T. D. Sale.

SANDY CROSS: Oglethorpe County. This name was selected for dual reasons: the white sandy soil in the area, and the fact that several roads cross at this point.

SANTA CLAUS: Toombs County. For the jolly Christmas gift bearer.

SAW DUST: Columbia County. So tagged because there were several sawmills in the vicinity.

SHAKE RAG: Fulton County. This railroad stop acquired its moniker from the custom of waving a handkerchief or some other piece of cloth as a signal to trainmen.

SHAKE RAG: Fayette County. Same as for Fulton County, above.

SILK HOPE: Chatham County. Christened in early days and expressed the anticipation of establishing a silk industry here.

SIX MILE: Floyd County. Originally known as Courtesy, the name was changed to reflect the distance by rail from here to Rome, Georgia.

SNAKE NATION: Fannin County. The community took its name from the old Cherokee Nation, which had chiefs with such names as Going Snake Speaker and Speckled Snake Chief.

SNAPFINGER: DeKalb County. For Snapfinger Creek. Storytellers relate that the stream was named in early times, when, as the county was being surveyed, a surveyor fell and broke a finger beside an unnamed creek. Because he "snapped" his finger near the water, the surveying party decided to christen the stream Snapfinger. Other sources claim the creek was named for a branch, or finger, of Snapping Shoals Creek.

SOCIAL CIRCLE: Walton County. One source states that the name was carried from Bulloch County. Another basis is that the title was derived from a meeting held at this spot in early times. The friendliness of the people attending the meeting was enhanced through the uncorking of kegs and bottles, making them more social.

SPRING PLACE: Murray County. The Moravian Brethren established the first mission in the area to educate the Cherokees. The church was named for a nearby spring, and later, when a settlement grew up a short distance away, it took the name of the mission.

STILLMORE: Emanuel County. When the town was first set up, postal authorities sent a list of possible names for the settlement. Officials stated that if none of the names on the list were suitable, they would send "still more." The names suggested were passed over in favor of Stillmore.

STOP: Cherokee County. For a chief of the "Old Sixes" Indian village located here in the early 1800s.

SUBLIGNA: Chattooga County. This is from the Latin *sub*, meaning "under," and *ligna*, meaning "wood," and was named by a Dr. Underwood for himself.

SUNSWEET: Tift County. This is a fruit industry trade name, which came from the bountiful crop of peaches harvested here in 1894.

SWEET GUM: Fannin County. For the sweet gum tree, found in abundance in the area.

SWORDS: Morgan County. Salutes John Buchanan Swords, settler and benefactor.

TADMORE: Hall County. In some sections of the country this word is used to express "a little more." This community, however, took its moniker from the biblical name of an ancient commercial center also known as Palmyra.

TALKING ROCK: Pickens County. There are several versions as to how this site acquired its name. One has it that Irishmen working on the railroad would leave money on a large rock, and Indians would replace the money with jugs of home-brewed whiskey. Another belief is that the label originated from a large rock in a nearby stream that made odd sounds as water rushed around and over it. An Indian legend claims the name comes from a rock with which Indians played tricks on each other. Finally, the assertion is made that the tag is a translation of a Cherokee name, *Nunygunswani-ski*, which means "the talker," or "place of the talker."

TAX: Talbot County. So named because county tax officials stopped at a store here to collect tax returns.

TEMPERANCE: Greene County. Once called Public Square, the name was changed after a great temperance revival was held here in either 1826 or 1827.

TEMPERANCE: Telfair County. Christened by a Methodist congregation, which had a large campground here before the Civil War.

THE ROCK: Upson County. So named because the community is situated on a rock, outcroppings of which appear over the site. Tradition has it that in early days mail was deposited in a secret opening in the rock, then covered with another rock. Stage drivers were told to leave mail at the rock, and later, when a post office was established on the site, the name was adopted.

THUNDERBOLT: Chatham County. The name for this community goes back to early days of settlement. James Oglethorpe, who led the colonization of Georgia, is credited with the name. Tradition says that a huge thunderbolt struck a rock near the site of the present community, shattering the rock, from which water gushed forth. Oglethorpe continued by saying that the water poured from the ground and emitted the "odor of brimstone."

TIGER: Rabun County. For the Cherokee chief Tiger Tail.

TOONIGH: Cherokee County. This is the railroad name for the town of Lebanon. There are differing versions as to how this name came about. It could have come from the name of a Cherokee chief, *Tooantuh*, which means "spring frog." Another explanation is that the hamlet was "too nigh" (too near) the village of Woodstock to be a part of Holly Springs and vice versa. Still another thought is that the train station building was brought to this site on a flatcar. As railroad workers struggled to situate the structure, one man marched along the tracks to make sure that it was not too close. As the engineer maneuvered the train back and forth, the man kept yelling, "Too nigh. Too nigh."

TRADERS HILL: Charlton County. Named for a trading post established when the community was a thriving trading center in the mid-1800s.

TRANS: Walker County. A prefix meaning "across." The community was christened by Professor E. I. F. Cheyenne, who "came across" the mountains to teach here.

TRICKUM: Walker County. Originally known as Graysville, for a man who operated a store here. The name was changed after this same store owner allegedly "tricked" and swindled some of his customers.

TY TY: Tift County. Another town name of conflicting origin. It could have been for the many railroad "ties" cut and sold here during early railroading days. Or it could have come from the phrase "Tight-Eye," used in early times to describe thickets or other dense growth that was hard to penetrate with the eye. The third possibility is that the name came from Ty Ty Creek. The stream was named for either the white titi (ironwood) or the black titi (wheat) trees that grew along the creek bank.

VILLANOW: Walker County. Two backgrounds to the origin of this handle: One source believes the name was taken from the novel *Thaddeus of Warsaw*, written by Jane Porter and published in 1803. In the novel is described a magnificent palace called Villanow. More traditional-minded folk lean toward the theory that the title was coined by Mrs. Constantine Wood, who is credited with saying, "It is no longer a hamlet, but is now a village, or village now."

VISAGE: Towns County. For the panoramic scene the town offers.

WAHOO: Lumpkin County. The label is believed to have come from the Creek Indian word *uhawhu*, which means "cork" or "winged elm."

WAX: Floyd County. A shortened form of "Waxhaw," birthplace of Andrew Jackson in South Carolina.

WAYCROSS: Ware County. So named because of the many crossroads located at this site.

WAYSIDE: Jones County. Was known, in succession, by two rather disparaging names, Lousy Level and Black Ankle. When the railroad came through, officials desired a less offensive name for their station. Wayside was chosen.

WELCOME: Coweta County. Some say the community was named for the friendly attitude of the Indians toward early settlers. Others believe it was christened for Welcome Carter, a farmer and one of the original settlers in the area.

YELLOW DIRT: Heard County. For nearby Yellow Dirt Creek; the stream acquired its designation because of the soil.

Idaho
THE GEM STATE

AMERICAN FALLS: Power County. Named for the falls on Snake River. The cascade was so tagged because a party of American trappers were descending the river and, having no knowledge of the existence of the falls, suffered heavy losses when they went over the rise.

ARROW: Nez Perce County. Name given to the site by builders of the Camas Prairie Railroad after they found a number of arrowheads in the vicinity.

ATOMIC CITY: Bingham County. Originally called Midway for its location between the towns of Blackfoot and Arco. An atomic reactor testing station was built here in 1949, and the community, not only to modernize its image but also to shuck the more common name of Midway, took the present name.

BAYHORSE: Custer County. By tradition, this community was so designated because while a man was searching for his strayed bay horse, he came across an outcropping of ore.

BENCH: Caribou County. Named for its location on a terrace-like "bench" between Bear River and Trout Creek.

BLISS: Gooding County. Honors David B. Bliss, a settler.

BLUE DOME: Clark County. In early days, a service station/diner was constructed here along State Highway 28. The name Blue Dome came from the original upper structure of the building.

BONE: Bonneville County. Family name.

CACHE: Teton County. Took its designation from the fact that most of the settlers migrated to this spot from Cache Valley, Utah.

CHALLIS: Custer County. For the founder, A. P. Challis.

CHILLY: Custer County. A group of men was in a cabin one night, sitting around a fire discussing possible names for a small settlement they planned to establish. Some other members of their group arrived late and upon entering the cabin exclaimed that it was "certainly chilly outside." Hence, the name.

COBALT: Lemhi County. Known as Forney, the town changed its name in 1950 for the locally mined mineral.

CORRAL: Camas County. Remembers a large stock corral located here when a branch of the Oregon Short Line Railroad was built.

COUNCIL: Adams County. In early days this was the meeting place for the Shahaptin Indians from the north and the Shoshoni from the south. It received its moniker because this is where the two tribes met to hold council.

CULDESAC: Nez Perce County. Name suggested by a Mr. Mellen, president of the Camas Prairie Railway Company. While traveling the proposed route for a branch of the railroad, he came to a natural end at this site, and stated that it formed a cul-de-sac.

CUPRUM: Adams County. No alcoholic beverages associated with this community. Instead, it was christened for the Latin word for copper, which has been mined in this area for many years.

DEARY: Latah County. While normally a term of endearment, this town salutes William Deary, manager of the Potlatch Timber Company.

DENT: Clearwater County. Remembers Charles Dent, a settler.

DINGLE: Bear Lake County. When first settled in 1871, the community was known as Dingle Dell. It was later called Cottonwood, but was changed to Dingle in 1896 when a post office was set up. The origin of the name is unknown, but since *dingle* means "small wooded valley," the town's location probably accounts for the label.

HEADQUARTERS: Clearwater County. This site was once the mail headquarters for the Potlatch Lumber Company.

MACKS INN: Fremont County. A tourist resort established in 1921 and named for its founder, W. H. Mack.

OBSIDIAN: Custer County. Relates to volcanic-like rock prominent in the vicinity.

POTLATCH: Latah County. A company town organized in 1905 by the Potlatch Lumber Company.

SINKER: Owyhee County. Takes its name from a stream that acquired *its* handle from the fact that early settlers used gold nuggets as "sinkers" on fishing lines.

SODA SPRINGS: Caribou County. At one time called Beer Springs. Either name would be expressive since early travelers tagged the springs for their bubbly gas and acidic taste.

SPIRIT LAKE: Kootenai County. For the lake. Although the lake name is said to come from Indian legend, there is doubt that Indians had anything to do with the tale. By folklore, the body of water received its handle when two escaping lovers drowned there. Their spirits supposedly hover over the spot to this day.

SQUIRREL: Fremont County. For the many squirrels found hereabout.

SUNBEAM: Custer County. For the Sunbeam Mine.

TENSED: Benewah County. First called Desmet, for the Jesuit missionary. The postal service refused to accept the name because it duplicated another location in the state. The townspeople resubmitted the name, only this time spelling it backward (Temsed). Through an error, officials in Washington recorded the name as Tensed.

THREE CREEK: Owyhee County. Once known as Seventy One, the cattle brand of Joe Scott, an early settler. Later settlers came across a rock located near a stream with the figure "3" written on it. They named the stream Three Creek, the name the settlement adopted.

TRIANGLE: Owyhee County. Stock brand used by the Triangle Ranch.

TRIUMPH: Blaine County. For the Triumph Mine.

UCON: Bonneville County. First known as Willow Creek, but the label had to be changed due to duplication. Around 1912, the postal department submitted a list of names for the townspeople to consider; from the list they selected Ucon.

USTICK: Ada County. Honors Dr. Harlan Page Ustick, who founded the community in 1908.

WHITE BIRD: Idaho County. Reportedly named for the Nez Perce chief.

WILDHORSE: Adams County. Named for the numerous wild horses roaming the area in early days.

Illinois

THE LAND OF LINCOLN

ANCHOR: McLean County. Anchor Township, formed around 1877 by Rev. George R. Buck, was named for a religious concept, the word *anchor* being found in the Bible, and the fact that a hymn by that name was popular at the time. In 1880, Daniel B. Stewart laid out a village on this site and named it for the township.

AROMA PARK: Kankakee County. Township named by James L. Romer as a play on the sound of his name.

ASSUMPTION: Christian County. Took its name from Assumption, Canada, former home of a local landowner. The Assumption, celebrated each August 15, is a ritual of the Catholic church.

BIBLE GROVE: Clay County. As sources tell it, this community received its handle when Gypsies camped in a grove near here, and after they left, a Bible was found in one of the trees.

BIG NECK: Adams County. Relates to a stretch (neck) of land, which is an extension of Bowen Prairie.

BLUE ISLAND: Cook County. Named by early settlers as they viewed the site from a distance, because it looked like an "island covered with blue flowers."

BLUE MOUND: Macon County. The community was christened by Isaac Goltree, who owned the land on which the village was established. Goltree was influenced by a nearby glacier formation that rose almost two hundred feet above the prairie floor. On top of the mound grew blue flowers.

BONE GAP: Edwards County. Hunters coming through this area as early as 1815 found several piles of bones near a gap in the timber. They named the spot Bone Gap, and when a village came into being, it took that name.

BUREAU: Bureau County. For the river, which received its tag from Pierre de Buero, a Frenchman who established a trading post near here.

BURNT PRAIRIE: White County. Township named as the result of a fire that burned a large part of the prairie in the area.

CARLOCK: McLean County. In the late 1800s, the Nickel Plate Railroad built through this area. Winton Carlock agreed to sell part of his land as right of way if the depot was put on his property. The company agreed and erected a sign that read "Carlock."

CAVE IN ROCK: Hardin County. Refers to a cave in a rock located nearby on the shore of the Ohio River.

CHERRY: Bureau County. Supposedly for James Cherry, an employee of the St. Paul Coal Company, which operated a mine near here.

ENERGY: Williamson County. Took its name from the trademark of a coal mine.

EQUALITY: Gallatin County. This moniker was suggested around 1797 by the French historian Etienne Volney. The word is part of the slogan of the French Revolution, which, when translated, reads, "Liberty, Equality, and Fraternity." The community name at the time was Saline, and Volney's suggestion was not carried through until 1827, when the name was officially changed.

GOLDEN EAGLE: Calhoun County. Supposedly christened by a riverboat captain who once saw an eagle perched on a high cliff at this point.

GOLDEN GATE: Wayne County. In 1881, the Louisville, Evansville and St. Louis Railroad surveyed this area for a track. Ethan Fowler, who owned forty acres of land where Golden Gate now sits, was opposed to the railroad because it meant a cut would have to be made through his farm. After the railroad completed its survey, Fowler erected a gate across the proposed road and padlocked it. Legal action ensued, but an out-of-court settlement was reached. Fowler agreed to the cut through his property, but payment for the right of way had to be made in gold. Because of this incident, residents called the place Golden Gate, the name it now carries.

GRAND CHAIN: Pulaski County. Took its name from an earlier settlement, which was designated for a grouping of large rocks in the Ohio River referred to as the "Grand Chain of Rocks." In days of heavy water travel, the rocks served as a landmark for the debarkation of passengers and supplies. The rocks are now covered with water backed up by dams on the Ohio River.

GRAND DETOUR: Ogle County. For a large bend (detour) in Rock River.

GRAND TOWER: Jackson County. Town's moniker was influenced by a large rock formation in the Mississippi River that resembles a tower.

IDEAL: Carroll County. Christened by Sylvanus R. Atherton, store owner and community's first postmaster, because he thought the people, living conditions, and environment were ideal.

JOY: Mercer County. For James F. Joy, an early president of the Chicago, Burlington and Quincy Railroad.

LITTLE AMERICA: Fulton County. A long time ago a man who lived in Canton, several miles north of this site, operated a tavern here. He commuted between the two towns daily and in those times travel was long and tiring. It became his custom each morning as he departed for work to say, "Well, I'd better get started for Little America." His reference was to the South Pole region and alluded to distance, but this community soon acquired the name Little America.

LONDON MILLS: Fulton County. In 1846, James Eggers built a grist-mill near this spot, which he called London, in honor of the English city. The present name was derived by combining the original name with Eggers's flour mill.

LOWPOINT: Woodford County. Tagged in early days for a "low point" of timber on the Peoria-Ottawa stage route.

MACKINAW: Tazewell County. This used to be a common term for a man's heavy coat, but the town was christened for the island in Lake Michigan. *Mackinaw* is from an Algonquian word meaning "turtle."

MARINE: Madison County. So designated because the village was first settled by several "sea captains" from the East.

MEDIA: Henderson County. In the late 1880s, the Santa Fe Railroad built a line connecting Kansas City with Chicago. The distance was exactly 412 miles. The true center of the line was 206 miles, and this is where the town of Media (middle) was established.

MOCCASIN: Effingham County. For Moccasin Creek. The stream was labeled by Griffin Tipsword when he discovered moccasin tracks along the bank.

MOOSEHEART: Kane County. This community was dedicated in July 1913 by the Loyal Order of the Moose. Often referred to as "Child City," its prime aim is to house, clothe, feed, educate, and train children of deceased members of the nonprofit organization. Its name was suggested by Congressman John J. Lentz of Ohio, and formally adopted in February 1913. Construction in the community, which is laid out in the shape of a heart, is ongoing.

NORMAL: McLean County. So designated because it was the site of the first state "normal" school.

OBLONG: Crawford County. Once called Hen Peck, for Henry Peck, the village was renamed for a large, flat stretch of land known as Oblong Prairie.

OLIVE BRANCH: Alexander County. It is believed this community was christened for an early Methodist church.

PICKAWAY: Shelby County. For the Piqua branch of the Shawnee Indian tribe.

PINKSTAFF: Lawrence County. For Owen Pinkstaff, who laid out the original site.

PREEMPTION: Whiteside County. This little community was designated for a federal program under which much of the surrounding area was settled. In the early 1800s, Congress passed a "preemption" law, which provided that any person settling on open land and farming it would have first right (preemption) to purchase that land.

PROPHETSTOWN: Whiteside County. This town received its name from a prominent Indian. However, there is debate whether the name was derived from "Shawnee Prophet," who was Tecumseh's brother, or from a Winnebago medicine man who served as advisor to Chief Black Hawk.

PROVISO: Cook County. Township named for the Wilmot Proviso of 1846, which was an unsuccessful attempt to ban slavery in any territory acquired by the United States in its war with Mexico.

REDBUD: Randolph County. For the redbud tree.

SAG: Cook County. For its location near "swampy" terrain.

SANDWICH: DeKalb County. First known as Newark Station, citizens prevailed upon Congressman "Long John" Wentworth to secure a post office for them. As enticement for his support, they promised that he could rename the town. Once the post office was granted, Wentworth christened it Sandwich, for his hometown in New Hampshire.

SCALES MOUND: Jo Daviess County. For a nearby mound located on land once owned by Samuel Scales.

SEMINARY: Fayette County. In a state constitutional convention in 1818, certain townships in Illinois were to be designated as sites for seminaries. This was one so designated.

THAWVILLE: Iroquois County. For William Thaw, a Pittsburgh railroad man.

TIMEWELL: Brown County. For the man who was in charge of the St. Louis office of the Wabash Railroad.

TRIUMPH: La Salle County. So named because the village was "triumphant" in a contest to secure a post office.

WHITE HEATH: Piatt County. A "heath" is an open tract of wasteland; however, this town was named for two local residents, White and Heath.

YELLOWHEAD: Kankakee County. For a Potawatomi chief.

Indiana

The Hoosier State

ADVANCE: Boone County. Originally called Osceola, for the Indian chief. The name had to be changed because of duplication. Advance was probably selected in anticipation of the progress expected with the coming of the Midland Railroad. 　IOI

ALERT: Decatur County. More than likely the moniker reflected the minds and attitudes of the townspeople.

AROMA: Hamilton County. Supposedly christened for the pleasing odors of freshly mown grass, budding trees, and flowering plants that swept over the area when a name was being considered.

AZALIA: Bartholomew County. For the flower, with a variance in spelling.

BANQUO: Huntington County. Originally known as Priceville, but some unknown local legend suggested the naming of the town for Shakespeare's ghost. Another version is that it was tagged for a Miami Indian.

BATTLE GROUND: Tippecanoe County. For the Battle of Tippecanoe, which was fought in the vicinity.

BEANBLOSSOM: Brown County. For the creek; the stream was named for the plant.

BIRDSEYE: Dubois County. As the story goes, several community names were submitted to postal authorities; all were rejected. Settlers finally decided on Bird, for Rev. "Bird" Johnson, postmaster at another settlement. The minister was asked to help select the new post office site. When Johnson decided on a location, he said, "This spot suits Bird's eye to a T-y-tee." Hence, the name.

BLACKHAWK: Shelby County. For the Sauk Indian chief *Ma-ka-ta-mi-kiak-kiak,* which translated to "Black Sparrow Hawk."

BLUEGRASS: Fulton County. Possibly refers to the tinge of area grassland.

BOUNDARY CITY: Jay County. For its location on an early Indian treaty (boundary) line.

BOURBON: Marshall County. For Bourbon Township, which, in turn, took its handle from Bourbon County, Kentucky.

BUCKSKIN: Gibson County. This name stems from early days when owners of a trading post hung deerskins on the side of the building to dry. When a town was formed, it took the name Buckskin.

BUD: Johnson County. For Bud Vandiver, son of the settlement's first merchant.

BUDDHA: Lawrence County. Tradition says that a tramp by the name of Budha used to wander through this area and that the town was christened for him. Others contend it is a derivative of the Hungarian capital, Budapest.

CARBON: Clay County. Founded in 1870 by the Carbon Coal Company.

CATARACT: Owen County. For a waterfall (cataract) on Mill Creek.

CELESTINE: Dubois County. Honors the Right Reverend Celestine Rene Lawrence de la Hailandiere, Bishop of Vincennes.

CENTER SQUARE: Switzerland County. Descriptive name, since the town was laid out in the form of a square and is near the center of the county.

CHILI: Miami County. This has nothing to do with the spicy Mexican food, but is an earlier spelling of Chile, the South American republic. Since there were communities in Miami County bearing the names Mexico and Peru, this probably had some influence on the selection of this town's name.

COLLEGE CORNER: Union County. Refers to a college once located here.

DAYLIGHT: Warrick County. Christened for the remark repeatedly made by a railroad engineer. Each evening, when he dropped off a construction crew at this site, he would say, "I'll pick you men up at daylight."

DEPUTY: Jefferson County. For James Deputy.

DIAMOND: Parke County. For the "black diamond" coal mined in the region.

ECONOMY: Wayne County. Supposedly named by Charles Osborn in 1825 when, finding himself short of funds, he platted his land into lots as the most "economical" way of selling them and raising needed capital.

EMINENCE: Morgan County. Probably named for its elevation.

EPSOM: Daviess County. Named for a well dug on this spot, the water from which tasted like Epsom salts.

FIAT: Jay County. Originally called Winona, the name was changed to Fiat in the mid-1880s. A petition was submitted by the townspeople, who also chose the name. Residents were adherents of the Greenback political party, which advocated "fiat" money. This is paper currency issued and made legal tender by government, but without promise of redemption.

FIVE POINTS: Marion County. For its location, where five roads meet.

FLOYDS KNOBS: Floyd County. The town is situated in a valley surrounded by hills, or knobs. Therefore, knobs, combined with the surname of Colonel Davis Floyd, provided the community its name.

FOUR POINTS: Boone County. For its location at a crossroads.

FRENCH LICK: Orange County. In the late 1700s, a trading post was established on this site. Settlers noticed that animals came to the springs to lick the water and rocks. The place was named "The Lick." In the early 1800s, the French built a fort here as protection against Indians, and the name eventually evolved into French Lick.

GAS CITY: Grant County. More than likely named for the gas industry.

HASHTOWN: Greene County. This small community, situated on the edge of Bloomfield, remembers the Hash family.

HOME PLACE: Marion County. The townspeople probably selected this name for sentimental reasons.

LAPEL: Madison County. Believed to have been named when the railroad was built through here, because a strip of land in the shape of a lapel was left between the railroad and the Pendleton Turnpike.

MAGNET: Perry County. Probably selected to "attract" settlers.

MECCA: Parke County. Two contradictory versions exist for this place name. The first revolves around a church erected here and nicknamed the Arabian Church, for its location on a dry, sandy hill. Nearby, Alexander McCune ran a general store. When the roads were passable, settlers near the church would journey to McCune's store. The storekeeper referred to those trips as the "Arabians coming to Mecca." The second rendition avers that in 1898 a tile plant was built here, and the owners, seeking the cheapest laborers possible, imported Moslems from the Near East. Another factor bearing on the selection of workers was that people from that part of the world are renowned for their tile. The laborers lived on the outskirts of this little settlement, and whenever they received their pay, would rush to town, as if "going to Mecca."

MONUMENT CITY: Huntingon County. Town site laid out in 1874, and christened for a monument erected nearby in 1869 that was dedicated to heroes of the Civil War.

OMEGA: Hamilton County. *Omega* is the last letter in the Greek alphabet. This community was originally called Dogtown, but when a post office was set up in 1870, that name was no longer acceptable. The moniker was changed to Omega, signifying the "last" of Dogtown.

ONWARD: Cass County. A tale has it that the name came from a comment by citizens after lounging around the local store: "I must now plug onward." The general feeling is, however, that the label was chosen to express a progressive nature.

PARAGON: Morgan County. A descriptive name.

PARIS CROSSING: Jennings County. Tagged for its location beside a railroad crossing about a mile northwest of Paris, Indiana.

PATRIOT: Switzerland County. Some think this name comes from the Patriots, veterans of the Revolutionary War, who settled here. Others opine it arose from the time citizens wanted to name the place Washington, the "greatest patriot of them all," but since there were already several towns by that name, they settled for Patriot.

PETROLEUM: Wells County. For the oil field in which the town was laid out.

PIMENTO: Vigo County. For the vegetable.

PINHOOK: La Porte County. Legend has it the handle came about when a woman left a store with a package of pins without paying for them. Another thought is that the hamlet name describes the roads converging at this point.

PINHOOK: Lawrence County. Several sources, including the one about when, in early days, it was illegal to sell liquor by the drink here. To get around this, merchants shrewdly concocted the idea of selling customers a "bent pin" to use as a fishhook, then giving drinks of whiskey as premiums. A story closely related to this, but eliminating the whiskey, is that the little hamlet was once known for making fishhooks from pins. A more logical explanation, if not as enticing, is that the name came from a peculiar twist in a nearby road.

POPCORN: Perry County. For the creek. The stream was christened when people from Vincennes who, while visiting a local family, began discussing the raising of corn. The two farmers argued over who grew the best corn, and the man from Vincennes asserted, "Your corn is popcorn compared to what we grow!"

PUNKIN CENTER: Orange County. Relates to the large number of pumpkins once grown here.

REDKEY: Jay County. Community has been called Half Way, Lick Skillet, Grand All, and Buzzard's Roost. The current name salutes James Redkey, who platted additional land here in 1867.

RETREAT: Jackson County. Title probably selected to denote a secluded, restful location or surrounding.

RISING SUN: Ohio County. One source states the community received its name because of the impressive sunrise over the nearby Kentucky hills. Another tenet is that some people were traveling down the Ohio River when the sun rose and they were awed by its beauty.

ROLL: Blackbird County. Rhymes with "doll," and honors Mathias Roll.

SANTA CLAUS: Spencer County. One version has it this moniker was chosen because it was around Christmas when a name was considered. Another choice is that the village was founded by German settlers on Christmas Eve, 1852. The villagers were meeting to select a name, it was cold, and a deep snow covered the region. After some time had passed, the door to their meeting place opened, and in walked a man dressed in a Santa Claus outfit.

SOUTHWEST: Elkhart County. The town is situated southwest of Goshen.

SPADES: Ripley County. Salutes Jacob Spade, a settler.

SPEEDWAY: Marion County. Platted in 1812, this is the home of the Indianapolis Motor Speedway, for which it was named.

SURPRISE: Jackson County. So named because the acting postmaster, Doc Isaacs, was "surprised" the town succeeded in having the railroad run its tracks through the community, and was "surprised" it was awarded a post office.

TAB: Warren County. Honors Harrison "Tab" Goodwine, who laid out the village in 1905.

TELL CITY: Perry County. Settled by Swiss colonists in 1857; named for their legendary hero, William Tell.

TOTO: Starke County. Some think this label stems from the English term for "borough"; others contend it is the translation of an Indian word meaning "bullfrog."

TREATY: Wabash County. For the creek, which received its name from a treaty with the Miami Indians that took place near the mouth of the stream in 1826.

TWELVE MILE: Cass County. More than a century ago, residents decided they were of sufficient number to warrant a name for their town. Since Logansport was the nearest city of any size, and that was where they had to travel for supplies, they decided to determine the distance between the two points. That, then, would be the name of their town. They estimated the distance to be 12½ or 13 miles. Since they were a superstitious lot, they wouldn't even consider a name such as Thirteen Mile; and 12½, when spelled out, would be too long. The only solution was to name it Twelve Mile, which they did.

WATERLOO: DeKalb County. According to legend, two drunks were hard at it in a bloody brawl when an onlooker remarked that the melee was worse than the Battle of Waterloo.

WINDFALL: Tipton County. The first settlement hereabout was known as Wildcat, established around 1848. Shortly thereafter, a devastating storm hit the region, uprooting many trees and doing much damage. The small creek that ran through the area was then christened Windfall, for the storm. Later, about three miles from the original site, a new village was built, and it was named for the stream.

YEOMAN: Carroll County. Remembers a man named Yeoman, who promised to buy the community a bell for the school if they christened the town in his honor.

YOUNG AMERICA: Cass County. Community name adopted in 1855, during the great expansionist movement in the United States. Thomas Henry, sawmill owner, purchased a steam boiler to operate his equipment. Someone wrote "Young America" on the implement, referring to the expansionist movement, so Henry decided that would be an appropriate name for the village.

ZULU: Allen County. Village name came through happenstance. Originally known as Four Corners, the name had to be changed when a post office was set up. A new name was selected by someone sticking a pin in a geography book, which happened to be open to an article on Africa.

AGENCY: Wapello County. For its location adjacent to an Indian agency in Iowa's earlier days.

AMBER: Jones County. J. C. Ramsey tagged this settlement not for the color, but for the name of a character found in a novel published in the *New York Tribune*. The previous label for Amber was Blue Cut.

CHARTER OAK: Crawford County. Moniker derived from early days when the site was first being surveyed. The surveyor, to protect his charts and maps when caught in a heavy rainstorm, bundled them up and tucked them into a hollow in a large oak tree that once stood on this site. The tree was cut down because of disease, but a symbolic tree was planted in its place several years ago.

COIN: Page County. Circumstance and convenience dictated this town's title. A workman digging a foundation came across a small silver coin. This was taken by townspeople as being symbolic of their settlement's future prosperity. Too, *coin* was a short word, easy to spell, and novel.

COLO: Story County. Supposedly named by John I. Blair for his dog, which was killed by a train.

CORRECTIONVILLE: Woodbury County. The town's name has nothing to do with a penal institution, having been christened by surveyors who platted the site. In the field of surveying, a mark, or line, is established and used to verify and correct markings in land surveys. This site happened to be on such a correction line.

CYLINDER: Palo Alto County. For the creek. The stream supposedly acquired its name when early automobile travelers attempted to cross during a time when the water was high and lost a cylinder in doing so. Another version is that not an automobile cylinder but one from a machine was lost as it was being moved across the water.

DIAGONAL: Ringgold County. For its location on the Chicago and Great Western Railroad, which crosses Iowa "diagonally."

EXLINE: Appanoose County. For David Exline, a merchant.

FERTILE: Worth County. For its location in the fertile Winnebago River Valley. More intriguing is the nickname for which the site was known for many years: Putsy.

GOLDFIELD: Wright County. Personal pride played a part in christening this town. It was the desire of settlers to honor a gentleman by the name of Brassfield. Knowing "brass" is often used in a derogatory sense, and not wishing to have such a connotation attached to their settlement, they substituted the most precious of metals—gold—and a city was named.

GRAVITY: Taylor County. For its location as the trading "center" of Washington Township.

HOLY CROSS: Dubuque County. In 1899, Bishop Loras erected a large wooden cross on the site of a future church; hence, the community name.

LONE ROCK: Kossuth County. For a solitary rock situated about two miles north of town.

LONE TREE: Johnson County. For a natural landmark. When settlers first traveled through this part of Iowa, the only break on the horizon for miles was a lone white elm tree, which was firmly rooted in the dark prairie earth.

LOST NATION: Clinton County. A most interesting name for a community, although none of the versions of its origin, of which there are at least five, are at all mysterious. One source believes the name came about because a tribe of Indians once starved and froze to death on this spot. Another avers that when hunters first spied the site from a distant hill, one of them commented that it was so lonely and isolated that it resembled a lost nation. Two other renditions go hand in hand. A Mr. Balm, searching for relatives in the area, lost his bearings for a period of time; or a Mr. Cook, looking for Mr. Balm, named the location because he had such a difficult time finding his quarry. The final version is that the town acquired its name because it was situated in wild and inaccessible country. Take your pick.

LOW MOOR: Clinton County. Christened for a foreign trademark. When tracks were laid for the first railroad through the area, workers used rails shipped from England; the brand name stamped on the rails was "Low Moor."

MORNING SUN: Louisa County. Two men, Cicero Hamilton and Henry Blake, were returning home early one morning following a night of searching for Hamilton's lost oxen. Apparently the rising sun left a deep enough impression on the men for them to name their settlement for that wonder of nature.

NEW HOPE: Appanoose County. Citizens jumped on this name as an expression of future aspirations, which failed to materialize.

NODAWAY: Adams County. For the creek. The stream tag is from the Indian *nodawa*, meaning "crossed without a canoe."

PROMISE CITY: Wayne County. Timmie Howland, storekeeper, suggested the site be called Town of Promise. Through time, usage slowly changed the name to Promise City.

RAKE: Winnebago County. Family name.

REMBRANDT: Buena Vista County. Originally called Orsland, for Barney Orsland. Postal authorities changed the name to Rembrandt, for the famous Dutch painter.

III

SERGEANT BLUFF: Woodbury County. The town is situated on bluffs along the Missouri River. It salutes Sergeant Charles Floyd, who accompanied the Lewis and Clark Expedition and died and was buried on a high bluff near here.

SOLDIER: Monona County. For a river. The stream is so called because an unnamed American soldier was buried along its banks in earlier days.

STEAMBOAT ROCK: Hardin County. Probably for a natural formation.

STORY CITY: Story County. Honors Judge Joseph Story.

STRAWBERRY POINT: Clayton County. More than likely named for the wild berries found growing on a nearby point of land.

WHAT CHEER: Keokuk County. On the surface, this would appear to be a puzzling place name. The intrigue is not deep, however. The community received its name from a Scot term meaning "How are you?" a phrase anticipating something hopeful. It was tagged to the town when a coal mine was discovered in the vicinity, and it was hoped the discovery would bring prosperity to the area.

Kansas
The Sunflower State

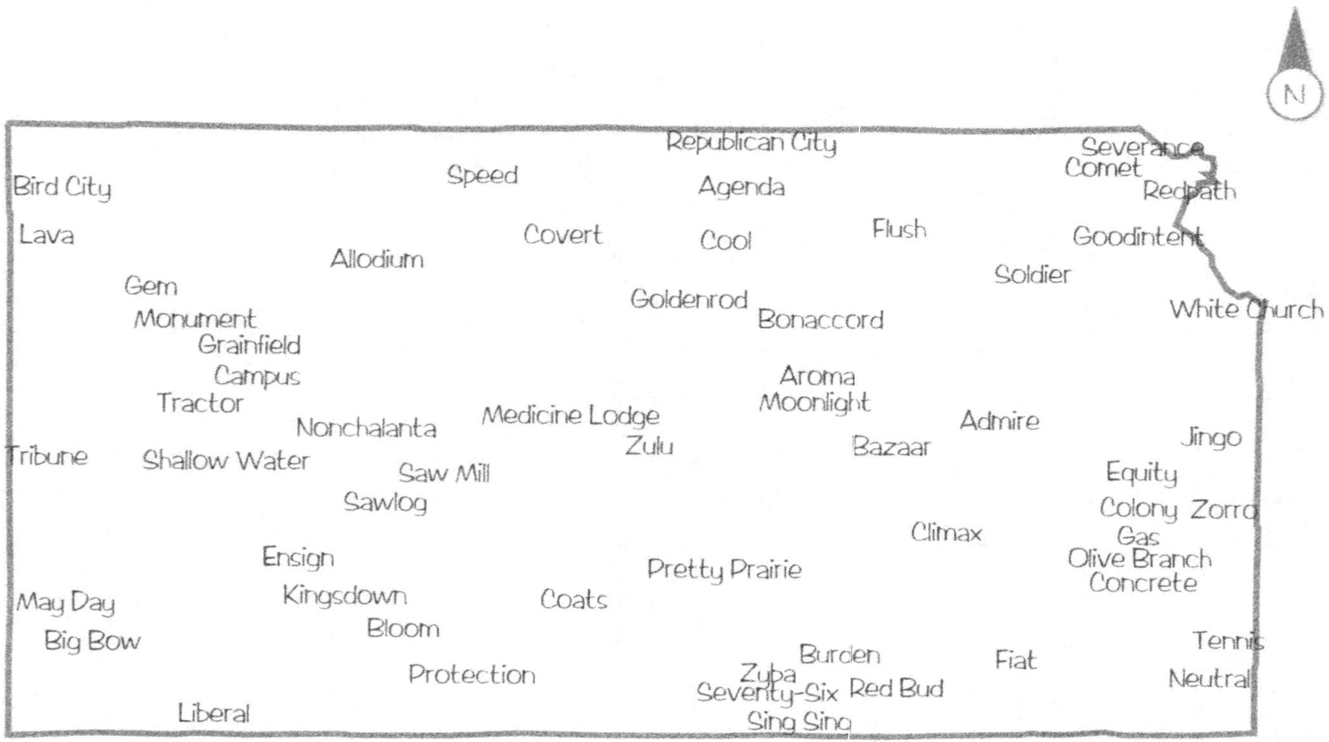

Republican City

Severance
Cornet
Redpath

Bird City

Lava

Gem
Monument
Grainfield
Campus
Tractor

Tribune
Shallow Water

Nonchalanta

Medicine Lodge
Zulu

Allodium

Speed

Agenda

Covert

Cool

Flush

Goldenrod
Bonaccord

Aroma
Moonlight

Bazaar

Soldier

Goodintent

May Day
Big Bow

Ensign
Kingsdown
Sawlog

Saw Mill

Bloom

Coats

Pretty Prairie

Climax

Admire

Jingo

White Church

Equity
Colony Zorro

Gas
Olive Branch
Concrete

Liberal

Protection

Zyba
Seventy-Six Red Bud
Sing Sing

Burden

Fiat

Tennis
Neutral

N

ADMIRE: Lyon County. For Captain Jacob V. Admire, one of the city founders.

AGENDA: Republic County. During a town meeting, the chairman asked what was on the agenda. One item mentioned was the selection of a name for the community. To avoid taking up a lot of time, it was decided to name the place Agenda.

ALLODIUM: Graham County. A term used in early days to refer to the holding of land title-free. Apparently this township was so named because it was ceded as a "grant without mortgage."

AROMA: Dickinson County. Because it was a "sweet"-sounding name.

BAZAAR: Chase County. Tagged by Martha J. Leonard for a shop, or bazaar, she once owned in Pennsylvania.

BIG BOW: Stanton County. For a Kiowa chief, *Zip-kay-yay*, called "Big Bow" by whites.

BIRD CITY: Cheyenne County. For Benjamin Bird, a settler.

BLOOM: Ford County. For Bloomsburg, Pennsylvania.

BONACCORD: Dickinson County. First called Bon Accord, and named for the harmony that existed among its citizens. In time the name became spelled as one word.

BURDEN: Cowley County. For Robert E. Burden, a pioneer.

CAMPUS: Gove County. According to lore, the community acquired its moniker because it was once a railroad "camp."

CLIMAX: Greenwood County. For its elevated location.

COATS: Pratt County. Remembers W. A. Coats, the town's builder.

COLONY: Anderson County. Relates to a colony of settlers from Ohio and Indiana.

COMET: Brown County. Christened from great expectations of the residents.

CONCRETE: Allen County. Remembers the Portland Cement Company.

COOL: Cloud County. For Joseph Cool, a pioneer.

COVERT: Osborne County. Family name.

ENSIGN: Gray County. Salutes G. L. Ensign, town founder.

EQUITY: Anderson County. First called Rich, the hardships brought on by the depression of 1893 caused residents to change the name to Equity, because after that setback, everyone was more "equal" economically.

FIAT: Elk County. This is from the Latin and means "let it be done." People living in this area in the mid-1880s were isolated as far as transportation and freight were concerned. They demanded that a loading point be established whereby they could transport livestock and crops. Their demands were heeded; thus, not only emerged a loading point, but also a small village that eventually became Fiat.

FLUSH: Riley County. For Michael Floersch. The simplified spelling of the name was done at the insistence of postal officials.

GAS: Allen County. For the presence of natural gas in the vicinity.

GEM: Thomas County. For Gem Ranch.

GOLDENROD: Lincoln County. For the plant.

GOODINTENT: Atchison County. Hattie Dorman, so pleased the community was starting a Sunday school, had the post office named Good Intent. The words were later joined to shorten the name, and then adopted by the village.

GRAINFIELD: Gove County. For vast grainfields in the region.

JINGO: Miami County. After a loud and sometimes heated discussion on a name for this town, one citizen commented, "By jingo, we'd better decide on a name in our next meeting!" The word *jingo* struck a chord and another resident exclaimed, "Why don't we call it Jingo?" The name was accepted by proclamation.

KINGSDOWN: Ford County. Designation for the small hamlet was created by drawing a playing card from a deck; the card drawn was a king.

LAVA: Sherman County. For a deposit of volcanic ash.

LIBERAL: Seward County. Early travelers through here were always faced with a shortage of water. In pioneering days, a rancher had a well on his property and freely let passersby quench their thirst. A comment often heard was that it was a "mighty liberal" gesture on his part. In time, the place became known as "the liberal well." When a town was established on the site, it took the name Liberal.

MAY DAY: Stanton County. So named by the postmaster simply because the choice was made on or around May 1, 1871.

MEDICINE LODGE: Barber County. The city was named for Medicine Lodge River. The stream came by its tag because it was on this site, near the stream, that Indian medicine men met to hold counsel. This city was the site of the signing of the Treaty of Medicine Lodge in 1867. The signatures on the treaty reflect representatives from the Plains Indians tribes—Apache, Arapaho, Cheyenne, Kiowa—and the United States government. Probably the best-known celebrity from Medicine Lodge is Carry Nation, the ax-swinging Prohibitionist of the early 1900s.

MONUMENT: Logan County. A monument honoring General John A. Logan was started near here in 1888. Although never completed, the town kept the name.

MOONLIGHT: Dickinson County. For Colonel Thomas Moonlight, a settler.

NEUTRAL: Cherokee County. Labeled for the agreement between whites and area Cherokees, avowing this as "everyone's land."

NONCHALANTA: Ness County. An attitudinal name, formed by adding "a" to nonchalant.

OLIVE BRANCH: Allen County. Believed to have been chosen by a "peace group," opposed to the more hawk-like "jingo" political element.

PRETTY PRAIRIE: Reno County. In 1872, Mary Newman Collingwood displayed courage superseding that of many of her male contemporaries. A widow with nine children, Mary left the security of a home in Indiana and with her brood migrated to Kansas. She settled in this area and was so impressed with the beauty of the open plains that she named the place Pretty Prairie. The name was adopted when a town was formed.

PROTECTION: Comanche County. Several versions abound for this community name's origin. Some believe the choice was influenced by the "protective" tariff that was reduced the year the town was founded. Indian lore has it the name was given to the place because of its location at the fork of a stream, which afforded protection from tornadoes and forest fires. A third claim is that the town offered protection for farmers and nesters against cattlemen and lawless elements trying to chase them off the land. Another source relates the name to the People's Grand Protective Union, a prohibition origination led by Governor St. John. Finally, the rendition that seems to get more backing than the others is that the site was so designated when two fortifications, or redoubts, were constructed in the area to give protection against Indian raids.

RED BUD: Cowley County. For the tree.

REDPATH: Doniphan County. First called Plowboy, the name was changed to honor James Redpath, a journalist and politician.

REPUBLICAN CITY: Republic County. For the river, which was christened for the Republican Pawnee.

SAW MILL: Pawnee County. Probably named for the sawmills situated throughout the heavily wooded area.

SAWLOG: Hodgeman County. The township was named for Sawlog Creek. Soldiers at Fort Atkinson, near Dodge City, used to get their firewood and timber along the south fork of the Pawnee River. Mules were used to pull the logs up from the riverbank, and when buffalo hunters passed the area and noticed the logs, they tagged the stream Sawlog Creek.

SEVENTY SIX: Sumner County. Probably named during the "Spirit of '76" fervor.

SEVERANCE: Doniphan County. For one of the owners of the town site.

SHALLOW WATER: Scott County. So named because the community sat where water was found no deeper than twenty feet below the earth's surface.

SING SING: Sumner County. Community handle has no connection to the infamous New York prison, having been named for John Sing Sing, Seneca Indian.

SOLDIER: Jackson County. Probably christened for the creek. The stream possibly received its name from the fact that soldiers from Fort Leavenworth often camped on the creek bank. Another legend claims the stream acquired its name from the time soldiers captured a quantity of illicit whiskey and dumped it into the creek.

SPEED: Phillips County. Relates to President Lincoln's attorney general, James Speed, who carried word of the president's death to Vice President Andrew Johnson.

TENNIS: Crawford County. For B. M. Tennis, a manager of the Santa Fe Railway.

TRACTOR: Scott County. This was the site of International Harvester's experimental station, and was named for the farm implement put out by IH.

TRIBUNE: Greeley County. Sources believe this community name came from the Greek word meaning "public defender." How or why it would be given as a place name is unknown. With the county moniker being Greeley, it's possible the town's citizens perpetuated the famous New York newspaperman by naming their town for the newspaper, since there are nearby villages named Horace and Greeley.

WHITE CHURCH: Wyandotte County. When Anglos settled here, there was an Indian church painted white situated on the site. As the settlement grew and reached sufficient size to warrant a name, White Church was a natural. The church was destroyed by a tornado, but the name remains.

ZORRO: Linn County. This adventuresome name was taken from the title of Johnston McCulley's novel, *The Mark of Zorro*.

ZULU: Rice County. Although there is no source for this community name, there is coincidence. The post office was established here in 1879. It was also at that time that the fearsome Zulu warriors in Africa were fighting against British and Dutch colonial rule.

ZYBA: Sumner County. Ingenuity contributed to the origin of this village name, since it consists of the last two and first two letters of the alphabet, reversed.

Kentucky

THE BLUEGRASS STATE

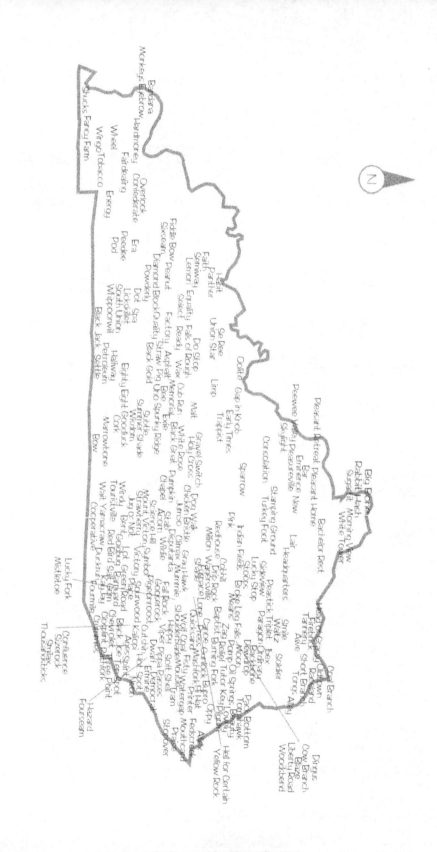

ACORN: Pulaski County. The naming of this little community closely resembles Sir Isaac Newton and the falling apple. The man nominated to select a title for the new post office was in the woods one day pondering various names. An acorn fell from a tree and hit him on the foot. Ergo, the name.

AFLEX: Pike County. Designation made by Colonel Leckie, settler and coal company owner. "Aflex" comes from the first letters of the names of two of his sons, Andrew and Frederick, and lex, for Leckie.

AGES: Harlan County. Family name.

ALLEY: Boyd County. Family name.

ASPHALT: Edmonson County. For an asphalt mine once in operation here.

AWE: Lewis County. Name selected by using the initials of the name of the postmaster, A. Wayne Everman.

BACHELOR REST: Pendleton County. Believed to have been so named simply because several bachelors lived in the area at the time.

BACKBONE: Elliott County. Designated for a large ridge running through the area that reminded residents of a backbone.

BANDANA: Ballard County. Originally known as Skillet. Some say the village acquired its name when hunters came through and one of the men left a red bandana behind. A resident picked up the handkerchief and from that event came the new name of the settlement. Another version is that in early days an old man used to pass through, carrying his belongings bundled in a large red kerchief tied to a stick. He spent many nights resting hereabout, sleeping with his head on his bundle. People used to say, "Here comes the bandana man." Thus, inspiration for the name. The word bandana is from the Hindustani, and refers to the process of tying cloth into knots before dying to give the material a spotted effect.

BAPTIST: Wolfe County. For a primitive Baptist church built here in the mid-1800s.

BAR: Henry County. Believed to have been tagged for the creek. In early days, several travelers camped near the stream and were attacked by a bear. They killed the animal, and because of the incident named the stream Bear Creek. With the passage of time, use of the local idiom of "bar" for bear changed the name to Bar Creek.

BARNYARD: Knox County. So designated because a resident had the largest barnyard in the area.

BEAUTY: Martin County. For the "Black Beauty" coal mined nearby.

BEE: Hart County. For a swarm of bees found on a ledge near here.

BENT: Pulaski County. For its location near a big bend in Buck Creek River.

BIG BONE: Boone County. Many centuries ago, a salt lick was located here. The lick attracted now-extinct mammals. In the early 1700s, French soldiers found bones on the site, and from that discovery Big Bone acquired its name.

BLACK GNAT: Taylor County. For the abundance of black gnats in this area in earlier times.

BLACK GOLD: Edmonson County. Asphalt mining around this site in the past made many people wealthy. Consequently, they decided to name the village Black Gold, after the black rock and the idea of wealth.

BLACK JACK: Simpson County. So named because the first school built here was made of blackjack logs. The school was then tagged Black Jack and the community later adopted the same name.

BLACK JOE: Harlan County. For the Black Joe Coal Mine.

BLAZE: Morgan County. Either a family name or the name of a horse.

BOW: Cumberland County. For Captain Ike Bow, Civil War veteran.

BROKE LEG FALLS: Menifee County. For nearby falls, so named when a man going downstream fell and broke his leg.

BURNING FORK: Magoffin County. Took its moniker from the fact that a spring in the fork of a road near here was always burning, for what reason no one seems to know.

BYPRO: Floyd County. For the By Products Coal Company.

CANOE: Breathitt County. Early settlers found a canoe tied to a tree near a stream.

CHEVROLET: Harlan County. Agreement on a community name could not be reached. A local mailman suggested Chevrolet, the make of his automobile, and it was accepted. The vehicle was a 1938 model, the only automobile in the area, and was used by residents as a "mobile mailbox."

CHICKEN BRISTLE: Lincoln County. Probably this name came about in early times, when residents had to resort to stealing to survive. For food, they absconded mostly with chickens; hence, the name.

CLIMAX: Rockcastle County. Label selected simply because it was one of several placed in a hat.

CLOSPLINT: Harlan County. For the Clover-Splint Mine. The mine took its tag from the fact that it was located on the Cloverfork River, and coal was mined from a "splint seam."

COAL BRANCH: Greenup County. For veins of coal found here.

COBHILL: Estill County. For an early day settler.

CONFEDERATE: Lyon County. Label selected in 1880 without any apparent significance.

CONFLUENCE: Leslie County. For its location near where a small stream enters (confluence) the Middlefork River.

CONSOLATION: Shelby County. As legend has it, a man stepped down from a train here and was unable to find lodging for the night. Looking around the small, uninviting site, he supposedly said, "Well, that is some consolation," apparently grateful that he wouldn't have to remain overnight. Another version is that at one time a road was supposed to have been built through here, but wasn't. The villagers were "consoled" in some other manner.

CO OPERATIVE: McCreary County. From the time two coal companies "merged."

CORK: Metcalfe County. Received its name when someone described it as a place lightly populated, as "light as a cork."

COW BRANCH: Morgan County. For the creek. The stream received its name because once, when cows from surrounding farms strayed, they could usually be found at this creek.

CRUMMIES: Harlan County. Family name.

CUB RUN: Hart County. When a name for this village was being discussed, a man happened to see a bear cub dart from behind a tree. When he raised his rifle to shoot, another man yelled, "Run, cub, run!" Ergo, inspiration for the name.

CUTSHIN: Leslie County. As lore has it, a hunter tripped over a rock near a stream and cut his shin. From that time on, the stream was called Cutshin, which eventually evolved into the community name.

DEMOCRAT: Letcher County. A former post office on this site was known as Razor Blade. The postmaster at the time, Ell King, was the only "democrat" in the small community. When a new office was built residents named it for King's political affiliation.

DEWDROP: Elliott County. Lewis Goodman, a leading figure in this at the time unnamed settlement, was having breakfast with his wife. They were discussing a suitable name for the community when Sara Goodman looked out the window and saw dew dropping from the roof of the house. "How about Dewdrop?" she suggested.

DIAMOND BLOCK: Muhlenberg County. For a nearby mine.

DINGUS: Morgan County. Family name.

DISPUTANTA: Rockcastle County. From the Latin, the hamlet received its name because of a "dispute" over a proper name for the site.

DO STOP: Grayson County. An invitation to passersby.

DOG WALK: Lincoln County. By tradition, two families once lived here that had several boys who had aversions to labor. All they wanted to do was walk from one house to the other, always accompanied by their dogs.

DOT: Logan County. Known as Masons Mill at the time a post office was put in. Advised by postal authorities that the name was too long, residents chose Dot, considering it about as short as any name could be.

DRIP ROCK: Estill County. For a nearby rock from which water dripped, apparently fed by an underground spring.

DUCKRUN: Whitley County. So named because the community "runs" along the Cumberland River, and ducks migrate through here every year.

DWARF: Perry County. Remembers Jerry "Shorty" Combs, a settler.

EARLY TIMES: Nelson County. From the brand name of a bourbon whiskey bottled by a local distillery.

EIGHTY EIGHT: Barren County. This name was suggested by Mr. Dabnie Nunnally, postmaster, because, ". . . I don't write very well and I will just use the figure 88." Figures are not used as community names and it has always been spelled out. Of interest is that in the 1948 election, the Eighty Eight precinct cast 88 votes for Thomas E. Dewey and 88 votes for Harry S. Truman.

EMINENCE: Henry County. For its location on a high plain on a railroad line.

ENERGY: Trigg County. Established by Rev. F. M. McCawley, and named for the "energetic" nature of the minister. Not only did McCawley spread God's Word, he also operated a farm, a store, and a mill.

EQUALITY: Ohio County. For Equality Church, which took its name from the fact that people in the community considered each other "equal."

ERA: Christian County. For a local newspaper, the *Kentucky New Era*, in 1880.

ERMINE: Letcher County. Family name.

EXIE: Green County. For Miss Exie Dowdy, a schoolteacher.

FACTORY: Butler County. Relates to an ax handle factory.

FAIRDEALING: Marshall County. Community tagged for the fair dealing of Enos Vaughn, store owner. Some question the basis of this compliment, considering he often traded a gallon of moonshine for an acre of land, and eventually owned as many as 10,000 acres in the area.

FAITH: McLean County. This hamlet had been awarded a post office when a government representative came on the scene. He met a

man and asked the name of the settlement. The man replied that
it did not have a name, whereupon the government agent
inquired as to the man's name. "John Faith," came the reply.
"Faith," the official mused. "That's a good name for a post office."
And it was a good name for the hamlet, as well.

FALL ROCK: Clay County. For a fall of water that runs over a rock.

FALLS OF ROUGH: Grayson County. For the falls on the Rough River.

FANCY FARM: Graves County. Settled by Catholics, they thought it
such a pretty farming community, they designated it Fancy Farm.

FEDSCREEK: Pike County. Believed to refer to a man named Fed.

FIDDLE BOW: Hopkins County. Labeled for a tree, the shape of
which closely resembled a fiddle bow, that once grew here. Sources
state the tree was eventually cut down and shipped to the
Smithsonian Institution in Washington, D.C.

FIREBRICK: Lewis County. For a plant that made firebricks for
chimneys.

FISTY: Knott County. For "Fisty" McCombs, a resident.

FOURMILE: Bell County. For its location four miles north of Pineville.

FOURSEAM: Perry County. A nearby mine took its coal from "four
seams."

FURNACE: Estill County. For an iron ore furnace.

GAP IN KNOB: Bullitt County. A "knob" is a large mound or hill.
Apparently this village received its name from a gap (opening) in
a nearby hill (knob).

GOLDBUG: Whitley County. Many years ago, a dispute arose
between the western and the eastern states. Those in the west
wanted silver as the basis for currency; eastern states pressed for
gold. People in this village pushed for the gold standard and were
called "goldbuggers," since Kentucky was, at the time, a western
state. In time, the hamlet became known as Goldbug.

GOODLUCK: Metcalfe County. Citizens had made several attempts to
have a post office brought in. When they finally succeeded, they
decided to call it Good Luck, because they felt fortunate in getting
the facility.

GOOSEROCK: Clay County. As the story goes, a goose nested on a
big rock in a nearby stream.

GRAVEL SWITCH: Marion County. Tagged for a railroad switch that
carried rock and gravel out of Beach Fork.

GRAY HAWK: Jackson County. Refers to a Mr. Gray and a Mr. Hawk,
landowners.

GREEN ROAD: Knox County. In early days, a road near here led to
some saltworks. People traveling the road commented how much

greener it was in this section than in any other. When a community emerged along the road, the comments served as inspiration for the place name.

GUNLOCK: Magoffin County. This was one of three names submitted by the postmaster, Roy Shepherd, but why it was sent is unknown.

HABIT: Daviess County. For Fred Habit, store owner.

HALFWAY: Allen County. For its location halfway between Bowling Green and the Tennessee state line.

HAPPY: Perry County. The first postmaster is credited with choosing this name, because the people here were always so happy.

HARDMONEY: McCracken County. Community name is politically connected, from the "hard money" slogan of the late 1830s.

HAZARD: Perry County. Honors Oliver Hazard Perry, naval hero of the War of 1812.

HEAD OF GRASSY: Lewis County. For its location at the head of Grassy Creek.

HEADQUARTERS: Nicholas County. This was once a meeting place (headquarters) for Indians.

HELL FOR CERTAIN: Lee County. Apparently named for Hell for Sartin Creek. The stream supposedly received its name because of all the "hell-raisin'" that took place at area dances.

HI HAT: Floyd County. Refers to the Hi Hat Elkhorn Mining Company.

HOLY CROSS: Marion County. Named by Maryland settlers in 1785. While this religious name was given in reverence, the first church wasn't built here until 1792. Today, a large cedar cross stands on a nearby knoll overlooking the town of Holy Cross.

HOT SPOT: Letcher County. Took its name from a coal company.

IBEX: Elliott County. Christened for a billy goat with long, curved horns that stretched to its shoulders, resembling the ibex found in Europe, Asia, and Africa.

INDIAN FIELDS: Clark County. For its location where there was once an Indian village.

JUG OR NOT: Pulaski County. As the story goes, this area was once known for its production of moonshine. When people hereabout met, they always asked each other if they had a "jug or not." Thus, inspiration for the village name.

JUMBO: Lincoln County. Originally called Green River School Community until around the Civil War. A post office was established about that time, and residents were asked to select a name for the facility and the community. It was also the year of the

famous elephant, Jumbo, and citizens decided that would be a good name.

KALIOPI: Leslie County. Christened by Sam Pilotos for his Greek mother.

KAYJAY: Knox County. For the initials of the Kentucky-Jellico Coal Company.

LAIR: Harrison County. Honors Matthias Lair.

LEMON: McLean County. A man by the name of Ray owned a store in which the post office was located. When asked what name he wanted for the office, he looked around until his eyes fell on a basket of lemons.

LIBERTY ROAD: Morgan County. Named for its status as a crossroads community near the town of West Liberty.

LICKSKILLET: Logan County. Animals licked salt deposits in a rock nearby; where they licked eventually formed the shape of a skillet.

LIMP: Hardin County. By tradition, some men were sitting on the porch of a store discussing names for their community. They looked into the distance and saw a man walking down the road. He had a limp; ergo, inspiration for the town's name.

LONE: Lee County. From sources available, it appears this hamlet was named by citizens because they were always in "loan" to each other. In time, the current spelling came about.

LOT: Whitley County. Refers to the biblical figure.

LOVELY: Martin County. Salutes Sam Lovely, a store owner.

LUCKY FORK: Owsley County. Daniel Boone, the famous frontiersman, was responsible for this name. Boone considered the nearby stream one of his favorite hunting spots and referred to the site as his "lucky fork." Later, when a community grew up here, residents remembered Boone's words.

LUCKY STOP: Montgomery County. For the Lucky Stop Tavern.

MALT: LaRue County. When a decision had to be made on a name for the new post office, someone noticed a can of Redtop Malt on a shelf in the local store. Thus, inspiration for the town name.

MARROWBONE: Cumberland County. One belief is that the community received its label from early days, when a family living here used to hunt bear for food. One of the young boys would eat none of the meat, preferring the area around the spinal cord. He ate so much of that section, he became very sick, after which he stated he would never again eat any of the marrowbone. Another rendition is that early scouts, looking for land grants for veterans of the Revolutionary War, considered the area bottomland "the marrow of the bone," meaning excellent farm acreage.

MASHFORK: Magoffin County. Supposedly acquired its name because a nearby fork of a creek is surrounded by high hills, and where the hills come together near one particular spot, they seem to "mash" into the fork.

MEANS: Menifee County. For Wilbur W. Means, first postmaster.

MEMORIAL: Hart County. For veterans of World War I.

MILLION: Madison County. Family name.

MISTLETOE: Owsley County. For the plant.

MONKEYS EYEBROW: Ballard County. This is probably the most unusual place name in America. The origin, on the other hand, is rather simple, at least, by local history. A country store here was situated below a bluff, which had trees and brush growing out over the ledge. One day, a man who had imbibed too much in the spirits looked up at the ledge and commented that it reminded him of a monkey's eyebrow. How far this is from the true origin of the moniker is unknown, but it's as good as any other.

MOON: Morgan County. This label was one of several on a list submitted to postal authorities, and was selected in Washington.

MORNING VIEW: Kenton County. So named when railroad officials, traveling through on a handcar, were treated to a beautiful sunrise.

MOUNT VICTORY: Pulaski County. Christened for two women missionaries who volunteered to carry the mail free of charge for a year if they would be assured a post office for the community. The name was chosen in honor of their "victorious" endeavor.

MOUSIE: Knott County. For Mousie Martin, daughter of the first postmaster.

MOUTHCARD: Pike County. For its location at the "mouth" of Card Creek. The stream supposedly acquired its handle because men used to play cards here.

MUMMIE: Jackson County. More than likely named when a "mummified" body was discovered in a stone house by settlers.

NEON: Letcher County. The town was probably designated for the gas discovered here in earlier days. There is an intriguing story, however, that accounts for a version of the hamlet name. When the railroad was built here, it was placed on a high plain to escape flooding. As a result, people boarding the train had to step up on a stool to reach the car. For some, the stool was not high enough, and they had to climb aboard by standing on the stool and putting a knee on the car to lift themselves into it. At the time, the place was known as Chips. Conductors, asking passengers their destination, and being told "Chips," would say, "Oh, you mean the place where people have to put their 'knee on' the

car to climb aboard." Some contend this is the source of the community tag.

NEW: Owen County. For Dick New, first postmaster.

OIL SPRINGS: Johnson County. Apparently oil was found in a spring near here.

OLDTOWN: Greenup County. Community was established in the 1780s, and was probably so labeled because traces of an earlier Indian village were found on the site.

OOLITE: Meade County. For the oolite limestone quarried here.

OPPY: Martin County. Refers to an early female resident called Oppy.

ORDINARY: Elliott County. When names for this site were being discussed, Dr. Wales S. Brown proffered, "It is only an ordinary place, so let's call it Ordinary."

OVERLOOK: Lyon County. For its location on a hill "overlooking" Barkley Lake.

PACK BOTTOM: Martin County. Remembers the Pack family that settled on bottomland.

PANTHER: Daviess County. Panthers were seen here long ago.

PARAGON: Rowan County. This community moniker could be derived from a family name, or from the settlement's relationship to nearby railroad tracks.

PATHFORK: Harlan County. For the creek, which took its name from a "path" that ran parallel to the "fork" of the stream.

PEANUT: Muhlenberg County. For a mine, which was so labeled because the owner was fond of goobers.

PEASTICK: Bath County. In earlier times, people came to this area to gather small poles with which to stick (support) pea vines.

PEEDEE: Christian County. Salutes P. D. Smith, founder of the community.

PETROLEUM: Allen County. For its location in an oil field, where oil was discovered in the 1880s.

PEWEE VALLEY: Oldham County. While residents were trying to decide on a name for the town, someone noticed the nest of a pewee bird.

PIG: Edmonson County. The story goes that many years ago, a political candidate promised that if elected he would see that a post office was established here. He was elected and kept his promise. When townspeople met to decide on a name for the facility, some wanted to honor the congressman, others did not. When no agreement was reached, the meeting adjourned until later. As some of the men were walking home, a razorback swine darted across the road. One of the men commented, "We remind me of that hog, so let's call the place Pig."

PIGEONROOST: Clay County. For the wild pigeons that once roosted here.

PILGRIM: Martin County. Supposedly the name was suggested by Betty Fannin, schoolteacher, because she liked the novel *Pilgrim's Progress.*

PINK: Jessamine County. One version is that the community was tagged for John "Pink" Overstreet, postmaster. More interesting, however, is local legend. Long ago, on the banks of a small spring, a pink hyacinth bloomed. Members of the community looked forward each spring to the blossoming of the flower because they depended on the spring for water and believed the flower kept the spring clean and pure. One day, a man rode along the bank and his horse stepped on the flower, killing it. Shortly thereafter, as the tale continues, the horse drank from the spring and fell dead. The townspeople, hearing what had happened, from then on refused to drink from the spring. The settlement took its name from the flower, the pink hyacinth.

PIPPA PASSES: Knott County. Alice Lloyd, founder of a small college bearing her name, christened the community for one of Robert Browning's poems, "Pippa Passes."

PLACE: Knox County. So labeled simply because residents believed this was a nice place to live.

PLEASANT HOME: Owen County. One source states the town was named for a Baptist church erected here in the early 1800s. Another belief is that it stems from the time the site was first settled by the Lowdenback family. Benjamin F. Lowdenback built a home for his family and when it was finished, his wife reputedly said, "This house . . . is such a nice place to live . . . Call it Pleasant Home."

PLEASANT RETREAT: Trimble County. Took its name from a school, which came to be called such when, in the process of moving books into the new school building, Mrs. Molly Fisher, alluding to the beautiful fall weather, commented, "Isn't this a pleasant retreat."

PLEASUREVILLE: Henry County. Took its name from a comment made by a traveling salesman, when he said the community looked like such a fun place.

POD: Christian County. Acronym for "Post Office Delivery."

POMP: Morgan County. Remembers Walter "Pomp" Kendally, a resident.

POWDERLY: Muhlenberg County. For Terrence V. Powderly, a resident.

PRAISE: Pike County. According to tradition, the name came from a preacher's favorite expression, "Praise the Lord."

133

PRESS: Breathitt County. For Press Howard, a settler.

PRINTER: Floyd County. For Printer Meade, a resident.

PUMPKIN CHAPEL: Casey County. For the Pumpkin Chapel School District.

QUALITY: Butler County. For the Quality Valley, named for its "fine" farming land.

QUICKSAND: Breathitt County. Many years ago, as legend relates, a man traveling through crossed a stream. In the middle of the stream he found himself and his horse slowly sinking. He cried for help, but before anyone could come to his rescue, both rider and horse disappeared. Ever since, the site has been called Quicksand.

RABBIT HASH: Boone County. Christmas of 1847 found this area both covered with a heavy snow and practically underwater from a flood. Spirits were low, and people gathered at this spot to watch their homes being washed away by the roaring water. Time passed, and since they had been without food for some time, that was the direction conversation turned. Dreaming, they chatted about what they would have for Christmas dinner—roast duck, turkey, ham—and, of course, all the trimmings. One gentleman, off to himself, had been quiet during the course of conversation. A man turned and asked what he planned for Christmas dinner. With a twinkle in his eye, and buoyed by spirits from a near-empty bottle, he answered, "Rabbit hash." Thus, inspiration for the settlement name.

RACELAND: Greenup County. Named for a racetrack no longer in existence.

READY: Grayson County. Citizens wanted their place named Simpson, for a local family. The name was submitted to Washington, but was returned because of duplication. So residents named it Ready, since there was "already" another Simpson.

RED BIRD: Whitley County. For the many redbirds hereabout.

REDHOUSE: Madison County. For a house built here painted red.

RELIEF: Morgan County. So christened because once a post office was established, it was a relief for residents not to have to travel so far for mail.

SALT GUM: Knox County. For the salt lick and gum trees in the vicinity.

SCIENCE HILL: Pulaski County. Took its name from a normal (science) school once located on a hill in the area.

SELECT: Ohio County. Citizens asked Washington postal officials for a name for their office. The officials replied, "Select a name," and they did.

SEMIWAY: McLean County. For its location "semi" distance between Calhoun and Sacramento.

SE REE: Breckinridge County. Known as Possum Trot, but when a post office was set up, residents didn't want a name like that attached to their community. A salesman traveling through the area had a daughter named Ree, so the community adapted that name; why "Se" was added is unknown.

SETTLE: Allen County. Remembers Felix T. Settle, first postmaster.

SHADE: Estill County. Salutes Dixie Kirby Shade Ingram.

SHORT BRANCH: Greenup County. For its location on a short branch (stream) of Little Sandy Creek.

SHOULDERBLADE: Breathitt County. For a creek; the stream acquired its name when someone found a bone on its bank.

SHUCKS: Fulton County. A family name, with an "s" added.

SIDEVIEW: Montgomery County. English Anderson and his family, early settlers in this part of the country, lived in a large house on a hill. One side of the house had a long porch that provided a panoramic view of the countryside. Since the porch was located on the "side" of the house, it was called "sideview," a name later taken by the community.

SIXSEAM: Hopkins County. It's doubtful that there's much of this hamlet left, but it took its name from a coal company.

SIZEROCK: Leslie County. Christened by Johnny Barnes, first postmaster, for a "large rock" located near the post office.

SKYLIGHT: Oldham County. Apparently acquired its moniker from the fact that the village is situated in a high area with plenty of open sky.

SMILAX: Leslie County. For a vine or plant.

SMILE: Rowan County. When finally granted a post office, residents were so happy they would no longer have to travel six to eight miles for mail that "they all smiled."

SOFT SHELL: Knott County. Community was comprised mostly of members of the Soft Shell Baptist Church.

SOLDIER: Carter County. In early days a detachment of soldiers camped nearby and had with them a dog they called Soldier. Since the village didn't have a name at the time, the military men decided to give it their mascot's name.

SOURWOOD: Clay County. Community name taken from the song "Chicken Crowing in the Sourwood Mountain."

SOUTH UNION: Logan County. This site was settled by Shakers from Union, Ohio (north of Kentucky). They named their new home South Union because it was "south of their former home."

SPA: Logan County. For a mineral spring.

SPARROW: Anderson County. When a name was needed for a new post office, a survey revealed that persons with the surname Sparrow were the most numerous, so that was the label chosen.

SPLINT: Harlan County. Term for a coal seam; village was named for local mines.

SPUNKY RIDGE: Green County. So named because schoolboys used to fight a lot—they were "spunky."

STAB: Pulaski County. According to lore, this site was first called Stab Eye, later shortened to Stab. As the story goes, a man was caught courting another man's woman and the offended stabbed the offender in the eye.

STAMPING GROUND: Scott County. In early days, buffalo were in abundance in this area. The animals used a regular route travel-ing to local springs, in which they rolled in the water and coated their rears with mud for protection against insect bites. The well-worn route was known as a "stamping ground," and when a com-munity grew up here around 1814, residents took the name Stamping Ground.

STOOPS: Montgomery County. For a Dr. Stoops.

STOPOVER: Pike County. Name suggested by David H. Blankenship, store owner, because people were always stopping at his crossroads place of business to ask various directions.

STRAW: Edmonson County. A long time back, a man named George owned a mill. People for miles around brought corn, wheat, and oats to the mill for grinding. As a result, there was always a pile of straw around the mill. One day some men were sitting on the pile trying to decide on a name for the hamlet. Suddenly, one of them realized they were on top of a good name; thus, Straw was born.

STRAWBERRY: Pulaski County. Named by Ned and J. W. Kelley for the beautiful strawberry patches in the vicinity.

SUBTLE: Metcalfe County. This handle was chosen simply because it was the shortest one submitted for consideration.

SUGARTIT: Boone County. Some believe the community designation comes from Utterback Creek, with *utterback* being from the German and meaning "sugar teat." Most feel the name comes from "sugar teat," but was related to a piece of sugar placed in a cloth and hung around the necks of young children as a pacifier.

SUMMER SHADE: Metcalfe County. For the many shade trees here-about.

SYMBOL: Laurel County. A Baptist minister recommended this name, hoping the community would serve as a symbol of progress.

TANNERY: Lewis County. For a tanning operation located here in the late 1800s.

TEN SPOT: Harlan County. Property was exchanged for money, either through gambling or deed transfer; ergo, the hamlet name.

THOUSANDSTICKS: Leslie County. Originally known as Gad, early day missionaries came here to gather sticks to use in arts and crafts. They tied the "sticks" in bundles of one "thousand."

THREE POINT: Harlan County. The points of three ridges meet at this site.

TOBACCO: Calloway County. Originally called Need More for the lack of merchandise in a local store, the town was renamed for a tobacco storage or curing house built nearby.

TOMAHAWK: Martin County. For a newspaper in nearby Inez, *The Tomahawk News.*

TONGS: Greenup County. Family name.

TOURISTVILLE: Wayne County. Apparently so named to reap benefits from tourists catering the nearby Mill Springs area.

TRAM: Floyd County. Christened for a long, winding wooden track located in Ivy Valley, which was used to transport logs in the early 1900s. The haulway was known as a tram.

TRAPPIST: Nelson County. For the Trappist Order of Catholic monks, which oversees the nearby Abbey of Gethsemane.

TRIPLET: Rowan County. Probably reflects on the prolificity of the mountain folk.

TURKEY FOOT: Scott County. For a three-pronged fork in Eagle Creek that resembles a turkey's foot.

TUTOR KEY: Johnson County. For a friend of the postmaster, with the word *key* added to make the name a little more unusual.

UNION STAR: Breckinridge County. First called Jackiesburg, the town split loyalties during the Civil War. The section that sided with the North petitioned for a post office. When it was granted, residents displayed their loyalty even further by naming the office and the settlement Union Star.

UNO: Hart County. When first settled, the village was known as Clear Pint, for the unblemished moonshine a resident made. The name was changed to Clear Point to get away from the moonshine image. When a post office was set up, the name had to be changed again, probably because of duplication. A man on the way to get a fresh jug of moonshine was asked his destination. When he replied, "You know," this gave inspiration for the new community name.

VICTORY: Laurel County. C. C. Nelson and a man named Pennington vied to have a post office placed here. Using political connections in Washington, Nelson was victorious and decided to name the office Victory, which the community also adopted. From latest reports, the post office has had a Nelson, or a Nelson relative, as postmaster ever since. 137

VIPER: Perry County. Inspiration for this tag came about when the postmaster happened upon a den of snakes.

WAGERSVILLE: Estill County. Derived from a family name.

WAIT: Wayne County. Village name taken from that of an early school. The school was so named because it was located near a river, and when the water was high, children on the opposite side of the stream had to wait until the water receded before crossing.

WALTZ: Rowan County. Family name.

WATERGAP: Floyd County. Apparently took its handle from a "gap" (opening in the mountain), through which "water" flowed.

WAX: Grayson County. Community received its name when a group of officials walked into a store and saw the owner weighing "beeswax."

WHEEL: Graves County. For a farm group called the "Wheelers."

WHIPPOORWILL: Logan County. For Big Whippoorwill Creek, which was christened for the bird.

WHITE ROSE: Taylor County. Either named for two families (White and Rose), or because wild, or white, roses grew plentifully in the region.

WHITE TOWER: Kenton County. For an early farmer, George White, who built large "barns" for his cattle.

WILDIE: Rockcastle County. From local yarns, two men went into business here in earlier times. The men's names were Will and Dee, and a combination of these was the basis for the town's title.

WINDY: Wayne County. Supposedly designated for a heavy storm that hit here in the early 1900s.

WINGO: Graves County. Salutes J. Wingo, settler.

WISDOM: Metcalfe County. For the superintendent of schools.

WOLF COAL: Breathitt County. Refers to the Wolf Valley Coal Company.

WOODSBEND: Morgan County. Known first as Flatswood, then as Bear Wallow, finally designated Woodsbend for a forest (woods) and for a "bend" in the Licking River.

YAMACRAW: McCreary County. For the Yamacraw Indians.

YELLOW ROCK: Lee County. For the yellow rock dug from a quarry.

ZAG: Morgan County. A long list of names for this community was sent to officials in Washington; all were rejected. A man by the name of Jeff Cox had a house here, the inside walls of which were covered with newspapers. A discussion was under way in the house regarding another name for the village when Cox's daughter, Pearl, saw the words *zig zag* printed in one of the newspapers. Both words were submitted to Washington, and Zag was approved.

Louisiana

THE PELICAN STATE

ACY: Ascension Parish. For William Acy, a settler.

AMITE: Tangipahoa Parish. One version for the origin of this name is that it came from the Amite River. How did the stream come by its moniker? It's either a Choctaw Indian word meaning "red ant," or a corruption of the French *amitié*, meaning "friendship," and was so named because of the friendliness of Indians in the region. There is a possibility that when recording the place name in their log, the French spelled the word phonetically as *himmita* and came up with Amite. Or it could stem from the Choctaw word *sagamite*, a type of corn eaten by Louisiana Indians. As is to be expected, folklore must have its own renditions. From this comes the theory that two roads once crossed here, and people living along the roads would meet at this spot and exchange news and gossip. The site became known as "A-meet," which could have evolved into Amite. Another tradition continues the previous one that in time a small settlement grew up on the site. It was very small, only "a mite" of a place, so residents called it Amite.

ARABIE: St. Bernard Parish. Supposedly so named because of news-paper headlines at the time that embellished the activities of an "Arabian" chieftain. It might just as well have come from the family name of Arabie.

BAPTIST: Tangipahoa Parish. Label was taken from the New Beulah Baptist Church.

BOOK: Catahoula Parish. Family name.

BULLION: Ascension Parish. Honors O. A. Bullion, a settler.

CONVENT: St. James Parish. For the Convent Du Sacre Couer (Convent of the Sacred Heart), founded by French nuns in 1825.

CUT OFF: LaFourche Parish. Christened for a proposed shortcut canal, or cutoff, intended for both navigation and drainage of farmland. Although two canals were started, at last count neither was finished.

DRY PRONG: Grant Parish. Two streams of water came together here to form Big Creek. During the 1870s, a family moved into the locality and began erecting a water mill on one of the streams. Having moved during the winter months, there was plenty of water to operate the mill. Before construction of the mill was com-pleted, however, summer arrived and the stream dried up. The family soon realized they had settled on the dry prong of the creek.

EMPIRE: Plaquemines Parish. Reportedly refers to one of the first gasoline launches, the *Empire*, that towed oyster boats through the river and past the town.

142

EROS: Jackson Parish. A post office was placed here in 1898, and Mrs. Mary Nash Collins, postmistress at nearby Nash, called the office Eros, for a recently discovered planetoid, not for the Greek god of love.

EXTENSION: Franklin Parish. So tagged because the new post office would be an extension of the Winnsboro office.

FORT NECESSITY: Franklin Parish. There was never a fort on this site, only a store called Fort Necessity. Jesse Moore built the store and named it in admiration of the fort built in Virginia by George Washington.

HAPPY JACK: Plaquemines Parish. Only legend vows to this community name origin, but supposedly a man by the name of Jack did live here at one time. His happiness is believed to have been brought on by frequent encounters with John Barleycorn.

HARDSHELL: Vernon Parish. For the Hardshell Baptist Church.

IOTA: Acadia Parish. Versions abound as to the origin of this village name. One is that when the railroad came through here, the community was known as Pointe aux Loupe. The railroad wanted the name changed because it was too long. *Iota,* one of the shortest letters in the Greek alphabet, was chosen. Another rendition states that railroad officials decided to skirt the nearby community of Cartville. One official rebelled, saying, "Not by one iota will I cut out this area." The railroad subsequently set the station between Cartville and Pointe aux Loupe and named the site Iota. The final version contends that the settlement was originally known as Fabacher. Railroad officials weren't particularly fond of that name and asked that it be changed. Citizens queried an official as to what name he would suggest, and he replied that it "made not one iota of difference" to him.

JESUIT BEND: Plaquemines Parish. For a settlement of Jesuit fathers on this site in the early 1700s.

JIGGER: Franklin Parish. In 1933, when the community was of sufficient size to warrant a post office, the postal department requested a list of twenty possible names, from which the department would select one. While Mr. and Mrs. Charles Harris were preparing the list, their son, called "Little Jigger" because of his size, interrupted with "Name it after me." The Harrises added their son's nickname to the list, and it was chosen.

LUCKNOW: Richland Parish. Robert Whoon and his wife were living with his brother when Robert's first child was born. The remark was made after the birth of the baby, "We're in luck, now!" Thus, the settlement's tag.

MANY: Sabine Parish. Pronounced "Man-e." Salutes Colonel Many, a soldier once stationed at then nearby Fort Jesup.

MIX: Pointe Coupee Parish. Remembers Thomas Mix, a settler.

NEW ROADS: Pointe Coupee Parish. Originally known as St. Mary, the name was changed in 1848 when a "new road" was constructed, connecting the False River with the Mississippi River. Through the years, the "s" came into use.

NICKEL: La Salle Parish. Around 1850, it was decided to set up a post office here, and to locate the facility in the general store owned by John Westbrook. Postal authorities asked Westbrook to suggest a name for the office, to which the store owner replied, "You know this whole place just isn't worth a nickel." The postal representative said, "That being true, we will just name the place Nickel." The community took the same name.

OIL CITY: Caddo Parish. Originally called Ananies, the name was changed to Oil City in 1910, when "black gold" was discovered.

OLIVE BRANCH: East Feliciana Parish. For a stream. There is some doubt about the authenticity of this name. At least one source believes it should be Oliver, the name of an ancestor of Daniel Cleveland, the original settler in the area.

PELICAN: De Soto Parish. The story is told that one time a hurricane blew a pelican onto the site, and it landed in a sawmill owned by W. R. Carroll. Because of this incident, Carroll named the small settlement Pelican.

PLAIN DEALING: Bossier Parish. Took its handle from the Plain Dealing Plantation, owned by George Oglethorp Gilmer. It is said that the Gilmer family attitude toward business "dealings" was "fair, honest and plain."

POINT BLUE: Evangeline Parish. Christened for its location near a strip of land that, when light shines on it at the right time, presents a blue hue.

PUMPKIN CENTER: Tangipahoa Parish. This title has nothing to do with pumpkins. It is believed the designation was taken from the hometown of an early comedy team known as "Uncle Josh and Aunt Nancy," whose phonograph records were once popular here.

RESERVE: St. John the Baptist Parish. For a plantation. Sometime between the years 1840 and 1844, a young peddler by the name of Leon Goudchaux was traveling through this region. It was his custom to spend the night at a plantation near where he happened to be when darkness arrived. One particular night, Goudchaux stopped at the Souvenir Plantation, owned by one Antoine Boudousqui. The owner was not cordial toward the young man and sent him scurrying from the premises. Goudchaux left, but called back the warning, "You had better reserve this plantation for me. I'm coming back some day and buy it." Boudousqui laughed at what he considered an idle boast by a common laborer. Twenty years later, Boudousqui found himself in financial straits and had to put Souvenir Plantation on the market. The buyer? Leon Goudchaux, who had, by this time, become a wealthy cloth and sugar merchant. So that neither time nor man would forget, Goudchaux christened his newly acquired estate Reserve, a reminder of the warning he levied years earlier.

START: Richland Parish. Took its label from the fact that with the new post office, the community would be making a fresh start.

SULPHUR: Calcasieu Parish. For a sulfur mine.

SUNNY SIDE: Iberville Parish. For the Sunny Side Plantation.

SUNSET: St. Landry Parish. One version for the origin of this place name is that when the railroad was marking its route, residents of Grand Coteau were divided. Some wanted the railroad to come through their settlement, others didn't. Those who favored the route believed if it didn't come through, then the village's "sun had set." The "againsts" prevailed; a station was set up two miles to the east and named Sunset. Another rendition is that railroad workers would name the stops each day as they completed sections of track. They happened to reach this point at sunset.

SUNSHINE: Iberville Parish. This moniker was selected for the post office set up here in 1881. It was the direct opposite of the earlier name, Forlorn Hope, and the change is understandable.

SUPREME: Assumption Parish. Refers to the Supreme Sugar Refinery.

TREES: Caddo Parish. For J. C. Trees, the area's first oil wildcatter.

UNCLE SAM: St. James Parish. At last knowledge, this is today the site of the Freeport Chemical Company. There was once a large plantation here owned by Samuel Pierre Auguste Fagot. It is generally believed the plantation took its name from its owner, "Uncle Sam." It could have come from the fact, however, that one of the Fagot male members returned from a trip to Europe sporting a fancy mustache, and women called him "Uncle Sam." Also plausible is the belief that Fagot, one of the first men to become wealthy in sugar, had his barrels stamped "U.S." to denote the country of origin, and this eventually led to Uncle Sam.

UNEEDUS: Tangipahoa Parish. Community developed by the Lake Superior Piling Company, Duluth, Minnesota, and took its name from the company's slogan, "You need us." It has been rumored that a short distance away, another small village once existed by the name of Weneedu. This has not been confirmed.

VIXEN: Caldwell Parish. At one time there was a family living here by the name of Fox. Possibly, someone dubbed the community Vixen, for a female fox.

WATERPROOF: Tensas Parish. Supposedly so named when Abner Smalley was standing on a strip of land waiting for a steamboat to dock. From where Smalley stood, he could see nothing but water. When the boat docked, the captain yelled, "Well, Abner, I see you're waterproof." From the comment came the town's name. The tag is misleading, according to available sources, since Waterproof has been inundated on more than one occasion and, at times, has been under as much as three feet of water.

WELCOME: St. James Parish. A translation from the French *Bon Secour,* and the name of a plantation.

WESTWEGO: Jefferson Parish. Acquired its moniker from the fact that in early days, it was the crossing point for travelers heading west.

WHITE CASTLE: Iberville Parish. Relates to the white castle home of the Vaughn family, which sat on a high bluff overlooking the Mississippi River.

Maine

THE PINE TREE STATE

ADMIRALTY VILLAGE: York County. For its early American naval history.

BIG TEN TOWNSHIP: Somerset County. For its large size and numerical designation.

BIG W TOWNSHIP: Somerset County. Received its label because it is larger than Little W Township and is designated by the letter W.

BINGO: Washington County. This moniker was pulled out of the air by a Mr. Ripley, who, when asked where he lived, replied, "Bingo," although the village had no name at the time.

BLACKSTRAP: Cumberland County. For William Blackstrap, a settler.

BLUE HILL: Hancock County. For a nearby hill covered with pine, spruce, and fir trees. From a distance the trees give off a "bluish" cast.

CONVENE: Cumberland County. When a post office was opened here, a name was needed for it and the settlement. Several women were discussing the matter when one of them said she hoped they could decide on a name, because having a post office would be very "convenient." In inspiration, another lady suggested they name the community Convene.

COREA: Hancock County. Village name derived from that of the Asiatic country Korea. Eva Talbut is credited with christening the town, but why she chose Corea is unknown.

DARK HARBOR: Waldo County. Named by seamen during the nineteenth century. In those days, sailors used the term "dark" to denote anything easily hidden, covered, or readily overlooked. Apparently, Dark Harbor sat in such surroundings.

DOG TOWN: Washington County. For the large number of dogs hereabout.

DOGTOWN: Somerset County. In early days a tannery was located here, and the carcasses spread out over the land attracted many dogs.

DUCKTRAP: Waldo County. So named because Indians once trapped ducks here during the molting season when they couldn't fly away.

FIVE MILE CORNERS: Hancock County. For its location five miles from Bucksport, and apparently for intersecting roads that create corners.

HAPPY CORNER: Piscataquis County. Community was apparently comprised of a bunch of happy people.

HASTY CORNER: Penobscot County. Family name.

HAY BROOK: Penobscot County. For the abundance of hay in the area, near a brook.

ICEBORO: Kennebec County. Remembers an ice plant once located here. The men who worked in the plant built their homes on the site.

LEATHER CORNERS: Penobscot County. Salutes J. S. Leathers, settler.

LITTLE W TOWNSHIP: Somerset County. So tagged because it is smaller than Big W Township, and for its letter designation.

LONG A TOWNSHIP: Penobscot County. For its geographical length, and because of its letter designation.

MEREPOINT: Cumberland County. Some believe the handle of this summer community situated on a peninsula came about because it is small (mere). Others opine it was derived from the French *mer*, meaning "sea."

MOOSEHEAD: Piscataquis County. One version of this name origin is that from nearby Mount Kineo, Moosehead Lake, for which the settlement is named, resembles a moose's head. In the opposite direction, from the lake to the mountain, some say Kineo resembles a crouching moose. Still others believe the tag came about because of the large number of moose horns found in the area in early settlement days. Yet another opinion is that the name comes from some legend that the Glooskap Indians connected to Mount Kineo.

MOOSEHORN: Piscataquis County. Records the time Joseph Bearce took a set of moose horns he found and placed them in a tree, where they were used to mark a small path off a major one.

OLD TOWN: Penobscot County. Hamlet name continues from early days when Indians referred to the site as their "old town."

OWLS HEAD: Knox County. A bay was so named by Governor Thomas Pownal in 1759, for the shape of the inlet. The name was later tagged to the settlement.

PULPIT HARBOR: Knox County. For the shape of a nearby rock.

RAZORVILLE: Knox County. For George Razor, who apparently changed the spelling of his name from that of the family, which was Reiser.

RED BRIDGE: Aroostook County. For a nearby bridge, the supports of which were painted red.

ROBINHOOD: Sagadahoc County. Settlement title taken from the English name of a local Indian.

SEAWALL: Hancock County. Village named for the many rocks lining the shore of Somes Sound.

SHAKER VILLAGE: Cumberland County. For a Shaker colony established here in 1791.

SHIN POND: Penobscot County. Family name, plus the town is located near a pond.

SLAB CITY: Oxford County. For a sawmill that cut slabs for buildings.

SODOM: Oxford County. This village received its moniker from outsiders, because neighbors thought the residents herein were downright "evil."

SOLDIER POND: Aroostook County. Originally called Little Lake. After three soldiers died here during the Aroostook Indian War, the lake name was changed to its present designation; the nearby community later took the same tag.

SPRUCE HEAD: Waldo County. For the many spruce trees in the area.

STARBIRDS: Piscataquis County. Remembers William Starbird, a landowner.

STETSON: Penobscot County. First inclination aside, this has nothing to do with Stetson hats. The settlement was christened for Amasa Stetson, landowner.

STRONGHOLD: Somerset County. Honors Rosie Stronghold.

SUCKERVILLE: Cumberland County. For the sucker fish, which are plentiful in nearby waters.

TEAR CAP: Oxford County. Dr. Joseph Benton was making house calls when he came across two women fighting. During the scuffle the women tore each other's lace caps; thus, encouragement for the hamlet name.

TOWN HOUSE: Oxford County. For a townhouse constructed here around 1858.

WELD: Franklin County. For Benjamin Weld, a landowner.

WHITE SCHOOL CORNER: Somerset County. For an early school building, painted white, that was situated on a corner lot.

WITCH ISLAND: Lincoln County. Relates to Mrs. Grace Courtland who, along with her husband, purchased this site as a summer home. Mrs. Courtland published a stock exchange paper in New York, and her uncanny judgment and predictions on stock earned her the sobriquet of the "Witch of Wall Street."

WONDERLAND: Hancock County. Ike Stanley, who owned an eatery here, gave the community its name as a publicity stunt.

Maryland
THE OLD LINE STATE

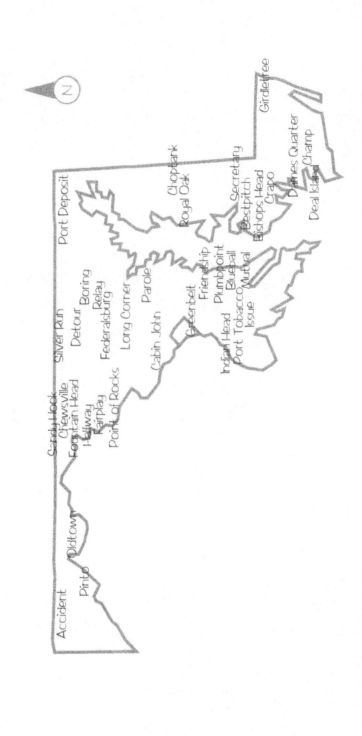

ACCIDENT: Garrett County. Named for a nearby tract of land. Around 1774, two separate surveying parties "accidentally" surveyed the same tract of land. The differences that occurred in the surveys were resolved in a friendly manner, and the tract was named for the mix-up that took place.

BESTPITCH: Dorchester County. All but deserted now, this hamlet remembers the Bestpitch family.

BISHOPS HEAD: Dorchester County. Supposedly acquired its name because the terrain is shaped like the headdress worn by bishops.

BLUEBALL: Calvert County. Probably took its name from an eighteenth-century inn.

BORING: Baltimore County. For David Boring, the first postmaster.

CABIN JOHN: Montgomery County. Mystery and interesting thought surround the different versions of how this community received its moniker. One source contends that a hermit named John once lived in a cabin here. Also, he disappeared from the area just as mysteriously as he arrived. Another rendition is that "John" was a pirate who deserted his fellow crewmen, made his way to this spot, and buried treasure somewhere in the vicinity. This belief was valid enough to persuade early land developers to put certain clauses in their contracts regarding any treasure that might be found by buyers. Through everything, the general consensus is that the name comes from a corruption of Captain (Cap'n) John, which came from a stream name recorded in early deeds and maps. Just who "Cap'n John" was, no one knows. Perhaps, as some believe, it was Captain John Smith, founder of Jamestown, and the first man to map this area.

CHAMP: Somerset County. Frank Beauchamp petitioned for a post office and suggested it be named for him. Authorities agreed, but considered his name too long, so they shortened it to Champ.

CHEWSVILLE: Washington County. This former factory town was named by Colonel Fitzhugh for his friend Mr. Chew. Fitzhugh owned a nail factory near here at the time.

CHOPTANK: Caroline County. For the river. The stream name is from an Indian word, the translations of which are many and varied: "flowing back strongly," "many bends," "wide waters," or "a deep stream."

CRAPO: Dorchester County. This community label could be a derivation of the French nickname Crapaud. Maybe it's from the French *crapeau*, meaning "amphibians." An intriguing version is that the postmaster, out for his evening constitutional, was walking near a pond when a large toad jumped from the bank into the water, making a noise that sounded like "crapo." This gave the postmaster the idea for the town's name.

DAMES QUARTER: Somerset County. Originally known as Damned Quarters, more religious elements changed the name, yet kept it in close proximity of its original designation.

DEAL ISLAND: Somerset County. First called Devils Island, religious conversion among villagers made them opt for a name change. Captain John Parks, a visiting minister, suggested Deils Island, pointing out that *deil* was a Greek word for "devil." Some disagree with this theory, stating simply that the "v" was dropped from Devil. Anyway, the place was known as Deils Island for many years, but eventually became listed as Deal Island.

DETOUR: Carroll County. Once called Double Pipe Creek, the tag had to be changed because it was too long for Western Maryland Railway timetables. Why Detour was chosen is unknown.

FAIRPLAY: Washington County. Acquired its handle in earlier times when farmers hereabout were "fair" in their dealings with friends and neighbors.

FEDERALSBURG: Carroll County. Named in 1812 for the Federal political party.

FOUNTAIN HEAD: Washington County. Believed to have been coined by Emmet W. Gans, the town founder.

FRIENDSHIP: Anne Arundel County. Two versions, closely related, account for the origin of this town name. One has it that a minister, stricken during Sunday service, lay down on the floor of the church and refused to move. The congregation, greatly concerned, tended to the minister through the night. The following morning he was completely healed and was so affected by the attention of the churchgoers, he named the small place Friendship. The other rendition has it that a minister was severely beaten by the town drunk and took ill during his sermon. He was so impressed by the care rendered by members of the church in nursing him back to health, that he named the community Friendship. It is quite possible both versions are one and the same.

GIRDLETREE: Worcester County. Some sources believe Indians "girdled" (debarked to stunt growth) a tree to allow for more garden space. Another version is that a wild grapevine grew around a tree, thus "girdling" it. The third rendition is that Charles and Mary Bishop "girdled" a tree to permit room for building their house. They named their home Girdle Tree Hill, which eventually evolved into the community name.

GREENBELT: Prince Georges County. During the New Deal era of the Great Depression, the Resettlement Administration built a planned community of 885 homes on this spot, housing more than 3,000 people. A complete community was established, including schools, shops, and other facilities. In 1953, the federal government sold all the land, including improvements, to the residents. The name Greenbelt comes from the fact that the houses were grouped around open spaces, grassy areas where no vehicles were allowed to enter.

HALFWAY: Washington County. For its location halfway between Hagerstown and Williamsport.

INDIAN HEAD: Charles County. A romantic but gruesome legend is associated with this town's handle. As the story goes, an Algonquin Indian chief was anxious to unite his tribe with another. One way to do this was to offer his daughter, a beautiful princess, as bride for the Piscataway prince. Before the marriage ceremony took place, an Indian brave from a tribe in Virginia happened to land his canoe on the shore of the Algonquin camp. It was love at first sight for both the brave and the princess, but because the new arrival was without title, the chief ordered him away. Love was not to be stopped so easily, however, and the young couple made plans to elope. One dark night, the brave canoed to the Algonquin camp but, instead of meeting the princess, he came upon the chief and his warriors. They cut off the young suitor's head, mounted it on a spear, and stuck the spear in the ground. It was a warning to all other Indians to stay away from the Algonquin camp. The next day, white settlers landed here and were greeted by the bloody head. They named the place Indian Head, the tag it retains to this day.

ISSUE: Charles County. Citizens chose this name simply because since the place now had a post office, mail would be "issued" from there, instead of being brought in.

LONG CORNER: Howard County. From information available, it appears the community acquired its name for its location in a long corner of the county, extending from the south branch of the Patapsco River to the north bank of the Patuxent River.

MUTUAL: Calvert County. So named because townspeople agreed that it was by mutual consent of all citizens to petition for a post office.

OLDTOWN: Allegany County. The oldest town in the county, it received its name as early as 1739, when Lord Baltimore issued a deed to "Old Indian Town." Through more than two centuries of history, the town has been called Indian Seat, Old Indian Village, King Opessa's Town, and Skipton, but retains the originally christened Oldtown.

PAROLE: Anne Arundel County. For nearby Camp Parole. During the Civil War, the federal government suspected Union solders were letting themselves be captured by Confederates so they could be paroled back home. Once the prisoners were released and returned

home, few ever reported back to duty. Camp Parole was established to curtail this practice, and Union soldiers paroled by the
Confederacy were kept at this post until they could be returned to
duty.

PINTO: Allegany County. This Mennonite community might have
received its name from a Shawnee Indian who used to ride a pinto
pony. Or, it might have come from a pony, but a pinto ridden by
the mailman along his route.

PLUMBPOINT: Calvert County. In very early days, there was a small
sheltered harbor here and, as legend dictates, it was protected by a
long bar (bank). The bar was reputedly covered with "plum" trees.
Old maps and other recordings listed the place as Plumb Point,
which was eventually written as one word and recorded as the
name of this small waterfront village.

POINT OF ROCKS: Frederick County. The town was named for a
large, pointed rock once located here that jutted out over the C &
O Canal and the B & O Railroad. It is believed the rock was blown
up during the Civil War to blockade the railroad and the canal.

PORT DEPOSIT: Cecil County. In December 1812, when discussion
was in progress over a suitable name, someone suggested, "It is a
port of deposit for lumber. Why not call it Port Deposit?"

PORT TOBACCO: Charles County. Supposedly this is a translation
from *Potapaco,* the name of an Algonquin Indian tribe or village.

RELAY: Baltimore County. For Relay House, which once stood on this
spot. Before inauguration of the steam engine, the B & O Railroad
erected Relay House to serve as a combination hotel and waiting
station for the comfort of its passengers.

ROYAL OAK: Talbot County. The exact origin of this small town's
name is unknown, although available evidence indicates a large
oak tree was used as a boundary marker as early as 1789. There is
some belief that "Royal" may have been attached to "Oak" when
a cannonball was fired into the tree, without doing any damage,
by British soldiers in the War of 1812.

SANDY HOOK: Washington County. Possibly acquired its name from
the fact that a driver lost a team of horses in a quicksand pool
near here.

SECRETARY: Dorchester County. Probably salutes Henry Sewall, early
secretary of state of Maryland.

SILVER RUN: Carroll County. For the stream, which reportedly took
its name from a silver mine.

Massachusetts

THE BAY STATE

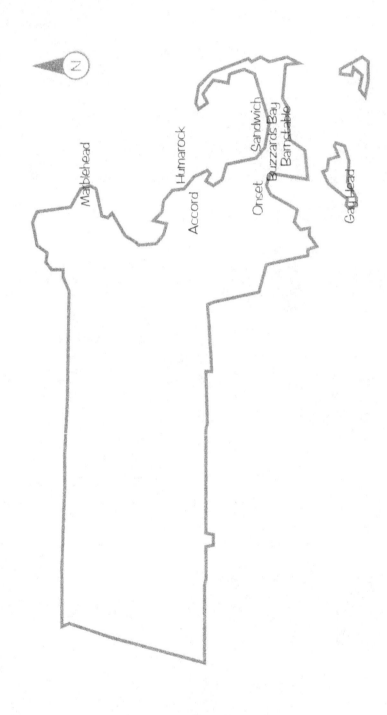

ACCORD: Plymouth County. For a pond. The pond name dates back to the seventeenth century, when colonists met at the site to discuss a disputed boundary claim. A settlement was reached with such amicability that the pond was named Accord.

BARNSTABLE: Barnstable County. For the English seaport.

BUZZARDS BAY: Barnstable County. Captain Thomas Dermer, English explorer, christened the site. In 1616, he entered the area and spotted a large number of birds sailing overhead. Thinking they were buzzards, he tagged the place Buzzards Bay. The birds were actually sea gulls. Another source contends the area was named by early Indians, who treasured a certain type of buzzard.

GAY HEAD: Dukes County. Took its name from nearby "gaily" colored cliffs.

HUMAROCK: Plymouth County. From "hummock," or sand hills.

MARBLEHEAD: Essex County. For gray granite rocks that early settlers mistook for marble stones.

ONSET: Plymouth County. From the Indian *oneset*, which means "summer home," and is probably descriptive.

SANDWICH: Barnstable County. For Sandwich, Kent County, England, former home of many of the early settlers.

Michigan

THE WOLVERINE STATE

ADVENTURE: Ontonagon County. For the Adventure Mine, which opened in 1850.

AFRICA: Ingham County. During the Civil War most of the voters in this community were black abolitionists; thus, the name.

AIR LINE JUNCTION: Jackson County. Took its name from the term used to describe a direct, or air line, route of a railroad run.

ALABASTER: Iosco County. From an alabaster mine.

ALOHA: Cheboygan County. Tagged by James B. Patterson, sawmill operator, who had once visited the Hawaiian Islands.

AMBLE: Montcalm County. Praises Ole Amble, a Lutheran minister.

ANTLERS: Marquette County. For the multitude of deer in the vicinity.

ANVIL LOCATION: Gogebic County. More than likely for a blacksmith's anvil.

AU TRAIN: Alger County. From the French and means "at the drag." Probably took its name from the fact that this spot was once where canoes had to be carried (dragged) across land from one body of water to another.

AZTEC: Houghton County. This copper mining community was named for the legendary Aztecs, believed to be the first copper miners in the Western Hemisphere.

BAD AXE: Huron County. In the early 1860s, a surveying party was mapping this area and made camp in a hunter's cabin, in which was found a much-used ax in bad shape. Lieutenant G. W. Park, a member of the party, suggested to Captain Randolph Papst, leader of the expedition, that the name Bad Axe Camp be used in the survey reports. This was done, and when a post office was set up on the site in November 1870, it was given the name Bad Axe. The state legislature didn't much care for the name and changed it to Huron in 1909, but local residents voted the old name back into use.

BLISS: Emmet County. For Aaron T. Bliss, lumberman and governor of Michigan.

BLOOMER: Montcalm County. When this town was no more than a small, struggling settlement, a dance was held, and several of the ladies wore bloomers, which were at the time symbolic of the female fight for recognition. Although appearance of the undergarments offended some church officials, *bloomer* became a household word. In 1852, the township was organized, and citizens voted Bloomer as its name.

BLUE JACKET: Wexford County. Probably an Indian chief's name. ·

BRAVO: Allegan County. Named to exemplify the spirit of early pioneers in establishing a settlement in the wilderness.

BRETHREN: Manistee County. For the Brethren Colony, sanctioned by the German Baptist Brethren Church, and founded by Samuel S. Thorpe.

BUTTERNUT: Montcalm County. For a butternut cheese factory.

CEMENT CITY: Lenawee County. For a cement plant erected here around 1901.

CENTER LINE: Macomb County. Christened by the French because it was on the middle (center) trail leading from the fort at Detroit to the northern trading posts.

CLIMAX: Kalamazoo County. Originally called Climax Prairie by early settlers because it was the end (climax) of their search for a homeland. "Prairie" was dropped from the name in April 1874.

COLDWATER: Genesee County. This community was not tagged by local residents but by their neighbors. Members of the settlement were known for their aversion to alcoholic drink, and the place was whimsically labeled Coldwater by other area residents.

COLON: St. Joseph County. When a name for this settlement could not be agreed upon, Lorensie Schellhouse opened a dictionary and his eyes fell on the word *colon*. He then commented, "We will call it Colon, for the lake and the river correspond exactly to the shape of a colon."

COON TOWN: Lenawee County. This is a nickname for the city of Addison, and came about during the political campaign of 1840. Practically the entire village consisted of Whig supporters, and since the coonskin cap was a symbol of that party, the headgear was prominently displayed.

CORAL: Montcalm County. First known as Stumptown, the community name was changed in 1862 by Charles Parker, merely because Coral was easy to spell.

COVERT: Van Buren County. This is a term often used to define a hiding place for game animals. The community was so named because of the many deer that once roamed the region.

CRISP POINT: Chippewa County. Salutes Captain Christopher Crisp, commander of the U.S. Coast Guard element posted here.

CROSS VILLAGE: Emmet County. In the late eighteenth century, members of a Jesuit order erected a large wooden cross on a bluff near this spot. The settlement was known for many years as La Croix (The Cross). It was changed to Cross Village in 1875.

CUBES POINT: Mackinac County. This label originally came from the name of an Indian, Animikiwab, who was called Kiob for short. Eventually, Cube became the accepted pronunciation and spelling.

DAFTER: Chippewa County. Family name.

DE TOUR VILLAGE: Chippewa County. Probably takes its name from the French term for "circuitous route," and was possibly so designated because of an early geographical feature. Once known as Detour, residents changed the community name to De Tour Village to avoid confusion with road signs.

DEVILS LAKE: Lenawee County. For the lake. According to legend, the water was christened by Meteau, a Potawatomi Indian chief. As the story goes, Meteau's daughter drowned in the lake, and her body was never recovered. The chief believed she was taken away by evil spirits; thus, the name.

DICE: Saginaw County. Family name.

DISCO: Macomb County. While disco fever was rampant years back, the word itself, without the full complement of "discotheque," comes from the Latin, meaning "to learn." The village was named for Disco Academy, a high school established here in the early days of settlement by Alonzo M. Keeler.

DOLLARVILLE: Luce County. Remembers Robert Dollar.

ECHO: Antrim County. For its location in hilly terrain, which produces echoes.

ELM HALL: Gratiot County. So named because some early pioneers lived in a long building, or hall, constructed of logs from elm trees.

EMPIRE: Leelanau County. In 1863, a schooner, *Empire*, became icebound in the adjacent harbor. It was abandoned and later used as a school by residents. When a name for the village was needed, Empire was chosen.

FOUR TOWNS: Oakland County. For its location at the corner of four townships: White Lake, Waterford, Commerce, and West Bloomfield.

FREE SOIL: Mason County. For Free Soil Mills, a lumber operation. The mill was named for the Free Soil (antislavery) party organized in Buffalo, New York, in 1848. When a village was officially established on the site, it took the name of the mill.

GANGES: Allegan County. Christened by Dr. Joseph Coates for the sacred river in India.

GERMFASK: Schoolcraft County. Community title derived from the initials of the surnames of the eight founding fathers: John Grant, Matthew Edge, George Robinson, Thaddeus Mead, Dr. W. W. French, Ezekiel Ackley, Oscar Shepard, and Hezekiah Knaggs.

GRAND LEDGE: Eaton County. For the Grand River, and an adjacent ledge of rocks.

GRAPE: Monroe County. For its township, Raisinville, with the word *raisin* being French for "grape."

HATMAKER: Branch County. Relates to the Hatmaker family, no member of which was ever a hatmaker (Aaron dealt in cider, Peter in groceries).

HELL: Livingston County. In the early 1800s, a group of men migrated from New York and settled here. They took over operation of a sawmill and added a flour mill and distillery. The town name came about from the "hell-raisin'" carried on with Indians in the vicinity of their operations.

HOLY ISLAND: Charlevoix County. In 1855, the island was set aside by Mormon "King" James J. Strang as the site for the Feast of First Fruits. Since this was a holy ritual, the place became known as Holy Island.

HONKY TOWN: Lenawee County. This site was first inhabited by a colony of Hungarians, sometimes referred to locally as "Honkies." In 1940, it became a home away from home for Mexican migrant workers from Texas.

HONOR: Benzie County. Refers to the daughter of J. A. Gifford, general manager of the Guelph Patent Cask Company.

HOUSE OF DAVID: Berrien County. This is part of a religious communal colony established in 1903 by Benjamin and Mary Purnell. In 1927, Benjamin died, and the colony split up. Mary Purnell set up a rival community and named it City (or House) of David.

ICEBERG: Bay County. The handle for this small transient fishing village on Saginaw Bay more than likely refers to the severe winters experienced in the area.

INTERMEDIATE: Charlevoix County. For its location midpoint (intermediate) between the north and south arms of Lake Charlevoix.

JAM: Midland County. From the initials of James A. Murphy, storekeeper and first postmaster.

KNOT MAUL: Montcalm County. Abraham Lincoln, the "great railsplitter," had many followers in this region during the presidential campaign of 1860. These followers, campaigning for Abe, put on an exhibition of chopping timber. A tree was axed just above a large "knot." Someone then stripped the bark from what was to be the handle of a "maul" (a large hammer) and displayed it beside the knot. Some people in the vicinity started referring to the place as Knot, others called it Maul. Eventually, the two words were brought together to form the place name.

MASS: Ontonagon County. For the Mass Mining Company, set up here in 1855. The company moniker came about because of the mass of copper produced. An interesting note to this venture is that the first discovery of copper ore in the region was made by

Noel Johnson, an escaped slave from Missouri. Johnson later sold his claims to the Mass Mining Company.

MATCHWOOD: Ontonagon County. A company town founded and named by the Diamond Match Company in 1888. The village was virtually destroyed by forest fires in 1893 and again in 1906, but was rebuilt after each devastation.

MAYBEE: Monroe County. For Abram Maybee, co-owner of the land on which the town is situated.

MESICK: Wexford County. Christened by Howard Mesick, who founded and platted the town site in 1890.

MINT: St. Joseph County. For the plant.

MIO: Oscoda County. Originally called Mioe, for the wife of Henry Dayarmond. It was renamed Mio in November 1883. No reason is given as to why the "e" was dropped, thus forming an Italian personal pronoun.

MOCCASIN: Berrien County. For an Indian chief.

NEWAYGO: Newaygo County. Believed to honor the Chippewa chief *New-wa-goo*, who signed the Treaty of Saginaw in 1812.

NEW ERA: Oceana County. Designated by a Dr. Spaulding for his former home, Erie, Pennsylvania. Apparently, Erie was converted to Era somewhere along the way.

NORTH STAR: Gratiot County. Supposedly labeled by Peter Hoffman because he considered the site "about as far north as any human being could possibly come."

NOVI: Oakland County. Some people believe this community tag came from "No. VI," the place being the sixth stop on the road from Detroit. Others opine it is from the Latin word for "new," and applied here because it meant a new start in life for the residents.

OLD MISSION: Grand Traverse County. Town was so named because it was the first white man's landing site in earlier days between Fort Wayne (now Detroit) and Fort Mackinac.

PARCHMENT: Kalamazoo County. Refers to the Kalamazoo Vegetable Parchment Company, a paper mill.

PAYMENT: Chippewa County. Salutes Roger G. Payment, the area's first permanent white settler.

PIGEON: Huron County. For the river, which was so named for the large number of wild pigeons in the area.

PINE STUMP JUNCTION: Luce County. In the late 1800s, many lumber camps were established along the Grand Marais–Paradise Road. Other roads met at this point, and at the junction was a large pine tree stump. The rural mailman nailed a huge iron mailbox to the stump, and loggers from the camps would pick up their mail there. Although mail is now delivered through the RFD system, at last account the stump still remains.

PIPESTONE: Berrien County. First called Shanghai Corners, having been named for a breed of chicken. The community was renamed for the township, which was probably christened for the clay found hereabout that Indians used to make smoking pipes.

PURITAN: Gogebic County. Founded by the Oliver Iron Mining Company in 1886, and named to honor America's early pioneers.

RATTLE RUN: St. Clair County. For the creek. The stream was so named because on a quiet night, water "running" over the creek bed caused the pebbles to make a "rattling" sound.

REMUS: Mecosta County. Remembers William J. Remus, who platted the township.

SEE WHY: Chippewa County. Name derived from the initials of C. Y. (Cornelius Y.) Bennett, sawmill and store owner.

SLAPNECK: Alger County. For John F. Slapneck, a logging land estimator.

STALWART: Chippewa County. Residents first suggested the community name of Garfield, for then President James A. Garfield. The name was rejected because of duplication. They next recommended Arthur, for Vice President Chester A. Arthur. It, too, was rejected for the same reason. The citizens then surmised that since Garfield and Arthur represented the "stalwart" wing of the Republican Party, the community should be named Stalwart, which was finally accepted by postal authorities.

TEMPERANCE: Monroe County. Land in this region was originally owned by Lewis Ansted and his wife. Mrs. Ansted was an ardent member of the Women's Christian Temperance Union (WCTU). As the Ansteds sold off their property for building plots, each deed contained a clause prohibiting the using, making, or selling of liquor on the land. Even the Ann Arbor Railroad agreed to such conditions when it purchased right of way from the couple. At last report, the village of Temperance was still dry.

TONE: Chippewa County. Christened by Irish settlers in admiration of their native patriot, Theodor Wolfe Tone.

TOPINABEE: Cheboygan County. Community was founded in 1881 as a resort and named for a Potawatomi chief. Translation of the name is thought to mean "Great Bear Heart." Chief Topinabee signed the treaty ceding Fort Dearborn, now Chicago, to the whites.

TWO HEART: Luce County. For its location on the Two Hearted River.

VICTORY CORNERS: Mason County. Commemorates the Northern victory in the Civil War.

WALTZ: Wayne County. For Josiah Waltz, a settler.

WATERSMEET: Gogebic County. For its location where the Ontonagon River and Duck Creek meet.

WHITE PIGEON: St. Joseph County. For the Indian chief who, in 1830, gave his life to protect the white settlement located here.

ZEELAND: Ottawa County. Early Dutch settlers of this town named it for their former home in the Netherlands.

Minnesota
THE GOPHER STATE

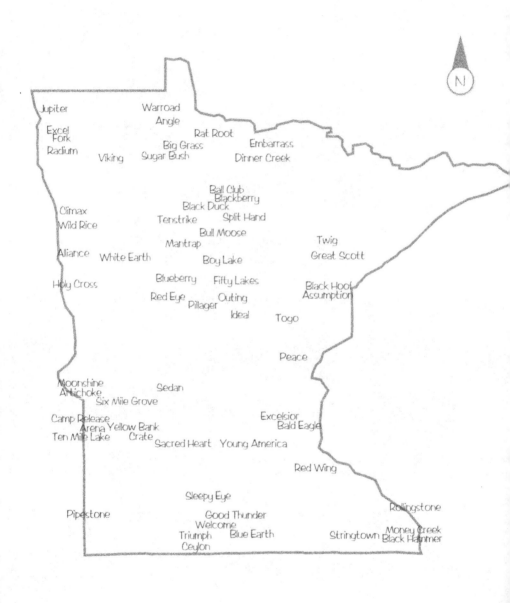

ALLIANCE: Clay County. During the late 1800s, farmers began agitating for lower railroad rates for their produce. This movement in Minnesota started in Clay County and gave birth to the Farmers Alliance, a political party of some influence in the state's 1890 political campaign. It was from this political group that the community took its name.

ANGLE: Lake of the Woods County. So tagged because its northern boundary is located on the inlet to the Lake of the Woods. Angle is the northernmost United States land area, excluding Alaska, lying ten to twenty-six miles north of the 49th parallel.

ARENA: Lac qui Parle County. Named by early pioneers from Arena, Wisconsin.

ARTICHOKE: Big Stone County. For the lake, which has since been drained. The lake name was probably translated from the Sioux language, and referred to the edible tuber roots of a specifies of sunflower that grew along the shoreline that were a prime source of food for the Indians.

ASSUMPTION: Carver County. A religious connotation, receiving its name from that of a Catholic church erected in the vicinity. The name Assumption refers to the ascent of the Virgin Mary into heaven.

BALD EAGLE: Ramsey County. For the lake, which took its name from the fact that when government surveyors were in the area, a number of bald eagles were nesting on an island in the lake.

BALL CLUB: Itasca County. For the lake. The Indians were fond of playing a ball game, and the lake is shaped like the bat or stick— which the French called "la crosse"—that was used in their game.

BIG GRASS: Beltrami County. Christened for the south branch of Roseau River. *Roseau* is the French translation of the Ojibwa word meaning "coarse grass" or "reed," which is common on the edges of lakes and streams in this northern section of Minnesota.

BLACK DUCK: Beltrami County. For the lake, which, in turn, was labeled for the ring-necked duck.

BLACK HAMMER: Houston County. Town tagged for a nearby bluff. Some say "hammer" is from the Norwegian for "bluff," and the feature was named by Knud Olson Bergo because it had been darkened by a forest fire. Possibly the bluff acquired its handle because of its shape.

BLACK HOOF: Carlton County. For the creek, with the stream being a translation of an Ojibwa phrase.

BLACKBERRY: Itasca County. For the lake. More than likely the lake acquired its name from the berry.

BLUE EARTH: Fairbault County. For the river, which the Sioux called *Mahkahto,* meaning "green" or "blue earth."

BLUEBERRY: Wadena County. For either Blueberry Lake or River, which was translated from the Ojibwa language.

BOY LAKE: Cass County. Translated from the Ojibwa *que-wis-uns,* which means "little boy." As the story goes, a Sioux war party invaded the Upper Mississippi region sometime around 1768. Three young boys were gathering wild rice near a lake and when discovered by the Sioux, were killed. The settlement took the name of the lake.

BULL MOOSE: Cass County. This community name refers to a political party, a division of the Republicans that broke from the main body in 1912 to back Theodore Roosevelt in his unsuccessful bid for a second term as president.

CAMP RELEASE: Lac qui Parle County. Township named for Camp Release. It was at this camp that captives taken during the Sioux uprising in 1862 were surrendered on September 26 to General Sibley.

CEYLON: Martin County. Citizens were sitting around the general store discussing names for their little settlement. One of the men noticed a box of tea from Ceylon (now Sri Lanka) on a shelf and suggested that name. This is the birthplace of Walter Mondale, former vice president of the United States.

CLIMAX: Polk County. From Climax Tobacco, which was sold locally.

CRATE: Chippewa County. Originally known as Willow Lake, the name had to be changed due to duplication. On July 23, 1888, townspeople chose Crate, honoring Fanning L. Beasley, homesteader. Beasley's middle name was Lucretius, from which his nickname, Crate, was formed.

DINNER CREEK: Koochiching County. For a creek. The stream took its name from early days, when timber cruisers and estimators met at a particular point along the creek for dinner.

EMBARRASS: St. Louis County. For the river. The stream was so named because at one time driftwood was so prevalent on parts of the stream that people in canoes had great difficulty navigating the waterway, sometimes being placed in the "embarrassing" position of having to swim away from an overturned boat.

EXCEL: Marshall County. For Excelsior, a village and township in Hennepin County. The name was shortened to avoid duplication.

EXCELSIOR: Hennepin County. On November 12, 1852, a settlement colony was formed in New York City. The colony, envisioning great things, named itself the Excelsior Pioneer Association, the seed for the name being Longfellow's poem "Excelsior." When the colony settled in Minnesota, a village and township took the name.

FIFTY LAKES: Crow Wing County. First known as Allen Township. In 1949, citizens wanted to open a liquor store. To do so, the law required that a municipal entity other than a township be formed. Therefore, they simply changed their governmental unit from a township to a village. They chose the name Fifty Lakes because supposedly there are that many lakes within a five-mile radius of the community.

FORK: Marshall County. For its location at a junction (fork) of the Snake and Red Rivers. Boatmen traveling north on the Red can juncture off in one of two directions, like tines on a fork.

GOOD THUNDER: Blue Earth County. Village named for a Winnebago chief, a friend of the whites who, in 1862, refused to join the Sioux attack on white settlers.

GREAT SCOTT: St. Louis County. Surprisingly, the origin of this community name is exactly as it would appear to be. The site was named by the board of county commissioners, because the expression "Great Scott" was a favorite of one of the board members

HOLY CROSS: Clay County. Across the state line, in North Dakota, a large wooden cross was placed in a small cemetery. Its size and location made it a standout on the prairie. The community where the cross was located was comprised of French-Canadian farmers following the Catholic faith. The Minnesota settlement was populated mostly by Norwegian Lutherans. Despite the differences in religious leanings, both communities became known as the "holy cross neighborhood." In time, the Minnesota township adopted that name.

IDEAL: Crow Wing County. At one time this township was called White Fish, for the lake. Ideal was apparently a whimsical designation.

JUPITER: Kittson County. Christened for the planet by Nels Hultgren, a Norwegian settler who was at one time a sea captain, a profession that acquaints its followers with the heavenly bodies.

MANTRAP: Hubbard County. For the lake. The lake was apparently well named. Sources reveal it is large and extremely difficult to skirt because of the wooded area surrounding it, thus capable of "trapping" travelers.

MONEY CREEK: Houston County. For a creek, which derived its label from an early incident. A traveler, after fording the stream, found that his personal effects, including money, had gotten wet. He spread the bank notes out on bushes along the creek bank to dry, but a wind came along and blew them into the water. Some of the money was never recovered.

MOONSHINE: Big Stone County. Derived its handle from a lake. D. K. J. Clark, upon first arriving in the area in 1876, camped along the lake. He intended to name the stream Moon Lake, Moon being his wife's surname. At night, the bright glow from the moon reflecting on the water caused the name to be changed to Moonshine. It isn't known whether Clark made the change or if it was done later by someone else.

OUTING: Crow Wing County. Site established in 1907 by William H. Andrews as a place for city dwellers to rest, relax, and picnic; hence, the name.

PEACE: Kanabel County. Designation chosen to counter a village within the township named Warman.

PILLAGER: Cass County. In the fall of either 1767 or 1768, a trader named Berti, who had a trading post on the Crow Wing River, was robbed by some Ojibwa Indians. Because of the incident, Ojibwa in the vicinity were termed "pillagers," and when a community was later established here, the name was applied to the settlement.

PIPESTONE: Pipestone County. For its location adjacent to the Pipestone Reservation and Indian Quarry.

RADIUM: Marshall County. For the element discovered in the region in 1902.

RAT ROOT: Koochiching County. For the river, which was christened by the Ojibwa, and refers to the roots eaten by muskrats.

RED EYE: Wadena County. This has no relation to the infamous stock whiskey sold in early day saloons. It is a translation of an Ojibwa term and refers to a species of fish called blue-spotted sunfish, green sunfish, or by some authorities rock bass.

RED WING: Goodhue County. For a Dakota Indian chief, who wore a swan wing dyed scarlet red for decoration.

ROLLINGSTONE: Winona County. Refers in no way to the magazine or rock group. The town was labeled for the river. The stream name in Dakota Indian language is *Eyan-omen-man-met-pah*, which, when literally translated, means "the stream where the stone rolls."

SACRED HEART: Renville County. One rendition of this community name origin concerns an early trader, Charles Patterson, who established a trading post around 1873 on the Minnesota River. Patterson usually wore a bearskin cap, and the bear, being a sacred animal to Sioux and Dakota Indians, caused the Indians to name the trader "Sacred Hat Man," which in time became Sacred Heart. The term was used by the Sioux when referring to Patterson's trading post, and later, when the township was established, the name was perpetuated. Another version of the name origin revolves around an early French priest who set up a mission of French half-breeds and Indians near a creek. The Frenchman saw the mouth of the stream as shaped like a heart and gave the site the name Sacred Heart. The surrounding locality then took the name of this early mission.

SEDAN: Pope County. For Sedan, France, site of a decisive battle between German and French forces in September 1870.

SIX MILE GROVE: Swift County. For a grove of trees located six miles from Benson.

SLEEPY EYE: Brown County. Sleepy Eye was a chief of the Lower Sisseton Sioux, and the city is named in his honor. Sleepy Eye died in 1860 in North Dakota, but several years after his death his remains were returned to this site and interred. A monument honoring *Ish-tak-ha-ba* ("Sleepy Eye") is situated near the town's railway station.

SPLIT HAND: Itasca County. For the lake, with the lake's moniker coming from an Ojibwa term meaning "cut hand," and probably harks back to an early incident.

STRINGTOWN: Fillmore County. So named because early settlers built their houses along a road in the ravine where the village is now located. Construction of the houses was said to "string out" for some distance.

SUGAR BUSH: Beltrami County. For maple trees used by both Indians and whites for the making of sugar.

TEN MILE LAKE: Lac qui Parle County. Labeled for a former lake, now drained, that was located ten miles from the Lac qui Parle mission and trading post.

TENSTRIKE: Beltrami County. Named for the game of bowling, its designation symbolizing a "strike."

TOGO: Aitkin County. Refers to Admiral Togo, the Japanese naval commander.

TRIUMPH: Martin County. For the Triumph Creamery Company.

TWIG: St. Louis County. Townspeople candidly named their village Twig because they looked on the local post office as just a "small branch" of the Post Office Department.

VIKING: Marshall County. Christened by Rev. Hans P. Hansen, a Norwegian Lutheran pastor. While the Scandinavian word is usually associated with men of valor and seaworthiness, its actual interpretation relates more to the pirates who at one time ravaged the western and southern coasts of Europe. The assumption is made that Reverend Hansen intended for the name to reflect goodness and boldness.

WARROAD: Roseau County. For the river, which was considered a neutral area by warring Ojibwa and Sioux.

WELCOME: Martin County. Honors Alfred M. Welcome.

WHITE EARTH: Becker County. For the White Earth Indian Reservation. During the period of the white man's roundup of the Indians and their resettlement on reservations, the Ojibwa were sent to this site, the first contingent arriving June 14, 1868. The reservation was named for White Earth Lake. The Ojibwa name for the lake translates "the place of white clay lake," referring to clumps of white clay found in various spots along the shore of the stream.

WILD RICE: Norman County. For the river, which is a translation from the Ojibwa language.

YELLOW BANK: Lac qui Parle County. For the river, which was named for the yellowish glacial drift seen on its eroded bluffs in earlier times.

YOUNG AMERICA: Carver County. So designated to personify the vigor and progressiveness of the young people in the United States.

Mississippi
THE MAGNOLIA STATE

ALLIGATOR: Bolivar County. For the lake, which was named for the abundance of alligators hereabout.

ALTITUDE: Prentiss County. For its extreme height, being situated on a ridge that crosses the county.

APPEAL: Bolivar County. A sawmill owner "appealed" so often to the Yazoo and Mississippi Valley Railroad for a spur line to move his logs, that when the line was finally built the adjacent community was named Appeal.

ARM: Lawrence County. For W. J. Armstrong, a landowner.

BASIC: Clarke County. Bob Oliphant, operator of a brick kiln, discovered iron ore on the site of the present settlement. A government analysis showed the ore to be of superior quality, and Oliphant had dreams of the emergence of a great city; hence, Basic. Since there was no coal in the area to run the furnaces needed to process the ore, however, and since the cost to have coal shipped in would have been prohibitive, Oliphant's dream never materialized.

BASIC CITY: Clarke County. Only a few miles from Basic, these two communities function as one. Basic City, which took its name from the larger town, was never big but because of the attraction of Mayerhall Springs, was once a great place for weekend picnics, annual gatherings, and political rallies.

BIRDIE: Quitman County. For the daughter of W. T. Dickerson, the town founder.

BLUE MOUNTAIN: Tippah County. Named for its location on a hill that, in the spring and fall, emits a bluish haze.

BOBO: Coahoma County. Salutes Colonel Robert E. Bobo, a landowner. *The Law of the Land,* a novel written by Emerson Hough, had its setting here and was dedicated to Colonel Bobo.

BOURBON: Washington County. For Bourbon County, Kentucky.

CHUNKY: Lauderdale County. Formerly a Choctaw Indian village called *Chanki-Chitto,* meaning "Big Chunky." The name comes from an old Indian game of Chunka, which was played at nearby Chunky Shoals.

D'LO: Simpson County. Possibly a family name, or might have been taken from the French *de l'eau,* meaning "of the waters."

DARLING: Quitman County. Remembers Jonathan W. Darling, engineer in charge of building a railroad through here.

DONT: Covington County. As the story goes, around 1900 a meeting was held by citizens to decide on a name for their little village. Many names were suggested, but after each recommendation, someone would say, "Don't name it that." Time passed and so many "don'ts" had been said, the people simply decided to call it Dont.

ECRU: Pontotoc County. *Ecru* means beige. The origin of this community handle seems to have come from the color of either the railroad depot or nearby clay deposits.

ELECTRIC MILLS: Kemper County. Took its moniker from an electrically operated sawmill located here.

EMINENCE: Jones County. For its elevation.

EXPOSE: Marion County. Honors Harry Expose, settler, store owner, postmaster.

FAIRGROUND: Neshoba County. Established in 1889 as the site of the Neshoba County Fair.

FRAIRS POINT: Coahoma County. Personal name, coupled with shape of terrain.

GUNTOWN: Lee County. Some say the community was christened for Louis McDaniel, a gunsmith who settled here in 1840. Consensus, however, favors the name as honoring Rhoda Gunn, a local beauty.

HARD CASH: Humphreys County. A small station stop on the Hard Cash Plantation, for which it was named. The plantation derived its tag from the fact that the original owners paid hard cash for the property.

HOT COFFEE: Covington County. Probably one of the most unusual place names in America. In 1870, enterprising E. L. Craft built a lunch counter on this site to serve travelers moving along the road between markets in Mobile and Ellisville. Craft's specialty was hot coffee, and his fame soon spread. The settlement that grew up around his lunchroom took the name Hot Coffee, and a large coffeepot was put up as a sign, letting travelers know they had reached the well-named community of Hot Coffee.

HUB: Marion County. Some people believe this community was named for a man who built a sawmill here in 1900. Others claim it was so called because the river crossing at this site was hub-deep on wagons. There are those who relate the tag to the often-present mud that came up to the hubs of wagons.

HURRICANE: Pontotoc County. For the creek.

HUSHPUCKENA: Bolivar County. From an Indian term meaning "little sunflower," apparently from local vegetation.

ISOLA: Humphreys County. Formerly known as Dawson Lake, there was a school located here in the late 1800s. After the county superintendent of education referred to the school as that "isolated schoolhouse," the village took its name from that description.

ITTA BENA: Leflore County. For a plantation around which the community grew up. The plantation label is from an expression meaning "home in the woods."

JAYESS: Lawrence County. From the initials of J. S. Butterfield, a lumberman.

KING BEE: Neshoba County. For a racehorse owned by Jim Mack Johnson, a sawmill operator.

KINGS OF ANDERSON: Coahoma County. For a plantation.

MIDNIGHT: Humphreys County. Derived its label from a poker game. In the 1880s, a group of hunters was camped near a swamp on the present site of Midnight. To pass the time, they decided to play poker. One of the men laid claim to the land on which they were camped, and at one point during the game threw his "claim" into the pot. He lost, and the winner, looking at his watch, said, "Well, boys, it's midnight, and that's what I'm going to call my land." The winner settled the land and later built his house on the exact spot where the poker game took place.

MISSIONARY: Jasper County. For the Six Town Missionary Station, established in 1825 by a man named Bardwell.

MONEY: Leflore County. Honors Senator Hernando DeSoto Money.

NEW SITE: Prentiss County. The name doesn't refer to the community, since it is more than one hundred years old. In early times, a schoolhouse located here was moved a short distance to be nearer the road. This move placed the building at a new site; thus, the name.

NITA YUMA: Sharkey County. From an Indian term that when freely translated means "trail of the bear." Appropriately tagged, since a bear trail was spotted near here sometime in the past.

NOXAPATER: Winston County. Name suggested by Dr. J. G. Gunn; however, there are differences of opinion as to its actual meaning. Some claim the word is Latin and means "dark father"; others aver that it is an Indian word meaning "trigger."

OLIVE BRANCH: De Soto County. Said to have been christened by Mrs. Frankie Blacker to symbolize peace with area Indians.

ONWARD: Sharkey County. Around 1875, three men from Virginia arrived in the vicinity and bought three plantations, which they named Alphin (Alpha?), Onward, and Omega. As a community developed, it apparently assumed the name of the second plantation.

PACE: Bolivar County. For James H. and Charles F. Pace, landowners.

PANTHER BURN: Sharkey County. Relates to the many panthers in the vicinity in earlier times. "Burn" was once a term for *creek*; apparently there was a stream close by.

PASS CHRISTIAN: Harrison County. For Christian L'Adnier, one of two brothers who explored this area in 1699. A second pass is named for the other sibling, Pass Marianne.

PENTECOST: Sunflower County. Family name.

PETAL: Forrest County. For Petal Polk, daughter of an early settler.

PINK: Tunica County. For Pink Bizzell, a storekeeper.

PROGRESS: Pike County. Apparently named with hopes that never materialized.

RED LICK: Jefferson County. Name influenced by the nature of the soil, which was red and contained salt deposits. Settlers brought their cattle to the site to let them lick the soil.

RED STAR: Lincoln County. For the large red star painted on a store by the Star Tobacco Company.

REFORM: Choctaw County. By tradition, Mr. Hanna, who organized a star mail route here, once made the statement that he was going to "reform" the people. When the village was organized, Hanna's comment was remembered.

REVIVE: Madison County. It seems this small hamlet acquired its name because each time the mail was delivered, in olden days, residents considered it "bringing new life to the town." One citizen, a deeply religious man of the Baptist faith, always thought of a hymn that had the word *revive* in it.

RISING SUN: Leflore County. Many years ago, an all-night poker game ended just as the sun was coming up. From that time on, the poker gathering was known as the Rising Sun Club. Later, when a community built up in the vicinity, it took its name from the club.

ROUGH EDGE: Pontotoc County. Although the accuracy is not verified, it is believed the community took its moniker from the first schoolhouse built here, which was constructed of "rough" lumber.

ROUNDAWAY: Coahoma County. For the lake, which was so named because of the "roundabout way" necessary to reach it from any direction.

SANDY HOOK: Marion County. This hamlet name is associated with a creek, the bed of which was so sandy that extra oxen had to be "hooked" onto wagons to get them across.

SEMINARY: Covington County. For Zion Seminary, an interdenominational school formed in 1847 by a New Yorker, Prof. A. R. Graves. At one time Zion Seminary was the leading college in southern Mississippi.

SHIVERS: Simpson County. Named for its founder.

SLEDGE: Quitman County. Remembers W. D. Sledge, a railroad engineer.

SOSO: Jones County. Refers to the expression often uttered by an early resident who, when asked how he felt, would reply, "Just so-so."

SPRING COTTAGE: Marion County. In the early 1800s, a small cottage was built by a spring. The building was used as a house of worship for many years and was referred to simply as "the cottage." When a more permanent structure was erected as a church, the cottage was then used by travelers and soon became known as "Spring Cottage," a name the community adopted.

SUNFLOWER: Sunflower County. For the plant.

TIE PLANT: Grenada County. The name is believed to be associated with a manufacturing plant that produced creosote, the substance used to preserve railroad ties.

TIPPO: Tallahatchie County. Translation of the Choctaw word *oktibbeha,* meaning "stream."

TOUCHSTONE: Simpson County. For T. N. Touchstone, son of Judge G. P. Touchstone, a settler.

TWIN: Marion County. Named for its location between two creeks that stem from the same source, later join into one, and flow into the Pearl River. Because of the similarity of these creeks, and the fact that they have their beginnings at the same source, the place was named Twin.

VALUE: Rankin County. Acquired its label in 1916 with the opening of the post office, just because there was no other such community name in the United States.

VENEER: Marion County. For a veneer mill located in the nearby city of Foxworth.

VETO: Franklin County. When the first post office was placed here, citizens submitted several names for consideration. All were "vetoed" for various reasons, so the postal department selected the name Veto for the community.

WHYNOT: Clarke County. While trying to decide on a name for the new post office, townspeople submitted a number of suggestions in writing. In one letter the writer penned, "WHY NOT call the office . . ." The words "why not" were written bolder than any of the names suggested. It attracted the attention of a reader in Washington, and Whynot was recorded as the official name.

Missouri
THE SHOW ME STATE

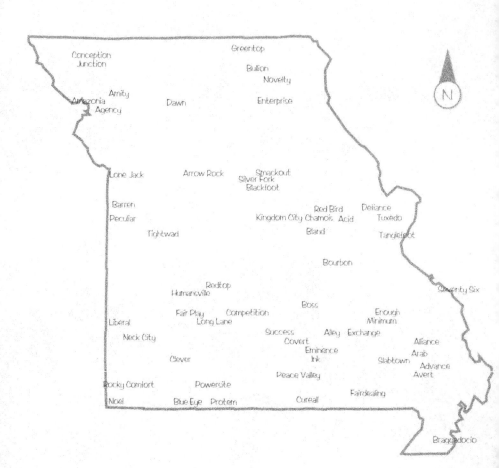

ACID: Franklin County. For the substance used in mines to process ore.

ADVANCE: Stoddard County. Reflects the positive attitude of its citizenry at the time.

AGENCY: Buchanan County. Was once the site of an agency for the Sauk and Fox Indians.

ALLEY: Shannon County. A personal name.

ALLIANCE: Bollinger County. Locally, this town is sometimes known as Jugtown. It received the name Alliance from the fact that following the Civil War, townspeople formed an alliance of their previous Union and Confederate loyalties.

AMAZONIA: Andrew County. Possibly this moniker came from the fact that in early times, a large Indian woman lived here by the name of "Zonia." Whites said she looked like an "Amazon"; thus, the name.

AMITY: DeKalb County. Either named for Amity, New York, having been christened by former residents thereof, or by a Mr. Wilcox. It is told that Wilcox decreed the name to be Amity as long as the residents lived in peace and harmony. However, should they ever veer from this path, then the name would be changed to Snarltown. Comradeship has evidently reigned for the more than 110 years the community has been in existence.

ARAB: Bollinger County. For Arab, Alabama.

ARROW ROCK: Saline County. An old Indian legend prevails. The community is situated on a very narrow point on the Missouri River. On the county side of the river sits a large white bluff. On the opposite side, in early days, was an Indian camp. The chief of the tribe offered his beautiful daughter's hand to any brave who could stand on one side of the stream and hit the bluff with an arrow. It was accomplished by a brave who not only hit the bluff, but lodged his arrow deep into the embankment. The French, knowing of the legend, named the site Pierrea á Flech in the early 1700s. The term translates into "Arrow Rock." On May 23, 1829, a town was platted here and named New Philadelphia. The townspeople didn't care much for that handle and in 1833 changed it back to Arrow Rock.

AVERT: Stoddard County. The village tag was chosen when the postmaster was instructed to select a name that would avert confusion.

BARREN: Cass County. For the "barrens" in neighboring Kentucky. This is a term used to describe land covered with brush and small timber.

BLACKFOOT: Boone County. Another name for Perche Township, and supposedly came about as a result of boys and girls hereabout dancing "barefoot."

BLAND: Gasconade County. For Richard Bland, U.S. congressman from Missouri.

BLUE EYE: Stone County. Supposedly refers to Elbert N. Butler, the first postmaster, who had blue eyes.

BOSS: Dent County. When the post office was put in place, the store owner in whose building it would be located was asked to name the facility. Looking around, he noticed a pair of Boss work gloves; thus, the name.

BOURBON: Crawford County. Christened for a former post office in the area, which, in turn, was named for a type of whiskey.

BRAGGADOCIO: Pemiscot County. Although the moniker of the individual choosing this village name is unknown, the source was probably Edmund Spenser's *Faerie Queen*. The word itself is a combination of the English *brag* and the Italian *-occhio*, meaning "swollen" or "inflated." As to how the community acquired such a name, there are two versions. One is that it was intended as a whimsical slap at the boastful or exceptionally optimistic attitude of some early settlers. The second rendition, an almost tongue-in-cheek one, is that a settler, having been blessed with a beautiful wife, constantly bragged on her. That his wife's name just happened to be Docio only completes the fantasy: "Bragging on Docio."

BULLION: Adair County. Honors one of Missouri's most famous senators, Thomas Hart Benton, known as "Old Bullion."

CHAMOIS: Osage County. The common usage of this word relates to a hide used to polish automobiles and is pronounced "shammy." However, Chamois, Missouri, comes from the French and is pronounced "sha-mwa." Local residents pronounce it "sha-moiz." The community was christened in 1856 by Morgan Harbor, who surveyed and laid out the town site. Harbor thought the area closely resembled the Alpine region of Europe, home of the sure-footed chamois, a goat-like antelope.

CLEVER: Christian County. At the time of the town's designation, around 1896, the word *clever* meant "friendly and accommodating" and related to the disposition of the town's inhabitants.

COMPETITION: Laclede County. Three businesses were established here many years ago. One was owned by R. L. Nelson, who named the place Newburg; a man named Roar built a store; and Ben Moore set up a mill. The Civil War came and went, and the people decided to erect a school. All three sections were considered, but Nelson's was chosen. The community name probably came from the competition among the three landowners.

CONCEPTION JUNCTION: Nodaway County. Relates to the Immaculate Virgin, the village having been founded by a Father Powers and his followers.

COVERT: Texas County. For J. A. Covert, a postmaster.

CUREALL: Howell County. For nearby mineral springs that supposedly had cure-all medicinal powers.

DAWN: Livingston County. One version of the origin of the community title is that a member of a hunting party shot a deer just as the sun was rising. The hunters were so impressed with the morning view that they named the place Dawn. Another report is that early residents, who were spread out over several miles, would meet at a crossing here to travel together to a gristmill at Utica. The common expression among the people was to "meet at dawn" to begin the journey. Later, when a settlement grew up at the crossing, and a name for the hamlet was needed, people remembered the saying and named it Dawn.

DEFIANCE: St. Charles County. As tradition goes, this little settlement derived its handle from a disagreement with the nearby town of Matson. Around 1892, the Katy Railroad started building a line through this region. People in Matson wanted a stop placed there; residents of what is now Defiance also wanted a depot. Despite influential opposition from certain elements in Matson, the Katy built depots at both locations, and the citizens of this community named their town Defiance, because of the opposition they had overcome.

EMINENCE: Shannon County. This town is located in a hollow, defying its name, which indicates an elevated situation. The name was taken from another community, no longer in existence, that sat on a hill.

ENOUGH: Iron County. Almost two hundred recommended names were submitted to authorities in Washington. After this number had been received, postal officials said that was "enough." Residents took the hint and named their hamlet Enough.

ENTERPRISE: Shelby County. Name suggested by the postmaster at Woodville, because he thought it was a good title for a new undertaking (the establishing of a post office).

EXCHANGE: Reynolds County. Evidently, this community enjoyed early day status as a "trading center."

FAIR PLAY: Polk County. Many years ago, a local store was the weekend gathering place for playing horseshoes and checkers. One day, two men got into a fight and were so evenly matched that it was soon apparent neither could win. They separated and shook hands. A bystander, so overcome by the display of friendliness, blurted, "Boys, that sure was fair play."

FAIRDEALING: Ripley County. This town acquired its name when a farmer had his mare stolen. The farmer went to his barn early one morning and discovered his horse gone. However, his well cared for saddle had not been touched. Later, and assumably in a sarcastic tone, the man related the event, but surmised that he had had a "fair deal," because the thief could have taken both his horse and the saddle. The farmer's "fair deal" comment was remembered when it came town naming time.

GREENTOP: Schulyer County. There was once an inn here that served as a way stop for travelers journeying to Iowa. The building was situated on a high hill surrounded by plush vegetation. One day, a woman waiting for the stagecoach commented that all she could see were green tops of trees in the valley below. Coach drivers began referring to the site as Greentop, and the community took that name.

HUMANSVILLE: Polk County. Derived from a family name.

INK: Shannon County. When this community was organized, the postmaster was advised that a short name was preferred. The postmaster called a meeting of the citizens to decide on a name. A lengthy discussion bore no fruit, and as they were about to adjourn, someone accidentally knocked over a bottle of ink. Ergo, the name.

KINGDOM CITY: Calloway County. For a brief period during the Civil War, Calloway County seceded from the United States and took the name Kingdom of Calloway. Many years later, Jack Lay built stores and residences here and named the town Kingdom City, connecting the name to its Civil War past.

LIBERAL: Barton County. One version of this name origin is that it reflects the liberal attitude of its residents in that they did not prejudge people, but accepted them on their own merits. The second tenet is that the name came from the liberal credit terms offered by an early storekeeper.

LONE JACK: Jackson County. Acquired its moniker from the fact that a solitary blackjack tree stood on the site when the town was laid out.

LONG LANE: Dallas County. Said to have acquired its handle because it was at one time a long lane of open land stretching about six miles toward the town of Buffalo.

MINIMUM: Iron County. A play on the name Minnie Farr, wife of Dr. N. A. Farr, postmaster.

NECK CITY: Jasper County. Originally called Hells Neck during early mining days because of the "hell-raising" that went on. When a post office was established, the government refused to approve the name Hell, and it was changed to Neck. Finally, in 1951, the postmaster added "City."

NOEL: McDonald County. Relates to "Uncle" Bridge Noel, who was instrumental in having a right of way cleared for the railroad. Although the town is small, Noel receives thousands of letters each Christmas for re-posting with a local postage seal that shows a Christmas tree and the words "Noel, MO. The Christmas City in the Ozark Vacation Land." It gained some popularity in the late 1930s when a movie on the life of Jesse James was filmed in the vicinity, and members of the cast, including the late Tyrone Power, were housed in Noel.

NOVELTY: Knox County. In the early or mid-1850s, Dr. Tom Pendry settled here, built a home, an office, and a store. It was such a wilderness at the time that Pendry hoisted a flag so the place could be seen from afar. Jane Ross Pendry, his wife, thought the flag was a "novel" idea, so they named the place Novelty.

PEACE VALLEY: Howell County. Relates to "Uncle" Billy Peace, a settler.

PECULIAR: Cass County. After several names for the settlement were submitted to Washington, and each rejected, postal officials suggested a name be chosen that was peculiar. The townspeople picked up on the recommendation, and Peculiar it became.

POWERSITE: Taney County. The community sits on a bluff overlooking one of the dams that provides electrical power to the White River settlements; ergo, the name.

PROTEM: Taney County. This village label was adopted when Washington officials advised the local postmaster that he could use the name Protem (in the interim) until an official name was decided on.

RED BIRD: Gasconade County. Named by E. R. Bowen, first postmaster, simply because he thought it would be easy to spell and remember.

REDTOP: Dallas County. Named by Mrs. Mary Frances Cassity, wife of the postmaster, when she looked out at the broad expanse of terrain and saw redtop hay growing in the fields.

ROCKY COMFORT: McDonald County. For Rocky Comfort, Arkansas.

SEVENTY SIX: Perry County. One belief is that the community took its name from a town in Clinton County, Kentucky, which, in turn, was named to commemorate the date of America's Declaration of Independence. The second verdict relates the name to a steamboat that hit a barrier in a nearby river and sank. Since the disaster occurred on the "76th crossing" of that voyage, the community took the number for its name.

SILVER FORK: Boone County. For Hugh Silvers, who settled here on the "fork" of a stream around 1816.

SLABTOWN: Wayne County. At one time this was a sawmill camp that produced "slabs" for construction.

SMACKOUT: Boone County. It is unknown if any of this hamlet still exists. It received its tag from the fact that a Mr. McKinsie operated a store here many years ago, and it seemed that his stock was always low. Whenever a customer asked for a particular item, McKinsie's standard response was, "I am just smack out of that."

SUCCESS: Texas County. A commendatory name.

TANGLEFOOT: Jefferson County. This is not a community itself, but is the local nickname for the town of Festus. The general belief is that the nickname comes from the tag hung on a raw whiskey prominent in many early settlements. The potency of the booze was said to make a person's "feet tangle" when he tried to walk.

TIGHTWAD: Henry County. One day, as the postman was carrying his mail, he stopped in the little general store and bought the last watermelon for fifty cents. He told the storekeeper he would pick it up at the end of his route. Upon his return, he found the storekeeper had sold it to someone else for more money, and called him an old tightwad.

TUXEDO: St. Louis County. Christened by settlers for their former home in New York.

Montana
THE TREASURE STATE

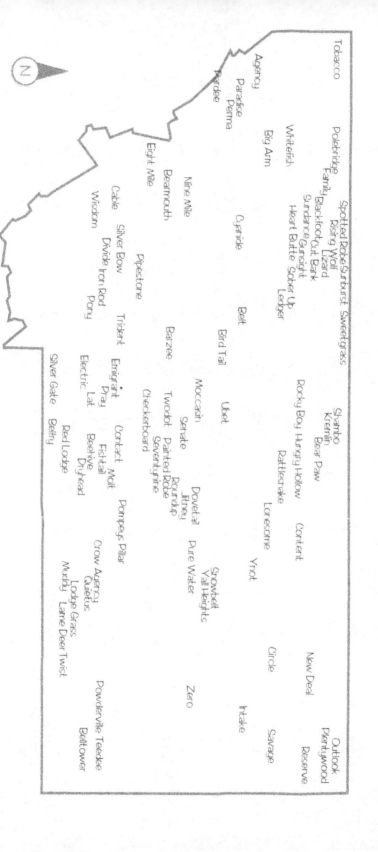

AGENCY: Sanders County. Remembers the time, in the 1870s, when the site was an Indian agency post office.

BARZEE: Meagher County. Relates to the Bar Z stock brand of a local ranch.

BEAR PAW: Blaine County. Moniker inspired by a range of mountains that, from their summit, look like a large bear paw spread out over the prairie.

BEARMOUTH: Granite County. Originally listed as Bear Mouth, the name officially became one word in 1892. There are a couple of stories as to how the town acquired its name. One is that the entrance to a nearby gully resembles a bear's mouth. The second version claims the name came from incidents involving a number of bears.

BEEHIVE: Stillwater County. Tag inspired by a rock formation shaped like a beehive.

BELFRY: Carbon County. Personal name.

BELLTOWER: Carter County. Relates to a bell-shaped butte.

BELT: Cascade County. The name comes from Belt Butte, which has a rim, or belt, of rocks around it.

BIG ARM: Lake County. Named for its location on a big extension, or arm, of Flathead Lake.

BIRD TAIL: Cascade County. Label inspired by Birdtail Divide, a group of hills with one of the peaks resembling a bird's tail as it is spread.

BLACKFOOT: Glacier County. Honors the Blackfoot Indians. There is an entertaining legend as to how this tribe became known as the Blackfoot. The lore accepted by most members of the tribe relates to the ancient Sun faith, and tells the story of an old Indian with three sons. The man sent his offspring to the plains area along the North Big River to hunt for game. The sons came across a large herd of buffalo but were not fast enough to catch any of the animals. When the sons reported the failure to their father, the old man had a vision. The Sun god told him to rub the feet of the eldest brother with a black magical medicine, which the Sun god provided. This done, the son returned to the plains, and with the speed brought on by the magic potion, easily caught up with the buffalo. Because of this incident, the old Indian decreed the descendants of the eldest son would be called Blackfoot.

CABLE: Deer Lodge County. Originally called Cable City, the name was shortened to Cable in 1872. Town was named for the Atlantic Cable Mine, which opened in 1866.

CHECKERBOARD: Wheatland County. Named for Checkerboard Creek. The stream was so christened because along its banks are located pieces of land, presenting a checkerboard mosaic.

CIRCLE: McCone County. Relates to the stock brand of an early Montana ranch.

CONTACT: Sweet Grass County. Designation inspired by its location where a limestone formation comes in contact with a quartz lode.

CONTENT: Phillips County. Christened by early settlers because they were so content living here.

CROW AGENCY: Big Horn County. Almost certainly named for the fact that it is the site of a former Indian agency.

CUT BANK: Glacier County. Relates to a nearby gorge that was made by Cut Bank Creek. The Blackfoot Indians called the stream "the river that cuts into the white clay banks."

CYANIDE: Lewis and Clark County. Although this is a poisonous chemical, the town was named for the cyanide treatment of ore. A large plant for this type operation was located here for many years.

DIVIDE: Silver Bow County. For its location near the Continental Divide.

DOVETAIL: Petroleum County. For a creek. The stream acquired its handle because it separates at a certain point, then comes together again, forming the shape of a dove's tail.

DRYHEAD: Carbon County. Named for the many buffalo skulls found at the base of a buffalo jump.

EIGHT MILE: Ravilli County. For the creek, so tagged because it empties into Bitterroot River eight miles from Stevensville.

ELECTRIC: Park County. Name inspired by Electric Peak, which acquired its label from the unusual electrical charge felt by a group of people during a storm in 1872.

EMIGRANT: Park County. Refers to Emigrant Peak.

FAMILY: Glacier County. Takes its moniker from the Holy Family Mission, established in the early 1800s to teach Indian children from the Blackfoot reservation. Only a few buildings of the original site remain.

FISHTAIL: Stillwater County. There are at least two versions for the origin of this name. Indians believe the title comes from a nearby mountain formation that resembles a fish tail. Others think a man named Fishtail once lived here and the town honors him.

GUNSIGHT: Glacier County. Relates to Gunsight Mountain in Glacier Park.

HEART BUTTE: Pondera County. This is an Indian town and is located near buttes shaped like inverted hearts; thus, the name.

HUNGRY HOLLOW: Blaine County. The first settlers in this area arrived in the spring of 1901. The scenery was green and lush, and farmers set about tilling the fields for crops. They didn't know the soil was too shallow for farming, neither were they aware of the lengthy winters common to this part of the country. Consequently, that first winter of 1901–1902 saw many of the settlers extremely hungry; ergo, the name.

INTAKE: Dawson County. Tagged for its location at the start, or intake, of the Yellowstone River irrigation system.

IRON ROD: Madison County. Remembers the town's Old Red Bridge, which was made of iron rods painted red.

JITNEY: Petroleum County. When Henry Ford's Model T was changing the life patterns of the American people, it was often called a "tin lizzie" or a "jitney." The town took its name from the latter.

KREMLIN: Hill County. Mirages are fairly common in this area, and when the Great Northern Railway was building tracks through here, most of the workers were Russian. One morning they looked out over the expanse of terrain and saw a mirage, which to them looked like a kremlin (fort) in their native land. The mirage was most likely brought on by a deep case of homesickness.

LAME DEER: Rosebud County. Honors the Indian chief who was killed on May 7, 1877, when General Miles attacked Lame Deer's camp.

LAT: Park County. This small community was christened when surveyors working the region marked "Lat," an abbreviation for "latitude," on their maps.

LEDGER: Pondera County. Originally named for Dan Ledgerwood, the moniker had to be changed when it was discovered there was a settlement by that same name in North Dakota. By dropping "wood," the present designation was adopted.

LIZARD: Toole County. Most likely refers to Lizard Lake, so tagged for the large number of lizards found there in earlier days.

LODGE GRASS: Big Horn County. For the creek. The Crow Indians called the stream Greasy Grass, but their words for "grease" and "lodge" are so similar that when translated into English, the word used was lodge. This is an old settlement and in early days was site of a summer hunting camp for the Crows. Today, Lodge Grass serves as the trading center for ranchers whose cattle graze on lush uplands grass that was once range for thousands of buffalo.

LONESOME: Phillips County. For its remote location on the Montana plains.

MOCCASIN: Judith Basin County. For a nearby mountain, which, with its low, rounded summits and dense pine trees, faintly resembles an Indian moccasin.

MOLT: Stillwater County. This has nothing to do with a bird shedding its feathers, having been named for Rudolph Molt, who donated land for the town site.

MUDDY: Big Horn County. Relates to Muddy Creek, which is descriptive.

NEW DEAL: Valley County. So named because the town was established in the early 1930s, during President Franklin Roosevelt's "New Deal" era. This was one of several towns that sprang up during the period and in this area, where people working on government projects, such as dams, lived.

NINE MILE: Missoula County. Remembers Nine Mile House, which was that distance from Frenchtown.

OUTLOOK: Sheridan County. The origin of this name is truly out of the Old West, if legend can be believed. As the story goes, a stranger rode into this unnamed settlement, tied his horse to a hitching rail, and ambled toward the saloon. At that particular moment some cowboys happened to be engaged in a slight disagreement, and as the stranger started to enter the building, someone yelled, "Look out!" Heeding the advice, the man ducked. He then walked in unharmed, and later, when citizens were considering names for their hometown, the advice of "look out" was remembered. For some reason, the townspeople reversed the words of the warning and came up with Outlook.

PAINTED ROBE: Golden Valley County. This is a station on the Great Northern Railroad and was named for Painted Robe Creek. The stream received its designation from the fact that in early days, Indian hunting parties painted their robes with clay from its banks.

PARADISE: Sanders County. This is a division on the Northern Pacific Railroad, and is where Mountain Standard Time (MST) changes to Pacific Standard Time (PST), or vice versa, depending on the direction of travel. The moniker Paradise is a corruption of "Pair O' Dice," the name of a roadhouse once situated on a local trail.

PARDEE: Mineral County. This mining community name was taken from the French *par dieu*, meaning "by God."

PERMA: Sanders County. Supposedly this is from the Latin meaning "ferry"; a ferry once served the site.

PIPESTONE: Jefferson County. For the creek, the stream being so tagged because clay found on its banks was excellent for making pipes.

PLENTYWOOD: Sheridan County. The name stems from early days when a cattle outfit, moving across the barren plains, met two riders coming from the opposite direction. The riders were asked if there was a good place to camp ahead, a place with water and wood for a fire. The cattlemen were instructed to continue on for another mile or so, where they would find "plenty of wood" in a small grove of trees near a creek bank. The cattlemen arrived at the spot and camped by the stream, where the town of Plentywood now stands.

POLEBRIDGE: Flathead County. This is a term usually applied to a bridge made of rough lumber, and apparently such a span once existed on this site.

POMPEYS PILLAR: Yellowstone County. This spot was named by Captain William Clark, of the Lewis and Clark Expedition, and was later adopted by the settlement. The term relates to the famous Roman general and statesman Pompey (106–148 B.C.), but why it was selected by Clark is unknown. Possibly some natural formation in the area reminded him of the monument in Alexandria, Egypt. There is at least one source that contends it was the nickname of an Indian baby who was part of the expedition.

PONY: Madison County. Applauds "Pony" Smith McCumpsey, who discovered gold in the region in either 1866 or 1867.

POWDERVILLE: Powder River County. The town, like the county, was tagged for the Powder River. It is believed the stream was named by Indians comparing the fine black sand in the river to gunpowder.

PRAY: Park County. Honors U.S. Congressman Charles N. Pray, who, it is reported, was responsible for having more post offices established in eastern Montana than any other individual.

PURE WATER: Garfield County. Remembers the unique discovery, considering it is located in an arid section of the state.

QUIETUS: Big Horn County. This is a term normally used when referring to halting or slowing some event, and is pronounced "kwi-eat-us." When the community was searching for a moniker, Frank Brittain, postmaster, sent fifteen suggested names to the Post Office Department in Washington; all fifteen were rejected. Brittain commented to his wife, "Well, they put the quietus on that." Almost as a joke Brittain submitted Quietus as the name for the town, and Washington accepted it.

RATTLESNAKE: Blaine County. For the abundance of rattlesnakes in the region.

RED LODGE: Carbon County. This is another old settlement and dates back to the time the Crow Indians came to this fertile valley.

There are several versions as to how the name Red Lodge came about. One is that the Crows painted their lodges with red clay from a nearby creek. Another story is that it was christened for the many "red" man "lodges" in the vicinity. It is also reported that the Crows once called the place "Bad Lodge" because a supply of meat they had stored spoiled and ruined one of their festivities. In 1866, James (Yankee Jim) George came to this area seeking gold; he found oil instead. Europeans from many counties came to work in the fields, and since 1951, this international heritage has been perpetuated by the annual Festival of Nations.

RESERVE: Sheridan County. So named because the town was established on the Fort Peck Indian "Reservation."

RISING WOLF: Glacier County. This is a Great Northern Railroad station and the title honors Hugh Monroe. Monroe was the first white man to explore what is today Glacier National Park. He lived among the Indians for many years, and they named him Rising Wolf. Later, they christened Rising Wolf Mountain in the park for him.

ROCKY BOY: Hill County. Pays homage to the Rocky Boy Indian tribe that once lived here.

ROUNDUP: Musselshell County. So named because this was once the gathering place for large herds of cattle that had grazed in the valley. The great cattle empires started their demise in this area around 1903, with the arrival of homesteaders who fenced the ranges and forced cattlemen behind barbed wire.

SAVAGE: Richland County. Remembers the first settler in the area.

SENATE: Fergus County. Christened for Postmaster James P. Sennot. Spelling of the name was apparently revised by postal officials.

SEVENTYNINE: Golden Valley County. Takes its name from John T. Murphy's "79" ranch.

SHAMBO: Hill County. Honors Louis Chambeau, a government scout. The Frenchman either suggested the simplified spelling of his name, or readily accepted it.

SILVER BOW: Silver Bow County. For Silver Bow Creek; the stream acquired its title when prospectors saw the sun shining on the water through an opening in the clouds.

SILVER GATE: Park County. This is a summer stopping place for visitors entering Yellowstone Park from Cooke City. The town took its moniker from Silver Mountain, and the fact that it is the "gateway" between the mountains.

SNOWBELT: Garfield County. Appropriately named, considering its location.

SOBER UP: Pondera County. This is a line camp from early cattle days in Pondera County. It acquired its name when a drunken cowboy went there after a wild drinking spree to sober up. It has been known by that title ever since.

SPOTTED ROBE: Glacier County. Formerly known as Kilroy, the name was changed in 1926 to honor a Blackfoot chief.

SUNBURST: Toole County. This title was suggested by William G. Davis because as the early morning sun rose, it shone brightly on the spot where the town was established.

SUNDANCE: Glacier County. Originally called Seville, the name was changed in 1925 to commemorate the Indian Sun Dance ceremony.

SWEETGRASS: Toole County. Relates to the special grass in this area so favored by cattle.

TEEDEE: Carter County. For the "TD" cattle brand.

TOBACCO: Lincoln County. For its location on Tobacco Creek.

TRIDENT: Gallatin County. For its location near the three forks of the Missouri River. At this point, the Missouri becomes the handle of the trident (a three-pronged weapon), and the Madison, Jefferson, and Gallatin Rivers the tines.

TWIST: Powder River County. Honors Oliver "Twist" Lawrence, owner of the land on which the post office was established.

TWODOT: Wheatland County. Remembers the stock brand of "Two Dot" Wilson. By branding one dot on the shoulder of his livestock, and one on the thigh, Wilson made alteration of his brand extremely difficult.

UBET: Fergus County. Takes its name from one of the most famous stage stations in Montana Territory. The name is a compromise of the expression "You bet," and was initiated by A. R. Barrows, who established the station in 1880. Residents accepted the name as short and unique, although not particularly dignified.

WHITEFISH: Flathead County. Relates to Whitefish Lake, which was coined by early settlers for the large number of whitefish making the lake home.

WISDOM: Beaverhead County. Took its title from the river, which flows through the town. The stream was named by Lewis and Clark for one of the three "cardinal virtues" of President Thomas Jefferson, the other two being philosophy and philanthropy.

YALL HEIGHTS: Garfield County. For its location on You All Creek, and the town name is a simplified spelling of the expression used by settlers coming from the southern states.

YNOT: Phillips County. A post office was established here in 1917. Thomas McMullen, postmaster, submitted names to Washington for consideration. Authorities notified him that none of the names could be considered, whereupon the postmaster wrote back, asking, "Why not?" His question gave inspiration for a name and officials recorded it as Ynot.

ZERO: Prairie County. When the railroad first moved into this region, there was "nothing" for miles around; thus, inspiration for the settlement name.

Nebraska

THE CORNHUSKER STATE

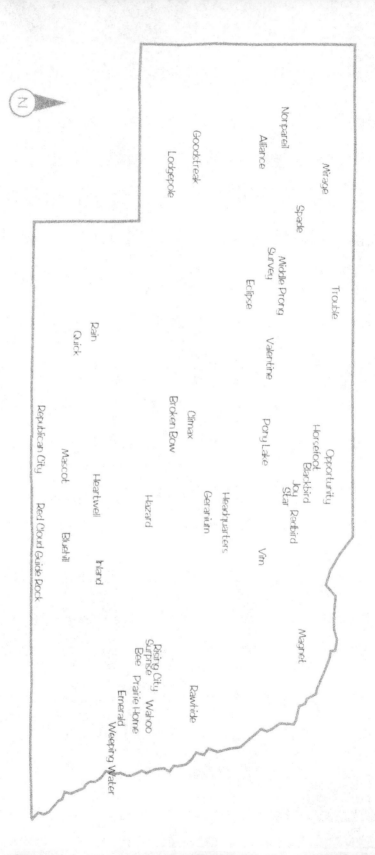

ALLIANCE: Box Butte County. The community was given this label by G. W. Holdrego because it was different from any other name in the state, was easy to spell and fairly short, and would be near the top, alphabetically, when listed with other place names in Nebraska.

BEE: Seward County. This county is comprised of sixteen precincts, each precinct designated alphabetically beginning with the letter A. Bee community is located in B precinct, and derived its phonetic spelling from the precinct designation.

BLACKBIRD: Holt County. For the river, which received its moniker from a chief of the Omaha Indians.

BLUEHILL: Webster County. Some believe the town acquired its name for its location on hills near the Blue River. Others think it was derived from the bluish atmosphere that surrounds the hills on which the town is located.

BROKEN BOW: Custer County. Christened by Wilson Hewitt, who came across an old Indian camping ground on which he found a broken bow and arrow.

CLIMAX: Custer County. Named by Mrs. William G. Ewing, postmistress, who thought the sandy, hilly site was the "limit" (climax).

ECLIPSE: Hooker County. Name selected at random, without any significance.

EMERALD: Lancaster County. A descriptive name, which places the town between green trees and rolling hills, with green foliated frog ponds scattered throughout the area. One source describes Emerald as "the most beautiful green spot in this country."

GERANIUM: Valley County. For the flower.

GOODSTREAK: Morril County. A Dr. Worth, physician and homesteader, discovered that fuel could be obtained from the surface, making digging unnecessary. Worth referred to this as his "good streak" of luck, and the name was later attached to the community.

GUIDE ROCK: Webster County. For a rock, measuring some seventy-five feet in height, that served as a landmark, or guide, for early settlers.

HAZARD: Sherman County. After several names were rejected for this town site, someone commented that they "should hazard some name." Another resident immediately suggested Hazard, which was accepted.

HEADQUARTERS: Wheeler County. This was once headquarters for the A. T. Cattle Company.

HEARTWELL: Kearney County. A family name.

HORSEFOOT: Rock County. The stock brand (horse's foot) of Mr. Best, the first postmaster.

INLAND: Clay County. This community took its handle from that of an earlier settlement in Adams County, which had been named by the railroad partly for its location and partly because it was railroad procedure to use alphabetical designations for its stations. Inland probably was phonetic for "I."

JOY: Holt County. Described the feeling of early settlers when they were finally awarded a post office.

LODGEPOLE: Cheyenne County. For the creek, so named because Indians used to cut poles on the bank for tepees.

MAGNET: Cedar County. Christened by B. E. Smith, owner of the town site, because he hoped to "attract" settlers to the area.

MASCOT: Harlan County. First known as Rouse, the railroad changed the community name to honor one of its officials.

MIDDLE PRONG: Cherry County. For the middle prong of the Loup River, which runs through the Middle Prong precinct.

MIRAGE: Sheridan County. Probably for Mirage Flats. The geographical feature was so named because a mirage lake would appear and disappear as travelers crossed the flatlands.

NONPAREIL: Box Butte County. This little hamlet was labeled by Eugene Heath, an early newsman who gave birth to *The Grip*, a local newspaper. Since the community was so small at the time, Heath christened it Nonpareil, taking the same name as the six-point type, the smallest used in printing.

OPPORTUNITY: Holt County. Opportunities looked good when a store and post office were opened on the site.

PONY LAKE: Rock County. For the lake, so named because once an Indian boy was thrown from a pony and died on the shore.

PRAIRIE HOME: Lancaster County. Designated by a man named Waite, presumably because at the time, the post office was located in a house situated on the prairie.

QUICK: Frontier County. Remembers M. W. Quick, first postmaster.

RAIN: Hayes County. A post office was set up here in 1895, at the time of a prolonged drought. The Reverend C. B. French, minister of the local Church of Christ, and the first postmaster, suggested the name Rain so residents would remember the drought.

RAWHIDE: Dodge County. For the creek. Origin of the stream name is an interesting one, to say the least. In earlier times, a group was traveling through the area. One of the men boasted that he would kill the first Indian he saw. Soon, a party of friendly Indians appeared on the scene and, true to his word, the braggart killed one of them. The Indians captured the travelers and demanded that the murderer be identified. Either through conscience, good sense, or both, the travelers turned the guilty man over, and the Indians virtually skinned him alive with a raw-hide whip. The beating took place on the creek bank.

REDBIRD: Holt County. For the creek, so named when surveyors spotted a redbird near the water.

RED CLOUD: Webster County. Honors a Sioux chief.

REPUBLICAN CITY: Harlan County. No politics involved in this town's name, it having been christened for the Republican River. The stream acquired its moniker from the Pawnee Republic, or Republican Pawnee, so called for its form of government.

RISING CITY: Butler County. For the Rising brothers, who owned the town site.

SPADE: Sheridan County. For the Spade Ranch.

STAR: Holt County. Name suggested by C. E. Downey because it was short and familiar.

SURPRISE: Butler County. Settlers were surprised to find the land so much better than they had thought it to be after their first visit here.

SURVEY: Cherry County. For the valley, which was so tagged as the result of a survey conducted through the valley by the Chicago, Burlington and Quincy Railroad.

TROUBLE: Cherry County. Supposedly tagged by Lerton Jay, first postmaster, because citizens had so much trouble deciding on a name for the settlement.

VALENTINE: Cherry County. For E. K. Valentine, three-term U.S. congressman from Nebraska.

VIM: Antelope County. For the energy, vigor, and spirit of the early settlers.

WAHOO: Saunders County. Some believe the community's name came from the wahoo plant (burning bush) found along Wahoo Creek. Others tend to think it was derived from the Indian word *pahoo,* meaning "a fairly level land." At least one source challenges this interpretation, pointing out that the surrounding terrain is rugged. Still another rendition believes *wahoo* to be an Indian word relating to a species of elm.

WEEPING WATER: Cass County. For the creek. A beautiful, but sad, Indian legend (concocted by whites) is attached to this creek. As the story goes, a tribe of Indians once lived here. The braves were heroic and the maidens beautiful and appealing, none lovelier than the daughter of the chief. Her beauty captured the heart of an Indian chief from a powerful tribe west of this location. When he asked for the hand of the princess, he was refused. Not to be outdone, he abducted the maiden one day while she was bathing with some other women of her tribe in a lake. When word of the kidnapping reached the camp, the chief and his warriors set out in pursuit. They caught up with the abductors but were slain in the battle that ensued. For three days women of the tribe awaited the return of their braves. When they didn't, the women started out in search. Upon arrival at this spot, they discovered the bodies of their men. It is said that the women wept so long, their tears formed Weeping Water Creek. Although only a legend, it is difficult to burst the beauty by stating that the name of the lake is a mistranslation of the Omaha and Otoe word *nigahoe*, "rustling water." White men confused the word with *nihoage*, which means "weeping water."

Nevada
THE SILVER STATE

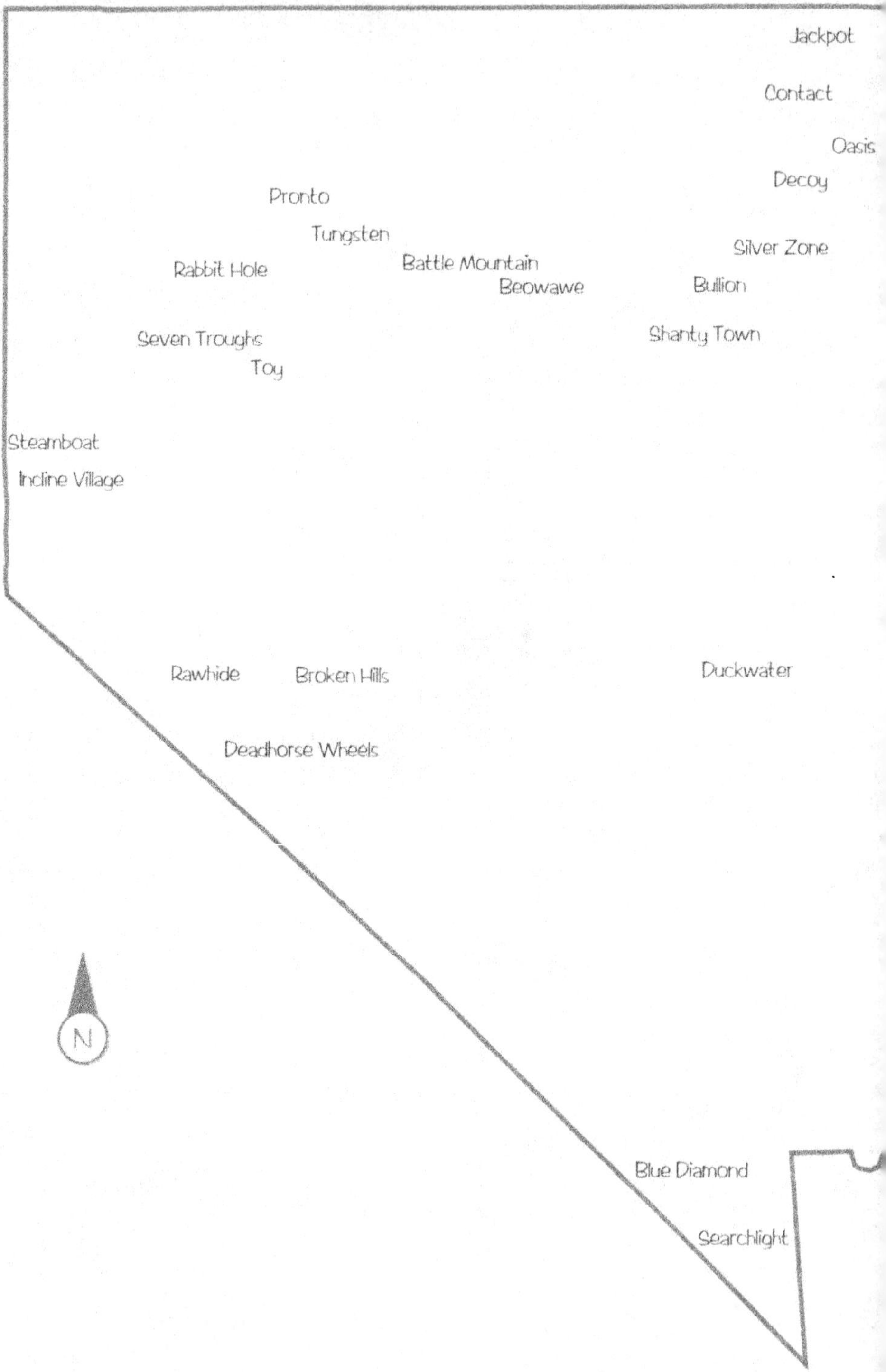

Jackpot

Contact

Oasis

Decoy

Pronto

Tungsten

Silver Zone

Rabbit Hole

Battle Mountain

Beowawe

Bullion

Seven Troughs

Shanty Town

Toy

Steamboat

Incline Village

Rawhide

Broken Hills

Duckwater

Deadhorse Wheels

N

Blue Diamond

Searchlight

BATTLE MOUNTAIN: Lander County. Relates to a battle that took place near here between Indians and a passing wagon train.

BEOWAWE: Eureka County. This hard-to-pronounce name had a comical, if questionable, origin. As the story goes, some officials were traveling by train when, at this stop, they saw an Indian woman lift her skirt, squat, and apparently answer nature's call. One of the men called out, "Beowawe!" That this is an Indian word for "bare bottom" is uncertain, but supposedly that was the intent. Regardless, the town later became known as Beowawe, and still carries that name.

BLUE DIAMOND: Clark County. For the Blue Diamond Corporation, which operated a plasterboard mill here.

BROKEN HILLS: Mineral County. For the surrounding terrain.

BULLION: Elko County. Refers to the Bullion Mining Company.

CONTACT: Elko County. In mining terms this word refers to a point where two or more minerals are found. The town was named for the Contact Mining District, which was the contact point of limestone and granite.

DEADHORSE WELLS: Mineral County. Probably took its name from the time an animal carcass was found here.

DECOY: Elko County. More than likely for the Decoy Manganese District.

DUCKWATER: Nye County. Indians named this site because of the number of ducks found here.

INCLINE VILLAGE: Washoe County. For a 1,600-foot steep incline, on which a system of hydraulically operated cars carried lumber to a flume.

JACKPOT: Elko County. First known as Unincorporated Town Number 1, the name was changed in 1959 by the Elko County commissioners to reflect winnings at slot machines.

OASIS: Elko County. For the Oasis Ranch.

PRONTO: Humboldt County. Believed to have been labeled for the Pronto Mining District. Another rendition is that railroad officials used to make runs to this stop for water because the service was "fast."

RABBIT HOLE: Pershing County. For Rabbithole Springs, christened by early travelers for the multitude of rabbits in the vicinity.

RAWHIDE: Mineral County. One version of the origin for this community name is that Charles Holman, rancher and prospector, created the name in 1903 when he nailed a steer's tail to a mailbox and placed a sign there reading, "Drop mail for Rawhide here." The second theory is that it was tagged for the brown, or rawhide, color of surrounding hills.

SEARCHLIGHT: Clark County. Some believe this name honors Lloyd Searchlight, who owned several mining claims in the area. Another thought is that a group of prospectors, unable to find silver ore in paying quantities, supposedly remarked that a searchlight would be needed to find any valuable diggings. The third version is that the community took its name from a box of matches with the brand name of Searchlight.

SEVEN TROUGHS: Pershing County. Seven troughs were once placed in a canyon near here for watering stock.

SHANTY TOWN: Elko County. For its general appearance.

SILVER ZONE: Elko County. For the Silver Zone Mining District.

STEAMBOAT: Washoe County. For the springs. The springs were so named because of steam emitted by hot water bubbling up into cooler air, giving the appearance of a steamboat.

TOY: Pershing County. There is an abundance of tule growth in the area, which Indians called *toi*; this is believed to be the origin of the community moniker.

TUNGSTEN: Pershing County. For the Tungsten Mine.

New Hampshire

THE GRANITE STATE

CENTER HARBOR: Belknap County. First called Senter Harbor, for the land grant given Colonel Joseph Senter. Through the years the spelling gradually changed to its present form.

EPSOM: Merrimack County. For Epsom, England.

LITTLE BOARS HEAD: Rockingham County. This old community, dating back to the early 1600s, was christened during early exploration. It acquired its handle from a glacial hill in the shape of a boar's head that is visible from the harbor.

SANDWICH: Carroll County. For Sir John Montague, the Earl of Sandwich.

SUNCOCK: Merrimack County. An Algonquin Indian word meaning "place of rocks" or "place of the wild goose."

New Jersey

The Garden State

ALLIANCE: Salem County. For the Alliance Israelite Universelle, an organization that brought many Jewish immigrants to the United States from Russia.

ATCO: Camden County. Derived its name from the Atlantic Transport Company.

BAPTISTOWN: Hunterdon County. Coined for followers of the Baptist denomination, who were the first settlers here in the 1720s.

BARGAINTOWN: Atlantic County. Acquired its title when town lots were sold at "bargain" prices.

BARLEY SHEAF: Hunterdon County. For the grain grown here in earlier times.

BEAR TAVERN: Mercer County. For an early day tavern.

BLACK HORSE: Middlesex County. For a colonial tavern.

BLUE ANCHOR: Camden County. For a colonial inn.

BLUE BELL: Gloucester County. For an early tavern.

BRAINY BORO: Middlesex County. This is actually the nickname for the borough of Metuchen. The title of Brainy Boro was attached to the place as a result of the large number of writers, executives, educators, and professional people living within its boundaries.

BRICKTOWN: Ocean County. Honors Joseph W. Brick, founder of the Bergen Iron Works.

BRIGANTINE: Atlantic County. Christened for an early fighting ship, known as a brigantine, that wrecked off the coast around 1710.

BURNT TAVERN: Monmouth County. Name was taken either from that of an early tavern, or from the event of one being destroyed by fire.

CHANGEWATER: Warren County. In early days, the Musconentcong River was navigable only to the present site of Changewater. Indians wanting to journey to the Atlantic Ocean had to carry their canoes overland from this point for a distance of about six miles to the Raritan River. Since this was the spot "where the water changed," that is how the community acquired its label.

COLTS NECK: Monmouth County. Some people associate the origin of this name with a tavern that displayed a sign of a colt's neck and head, and the date 1817. Some sources deny this, stating that there is mention of Colts Neck as early as 1777.

CREAM RIDGE: Monmouth County. For the dairy industry once located here.

DEAL: Monmouth County. Supposedly designated for the English city.

DEERFIELD STREET: Cumberland County. For the Deerfield Plantation built by Benjamin Davis around 1725. In 1737, a Presbyterian church was erected here, and the road leading to it was referred to as Deerfield Street. In 1803, a post office was set up on the site, and the village was officially recognized by its present name.

DOUBLE TROUBLE: Ocean County. This community handle came about after a dam suffered two simultaneous breaks, apparently causing serious damage to the surrounding area.

DUTCH NECK: Mercer County. For the strip of land on which Dutch settlers from Long Island established a community.

EGG HARBOR: Atlantic County. For the prominence of sea gull eggs in earlier times.

FAR HILLS: Somerset County. Reportedly named by Mrs. Grant Schley, because she thought it descriptive of the area's far hills.

FELLOWSHIP: Burlington County. Christened by Quaker settlers and is a term often used by that sect.

FOUR MILE: Burlington County. For a colonial tavern.

FOUL RIFT: Warren County. For the treacherous (foul) rapids in the Delaware River, "rift" being a rocky place in a stream.

FRIENDSHIP: Burlington County. For the Society of Friends, more commonly known as Quakers.

GOOD INTENT: Camden/Gloucester Counties. Refers to the Good Intent Woolen Factory.

GREAT NOTCH: Passaic County. For its location at the opening (notch) in the Watchung Mountains.

HALF ACRE: Middlesex County. Community acquired its moniker when an innkeeper fenced off a half-acre lot from a nearby road.

HEAD OF THE RIVER: Atlantic County. Geographically named for its location at the head of the Tuckahoe River.

HEADQUARTERS: Hunterdon County. So named because George Washington, retreating from New Jersey in 1777, made his temporary headquarters in a stone building located on this site.

HICKORY TREE: Morris County. Community tag taken from a former symbol of the Democratic Party.

HIGH BRIDGE: Hunterdon County. For a railroad bridge built here in 1853, which spans 182 feet above a river.

HIGH CROSSING: Burlington County. For an elevated Central Railroad crossing.

HOG WALLOW: Burlington County. Took its name from wild hogs that once roamed the region.

LIBERTY: Somerset County. Named in a patriotic vein following the Revolutionary War.

LITTLE SILVER: Monmouth County. Early colonists purchased goods from local Indians for a little silver. Another way of thinking is that the village was named for a river, the stream being so named because of its stillness and shimmering appearance.

MAXIM: Monmouth County. No proverbial influence here, with the hamlet having been named for Hudson Maxim, inventor.

PHALANX: Monmouth County. Relates to the North American Phalanx, organizer of a commune here in 1844. The socialistic society had a brief existence, lasting only eleven years.

POINTERS: Salem County. Refers to a sign once located on this spot that "pointed" to three roads.

PORCHTOWN: Gloucester County. For John Porch, a settler.

PUMPTOWN: Middlesex County. Took its label from an old pump that once sat in the middle of a road.

RED BANK: Monmouth County. Refers to the color of soil on the banks of the Navesink River.

RED LION: Middlesex County. For a colonial tavern.

ROCKAWAY: Morris County. Supposedly from the Algonquin word for "sandy place."

SCOTCH PLAINS: Union County. Township christened for George Scott, settler.

SEA BRIGHT: Monmouth County. Named by settlers for their former home in England.

SERGEANTSVILLE: Hunterdon County. First called Skunktown, the moniker had to be changed when a post office was established in 1827. Since the Sergeant families outnumbered any others in the area, that was the name chosen.

SEVEN STARS: Ocean County. For a once-famous hotel located here.

SHIP BOTTOM: Ocean County. This borough was named when the hull of a ship landed on the beach, bottom up, following a terrible storm at sea in 1817.

STRAW CHURCH: Warren County. Remembers the first place of worship built in the settlement. A thirty- by forty-foot building was erected here prior to 1790, and the roof was thatched with straw, resulting in the structure being called the Straw Church. Later, residents took that name for their community.

TABERNACLE: Burlington County. The only agreement on the origin of this village name is that it came from a chapel. The dispute arises as to whether the church was built by Quakers, Mormons, or some other religious sect.

TEN MILE RUN: Somerset County. For its distance from the city of New Brunswick.

THOROFARE: Gloucester County. For its location at the intersection of several roads.

THREE TUNS: Burlington County. Refers to an early tavern.

TIMBUCTOO: Burlington County. This place name usually refers to a destination of almost infinite distance, i.e., "I'd travel to Timbuctoo just to . . . ." This thought must have been on the minds of villagers when they selected the name, although records indicate it was named for Timbuctoo, a real location in Mali, Africa, but with a slightly different spelling.

TRANQUILITY: Sussex County. For a church of days long past.

TURPENTINE: Burlington County. For a turpentine plant in operation here during colonial days.

New Mexico

THE LAND OF ENCHANTMENT

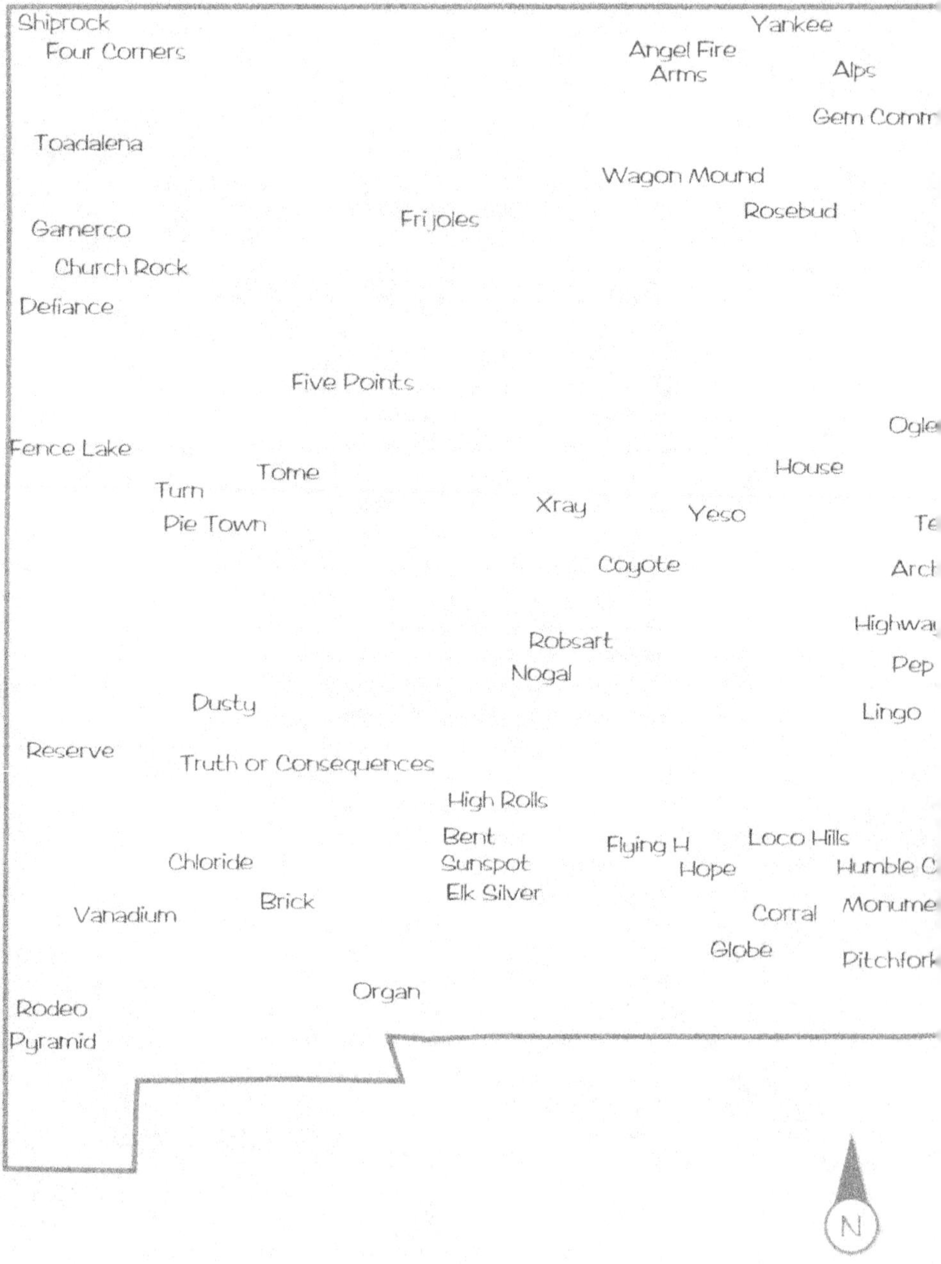

Shiprock

Yankee

Four Corners

Angel Fire

Arms

Alps

Gem Comm

Toadalena

Wagon Mound

Rosebud

Gamerco

Frijoles

Church Rock

Defiance

Five Points

Ogle

Fence Lake

House

Tome

Turn

Xray

Yeso

Te

Pie Town

Coyote

Arch

Highwa

Robsart

Pep

Nogal

Dusty

Lingo

Reserve

Truth or Consequences

High Rolls

Bent

Flying H

Loco Hills

Chloride

Sunspot

Hope

Humble C

Brick

Elk Silver

Vanadium

Corral

Monume

Globe

Pitchfork

Organ

Rodeo

Pyramid

N

ALPS: Union County. This railway station was named for its location in terrain similar to the Swiss Alps.

ANGEL FIRE: Colfax County. Before a white man ever stepped foot in this region, the Moache Ute Indians gathered here each autumn for a celebration. In the 1780s, during one of these rituals, three braves returned to the camp with tales of seeing a bright glow coming from the top of a nearby mountain. As the Indians gazed at the unusual sight, one of the elders interpreted it as an omen of the gods, blessing their celebration. Later, when Spanish Franciscan friars entered the area to teach Christianity to the natives, they used legend to make their point, and this strange phenomenon was one of their favorites. Such famous trailblazers as Kit Carson, as well as many other travelers, reported seeing the eerie light, and Carson attributed it to sunlight reflecting off frost gathered on branches of trees. Today, the legend is perpetuated from Indian lore, through Spanish conquests, to Anglo settlement, and Angel Fire is still a big part of local heritage, culminating in that name being applied to the small community.

ARCH: Roosevelt County. This community label might have been proffered by Ila Nicholas to honor Arch Williams, a settler. Or maybe Ila didn't name it for an individual, but chose Arch because she liked the name and it fit the desire of postal authorities for a short, easy-to-spell name. Another rendition is that the spot remembers Arch Grag (or Gregory), an early county sheriff. The county was named for Theodore Roosevelt; there are those who think the village honors his son, Archie.

ARMS: Colfax County. For Henry M. Arms, first postmaster.

BENT: Otero County. Salutes George B. Bent, a mine operator.

BRICK: Dona Ana County. Relates to a brick plant once located here.

CHLORIDE: Sierra County. For the type of coal once dug from local mines.

CHURCH ROCK: McKinley. For a natural rock formation.

CORRAL: Eddy County. For the animal enclosure. Evidently this was once the site for the gathering of cattle and/or horses.

COYOTE: Lincoln County. Probably named for the animal.

DEFIANCE: McKinley County. For a fort once located across the state line in Arizona.

DUSTY: Socorro County. Descriptive of the prevailing weather conditions.

ELK SILVER: Otero County. For elk and silver spruce trees in the vicinity.

FENCE LAKE: Cibola County. For a reservoir enclosed by a fence.

FIVE POINTS: Bernalillo County. A suburb of Albuquerque, this is the site where five highways meet.

FLYING H: Chaves County. For the Flying H Ranch.

FOUR CORNERS: San Juan County. Appropriately named, since it is the only place in the United States where four states meet. At this point, individuals standing in Arizona, Colorado, New Mexico, and Utah would literally be nose to nose.

FRIJOLES: Los Alamos County. Spanish for "beans"; the village was christened for the area's principal crop.

GAMERCO: McKinley County. Community name derived by using letters from the Gallup Amerco Coal Company.

GEM COMMUNITY: Union County. For George E. Merrilatt, a homesteader.

GLOBE: Eddy County. Harks back to the Globe Mill and Mining Company, which mined gypsum and made it into plasterboard.

HIGH ROLLS: Otero County. This village is situated at a high elevation, where the trip from Cloudcroft to La Luz is over a road that descends almost 4,000 feet. The postmaster gave the rather facetious explanation for the naming of the village: "If you ever lie down and start rolling, you won't stop until you reach the next county, forty miles away!" Tongue-in-cheek version aside, "rolls" in local jargon refers to the rapids of a mountain stream. Fresnol Creek flows along these slopes quite rapidly, making "high rolls."

HIGHWAY: Roosevelt County. Named for its location along a state highway.

HOPE: Eddy County. Originally called Badgerville because the first settlers lived in hillside dugouts like badgers. Renaming of the town was decided on in a simple, yet unique, manner. Two of the settlers, Elder Miller and Joe Richards, threw a dime into the air and agreed that the first one to shoot a hole in it would have the honor of christening the settlement. As the coin sailed upward, Richards blurted, "I hope you lose." Miller did, and as a consequence, Richards named the place Hope.

HOUSE: Quay County. For either Lucie J. House, who settled here in 1902 and was the first postmistress, or for John L. House, who built a store here in 1904.

HUMBLE CITY: Lea County. For the Humble Oil Company.

LINGO: Roosevelt County. First called Need, postal officials requested that the name be changed because it was too similar to Weed in Otero County. The present designation was recorded in March 1918. Some believe Lingo was chosen because of the accent of the people living on the eastern slope of a nearby ridge. Others contend it was a family name.

LOCO HILLS: Eddy County. Christened for a range of sand dunes. The small hills were not named for the locoweed. It is believed the moniker was derived by the Spanish from the wind blowing the sand and continually changing the appearance of the dunes, which the Spaniards called crazy, or loco.

MONUMENT: Lea County. For a white stone monument erected by Indians to mark a spring.

NOGAL: Lincoln County. Spanish for "walnut tree," the community was labeled for a tree that served as a landmark for many years.

OGLE: Quay County. A family name.

ORGAN: Dona Ana County. This old mining community was tagged for the Organ Mountains. The hills acquired their moniker because of peaks in the range that resemble pipes of an organ. This vicinity received a breath of fame when in 1908, Pat Garrett, the sheriff who killed the infamous outlaw Billy the Kid, was ambushed and slain on the road leading from Organ to Las Cruces.

PEP: Roosevelt County. Village is said to have been christened by Harold Radcliff during the depression of the 1930s for a breakfast cereal popular at the time. Another outlet opines it could be an abbreviated form of "pepper."

PIE TOWN: Catron County. Not too many years ago, a baker here specialized in pies. His fame was renowned among local workers and travelers. He had a large sign on the highway advertising his specialty, and when a name was needed for the small hamlet, Pie Town was a natural.

PITCHFORK: Lea County. For the stock brand used by an area ranch.

PYRAMID: Hidalgo County. For the Pyramid Mountains, so named because one of the peaks is shaped like a pyramid.

RESERVE: Catron County. For the U.S. Forest Reserve, which was placed here.

ROBSART: Lincoln County. The origin of this community handle will raise some eyebrows, but could very well have come out of the Old West. The story goes that there was once an old Indian fighter living in these parts, and he would ride his mule to this section to watch workers lay railroad track. The old man had a speech impediment, and his mule, named Rob, often displaying the stubbornness so much a part of his breed's nature, frequently balked at his owner's commands. The Indian fighter would rant, rave, and cuss, because he couldn't get "Rob" to "sart" (start). Hence, the brainstorm behind the place name.

RODEO: Hidalgo County. Spanish for "roundup," and the settlement was so labeled because it was here that cattlemen used to gather to round up and brand their cattle for shipment to market.

ROSEBUD: Harding County. This hamlet was settled in 1908 by three sisters. In the area, a new barn was being painted, and when the painters finished, they added three green rosebuds, one for each of the sisters, on the end of the barn. Later, when application was made for a post office, Rosebud was submitted as the name and was accepted.

SHIPROCK: San Juan County. Named by Navajo Indians for a large rock. The rock is part of the history of the Navajo and is surrounded by three related legends. One story is that the Navajo, once stranded in a foreign and unfriendly land, were rescued by a large stone ship built by the Great Spirit. The ship brought them to this spot. The second legend has the tribe brought here by a great bird and the bird turning to stone when its mission was complete. The third legend has it that the Navajo were placed here as an original homestead and the ship is a symbol of their journey.

SUNSPOT: Otero County. This is the site of the Sacramento Peak Observatory, which is part of the U.S. Air Force's Cambridge Research Laboratories. The main purpose of the observatory is to study and predict solar (sunspot) disturbances in the earth's atmosphere.

TEXICO: Curry County. For its location on the Texas–New Mexico border.

TOADLENA: San Juan County. Town title derived from the Navajo word meaning "water bubbling up," and was probably related to a nearby spring.

TOME: Valencia County. Remembers Tome Dominquez, a settler.

TRUTH OR CONSEQUENCES: Sierra County. Originally called Hat Springs, but changed its name in March 1950 solely as a publicity stunt. *Truth or Consequences,* a radio and later television show of exceptional longevity, was hosted for many years by its founder, Ralph Edwards. Edwards offered to hold an annual "Truth or Consequences" festival in Hat Springs if the name of the town was changed to honor his show. The citizens accepted his offer.

TURN: Valencia County. For the sharp turn in the highway at this point.

VANADIUM: Grant County. For the mineral found in the area, which is used as an alloy in the making of steel.

WAGON MOUND: Mora County. Christened around 1859 for a rock formation that resembles a covered wagon.

XRAY: Torrance County. Tagged by settlers for their former home in
Texas.

YANKEE: Colfax County. Community founded in 1904 by the New
York Wall Street brokerage firm of E. D. Sheppard and Company. It
was so named because several Boston men (Yankees) were
involved in local mining ventures.

YESO: De Baca County. This is an Indian word meaning "white
rock," and the town is believed to have been named for a nearby
geographical feature.

New York

THE EMPIRE STATE

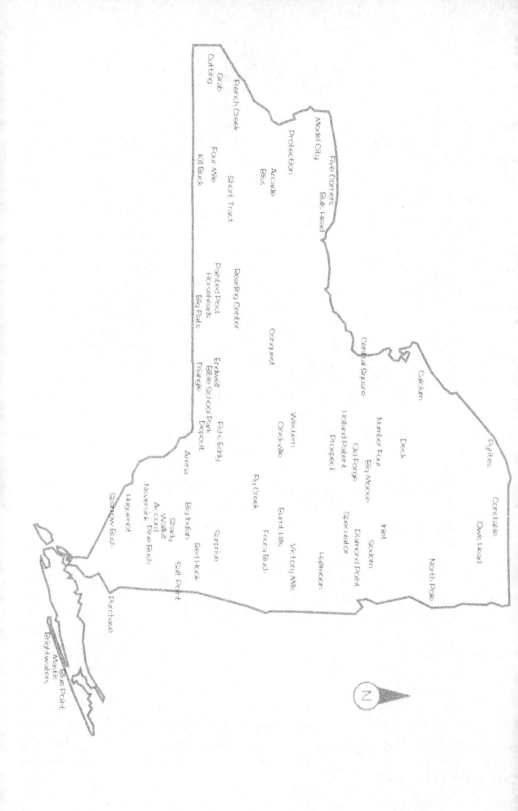

ACCORD: Ulster County. It would seem this community received its handle through a bit of irony. When the people couldn't decide on a proper name for the settlement, one citizen wrote postal officials suggesting the name Discord. Despite all the squabbling done by residents, however, the name that came back from Washington was Accord.

ARCADE: Wyoming County. Christened by Horatio Waldo because he was highly impressed with the shopping arcade in the Reynolds Building in Rochester, New York.

ARENA: Delaware County. As the story goes, early residents of this hamlet had so many fights that one man thought Arena would be a good name for the place.

BIBLE SCHOOL PARK: Broome County. In the early 1900s, on the outskirts of Binghamton, a place called White City Amusement Park was a magnet for the lower elements of society. A few years earlier, John A. Davis, evangelist, had established a school for the teaching of the Bible. By 1910, the school had outgrown its quarters. As divine providence would have it, the amusement park fell on hard financial times, and the Davis school took over the property. Hereon was established the Practical Bible Training School, and the community in which the school was situated was called Bible School Park.

BIG FLATS: Chemung County. This old area, traversed in ancient times by the Great Mammoth, and settled before the beginning of the nineteenth century, took its title from that of an early settler by the name of Flatts.

BIG INDIAN: Ulster County. For Big Indian Hollow.

BIG MOOSE: Herkimer County. For Big Moose Lake.

BLISS: Wyoming County. Remembers Sylvester Bliss, a settler.

BLUE POINT: Suffolk County. In earlier times, seamen sailing toward the shore noticed a blue haze over this point of land.

BRIGHTWATERS: Suffolk County. Some believe the community name comes from the Indian *wohseepee*, meaning "bright waters." One source contends, however, that the Indian word for water at the time was *niep*. This source goes on that the town received its tag when a woman came here and, seeing the many ponds with the sun shining on them, suggested the place be called Brightwaters.

BULLS HEAD: Monroe County. This section of the city of Rochester was named for an 1800s tavern.

BURNT HILLS: Montgomery County. So named because in early days Indians would burn dead vegetation in surrounding hills to clear ground for a better growth of berries. The berries would then attract wild game that Indians killed for food. The community took its moniker from the "burning of the hills."

CALCIUM: Jefferson County. First called Sanfords Corners. Madison Cooper, a pioneer in refrigeration and a citizen of the town, used calcium chloride in his cooling process. Because of his renown, he received much mail, most of which was addressed to Sanfords, New York. This irritated Cooper to the point that he petitioned the postal department to change the name of the community to Calcium, which it did.

CENTRAL SQUARE: Oswego County. Believed to have acquired its name because it was the intersection (center) between Syracuse to the north and the east-west road to Oswego City.

CLOCKVILLE: Madison County. A family name.

CONQUEST: Cayuga County. Originally part of the city of Cato, Conquest was named by a faction of the city fathers for their success in getting this section separated from the rest of Cato.

CONSTABLE: Franklin County. Personal name.

CUTTING: Chautauqua County. Christened by Henry R. Case for his mother, Lucy Cutting Case.

DECK: Herkimer County. Personal name.

DEPOSIT: Delaware County. This was once the deposit point for timber from the Susquehanna region, which was later sent by raft to markets in Philadelphia.

DIAMOND POINT: Warren County. The village was named for a point of land that juts into Lake George, on which can be found quartz crystals that settlers thought resembled diamonds.

ENDWELL: Broome County. Henry B. Endicott, partner in the Endicott-Johnson Shoe Company, had a son named Wendell. When a post office was established here in 1921, the letters of *Wendell* were rearranged to form *Endwell*, and this became the hamlet name.

FEURA BUSH: Albany County. This is a term meaning "fiery wood," and it is believed Indians gave the name to the area. In earlier times, a large growth of pine trees stood where the village is now located, and when the sun struck the trees, they appeared to be on fire.

FISHS EDDY: Delaware County. A family name connected to a stream (eddy).

FIVE CORNERS: Orleans County. For its location where three roads meet, forming five corners.

FLY CREEK: Otsego County. For Fly Lake, a "small" stream of water that reportedly once existed here.

FOUR MILE: Cattaraugus County. Tagged for one of the stops on the Olean, Bradford and Warren Railroad.

FRENCH CREEK: Chautauqua County. For the creek. The stream was labeled as such by George Washington in December 1753 because of the many French settlers in the area.

239

GRAB: Chautauqua County. From sources available, this place is often referred to as Grab Gut, and acquired its name from the high prices a store owner charged, often causing a person to "grab his very guts."

HALFMOON: Saratoga County. The town was supposedly named for the *Half Moon,* the ship that brought Henry Hudson to this part of the state.

HOLLAND PATENT: Oneida County. In 1769, England's King George III granted a patent of 20,000 acres of land to Henry Fox, Lord Holland. Through the years the land passed from hand to hand, and a community was eventually set on the present site and came to bear the name Public Square. In 1845, citizens decided to change the name to Holland Patent, thus relating back to its beginning.

HORSEHEADS: Chemung County. In 1779, American forces were campaigning against the Iroquois as well as against the British. After one especially arduous maneuver, General Sullivan and his tired troops camped near this spot. Their horses were so exhausted that many fell over dead. Several others were in such bad shape that they had to be killed. The bodies of the animals were left where they fell. Eventually, all that remained of the animals' bodies were bleached skeletons. Indians called the place the "Valley of the Horses' Heads." This little hamlet adopted the name Horseheads.

HUGUENOT: Orange County. For the Huguenots, French exiles who settled in this area long ago.

INLET: Hamilton County. Located at the northern end of a lake, the place was informally known as Head of the 4th Lake. When asked for more explicit directions, the name given was "at the inlet."

KILL BUCK: Cattaraugus County. For an Indian chief.

MASTIC: Suffolk County. Mastic is a resin used in making varnish. This place name, however, evolved from an Indian word meaning "great river," and relates to what is now known as the Forge River.

MODEL CITY: Niagara County. Also known as Modeltown, this community was part of a grandiose plan in the 1890s to build a great industrial city with a population in the millions. Unfortunately, financial difficulties prevented finalization of the plan.

240

NEVERSINK: Sullivan County. Throughout its long history, this town has had its name spelled a couple of different ways— Narvasvasing, Nevisinck. There are more than a couple of versions of its origin, but none have been accepted as any more valid than the others. It could mean "mad river," referring to a turbulent stream; maybe it is expressive of its very literal translation, a running stream, unbroken, that "never sinks" into the ground. Possibly it could be defined as meaning "water between highlands." Possibly it simply means a "fishing place," or a "western place where the sun never sets." All are of Indian origin.

NORTH POLE: Essex County. Located at the foot of White Mountain, this community was opened in 1949 as a Christmas fairyland, housing Santa Claus's workshop, home, and so on.

NUMBER FOUR: Lewis County. In December 1798, John Brown purchased 210,000 acres of land. He had the acreage surveyed into eight townships, the names of which were (1) Industry, (2) Enterprise, (3) Perseverance, (4) Unanimity, (5) Frugality, (6) Sobriety, (7) Economy, and (8) Regularity. *Unanimity* is not only tricky to pronounce, it is also difficult to understand. Because of this, it was always referred to as "Number Four," by which the village is known today.

OLD FORGE: Herkimer County. Commemorates a forging iron ore processing plant.

OWLS HEAD: Franklin County. For the shape of a mountain.

PAINTED POST: Steuben County. This community took its handle from the "Painted Post" landmark. Although there have been several painted posts on this site, history states that the original was placed here to celebrate an early Indian victory. The chief had a tree felled, peeled, squared off, and painted red. The Indians took thirty prisoners and killed twenty-eight others during the battle. The latter the chief had represented on the pole as headless figures; symbols of the prisoners taken were painted on the post, but with heads. The village that eventually grew up here took Painted Post as its name.

PINE BUSH: Orange County. For the number of pine trees that once grew here.

PROSPECT: Oneida County. Colonel Adam Mappa, pioneer, upon arriving at this site exclaimed, "What a beautiful prospect."

PROTECTION: Erie County. Charles Fuller christened this village around 1840. It was known as Protection Harbor, but the latter was dropped long ago. Probably acquired its title because the harbor was safe from high winds or underwater trappings.

PURCHASE: Westchester County. Quakers under the leadership of John Harrison purchased a tract of land from the Indians in 1695.

The following year the provincial governor of New York awarded a patent to the area and the words "Harrison's Purchase" were written across the face of the plat, from top to bottom. In time, each section acquired its respective name.

PYRITES: St. Lawrence County. For pyrites (sulfide) mining activities conducted hereabout in earlier days.

READING CENTER: Schuyler County. Christened by settlers from Reading, Pennsylvania.

RED HOOK: Dutchess County. At one time the town of Schuyler's Patent existed here. A section of the town was known as Red Men's Corners, or "Red Hook," because most of the residents were Indians. Red Hook became a separate township and town in 1812.

SALT POINT: Dutchess County. One thought is that the community took its name from a salt lick. Another belief is that during the 1800s, cattle were driven to the market in Poughkeepsie from Connecticut, and cowboys would stop here before moving the cows on. They would try to get the cattle to put on as much weight as possible, since the animals were bought by the pound. Salt bricks were placed throughout the campground for the cows to lick, thus increasing their thirst, making them drink large quantities of water; ergo, added weight.

SHADY: Ulster County. For its location in a deep valley with high mountains on each side, which provide a natural "shade."

SHORT TRACT: Allegany County. So named because a plot (tract) of land was once owned by William Short.

SODOM: Warren County. The biblically wicked name for the city was supposedly supplied by a local family for their former home in Dutchess County.

SPARROW BUSH: Orange County. Probably christened by a Mr. Sparrow, landowner and ship parts manufacturer.

SPECULATOR: Hamilton County. This name could glorify the magnificent mountains that overlook the homes of early settlers, or it could have been named for a land speculator.

SURPRISE: Greene County. Named by the first postmaster for no apparent reason.

TRIANGLE: Broome County. For Triangle Township, which was probably coined for its location between a tract of land and the Chenango and Tioughnioga Rivers.

VICTORY MILLS: Saratoga County. Some businessmen set up a factory (mill) here to produce and process cotton. They named their factory Victory Mills, relating the name to the Revolutionary War battle conducted nearby in 1776, where General Gates defeated General Burgoyne. The community took its name from the factory.

WALLKILL: Ulster County. For the river, which was probably named by or for the Dutch (Walloons) and the word *kil*, meaning "channel."

WESTERN: Oneida County. For its location in the western part of the township.

North Carolina

THE TARHEEL STATE

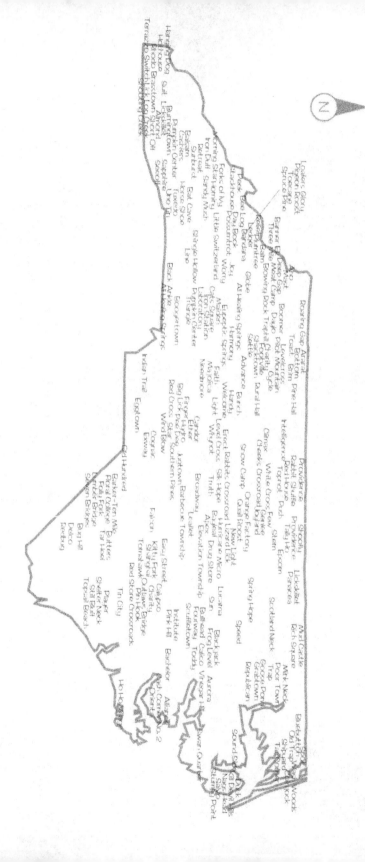

ADVANCE: Davie County. There are two schools of thought on the origin of this place name. Some think it was so called because townspeople believed the establishment of a post office would help the town grow, or advance. Another idea is that it could have been named for a ship used for blockade-running during the Civil War.   245

AHO: Watauga County. As the story goes, a lengthy meeting was held to decide on a name for the new community, but no agreement was reached. It was finally decided that the next word spoken would be adopted. A long silence prevailed until B. B. Doughtery rose from his chair, stretched, and yawned, "Aho." Thus, the name.

ALL HEALING SPRINGS: Alexander County. This resort was developed by Milt Milstead and named for the assumed healing powers of the water.

ALL HEALING SPRINGS: Gaston County. Tagged for nearby mineral springs.

ALLIANCE: Pamlico County. Named for the Farmers Alliance Movement, an organization with some political clout in the late 1800s.

ALMOND: Macon County. Remembers Bud Almond, who donated land for the town site.

APEX: Wake County. Took its moniker from its location as the highest point on the railroad line between Richmond, Virginia, and Jacksonville, Florida.

ARARAT: Surry County. Relates to the Ararat River, which was christened for the biblical mountain situated between Turkey and Russia.

AURORA: Beaufort County. Remembers an early county newspaper, *Aurora Borealis*. This was once a free black settlement known as Betty Town.

BACHELOR: Craven County. Salutes Edward Batchelor, an early settler, with a slight change in the spelling.

BALM: Avery County. Community name could have come from some biblical reference, such as Jeremiah 51:8, or because of the soothing, easy-living interpretation of the word.

BALSAM: Jackson County. Relates to the Balsam Mountains, which were apparently named for the tree from which balsam wood is obtained.

BANDANA: Mitchell County. Supposedly, the village was named from the fact that a railroad worker once tied a bandana to a bush to mark the site for a station.

BANNER ELK: Avery County. Christened for the Banner family, early settlers on the Elk River.

BARBECUE TOWNSHIP: Harnett County. The community label more than likely comes from Barbecue Swamp. Around 1750, a man by the name of Red McNeill came across the swamp early one morning. A heavy mist rising from the water reminded him of smoke from barbecue pits he had seen in the West Indies.

BARKER-TEN MILE: Robeson County. This settlement was named for two churches, Barker Methodist Church and Ten Mile Baptist Church.

BAT CAVE: Henderson County. Named for a cave inhabited by bats and other wild and rare animals; the cave is under protection as a natural preserve.

BAYLEAF: Wake County. Tagged for area bay trees.

BEE LOG: Yancey County. Named for a fallen tree that contained bees and honey.

BIG LICK: Stanly County. Named for the salty makeup of soil in the area that attracted deer and buffalo.

BLACK ANKLE: Cleveland County. While the true origin of this moniker is unknown, speculation thrives as to its derivation. Some believe the name refers to a strip of dark, fertile soil that left farmers' ankles black after a day of plowing. There is a local story that the village was coined for a section in Randolph County. This story is related to moonshiners who operated during prohibition days. The bootleggers would set fires throughout the area to prevent lawmen from finding their stills. The term "black ankle" came about when moonshiners walked through the ashes of old fires to set new ones; thus getting their "ankles black."

BLACKJACK: Pitt County. Apparently received its name from the fact that early settlers built their cabins near and under large oak trees, a species of which is known as blackjack.

BLOWING ROCK: Watauga County. Takes its tag from a rock, which acquired its name from the fact that anyone standing on the rock and throwing an object of light weight into the wind will have the object brought back by strong currents.

BLUEBUTTON: Camden County. Relates to the Bluebutton Plantation, established in 1722 by Stephen Anderson; the plantation was named for a small flower common to the area.

BOOGERTOWN: Gaston County. As folklore has it, many years ago a man had a moonshine still on a mountain near the present site of Boogertown. Concerned that someone might discover his enterprise, he spread the story that evil spirits (boogers) roamed the mountain. In time, the hill became known as Booger Mountain, and the hamlet that grew up nearby was called Boogertown.

BOOMER: Wilkes County. For "Boomer" Matheson, postmaster.

BOTTOM: Surry County. For its location in bottomland.

BRASSTOWN: Clay County. This community supposedly received its title because of some confusion in translating two Indian words. The Cherokee word *itse'yi* means "a place made green with vegetation," while *untsai'yi* means "brass." Apparently, white men took the latter and translated it into a community name.

BRIM: Surry County. A family name.

BROADWAY: Lee County. Named for a broad, level opening in a pine forest that once covered the area.

BUG HILL: Columbus County. This community received its name from Bug Hill School. Long ago, when settlers first arrived in the area, there was a large clay hill here. The ground was so infested with bugs that no crops would grow on it, so citizens decided it would be a good place to build a school.

BULLHEAD: Greene County. The origin of this village handle dates back to early America. British soldiers were in the region during the Revolutionary War, and as they approached a farmhouse near here, the owners turned loose a bull, hoping it would scare off the soldiers. Undaunted, the redcoats killed the bull, cut off its head, and placed it on a fence post. When a community was established here later, that event gave inspiration for the name.

BUNCH: Davidson County. A family name.

BURNINGTOWN: Macon County. In early days, settlers were cutting a road through dense forest when they came upon an Indian town that was afire. They bypassed the burning town, later made a treaty with the Indians, and settled along a creek they named Burningtown, after the incident at the Indian settlement. In time, the community acquired the same tag.

BUTTERS: Bladen County. Salutes the Butters Lumber Company.

CALICO: Pitt County. This small community was so named because at one time there existed a store here owned by Henry Venters and his father. Reputedly, the Venters sold more calico cloth than any other store in the county.

CALYPSO: Duplin County. A student of Greek mythology must have been responsible for this name, since it comes from that of the sea nymph in Homer's *Odyssey.*

CANDOR: Montgomery County. Three merchants were responsible for selecting this name, and did so because they wanted members of the community to be "frank and sincere."

CASH CORNER NO. 2: Pamlico County. This small spot was so christened because a storekeeper sold merchandise cheaper for cash than on credit.

CASHIERS: Jackson County. Some credit this name to the fact that a horse by the name of Cash used to graze here. Others believe the tag was derived from a hermit named Cashier who once lived in the vicinity.

CATS SQUARE: Lincoln County. So named because unwanted cats were often left at a local crossroads.

CHARITY: Duplin County. Remembers the Charity Methodist Church.

CHARITY: Yadkin County. Remembers the Charity Baptist Church.

CHEEKS CROSSROAD: Orange County. A family name and location.

CLIMAX: Guilford County. For its elevated height.

COGNAC: Richmond County. Originally known as Eight-Nine Mile Siding due to its distance from Richmond, the community name was changed to Cognac, honoring either the French city or the French brandy.

COINJOCK: Currituck County. This town's name has been spelled several different ways in times past: Coenjock, Cowenjock, or Cornjack. Coinjock is from an Indian word meaning "place of the blueberry swamps." Tradition is that wild blueberries were once abundant here.

CYCLE: Yadkin County. Originally known as Pea Ridge. A post office was established around 1913 and named Cycle because its patrons lived in a "circle" surrounding the office. Ultimately, the settlement changed its name to that of the post office.

DAY BOOK: Yancey County. Two versions exist as to why this community has such an unusual moniker. Some contend that a post office was opened around 1815 and christened for a book used to log names of people moving west. The second thought is that the name was derived from an employee "time book" kept by a lumber company.

DAYLO: Wilkes County. This settlement was established in 1924 by E. N. Vannoy, who owned a store. Vannoy named the community for a brand of flashlights he sold.

DEEP GAP: Watauga County. Relates to a large gap (opening) in the nearby Blue Ridge Mountains.

DELCO: Columbus County. First known as Brinkly, the community was renamed New Berlin by the many German settlers when it was incorporated in 1918. Not long thereafter, World War I broke out, and residents wanted to change the name to show their loyalty to the United States. They selected Pershing, honoring General "Black Jack" Pershing. This name was to bring them discomfort because railroad conductors would call out loud and clear, "Perishing." This upset the townfolk, and once again they looked around for a new name. At the time, electricity for the town was

provided by batteries in a local light plant. L. R. Hobbs owned the Delco light plant and also sold Delco batteries. One night, as he drove to a town meeting, he happened to have a Delco battery on the seat beside him. Thinking of this, he suggested Delco as the community name and the city fathers quickly agreed.

DRUG STORE: Johnston County. It is doubtful that this was ever more than a stop in the road. A drugstore was built here as early as 1886 and probably housed the post office that served the surrounding community. A historical marker is located at the intersection of Highway 42 and State Road 1010, denoting where the original drugstore stood.

DUCK: Dare County. Titled for the number of wild ducks in the region.

EASY STREET: Sampson County. So named because in earlier times it was easy to buy illegal liquor here.

EGGTOWN: Anson County. From the fact that many residents raised chickens and sold eggs.

ELEVATION TOWNSHIP: Johnston County. Geographically named for its location in a hilly section of the county.

EPSOM: Vance County. Originally known as Dukes Crossroads, the name had to be changed because of duplication when a post office was established. The new title was suggested by Dr. Bennet P. Alston, who happened to spy a box of Epsom salts in a local store.

ERECT: Randolph County. The community was christened by C. M. Taylor, merchant, in recognition of the splendid posture of his neighbor, Tom Bray.

ETHER: Montgomery County. This medical name was given by Dr. F. E. Asbury, a local physician.

EUPEPTIC SPRINGS: Iredell County. Earlier known as Powder Springs, but when it was developed into a health spa by Dr. John Ford, he changed the name to Eupeptic, a generic term for "good digestion."

EXWAY: Richmond County. Citizens of this small crossroads community suggested the name X-Ray because of the crossroads. Postal authorities accepted the name but altered the spelling.

FAITH: Rowan County. Named for the gumption displayed by J. T. Wyatt. Without previous experience, Wyatt started a quarry and worked it, initially, on faith alone.

FALCON: Cumberland County. A discussion was being held in the local store to decide on a name for the new post office. J. A. Culbreth glanced at a box of Falcon pens on one of the shelves and said, "Name it Falcon."

FEW: Durham County. Originally known as Oyaya, having been named for a city in Japan. After the Japanese attack on Pearl Harbor on December 7, 1941, citizens voted to change the title and honored Dr. William Few, the first president of Duke University.

FINGER: Stanly County. Bows to a local minister.

FLORAL COLLEGE: Robeson County. Named for one of the first women's colleges in the South, which operated here 1841–1878. The school was designated for the many wildflowers that grew in the area.

FOLLY FORK: Robeson County. This is an early place name and, at the time, *folly* was from the French *folie*, meaning "delight" or "favorite abode." Apparently, Folly Fork took its name from an early estate or plantation.

FOOTVILLE: Yadkin County. Salutes Colonel George Foot, Revolutionary War veteran.

FORKS OF IVY: Buncombe-Madison Counties. Named for its location near the junction (fork) of the Ivy and Little Ivy creeks.

FOURWAY: Greene County. Took its name from a gasoline service station built here in the late 1920s or early 1930s.

FROG LEVEL: Pitt County. Relates to a nearby pond, located on a level piece of land, at which great numbers of frogs gathered every time it rained.

GENLEE: Durham County. This is another town that once had a Japanese name. Formerly known as Togo, the moniker was voted out by citizens after Pearl Harbor and renamed in honor of the Confederate hero General Lee.

GLOBE: Caldwell County. So named because early pioneers cleared an area that was practically "round."

GOOSE POND: Bertie County. Titled for the goose pond on a plantation.

GRABTOWN: Bertie County. The source for the origin of this community name presents a colorful picture. It seems that Dave Worthington used to live here and was what modern-day thinkers would call a "free soul." He was witty, a banjo player, fiddler, world traveler, never found without his little brown jug, and cared less about work, preferring the fun side of life. The village came by its name through an oft-expressed feeling of ol' Dave: "Anything in the immediate vicinity that wasn't tied down was subject to grabs."

HANDY: Davidson County. So named because when the post office was established, it was much handier than the earlier office located at Jackson Hill, some three miles distant.

HANGING DOG: Cherokee County. More than likely relates to Hanging Dog Creek. The stream was christened when an Indian's hunting dog became hung up in a mass of jammed logs and vines in the stream.

HARMONY: Iredell County. In 1846, a revival camp meeting was held here, sponsored by the Methodist and Baptist faiths. One of the hymnals used during the revival was the *Christian Harmony Hymnbook;* thus, the name.

HO HO VILLAGE: Carteret County. Name has nothing to do with Santa Claus, having come from the first two letters of the names of the developers, Hodges and Howard.

HOMINY: Buncombe County. Said to have been tagged for Hominy Creek, which was supposedly named for a rather mundane event that took place prior to the Revolutionary War. A hunting party from South Carolina stopped along the creek bank. For supper, they cooked hominy.

HORSE SHOE: Henderson County. Christened for its location at a sharp bend in the French Broad River.

HOTHOUSE: Cherokee County. Supposedly takes its name from Hothouse Creek. The stream was named in early days when Indians heated stones and placed them in the stream. This resulted in "sweat baths," and was used to refresh tired hunters and warriors.

HURRICANE: Wake County. Remembers a devastating hurricane that hit this area more than a century ago.

HYDRO: Montgomery County. For a power generating plant.

INDIAN TRAIL: Union County. Relates to an Indian trail that once ran through here.

INSTITUTE: Lenoir County. For Lenoir Collegiate Institute.

INTELLIGENCE: Rockingham County. So named because the first modern school in this rural part of the county was located here.

IRON DUFF: Haywood County. This community moniker came about through an error by Washington postal officials. The townspeople wanted to honor Aaron MacDuff, an early settler. Somehow, post office authorities confused the name, and it was recorded as Iron Duff.

IRON STATION: Lincoln County. Harks back to the many ironworks and forges in operation in this vicinity for almost a century (1790–1880).

JOY: Burke County. Reportedly named for Joy Henderson, daughter of a prominent family.

JOYLAND: Durham County. This is now a section of the city of Durham, but is still known as Joyland. Apparently the name

252

stems from the feeling that a proposed orphanage was to bring. Foundation for the home was laid, but for some reason the building was never completed.

JUGTOWN: Moore County. Following the Civil War a depression hit this pottery-making area. Farmers who couldn't sell their corn turned to the illegal business of moonshine. Several pottery makers began turning out jugs for the illicit whiskey; therefore, the name Jugtown.

KILL DEVIL HILLS: Dare County. Of the many legends concerning this name, the one recorded by William Bird of Virginia in 1728 seems to be the most accepted. It appears that rum consumed in this part of Carolina was shipped in from New England and was so potent, it bred the saying, "That thar rum is powerful enough to kill the devil." Thus, the name. It was from this site that the Wright brothers made their famous airplane flight in 1903.

KITTY FORK: Sampson County. The hamlet was named for Miss Kitty Royal, a lady of some means, who once lived in a house located at the fork of a road.

LABORATORY: Lincoln County. Refers to a Confederate drug manufacturing facility located here during the Civil War.

LEAFLET: Harnett County. There are a couple of versions as to how this community received its title. Suggested names were submitted three or four times, and each was rejected by postal officials. Finally, the name Leaflet was sent forth because it was not duplicated by any other locale. Another version has it that citizens decided on the name Little Leaf, but the man designated to record the name lost the slip of paper on which the words were written. He recollected that the name referred to some type of leaf, so he recorded "Leaflet."

LEDGER: Mitchell County. Citizens wanted a post office. A man by the name of Phillips recorded all mail sent out and received by the settlement through another post office. He then sent his ledger to postal officials. Not only did the record influence the decision to establish a post office here, it also inspired the Post Office Department to name it Ledger.

LEVEL CROSS: Randolph County. Named for the level intersection of several roads at this point.

LEVELCROSS: Surry County. So named because two roads cross here, and the terrain is level.

LICK LOG CREEK: Clay County. From a nearby stream, which, in turn, was so named because a pioneering family by the name of Davis cut trees along the creek bank, then hollowed out the logs and filled them with salt for their stock.

LICKSKILLET: Macon County. This name came about when a hunting party left unwashed cooking utensils in camp while they searched for game. When they returned they found that the utensils had been licked clean by animals. The oft-repeated story was inspiration for the community name.

LICKSKILLET: Warren County. Basically the same as above.

LIGHT: Davidson County. As legend has it, the post office and, ultimately, the community, took their names from a mysterious light that used to be seen moving up and down a small stream. There is no evidence that the source of the light was ever discovered.

LINE: Rutherford County. Remembers an old tavern once located here that sat on the Rutherford-Cleveland county lines.

LITTLE SWITZERLAND: McDowell County. This is a summer resort founded in 1910 by Heriot Clarksun. He gave it this name because of the supposed resemblance of the mountains to those in Switzerland.

LIZARD LICK: Wake County. This odd name was given to the village by a passerby, who happened to notice a number of lizards sunning and licking themselves on a rail fence.

LOAFERS GLORY: Mitchell County. The settlement was named by a female resident of the community, because the menfolk liked to "while away their time" on the porch of the general store.

LUCAMA: Wilson County. Designation derived from the names of three sisters of Josephus Daniels: Lucy, Carrie, and Mary.

LUMBER BRIDGE: Robeson County. Named for the wooden bridge that spans the Little Marsh Swamp.

MAIDEN: Catawba County. Named for Maiden Creek, which was christened by settlers for the maiden cane found growing here.

MAJOLICA: Rowan County. This is a type of ornately decorated pottery, usually of Italian origin. As the story goes, V. C. McBee, railroad superintendent, was considering a name for a siding at this point. T. C. McNeeley, his clerk, walked into the railroad car carrying a green majolica jar of drinking water. McNeeley suggested the water be used for christening and the place be named for the pot—and it was.

MAST: Watauga County. Family name.

MEAT CAMP: Watauga County. For the creek, with the stream getting its title from the time early hunters brought their animal hides and salted meat to this spot.

MICRO: Johnston County. So named because it accurately applies to this "small" community near Durham. This micro post office, at least a few years back, didn't even have a toilet. When the postmaster felt the call of nature, he had to close the office, walk across the street, and use the facilities at a service station.

MINK NECK: Hertford County. Christened by early settlers for the many minks found in this neck of the woods.

MORNING STAR: Haywood County. The Reverend Levi Bohham was a circuit minister in this region during early days. When a church was built here, he named it Morning Star for another of his churches in or around Virginia. The community took its name from the church.

MUD CASTLE: Northampton County. For an early plantation.

NAGS HEAD: Dare County. A rather fanciful legend surrounds the name of this popular summer resort. It is told that once some of the local populace tied lanterns around the necks of ponies (nags) and, at night, walked them up and down the beach. The swinging lanterns resembled those of vessels and lured ships onto the shore, where they beached and became easy prey for looting.

NEEDMORE: Rowan County. This hamlet got its name when Jeff Smart stopped at a store and asked for several items, none of which were in stock. Smart is reported to have commented that the storekeeper "needed more" in his store.

NEW LIGHT: Wake County. This community received its name from the Newlights, a branch of the Baptist faith that refused to admit membership to its church until individuals could testify to a religious experience and conversion.

OLD HUNDRED: Scotland County. So named because this was the site of the 100-mile marker when the railroad from Wilmington was built.

OLD TRAP: Camden County. This is an early settlement dating back to the mid-1600s. It was an active maritime center in the eighteenth century, and a tavern provided the men with West Indian rum. There was a windmill here at the time, and tradition has it that men on the way to the mill with grain often stopped at the tavern to get their strength revitalized by rum. This "revitalization" often took a long time, and the tavern was soon referred to as a "trap," probably by womenfolk. By the end of the Revolutionary War, "The Trap" was used when referring to the community, and after 1800, Old Trap became the accepted name.

ORANGE FACTORY: Durham County. This small community north of Durham received its name when a cotton mill (factory) was built in a grove of orange trees.

ORIENTAL: Pamlico County. In 1862, the Federal transport *Oriental* sank near Bodie Island. The ship's nameplate was later found by

Rebecca Midgett, wife of the town's first settler, and this gave inspiration for the community name.

OUTLAWS BRIDGE: Duplin County. Refers to a bridge built here by early settlers whose family name was Outlaw. The family doesn't lend itself to evil in real life. In fact, from the Outlaw family have come war heroes, patriots, judges, professional people, and congressmen.

PANACEA: Warren County. For Panacea Springs. In the early 1900s, this was a popular resort community, which gained its fame from the curative (panacea) powers of a mineral spring nearby. Little remains of the settlement, but mineral water from the spring is still bottled and sold.

PEE DEE: Montgomery County. For the creek. There is some confusion over the stream name. It comes from a Catawba Indian word, but it is uncertain if the word is *pi'ri*, which means "something good," or *pfhere*, which means "smart," "expert," or "capable."

PEEK: Madison County. A family name.

PIGEON ROOST: Mitchell County. So named because this used to be the gathering place for a large number of now-extinct carrier pigeons.

PILOT MOUNTAIN: Surry County. For the mountain, so named because it served as a guide (pilot) for early travelers.

PIN HOOK: Duplin County. This name could have come from the sharp bend in a nearby river, or it might be associated with a locally used fishhook, sometimes referred to as a pin hook.

PINE HALL: Stokes County. Salutes the many Hall families living in the area, and for the nearby multitude of pine trees.

PINK HILL: Lenoir County. For a plantation.

PLAYER: Pender County. Probably a family name.

PLUMTREE: Avery County. The town was named for Plumtree Creek, but it is a misnomer, in a way. While the stream was named for the plum trees growing nearby, the town has never had a wild plum tree growing within its limits.

POOR TOWN: Hertford County. Apparently acquired its moniker during a communal dinner held by Ed Newsome and Margaret Early, local storekeepers. It was during the dinner that the comment, "It was a poor meal at the poor town," was heard. The name has stuck to this day, despite efforts to change it.

POSSUMTROT: Yancey County. As the story goes, this community name came about from the time a man on horseback was riding along a wooded trail. A possum came out of the woods and trotted just ahead of the horse and rider for some distance.

256

PROVIDENCE: Caswell County. In the very early part of this century, a Methodist congregation split over the issue of doctrine. One group moved north of the site of the church located near here, while the other group moved a short distance south. This latter group took the name Providence Church, which was adopted by the village.

PROVIDENCE: Granville County. Named for the Providence Presbyterian Church, established here in 1767.

PUMPKIN CENTER: Lincoln County. This title was born on the spur of the moment in either 1917 or 1918. A large field was, at the time, full of pumpkins. A traveler passing through stopped to watch a baseball game being played in the field. Approaching some of the players, he inquired as to the name of the community. "Pumpkin Center," they responded, and Pumpkin Center it became.

PUMPKIN CENTER: Jackson County. A post–Civil War doctor lived here and owned a large area of land. He and his family raised many pumpkins and he often boasted that he lived in the pumpkin center of the world.

PUSH: Person County. A tongue-in-cheek explanation for the name is that when it rained, anything that moved became mired in the mud and had to be "pushed" out of the ruts.

QUAIL ROOST: Durham County. For a former hunting club.

RABBIT SHUFFLE: Caswell County. Supposedly refers to the land, which was so poor, a "rabbit had to shuffle" to find something to eat.

RABBITS CROSSROAD: Chatham County. This place name is said to have come about one winter, when a hunting party saw a large number of rabbit tracks crisscrossing in the snow.

RED CROSS: Stanly County. For a crossroad sided by red clay banks.

RED HOUSE: Caswell County. For the Red House Presbyterian Church.

RED STORE CROSSROADS: Duplin County. More than likely named for a store, painted red, situated at a crossroads.

REDBUG: Columbus County. Acquired its tag when a lumberman working near here sat under a pine tree to rest. He was soon attacked by a horde of "red bugs" and suffered several severe bites.

RELIEF: Mitchell County. Designated for the patent medicine "Hart's Relief," sold here in John Peterson's store around 1870. The reason for the popularity of Hart's Relief could have been its high content of alcohol.

REPUBLICAN: Bertie County. Salutes the Republican Baptist Church. The church was so named because it served as a "public" meeting place for the surrounding area.

RETREAT: Haywood County. So named because the original post office sat at the center of four small communities. There was no way to get from the office back to the communities except to "retreat."

RHODO: Cherokee County. As the story goes, this settlement was named for the "raw dough" biscuits once served at a boarding house.

RICH SQUARE: Northampton County. This term was used in the original land deed of 1766, and probably refers to the fertility of the soil. The name was taken from the deed.

ROARING GAP: Alleghany County. The hamlet was tagged for an opening (gap) in nearby mountains through which the wind blows (roars).

RURAL HALL: Forsyth County. In March 1875, a man by the name of Bitting was appointed postmaster for this community. He lived in a house that had a large hall, which was also a popular gathering place for the townspeople. Mail to the site was addressed simply to "Hall." Confusion soon arose as to whether the mail was destined for Salem Hall, which was in the community, or for the Bitting home, which was in the country. To resolve the issue, mail for Bitting's post office was marked "Rural Hall."

SALVO: Dare County. According to tradition, this town was so named when, during the Civil War, a Union gunboat in the harbor shot a barrage (salvo) of cannon across a nearby beach.

SANDY MUSH: Buncombe County. For Sandy Mush Creek. Often early place names came from simple events; such is the case here. In the long ago, a hunting party was cooking on the creek bank, and sand from the stream got into the mush they were cooking.

SAPPHIRE: Transylvania County. This name came about either because of the vivid blue sky and water, or because sapphires were found in the vicinity.

SCOTLAND NECK: Halifax County. So named because the original Scot settlement in 1722 was on a stretch (neck) of land.

SCUFFLETOWN: Greene County. This place name is said to have resulted from an earlier disagreement among members of the Free Will Baptist Church. Today, the community is popularly known as Ridge Spring.

SEEOFF: Transylvania County. So designated because from a nearby mountain a person can "see off" a long distance.

SETTLE: Iredell County. Honors Thomas Settle, a prominent North Carolina Republican.

SEVEN BRIDGES: Robeson County. Apparently named for the seven bridges that span a road near this small hamlet.

SHACKTOWN: Yadkin County. Salutes B. G. "Shack" Colvard, a businessman.

SHANGHAI: Sampson County. Probably named for a breed of chicken.

SHELTER NECK: Pender County. There is a plot of land near here where Revolutionary War soldiers camped. The spot was covered with holly trees and acquired the name Holly Shelter. Apparently this small town was, at that time, located on a neck of land and was part of the Holly Shelter area that broke away and became known as Shelter Neck.

SHINGLE HOLLOW: Rutherford County. For a shingle mill located in a hollow (small valley).

SHIPYARD: Camden County. This was a center for the building of small sailing vessels during the eighteenth century.

SHOOFLY: Granville County. This name could have been derived from several sources: a plant that repels flies, the famous German pie, or a child's rocking toy.

SHOOTING CREEK: Clay County. For a creek. The stream name is thought to be a translation of the Cherokee word *du-stagalan'yi*, which means "where it made a great noise."

SHORT OFF: Macon County. So designated for a mountain that was named for C. W. Short, an American botanist of the 1800s.

SILK HOPE: Chatham County. The name more than likely evolved from the mid-1800s, when home cultivation of silkworms was being promoted.

SNOW CAMP: Alamance County. This community moniker is believed to be associated with an early incident, when travelers were caught in a heavy snowstorm and camped here.

SOUND SIDE: Tyrrell County. For its location on the south side of Albermarle Sound.

SOUTHERN PINES: Moore County. John T. Patrick, a promoter, developed this site and named it Vineland. He later changed the name to Southern Pines, possibly to make it more attractive to out-of-staters, primarily New Englanders.

SPEED: Edgecombe County. Remembers E. T. Speed.

SPOT: Currituck County. Originally known as Hog Quarter, the moniker was changed to Spot in 1920, being named for a fish found in local streams.

SPRING HOPE: Nash County. This name is said to have been given by early settlers for a nearby spring, which they hoped would forever keep them supplied with water.

SPRUCE PINE: Mitchell County. When settlers first arrived here, they saw a growth of trees on a nearby hill. Thinking they were spruce

pines, they called the settlement by that name. However, the trees they saw were hemlocks.

STACKHOUSE: Madison County. A family name.

STAR: Montgomery County. Named by Angus Leach, merchant, for the fact that the settlement is situated on a high hill and can be seen from all directions, like a star.

STEM: Granville County. A family name.

STILL BLUFF: Pender County. So named because it is considered to be a quiet (still) place situated on a bluff.

STUMPY POINT: Dare County. This place was probably named by Indians for the many tree stumps and points that jut out all over the place.

SUIT: Cherokee County. Honors Johnson Suit, the first postmaster.

SUN: Wilson County. Designated for the Sun Chapel, established here in earlier days.

SUNBURST: Haywood County. So named because the town is located where the sun seems to suddenly "burst" forth from behind a mountain range.

SWAN QUARTER: Hyde County. Some people believe this community name came from Samuel Swann, who settled here in the 1700s. Others think it came about when early settlers found a large number of swans using it as winter quarters.

TALLY HO: Granville County. Foxhunting was a popular sport in this region in early days, and the village is named for the words hunters call out when they sight their quarry.

TAR CORNER: Camden County. Name supposedly derived from a barn once situated here that was covered with tar and stood at the intersection of two roads.

TAR HEEL: Bladen County. This is North Carolina's nickname and is said to have come from one of two events. During the American Revolutionary War, General Cornwallis and his forces crossed a river in the state and came out with tar on their feet. Another source avers that the title came about when tar made in this area was taken to Cape Fear River, where it was put aboard rafts for shipment to Wilmington. The river waterfront was, naturally, covered with tar, which quickly adhered to the feet of anyone stepping in it.

TERRAZZO SWITCH: Cherokee County. Named for the terrazzo flooring made from marble chips by the Columbia Marble Company, and the fact that the settlement was located on a "switch" of the Southern Railroad.

THREE MILE: Avery County. Believed to have been christened for Three Mile Creek, so called because of its length.

TIN: Henderson County. Salutes Joseph Youngblood, tinsmith, who submitted a bid to supply tin cups and plates to the community jail.

TIN CITY: Duplin County. Hamlet was so designated because, when first established, a large number of buildings were constructed of sheet metal.

TOAST: Surry County. This community post office was named by a Washington official. When the name was returned, an editor of the local newspaper quipped that the bureaucrat was probably eating toast when he named the new office. The community later took the same name.

TODDY: Pitt County. So tagged because a local store always had a drink of whiskey (toddy) for its customers.

TOECANE: Mitchell County. For its location at the junction of the Toe River and Cane Creek.

TOMAHAWK: Sampson County. Supposedly for the creek, which acquired its name from its shape.

TOPNOT: Caswell County. Probably christened for its location on or near the top of a hill.

TOPSAIL BEACH: Pender County. Named for Topsail Sound, so called because that was the site where residents watched for the topsails of approaching ships.

TRAP: Bertie County. From the story passed down by early wives, the village received its name from the activities of a tavern once located here that used to trap their menfolk.

TRAPHILL: Wilkes County. For a snare (trap) laid out on a hill by a hunter named William Blackburn.

TRIANGLE: Lincoln County. Refers to the triangle formed by roads running through the town.

TRUTH: Chatham County. Moniker suggested by a resident more as a joke than anything else, but other citizens took him seriously.

TUXEDO: Henderson County. Name chosen simply because residents liked it.

UNO: Henderson County. According to folklore, this little settlement was so named because two young girls who once lived here had a small mongrel dog they called Uno. Why they christened the mutt with that name is not known.

VINEGAR HILL: Beaufort County. This name is believed to have come from the fact that there was once a cider press here.

WASH WOODS: Currituck County. So titled because of the hundreds of old tree stumps visible at low tide.

WELCOME: Davidson County. When a name for the community was being discussed, some disagreement arose. Finally, Welcome was chosen, first, because of a "Welcome" sign hanging over the door of the general store and, second, because one citizen commented that "everybody's welcome here." 261

WHITE CROSS: Orange County. Sources indicate that this community acquired its name because of the soil. However, how white cross relates to soil is unknown.

WHYNOT: Randolph County. During discussion on a name for the town, many suggestions were forthcoming, with "Why not name it . . ." After a period of time in which no decision had been reached, Alfred Yow rose and said, "Let's name it Whynot and go home."

WIND BLOW: Montgomery County. Received its tag around 1920 from S. R. Gaddy, because he believed that if the wind was going to blow anywhere, it would blow here.

WORRY: Burke County. Named by Jane Elizabeth Caldwell, who, after having had several suggested names rejected, was concerned that an acceptable one might never be forthcoming. Her concern inspired the name Worry, which was submitted and accepted. Some say the post office was named by a Mrs. Henderson for basically the same reason.

North Dakota
The Flickertail State

Sodhouse   Dunker Colony   Smugglers Point

Rival

Spiral   Bowbells   Overly   Bachelor   Willdo   Backoo

Bonetrail   Boundary
Persevere   Pennyhill   Dash
                                    Cardio
Plaza   Rugby   Concrete
White Earth   Goa

Nameless

                    Killdeer
            Greatstone   Fort Defiance   Shake
South Heart   Flasher   Dornybrook   Twist   Tokio   Devils Lake   Bachelors Grove
New England   Hub   Expansion   Divide   Why Not
Regent   Zap
Coalbark   Heart

Trotters
Riders

                Nosodak   Arena

                        Cannon Ball   Past   Community   West Edge

                                Silverleaf

                                            Prosper   Wild Rice

N

ARENA: Burleigh County. This moniker could have come from the surrounding mountains, which form a natural arena around the site. Since *arena* means "sand," and there are several sandy areas in the vicinity, that could have been the origin.

BACHELOR: Rolette County. At the time a name was considered for the site, there were a number of unmarried men in the area.

BACHELORS GROVE: Grand Forks County. A grove of trees once stood along Turtle River, and the community was so named because at the time only one man had his family with him.

BACKOO: Pembina County. Christened, with a variation in spelling, by John Mountain for the Borcoo River in his former home, Australia.

BONETRAIL: Williams County. For its location on a trail over which buffalo bones were once hauled to market.

BOUNDARY: Rolette County. For its location near an iron boundary post, which served as the international marker between the United States and Canada.

BOWBELLS: Burke County. Relates to the famous church bells of Saint Mary-le-Bow, Cheapside, London, England.

CANDO: Towner County. During earlier times, disagreement arose as to the site of the county seat. P. T. Parker, one of the county commissioners, made a statement that the commission had the power to designate the county seat, and "we can do it. And furthermore will name the county seat Cando."

CANNON BALL: Sioux County. For the limestone cannonballs found in and near the Cannonball River.

COALBANK: Hettinger County. For lignite coal in surrounding hills.

COMMUNITY: Stutsman County. A name that sounded good at the time.

CONCRETE: Pembina County. For a cement plant.

DASH: Towner County. For a rabbit-chasing dog owned by an early settler.

DEVILS LAKE: Ramsey County. For the lake, which comes from the Sioux *minne*, meaning "water," and *waukan*, meaning "spirit."

DIVIDE: Eddy County. For its location at the divide of the drainage of the James and Sheyenne Rivers.

DONNYBROOK: Ward County. For the Donnybrook Fair of Ireland.

DUNKER COLONY: Towner County. Relates to the German Baptist Brethren sect, also known as "Dunkards" because of their baptismal rites. The name comes from the German *tunken*, meaning "to dip."

EXPANSION: Mercer County. Christened by residents expressing their hopes for the future, which proved futile, since the site is little more than a ghost town today.

FLASHER: Morton County. This has nothing to do with exposing oneself in the nude, having been named by its founder, William Brown, for Mabel Flasher, his niece and secretary.

FORT DEFIANCE: Mercer County. Received its tag when Alexander Harvey and Francois Chardon established a fur trading post on the site in 1845. They had been fired from nearby Fort McKenzie for allegedly mistreating Indians and other lawless acts. In "defiance" of their dismissal, they erected this post.

GOA: Benson County. "Goa" is both a city in India and a member of the gazelle family. Neither of these applies to Goa, North Dakota. Robert Hunter, an early settler, petitioned for a post office, and when it was granted residents thought it should be named for him. Hunter believed the more deserving individual was William Preause, who, for quite some time, had been bringing mail weekly by horse-drawn wagon twenty-five miles from Minnewaukan. For this he received a salary of thirty-five dollars a year. When Preause was approached about naming the office for him, he replied that he didn't care about the name as long as the office was "a go." For some reason residents reversed the words and came up with Goa.

GREATSTONE: McLean County. Early homesteaders found many "great stones" that had to be removed before tilling could begin.

HEART: Grant County. For its location near the Heart River.

HUB: Mercer County. Honors Hub Brown, husband of the first postmistress.

KILLDEER: Dunn County. For the mountains, which were named by the Sioux because that was where they hunted for deer.

NAMELESS: McKenzie County. Christened by Robert Stroud for his former home, Nameless, Texas.

NEW ENGLAND: Hettinger County. Settled in 1887 by members of the New England Colony Association.

NOSODAK: Sioux County. Acquired its name from the fact that it is on the borderline of North and South Dakota.

OVERLY: Bottineau County. The hamlet could have acquired its name from the time it was the site of a day layover (overlay) for train crews, or it may have been named for a land commissioner on the Soo Railroad. Another possibly is that it was named for Hans Overlie, an early settler, and the spelling was changed at the request of the Post Office Department.

PAST: Stutsman County. For William H. Past, postmaster.

PENNYHILL: Rolette County. For a range of hills. The hills could have been named by Father Campeou, who, during a dry, hot summer, toured the range. Noticing the bareness of the landscape, Campeou reputedly remarked, "I can't see how anyone could make a penny in these hills. Pennyhills—that should be a good name for them."

PERSEVERE: Williams County. Recognizes the ruggedness and stamina of early pioneers.

PLAZA: Mountrail County. The original town site was laid out with a park (plaza) in the center of the business district.

PROSPER: Cass County. For the prosperous farmland on which early arrivals settled.

REGENT: Hettinger County. Labeled by residents with the expectation of its becoming the queen (regent) city and county seat of Hettinger County. Despite its central location, its dreams never came true.

RIDERS: Golden Valley County. Named by railroad officials in 1914. There was a railroad siding called Ranger, and since this was cowboy country, officials decided to honor them.

RIVAL: Burke County. This hamlet was on the Soo Railroad line and was meant to rival Lignite, a town on the Great Northern line.

RUGBY: Pierce County. For Rugby, England.

SILVERLEAF: Dickey County. While visiting a neighbor, Don Keenan spied an empty can of lard with a label reading "Silverleaf." He cut the label from the can and nailed it to the side of the depot. In time, this became the accepted community name.

SMUGGLERS POINT: Pembina County. This was once an easy spot for smugglers to cross the Canadian border.

SNAKE: McLean County. For the creek, so named because of the large number of garter snakes in the vicinity.

SODHOUSE: Rolette County. The first post office, set up here in May 1891, was located in the "sod house" of Ingebret Ingbretson, the first postmaster.

SOUTH HEART: Stark County. For its location at the mouth of the south fork of the Heart River.

SPIRAL: Burke County. Name possibly suggested by the spiral outline of the Soo Railroad track.

TOKIO: Benson County. As the story goes, a railroad official heard the Indian word to-ki, which means "gracious gift." He liked the sound of the word as well as the meaning and commented, "We'll just add an 'o' and call this place Tokio."

TROTTERS: Golden Valley County. Remembers Francis L. Trotter, the first postmaster.

TWIST: Wells County. For Jesse D. Twist, the first postmaster.

WEST EDGE: Barnes County. For its location on the west edge of the Sheyenne River Valley.

WHITE EARTH: Mountrail County. For the creek, which is a translation of the Indian word *maskawapa*, for the white clay sand of the creek bed.

WHYNOT: Grand Forks County. Received its moniker from a terse comment made by Erik K. Larsgaard, when asked why he was building a store on his homestead: "Why not?"

WILD RICE: Cass County. For the river. The stream was named for the heavy growth of wild rice on its banks.

WILLDO: Towner County. To challenge the name of the county seat, Cando.

ZAP: Mercer County. This handle came from either a coal mining hamlet in Scotland, or from a prominent Minnesota banking family.

Ohio
THE BUCKEYE STATE

ALLIANCE: Stark County. For an alliance formed by three villages: Williamsport, Freedom, and Liberty.

ANTIQUITY: Meigs County. For a rock; named by early settlers because of the ancient carvings found thereon.

BIG PRAIRIE: Holmes County. Descriptive of a large, flat section of land for which the community was named.

BIRDS RUN: Guernsey County. "Run" is usually associated with a stream or creek. This village name has a more unsavory connection. Long ago, two settlers were located here. One, Robert Atkinson, was married; the other, a man named Bird, was single. Atkinson's wife died and Bird and some local Indians assisted in the burial. After a time, the widower returned to Virginia to get himself another bride, leaving his land, home, furnishings, and everything else he owned in the care of his neighbor. No sooner had Atkinson departed than his "friendly" neighbor, Bird, loaded all the widower's possessions onto a boat and sailed down the Muskingum River, never to be seen again. From this incident, "Bird's run," came the community name.

BLACK HORSE: Portage County. In 1830 David Grier built a tavern on this spot. One of his tenants, unable to pay his keep, painted a sign for the outside of the tavern. The sign depicted a black horse, and from this is said to have come the community's handle.

BLACKLICK: Franklin County. For a creek, which was christened for the black salt stones in the stream that deer licked.

BLOOMERTOWN: Darke County. For the dress code adopted by Amelia Bloomer and her followers in their 1800s fight for women's rights.

BLUE ASH: Hamilton County. For the blue ash trees that once grew here.

BRILLIANT: Jefferson County. Relates to a glass company of long ago.

BROKENSWORD: Crawford County. For the creek. The stream was so labeled from the fact that Colonel Crawford, for whom the county is named, having been taken prisoner by Delaware Indians, "broke his sword" on a rock on the creek bank. Another version is that Indians found a broken sword left behind by a member of Crawford's army.

CABLE: Champaign County. Remembers Hiram Cable, the town founder.

CARBON HILL: Hocking County. For coal found in nearby hills.

CHARM: Holmes County. The origin of this little Amish town's name is believed to be descriptive. There is supposition, however, that the name came about around 1886 when Joni J. Yoder, watch repairman, used to attach ornaments to the rather large watch chains worn by men. The ornaments were called "watch charms," and the association with Yoder's occupation gave the idea for the community name.

COLLEGE CORNER: Butler County. For a now-defunct college.

CONVOY: Van Wert County. Christened by John Nesbit for his former home, Convoy, Ireland.

COOLVILLE: Athens County. Village handle derived from that of Simeon Cooley, father of an early settler.

DEFIANCE: Defiance County. Named for historic Fort Defiance. The fort received its name from General "Mad" Anthony Wayne's famous challenge: "I defy the English, the Indians, and all the Devils in Hell to take it!"

EMPIRE: Jefferson County. Relates to the Empire Sewer Pipe Plant established here in 1885.

FELICITY: Clermont County. Name is commendatory, suggested by the name of the founder, William Fee, combined with "-city," and at one period was spelled Feelicity.

FORT RECOVERY: Mercer County. On this site in November 1791, troops under General Arthur St. Clair were badly beaten by Indians. President Washington dispatched another force to the area under the command of General "Mad" Anthony Wayne. In December 1793, a detail led by Major Burbeck reoccupied the site lost two years earlier. The place was named Fort Recovery, because American troops "recovered" the ground from the Indians.

GRATIS: Preble County. This is from the Latin, meaning "free," and the community was more than likely named because the land for the town site was "donated" by three local landowners.

KILLBUCK: Holmes County. For a Delaware Indian chief.

LIBERTY CENTER: Henry County. Believed to have been so named to conform with other patriotic names: Henry County, for Patrick Henry, located in Liberty Township, and bordered by Washington and Freedom Townships. A couple of interesting notes regarding this village: In 1976, Craig Myers, an eighteen-year-old, was elected mayor, believed to be the youngest person to ever hold such a high elective office. This is also the home of Marjorie Whiteman, an authority on international law, who served in most of the presidential administration of Franklin D. Roosevelt.

LIGHTSVILLE: Darke County. For William B. Light, who platted the town site in 1874.

LONG BOTTOM: Meigs County. Designated for a long stretch of "bottomland" along the river that runs through here.

MARBLE FURNACE: Adams County. For a marble furnace that operated here until about 1834.

MOUNT HEALTHY: Hamilton County. Originally known as Mount Pleasant, postal officials in 1884 requested that the name be changed, probably due to duplication. Residents selected Mount Healthy because the village escaped a cholera epidemic that ravaged the area in the 1850s.

MOUNT VICTORY: Hardin County. The land on which Mount Victory is located once belonged to Cyrus Dille. When he died it was put up for sale. Around this same time, Samuel McCullough laid out the town of Ridgeway. Not wanting another town so close (for economic reasons), McCullough attempted to outbid all interested parties for the Dille land. Ezra Dille, a descendant of Cyrus, outbid McCullough. Later, when Ezra was asked who won, he replied, "We did." "Victory!" the inquirer excitedly claimed. "We will call the town Mount Victory!"

NEWCOMERSTOWN: Tuscarawas County. Sometime between 1730 and 1740, when the Delaware Indians roamed this valley, Chief Eagle Feathers took Mary Harris, a white captive, as his wife. A decade or so later, he acquired another white woman prisoner and brought her to share his wigwam. This didn't set too well with Mary, and she jealously named the recent arrival "New Comer." This jealousy persisted, and there was no peace in Eagle Feathers's tepee. One morning he was found dead, with an ax buried in his skull. Mary accused New Comer of the violent deed and inflamed the tribe against her. The accused girl fled but was captured by another tribe along the Tuscarawas River. Her capture caused the small Indian settlement to be called *Ge-kel-e-muk-pe-chunk*, or "Newcomerstown." The girl was returned to Eagle Feathers's village and eventually sentenced to death. The place of her second capture has been henceforth called Newcomerstown.

NORTH STAR: Darke County. The village received its moniker both because it is as far north in Darke County as you can go before hitting swampland, and because of a sign that hung in the front of a local store. The sign was made from the wood of a crate of Star Tobacco, and had a large star on the side.

PURITY: Licking County. Name suggested by Cary Stevenson after he noticed a can of Purity tea (or coffee) on the shelf of a local store.

PUT IN BAY: Ottawa County. Some believe the origin of this community name is that it was an offshoot of Pudding Bay. Another tenet is that the name came about when, during the Revolutionary War, Commodore Perry had his ships "put in" here for safety.

REPUBLIC: Seneca County. Christened by General Sidney Smith when he had the town site platted in 1834, because he thought it would be for the "public good."

RISINGSUN: Wood County. First known as Black Swamp, then as Coon Town, several ladies wanted a more dignified designation for their community. In 1874 they sponsored a contest for a new moniker. A young man in the village suggested Risingsun because this is the first community in the county to view the morning sun.

ROOTSTOWN: Portage County. Honors Ephraim Root. A home in this little hamlet once served as a stop on the Underground Railroad before the Civil War. Another interesting fact about the community is that an organ donated by Mrs. John D. Rockefeller in 1897 was, at last report, still being used in the Congregational Church.

ROUNDHEAD: Hardin County. For an Indian chief.

SEAMAN: Adams County. Franklin Seaman donated land for a railroad right of way and asked that the town be named for him.

SEVEN MILE: Butler County. So tagged because General Wayne once instructed his troops to meet him seven miles north of Fort Hamilton, and that brought them to this point.

SEVENTEEN: Tuscarawas County. Hamlet took its handle from Lock Seventeen, which was constructed on the Ohio and Erie Canal in 1829.

SHADYSIDE: Belmont County. For an early farm.

SHINROCK: Erie County. Salutes Joseph Shinrock. As the story goes, the community was not named until a post office was placed here in 1884, although Shinrock actually settled in the area twelve years earlier. The name suggested for the new office, and thus the settlement, was Shinrock, because citizens believed he would be the new postmaster. Because Shinrock's wife couldn't read English (they were of German extraction), and she would be required to handle mail at least two days a week, the new postmaster appointed was Christen Koppenhafer. Shinrock had been recorded as the official name in Washington, and so it remains.

TRANQUILITY: Adams County. Named By John T. Wilson, store owner, in 1848, and is thought to be commendatory.

UNION FURNACE: Hocking County. For an early iron furnace.

WINDFALL: Medina County. One version of the community label is that the wind blowing here always provided a "windfall" of apples on the ground. Another tenet is that many years ago a heavy windstorm hit the area, blowing over most of the trees and several buildings. A final contention is that due to its location on a high elevation, the wind always blows here.

Oklahoma
The Sooner State

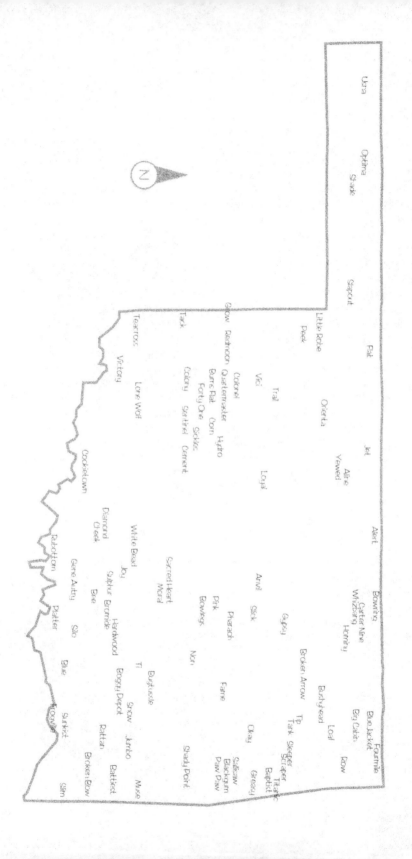

ALERT: Kay County. For Alert, Kansas.

ALINE: Alfalfa County. Relates to Marie Aline Hartshorn, daughter of an early settler.

ANVIL: Lincoln County. For a rock shaped like an anvil.

BAPTIST: Adair County. For the Baptist Mission, once located near this site.

BATTIEST: McCurtain County. This has nothing to do with craziness, having been christened for Byington Battiest, a Choctaw jurist.

BEE: Johnston County. Community was supposed to have been designated Dee, for the daughter of a local family, but was misspelled by a postal employee.

BIG CABIN: Craig County. For Big Cabin Creek; the stream was named for a large cabin situated on the Texas Road near here.

BLACKGUM: Sequoyah County. For blackgum trees.

BLUE: Bryan County. For the river.

BLUEJACKET: Craig County. Honors Rev. Charles Bluejacket, a Shawnee minister and the town's first postmaster.

BOGGY DEPOT: Atoka County. For the creek. The stream name comes from the French *vaseux*, meaning "muddy" or "rainy," and applies to the makeup of the water.

BOWLEGS: Seminole County. This oil field was so designated because the discovery was situated on a farm owned by Billy Bowlegs, a Seminole chief. Some sources claim the tag came from the Bowlegs Prairie, which had been named for Sarah Bowlegs.

BOWRING: Osage County. Believed to be derived from a combination of personal names, Bowhan and Woodring.

BROKEN ARROW: Tulsa County. This is an Indian symbol for peace. Following the end of the Civil War, some Creek Indians held a ceremony on this site at which they "broke an arrow." The community took its name from the event.

BROKEN BOW: McCurtain County. Christened by the Dierks brothers for their former home in Nebraska.

BROMIDE: Johnston County. For a bromide spring.

BUGTUSSLE: Pittsburg County. A descriptive title meaning a peaceful, rustic, or backwoods area. The boyhood home of Carl Alberts, former Speaker of the U.S. House of Representatives, is located here.

BURNS FLAT: Washita County. Community took its name from the former post office of Burns, which was located nearby.

BUSHYHEAD: Rogers County. Remembers Dennis W. Bushyhead, Cherokee chief.

CARTER NINE: Osage County. Refers to the Carter Oil Company, which was situated on Section 9 of Township 26.

CEMENT: Caddo County. Tagged for gypsum deposits.

CHEEK: Carter County. Family name.

COLONEL: Custer County. Refers to "Colonel" D. Garvin, the first postmaster.

COLONY: Washita County. Relates to the Seger Colony, which was started here in the 1890s.

COOKIETOWN: Cotton County. Around 1928, Marvin Cornelius opened a mercantile store and named it Cookietown.

CORN: Washita County. Originally spelled Korn, the name was changed to its present spelling in 1918. Took its name from the fact that the original post office was located in a cornfield.

DIAMOND: Stephens County. Christened by a religious group in commemoration of its 75th (diamond) anniversary.

FAME: McIntosh County. For the surrounding "famous" bottomland of the North Canadian River.

FLAT: Harper County. Descriptive, referring to the adjacent country-side.

FORTY ONE: Washita County. For its location on former Highway 41.

FOURMILE: Ottawa County. For its location four miles from the Kansas state line.

FROGVILLE: Choctaw County. For the abundance of frogs in the area. Legend has it that the frogs were so big, they gobbled up small ducks.

GENE AUTRY: Carter County. Originally known as Berwyn, the moniker was changed in January 1942 to honor the famous cowboy movie star, who later became owner of the California Angels baseball club.

GREASY: Adair County. For the creek; the stream name harks back to the days when a lard rendering plant was operated in the area.

GROW: Roger Mills County. Christened by Charlie Dunagan, first postmaster, because he felt the little town had plenty of room to grow.

GYPSY: Creek County. Name origin relates either to an oil company or to the oil field owned by the company.

HARDWOOD: Coal County. For the hardwood trees.

HOMINY: Osage County. A corruption of "Harmony" Mission, which was first established among the Osage Indians then living in Missouri.

HYDRO: Caddo County. Relates to the almost limitless amount of good water from vicinity wells.

JET: Alfalfa County. For W. J. Jett, the first postmaster.

JOY: Murray County. When the districts of Carr Flats and Wheeler were consolidated, a contest was held to determine a name for the new school. Joy was the winning entry, and also the name adopted by the community.

JUMBO: Pushmataha County. Remembers the Jumbo Asphalt Company.

LITTLE ROBE: Ellis County. For a Cheyenne chief.

LOAF: Mayes County. Citizens wanted the post office named Sugar Loaf, but postal officials deleted "Sugar" for some unknown reason.

LONE WOLF: Kiowa County. For *Mam-a-day-tre*, a Kiowa chief known as Lone Wolf.

LOYAL: Kingfisher County. Originally called Kiel, the German name was changed during World War I to show "loyalty" to the United States.

MORAL: Pottawatomie County. Christened by Brooks Walker for a moral issue: his success in keeping saloons out of the town.

MUSE: Laflore County. For Rev. Joseph Muse, a Baptist minister.

NON: Hughes County. Community title taken from the last syllable of John W. Cannon's name; he was the first postmaster.

OKAY: Muskogee County. Refers to the Okay Truck Manufacturing Company, and not to the state's nickname, as might be supposed.

OPTIMA: Texas County. This is from the Latin, meaning "best possible results," and reflected the optimistic outlook of the townspeople at the time the community was christened.

ORIENTA: Major County. Refers to the popular designation of the Kansas City, Mexico and Orient Railroad.

PAW PAW: Sequoyah County. Harks back to the Paw Paw Society, a secret organization with Southern sympathies during the Civil War.

PEEK: Ellis County. Salutes Vest Peek, a landowner.

PHARAOH: Okfuskee County. For O. J. Pharaoh, a rancher.

PINK: Pottawatomie County. Possibly acquired its name because surrounding communities had such "color" tags as Brown, Black, etc.

PLATTER: Bryan County. Remembers A. F. Platter, a businessman.

QUARTERMASTER: Custer County. For the creek, the stream having been named for James M. Bell, General Custer's quartermaster at the Battle of Washita.

RATTAN: Pushmataha County. Tagged by settlers from Rattan, Texas.

REDMOON: Roger Mills County. Honors a Cheyenne chief.

ROW: Delaware County. Pronounced "rou," this town was christened by James R. Wilson, first postmaster, because of the many fights and brawls (rows) taking place in the community's early days.

RUBOTTOM: Love County. Remembers William P. Rubottom, landowner.

SACRED HEART: Pottawatomie County. For the Sacred Heart Mission, established by Father Isidore Robot in 1876. "Mission" was dropped from the name in May 1888.

SALLISAW: Sequoyah County. From the French *salaisiau*, meaning "salt provision," and so named for the many salt deposits found along nearby streams.

SCRAPER: Cherokee County. Salutes Captain Archibald Scraper, a member of the Union Indian Brigade during the Civil War.

SENTINEL: Washita County. For an area newspaper, the *Herald Sentinel*.

SHADE: Texas County. For the Shade Well, which, in turn was christened for J. N. Shade, an official of the Rock Island Railroad.

SHADY POINT: Leflore County. Politics might have played a part in this community designation. First called Harrison, for then President Benjamin Harrison, a Republican. In 1896, the name was changed to Shady Point by the postmistress, a Mrs. Leonard, supposedly for the many shade trees situated along nearby railroad tracks. However, in 1896, Grover Cleveland was president, and he was a Democrat, the same party affiliation as Mrs. Leonard.

SICKLES: Caddo County. Recognizes Frank C. Sickles, land office registrar at El Reno.

SILO: Bryan County. For Albert B. "Silo" Gates, a resident.

SLAPOUT: Beaver County. By tradition, this community moniker came from an expression uttered by a store owner. It seems that just about every time a customer walked into the store to buy something, the storekeeper was always "slap out" of whatever the customer wanted.

SLEEPER: Cherokee County. Remembers Gid Sleeper, a cattleman.

SLICK: Creek County. Pays tribute to Thomas B. Slick, an oilman.

SLIM: McCurtain County. Honors "Slim" Herndon, a resident.

SNOW: Pushmataha County. Relates to George Snow, who was instrumental in having a post office set up here.

SULPHUR: Murray County. For the character of water found in a medicinal spring located in Platt National Park.

SUNKIST: Choctaw County. From the commercial name made popular in the orange industry.

TACK: Beckham County. For Tack Hodgson, son of the town site owner.

TANK: Mayes County. Refers to a water tank located on the Kansas, Oklahoma and Gulf Railroad.

TEACROSS: Harmon County. For the "T+" Ranch.

TI: Pittsburg County. Took its tag from the reversed initials of Indian Territory.

TIP: Mayes County. For William H. H. "Tip" Mayes, a Cherokee Indian.

TITANIC: Adair County. Refers to the ill-fated, "unsinkable" *Titanic*, the luxurious cruise ship that sank in the North Atlantic on April 14, 1912.

TRAIL: Dewey County. Harks back to the Trail Store, once located on the Dodge City cattle trail.

USNA: Cimarron County. Community label taken from the initials of United States of North America.

VICI: Dewey County. A whimsical handle, selected by Burt Vincent from the Latin phrase *Veni, vidi, vici,* "I came, I saw, I conquered."

VICTORY: Jackson County. Christened by residents to commemorate their victory in attaining a post office.

WHITE BEAD: Garvin County. Honors White Bead, a Caddo chief.

WHIZBANG: Osage County. This is a local name for the town of Denoya, and its designation comes from a magazine popular at the time, *Captain Billy's Whizbang.*

YEWED: Alfalfa County. When a community was first organized here, residents wanted it named Dewey, honoring Admiral George Dewey, hero of the Battle of Manila Bay. Postal authorities rejected the name because of duplication. The townspeople realized a semblance of success when they simply reversed the spelling of "Dewey" and came up with "Yewed," which the Post Office Department accepted.

Neverstil

Mist

Aloha Pleasant Home Tanks Cayuse Promise

Bridal Veil Idea Eightmile

Liberal Rhododendron

Yamhill Alms

New Era

Mount Angel

Fossil Monument Halfway

Sublimity Spray Cornucopia

Burnt Woods Haystack Horse Heaven Courtrock

Sweet Home

Otter Rock Grizzly Izee

Tangent Top Ironside

Sisters Brogan

Noti Bend

Swisshome

Pawn

Drain Brothers

Tenmile Tiara Arock

Starvout Paisley

Sixes Eolate Follyfarm

Steamboat

Lookingglass Yoncalla Blitzen

Remote Glide

Swastika Wagontire

Gold Hill

Plush

Persist

Wonder

Talent

AIMS: Clackamas County. Took its tag from the fact that it was the "aim" of citizens to establish a thriving community.

ALOHA: Washington County. Christened by Robert Caples in 1912, apparently because he liked the sound of this Hawaiian word.

AROCK: Malheur County. For a nearby rock, on which was picture writing said to be of Indian origin.

BEND: Deschutes County. For Farewell Bend, a point on the Deschutes River. The bend was so named because it was at this point that early travelers had their last glimpse of the river.

BLITZEN: Harney County. For the Donner and Blitzen River. The stream handle is taken from the German words for "thunder" and "lightning," and was named during the Snake War of 1864, when Colonel George B. Currey and his troops crossed the river during a heavy thunderstorm.

BRIDAL VEIL: Multnomah County. For the falls, which probably took its name from its appearance.

BROGAN: Malheur County. Community label has no relation to the heavy work shoe, having been named for D. M. Brogan, settler.

BROTHERS: Deschutes County. So named because so many brothers (male relatives, not religious) settled in the area.

BURNT WOODS: Lincoln County. Relates to a devastating forest fire that scarred timber hereabout.

CAYUSE: Umatilla County. Honors the Cayuse Indians. This is also the source for the term "cayuse," used when referring to an Indian pony.

CORNUCOPIA: Baker County. Tagged by miners from Cornucopia, Nevada. This term is derived from the Latin, meaning "horn of plenty," and expressed the expectation of the miners.

COURTROCK: Grant County. For a rock formation.

DRAIN: Douglas County. Remembers Charles Drain.

EIGHTMILE: Morrow County. For the canyon, which derived its name from the fact that the mouth of the canyon is about eight miles from the Columbia River.

FOLLYFARM: Malheur County. This name came about because J. H. Neal attempted to irrigate his farm under less than suitable conditions. Realizing his failure, and possessing a sense of humor, Neal christened his place "Neal's Folly." In time, Folly Farm was the popular name of the community. When a post office was granted, Neal suggested Folly Farm as the name; postal officials agreed, but united the two words into one.

FOSSIL: Wheeler County. Thomas B. Hoover was digging up fossils when a post office was placed on his ranch in February 1876. The coincidence gave him the idea of Fossil as the name for the facility, which the tiny hamlet also adopted.

GLIDE: Douglas County. Virginia C. Laird, first postmistress, was having a difficult time selecting a name for the new office. She happened to overhear her small son singing "The River Goes Gliding Along." Her problem was solved.

GOLD HILL: Jackson County. The village name reflects on the "Gold Hill Lode," which was located a short distance from the present town site. The amount of gold taken from this lode was so great that the exact wealth it produced isn't known even today.

GRIZZLY: Jefferson County. For the Grizzly Mountains.

HALFWAY: Baker County. The community was, at the time, situated halfway between two designated points.

HAYSTACK: Jefferson County. For the mountain, which was named for its shape.

HORSE HEAVEN: Jefferson County. This area acquired its name early in this century when the grass was truly a heaven for grazing horses. Over the years, drier climates, fencing, and overgrazing depleted the once-beautiful grassland.

IDEA: Gilliam County. When a handle for the post office was submitted, it was spelled "Ida," the name of the wife of a settler. By the time the title was officially recorded and returned, it had been changed to its present form.

IRONSIDE: Malheur County. For the mountain, which carried the name of an army officer who once bivouacked his cavalry unit near here.

ISOLATE: Douglas County. For its remote location.

IZEE: Grant County. For the "IZ" stock brand of M. N. Bonham.

LIBERAL: Clackamas County. For Liberal, Missouri.

LOOKINGGLASS: Douglas County. For the canyon. The valley was named by Hoy B. Flournoy, who explored the area around 1846. The site reminded him of a looking glass.

MIST: Columbia County. Descriptive of atmospheric conditions in the Nehalem Valley, where the settlement is located.

MONUMENT: Grant County. For a large, towering hill known as Monument Mountain.

MOUNT ANGEL: Clackamas County. Originally settled by German religionists; the name personifies their beliefs.

NEVERSTIL: Columbia County. This was once the site of repair shops for A. S. Kerry's logging railroad, and was supposedly designated by him for the noise and commotion generated by the shops.

NEW ERA: Clackamas County. One source claims that this community handle came about when the railroad was completed to this spot on the mouth of Parrott Creek, where boats could then stop and unload their cargo. This was viewed as a new era in river transportation, since it greatly reduced the distance boats had to travel. Another rendition is that the name was given the village by a local family, members of which were spiritualists, and inspiration for the name was a publication called *New Era*, of which they were devoted readers.

NOTI: Lane County. A rather traditional story is told about how this town received its name. In early days, a white man and an Indian were traveling through the Willamette Valley with only one horse between them. They had worked out a system whereby one would ride for a while, stop, tie the horse to a tree, and then walk ahead. When his companion reached the spot where the horse was tied, he would mount up and ride some distance beyond where his partner was walking, tie the horse, then continue on foot. This routine was to be repeated until they reached their destination. As the story continues, the white man had agreed to tie the horse at a spot where the town of Noti now stands. Instead, he continued his journey until he reached the city of Eugene. When the Indian arrived at the designated site, there was no horse. Realizing he had been double-crossed, the Indian supposedly uttered, "Him no tie!" Ergo, the source for the community name.

OTTER ROCK: Lincoln County. Believed to have been christened for sea otters that once were in abundance here.

PAISLEY: Lake County. The only conflict in the origin of this name seems to be over who the author really is. It was named for Paisley, Scotland, and not for the multicolored cloth, but Charles Mitchell and a Mr. Steel, both Scots, are each given credit for having selected the name.

PAWN: Lake County. This name, which is both a chess piece and a token of collateral, came about in a rather unique way. Long ago, four residents were responsible for having a post office put in place here. Those four individuals were named Poole, Akerley, Worthington, and Nolen. The townspeople honored the quartet by taking the first letter of each name and forming the word *Pawn*.

PERSIST: Jackson County. Some say the community label is a compliment to early settlers, applauding their "persistence" in taming the land, building settlements, schools, and so on. Others claim that the name came about because residents "persisted" for eighteen years before they were finally granted a post office.

PLEASANT HOME: Multnomah County. Descriptive.

PLUSH: Lake County. Named for a Piute Indian. How the Indian became known by such an unusual name is part of the community folklore. It seems that in times gone by the Indian was conned into a rigged poker game. One of the players dealt the novice a flush, a strong poker hand as any manipulator of the pasteboards is well aware. The only problem was, the dealer dealt another player a better hand. The Indian, in calling his cards, couldn't say "flush," and said "plush" instead. Thereafter, he was known as Plush and later, so was the hamlet.

PROMISE: Wallowa County. When this site was first settled by John C. Phillips and W. Mann in 1891, the latter called the place "Promised Land" and "Land of Promise." When a post office was established, it took the name Promise, as did the town.

REMOTE: Coos County. For its isolated location at the time of christening.

RHODODENDRON: Clackamas County. For the flower.

SISTERS: Deschutes County. For the Three Sisters Mountains, which were named for their similarity in size and shape.

SIXES: Curry County. For the river. Some people believe the stream refers to an Indian chief, while others opine that the name was derived from a Chinook Indian word meaning "friend."

SPRAY: Wheeler County. For John Fremont and Mary E. Spray, town founders.

STARVOUT: Douglas County. For the creek. The stream was named sometime in the 1850s, when George Walton was grubstaked by Hardy Eliff in a gold prospecting venture. Little, if any, gold was found, and after a severe winter, Walton abandoned his diggings. Residents said the prospector had been "starved out," and the name was given to the creek and later to the settlement.

STEAMBOAT: Douglas County. This term was used by early miners when referring to a mine that had not produced as expected. Apparently, this happened to a mine at the present site of Steamboat.

SUBLIMITY: Marion County. For sublime scenery.

SWASTIKA: Jackson County. For the swastika stock brand used by rancher C. E. Burton. Adolf Hitler and his madness probably forever hexed this onetime, pre-Roman symbol of good fortune.

SWEET HOME: Linn County. As legend has it, William Clark was visiting in the cabin of John Gilliland. Gazing at the serene, panoramic view of the Santiam Valley, Clark commented, "You certainly have a sweet home here, John." Thus, inspiration for a settlement name.

SWISSHOME: Lane County. So named when a family from Switzerland, Mr. and Mrs. Heinrich Zweilder, settled near the present site of the post office.

TALENT: Jackson County. For A. P. Talent, who platted the town.

TANGENT: Linn County. For the twenty-mile stretch of railroad track laid out in a straight line (tangent) that runs through the town.

TANKS: Umatilla County. For water tanks once used by freight haulers.

TENMILE: Douglas County. In pioneer days, a rancher used to drive cattle from his home in Happy Valley to this spot for grazing. The name Tenmile came about because it was ten miles from his home to this spot.

TIARA: Harney County. This is a term associated with a jeweled crown or headdress worn by women. The moniker was chosen for this village by Hill M. Bensen because it is situated at the "head" of a valley, and he considered the place a "jewel" in its setting.

TOP: Grant County. Honors Top Reasner, a resident.

WAGONTIRE: Harney County. This thriving metropolis of less than a half dozen residents was named for an old wagon tire that lay for years beside the road.

WONDER: Josephine County. In 1902, John T. Robertson established a store here. Residents called the place "Wonder Store" because they wondered where he expected to get his customers, since the area was so sparsely populated. This later became the hamlet's name, minus "Store."

YAMHILL: Yamhill County. Has nothing to do with sweet potatoes, taking its name from that of an Indian tribe, the Yamhela.

YONCALLA: Douglas County. For a mountain, the Indian translation of which means "haunt of eagles."

Pennsylvania
THE KEYSTONE STATE

North East

Torpedo
Complanter
Tuna
Cyclone
Spindlehouse
Roulette

Asylum
Toodleytown
Sugar Run
Hop Bottom
Starlight
Autumn Leaves

Transfer
Oil City
Allemagoozelum
Endeavor
Pigeon
Deadman's Corner
Cherry Tree
Climax
Turnip Hole
Pit Hole City
Turtle City
Slippery Rock
Crown
Big Run
Panic

Warpum
Harmony
Distant
Smoke run
Snow Shoe

Eighty Four
Coal Center
Lettrie
Prosperity
Library
Homestead
Glassport
Apollo
Nu Mine
Export
Green Tree
Large
Presto
Slickville
United
Plum
Black Lick
Loop
Chest Springs
Nanty Glo
Scalp Level
Drifting

Fallentimber
Defiance
Fairhope
Confluence
Broad Top
Burnt Cabins
Warriors Mark

Crucible
Indian Head
Shrock
Cleat Haven
Fairchance
Outcrop
Greenstone
New Freedom
Seven Stars
Airville
Railroad
Willow Street
New Garden
Media
Pilgrim Gardens
Darling
Mount Wolf
Red Lion
Peach Bottom
Smoketown
Ninepoints
Intercourse
Compass
Center Square
Flourtown
Bird in Hand
Blue Ball
Blue Bell
Broad Axe
King of Prussia
Doublingap
Union Deposit
Highspire
Pillow
Mary D
White Deer
Exchange
Mazeppa
Shaft
Seltzer
Ringtown
Light Street
Sugar Notch
Sugarloaf
Rough and Ready
Shickshinny
Forty Fort
Drums
Freeland
Delaware Water Gap
Skytop

Picture Rocks

Virginville
Yellow House
Dryville
Upper Black Eddy
Cooksy
Effort
Old Forge
Factoryville
Chinchilla
Funfony
Panther
Notch
White Horse

N

AIRVILLE: York County. Supposedly tagged for the surrounding clean, pure air.

ALLEMAGOOZELUM: Venango County. Two settlers were conversing, trying to see who could come up with the most outlandish name for their little community. One, who owned most of the land hereabout, suggested Allemagoozelum. He won the contest, hands down.

APOLLO: Armstrong County. Christened for the Greek god by Dr. Robert McKisson, a physician and student of mythology.

ASYLUM: Bradford County. This hamlet was established as a haven (asylum) for French revolutionary exiles in 1794. At one time, the colony comprised some 400,000 acres of land. Unfortunately, the colonists had been reared in the French aristocracy and were unable to adapt to the hard labor and sacrifices this new country of America demanded as prerequisites for survival. The colony was nothing more than a small settlement within a few years.

AUTUMN LEAVES: Wayne County. For the aroma and scenery provided during the fall when leaves cover the ground.

BIG RUN: Jefferson County. Labeled for a large stream (big run) that empties into Stump Creek.

BIRD IN HAND: Lancaster County. Relates to a hotel in place here at least as early as 1734. The inn had a sign in front that read, "A bird in the hand is worth two in the bush." At least four buildings have been erected on the hotel's original foundation, and at last count, a Bird In Hand hotel building was still standing.

BLACK LICK: Indiana County. For the dark-colored rocks located in a stream that deer and other animals used to favor because of salt deposits.

BLUE BALL: Lancaster County. For the 1700s Blue Ball Tavern, a favorite stopping place on the old Paxtang Road.

BLUE BELL: Montgomery County. Known as Pigeontown until 1840, when it was renamed for its present moniker, taking that from an inn located here around 1743.

BROAD AXE: Montgomery County. For an inn established here in the late 1700s. A sign outside the building depicted a broadax, square, and compass.

BROAD TOP: Huntingdon County. For the mountain, which is descriptive.

BURNT CABINS: Fulton County. This old community received its name prior to the American Revolution. The English made certain agreements with the Indians, which prohibited white settlement or movement west into certain designated sections. When whites violated the agreement and erected cabins on Indian lands, the

English provisional governor burned the cabins of the squatters. From that event evolved the town name.

CENTER SQUARE: Montgomery County. Supposedly relates to the time when two roads crossed at this point.

CHEAT HAVEN: Fayette County. For the Cheat River. The stream received its name because in early days, the water was subject to sudden risings. People attempting to cross at those times were often deceived (cheated) because of its treachery.

CHERRY TREE: Venango County. For Cherrytree Township, in which it is located. The township was christened for the abundance of cherry trees hereabout.

CHEST SPRINGS: Cambria County. Tagged for three springs and for the many "chestnut" trees in the vicinity.

CHINCHILLA: Lackawanna County. As legend has it, this village was named by George Tanner, first postmaster, because his wife owned a chinchilla coat.

CLIMAX: Clarion County. Harks back to the Climax Fire Brick Company, founded in 1840 and one of the oldest brick companies in the United States.

COAL CENTER: Washington County. Appropriately named, since this was once one of the largest coal producing centers in the world.

COMPASS: Chester County. For an old tavern that had a sign with a mariner's compass depicted on it.

CONFLUENCE: Somerset County. For its location at the junction (confluence) of three streams: Laurel and Casselman Creeks, and the Youghingheny River.

COPLAY: Lehigh County. The borough designation comes from a creek, which took its name from an old Indian word meaning "smooth-running stream"

CORNPLANTER: Warren County. Honors *Gar-gan-wah-gah*, a Seneca Indian chief called "The Cornplanter" by whites.

CROWN: Clarion County. In the 1880s, a post office was approved for this site, and postal authorities asked Joe Shillinger, a merchant, for a name. The storekeeper spied a spool of Crown thread on the counter.

CRUCIBLE: Greene County. Refers to the Crucible Mining Company.

CYCLONE: McKean County. For a cyclone that hit the area in 1884.

DARLING: Delaware County. The rural post office at this site is probably the smallest in the United States, yet letters flood into it around Valentine's Day for the "Darling" postmark. It was named for Jesse Darlington, the first postmaster. The shortened form was registered because another Darlington post office already existed.

DEADMANS CORNER: Forest County. Supposedly christened when two men fought a bitter battle and one of them died. A grave marks the spot either where the battle took place, or where the unfortunate combatant is buried.

DEFIANCE: Bedford County. Supposedly tagged for a fort built here at one time, the exact location of which is unknown.

DELAWARE WATER GAP: Monroe County. Takes its label from the water divide (gap) in the Blue Mountains.

DISTANT: Armstrong County. This was one of several names submitted to Washington postal officials, and was selected by them.

DOUBLINGGAP: Cumberland County. Named for the fact that two mountains meet here, and the "gaps double" up on each other.

DRIFTING: Clearfield County. This German settlement was titled for the snowdrifts that frequent the area.

DRUMS: Luzerne County. For Abram Drum, a tavern owner.

DRYVILLE: Berks County. Remembers Benjamin Dry, the first postmaster.

EFFORT: Monroe County. Christened for the great effort exerted to have a post office set up here.

EIGHTY FOUR: Washington County. Did this unusual community name come about because, as some believe, the post office was established here in 1884? Or, as others contend, was the name tagged to the settlement to honor Grover Cleveland's presidential election in the same year? There is a feeling that the naming predates both the post office and Cleveland's election, to the time postal workers threw mailbags from trains traveling between the villages of Clokeyville and Wylandville. This spot, at the time, was known as "Drop 84."

ENDEAVOR: Forest County. Relates to the Christian Endeavor Society, established here in the early 1900s by Rev. J. V. McAnich.

EXCHANGE: Montour County. For its location, where an early stage route horse-exchange station once existed.

EXPORT: Westmoreland County. So named because it was the first place in the region to mine coal for nonlocal (export) use.

FACTORYVILLE: Wyoming County. Harks back to a wool factory that opened here around 1825.

FAIRCHANCE: Fayette County. Believed to have acquired its title from the fact that once settlers made it to this point, they had a "fair chance" of reaching their western destination.

FAIRHOPE: Someset County. Citizens chose this name because they held a "fair hope" that the railroad would build through here.

FALLENTIMBER: Cambria County. Supposedly acquired its moniker after a heavy windstorm ripped through the area, uprooting much virgin timber.

FLOURTOWN: Montgomery County. Relates to the flour industry of earlier times.

FORTY FORT: Luzerne County. Remembers Forty Fort, a stockade built here around 1769, and named for the first forty Connecticut settlers coming into the area.

FREELAND: Luzerne County. This community label came about in the late 1860s. Freeland is built on land that was formerly the Joseph Birbeck farm. The farm was completely surrounded by land owned by coal mining companies. In 1868, Mr. A. Donop purchased the Birbeck farm and subdivided it into town plots. Since this was the only land around that was for sale, it was known as "free land." Donop named the town Freehold, which it held until a post office was set up in 1874. Postal officials requested that the name be changed to avoid conflict with Freehold, New Jersey.

FURLONG: Bucks County. So named simply because the word *furlong* happened to come up during the discussion on a community name.

GLASSPORT: Allegheny County. Refers to the United States Glass Company plant set up here in 1888.

GREEN TREE: Allegheny County. Took its moniker from a large sycamore tree that once grew here, and under which townspeople gathered to await the stagecoach carrying mail.

GREENSTONE: Adams County. For the green rock in the vicinity, which is used in making tennis court surfaces and roofing shingles.

HARMONY: Butler County. For an early communal settlement, the Harmony Society.

HIGHSPIRE: Dauphin County. This old village supposedly acquired its designation from a church spire that served as a landmark for boatmen sailing the Susquehanna River.

HOMESTEAD: Allegheny County. Town moniker more than likely relates to the Homestead Bank and Life Insurance Company, which laid out the site in 1871. Another tenet is that the community was christened for an early farmhouse known as the McClure homestead, but few accept this theory.

HOP BOTTOM: Susquehanna County. For the creek, which was named for the hops, used in brewing beer, that grew there.

INDIAN HEAD: Fayette County. For its location at the head of Indian Creek.

INTERCOURSE: Lancaster County. Versions abound as to the origin of this city's rather provocative (by today's terminology) name. One belief is that it came from a racetrack once located here, one entrance to which was marked "Enter course." Another rendition is that two famous roads, the Kings Highway and the Old Newport Road, intersected here, and the town was named for the intersection, or "intercourse." A feeling with much justification attributes the moniker, which was recorded in 1814, to the congeniality, mutual friendship, and people-to-people intermingling, commonly known as "intercourse" in early days, that existed at the time.

KING OF PRUSSIA: Montgomery County. For an early day inn.

LARGE: Westmoreland County. Family name.

LIBRARY: Allegheny County. Around 1833, residents of Loafers Hollow, wanting to better themselves, joined together and established a library of some 2,000 books in the home of John Moore, who also became the community's first librarian. Later that same year, a post office was set in place here. No longer wanting their home to be known as Loafers Hollow, the townspeople voted to change the name to Library, honoring their most beneficial endeavor of a few months earlier.

LIGHT STREET: Columbia County. Named by Rev. Marmaduke Pearce, who once lived on Light Street in Baltimore.

LOOP: Indiana County. For the bend (loop) in Mahoning Creek.

MARY D: Schuylkill County. Community tag derived from Mary Dee, daughter of a coal mine owner named Dee.

MAZEPPA: Northumberland County. Christened for the historical, true-to-life character in Lord Byron's poem by the same name. Ivan Mazeppa, who was born in the seventeenth century and died in 1709, was a Ukrainian hero, and the anniversary of his death is still celebrated by many of those of that heritage.

MEDIA: Delaware County. From the Latin, meaning "central," the community acquired its moniker for its location in the county.

MOUNT WOLF: York County. Derived from the family name of Wolf.

NANTY GLO: Cambria County. From the Welsh, meaning "coal brook," and relates to the coal mining region.

NEW FREEDOM: York County. First called Freedom, being named for the Free family, the name was changed to New Freedom to prevent duplication.

NEW GARDEN: Chester County. Hamlet was colonized in the early 1700s by Irish immigrants, who tagged it for their former home in County Carlow.

NINEPOINTS: Lancaster County. For the many roads that merged at this spot.

NORTH EAST: Erie County. Borough named for North East Township, in which it is located. The township received its name because of its situation in the northeastern section of the county.

NOTCH: Pike County. Named for a mountain gap (notch) near here.

NU MINE: Armstrong County. So labeled because it was the "newest" mine opened by a coal mining company. Why *Nu,* the thirteenth letter of the Greek alphabet, was chosen as the spelling is unknown, unless that number was significant.

OIL CITY: Venango County. Appropriately named, since it is the center of Pennsylvania's oil industry. Nearby Oil Creek, which has a natural petroleum outflow, was used by Seneca Indians as early as the mid-1600s as a source of "black gold." It was here in Oil City that John D. Rockefeller set up his first operation on the way to reaping a fortune in petroleum.

OLD FORGE: Lackawana County. Relates to an iron forge built here in 1789.

OUTCROP: Fayette County. Took its name from an "outcropping" of coal.

PANIC: Jefferson County. So named because a depression, or panic, was the concern at the time the small community was christened.

PANTHER: Pike County. For the bounty of panthers found here in early days.

PEACH BOTTOM: Lancaster County. For a peach orchard owned by John Kirk.

PICTURE ROCKS: Lycoming County. Borough tagged by settlers who found Indian pictures painted on rocks.

PIGEON: Forest County. Community is located in a heavily forested area and during the years 1868–1871, millions of wild pigeons roosted in the trees. The village took its handle from this migration phenomenon.

PILGRIM GARDENS: Delaware County. Named by the developer.

PILLOW: Dauphin County. Supposedly salutes Admiral Pillow.

PIT HOLE CITY: Venango County. For the creek, the stream being so named for a deep hole in the rocks along the creek bank.

PLUM: Allegheny County. For the creek, with the stream moniker probably coming from a growth of plum trees.

PRESTO: Allegheny County. Postal authorities requested a name change from the old name of Rosevale because of duplication. At a town meeting, the owner of the store in which the gathering was being held noticed a sack of Presto flour on one of his shelves. "Let's name the place Presto," was his suggestion, and so they did.

PROSPERITY: Washington County. Named by postal officials from exaggerated reports of prosperity by citizens wanting a post office.

RAILROAD: York County. First called Shrewsbury, the name had to be changed because of duplication. An oft-repeated saying by the townspeople was, "We're going to the railroad to meet . . ." So, they decided to call the place Railroad.

RED LION: York County. For a tavern.

RINGTOWN: Schuylkill County. Originally called Bittlersville. When a farmer secured a wagon wheel "ring" from a blacksmith, this was inspiration enough for residents to change the name.

ROUGH AND READY: Schuylkill County. Supposedly coined for the town in Calfornia, which honored General Zachary "Rough and Ready" Taylor.

ROULETTE: Potter County. No gambling here, the village having been named for Jean Roulette, an early French settler.

SCALP LEVEL: Cambria County. So designated when trees in the area were cut down, or "scalped."

SELTZER: Schuylkill County. Family name.

SEVEN STARS: Adams County. Remembers the Seven Star Tavern, located here in the 1830s–1840s. The history of the tavern name almost sounds spicy. Seems the owner had seven daughters who enticed and entertained men in the area, as well as passersby. One patron made a complimentary comment regarding their singing, calling them the "seven stars"; thus, the tavern name.

SHAFT: Schuylkill County. Named by the Susquehanna Mining Company when a shaft was sunk here in 1900 to haul coal to the surface.

SHICKSHINNY: Luzerne County. For the creek, which is a translation of the Algonquian word meaning "plenty turkeys."

SHINGLEHOUSE: Potter County. Relates to an old house built on this site in 1806 by a Frenchman, and sided with shingles.

SKYTOP: Monroe County. For its high elevation.

SLICKVILLE: Westmoreland County. Honors the superintendent of a coal mining firm.

SLIPPERY ROCK: Butler County. For the creek. The stream was named for a rock in the creek covered with algae, which made it extremely slippery. Up until several years ago, Slippery Rock College was known by few people outside this region. When, almost as a joke, a national television network sportscaster picked up the score off the wire service of a Slippery Rock football game, future renown was assured.

SMOCK: Fayette County. Family name.

SMOKERUN: Clearfield County. It is believed the community title comes from either the smoke puffed out by steam engines crossing the valley's railroad line in earlier days, or from the fog that covers the valley most of the time.

SMOKETOWN: Lancaster County. One belief on the origin of this town handle is that in early days, when a stagecoach stop was located here, Indian women sat on the porch of the stop and smoked pipes. Passengers referred to the place as Smoketown. Another version, one more acceptable, contends that trains used to stop near here to refill their water tanks. The smoke from the engines drifted down over this little hamlet; thus, the name.

SNOW SHOE: Centre County. This village name comes from one of two incidents of long ago. As legend has it, hunters were caught in a snowstorm around here and had to make snowshoes to get to the nearest settlement. The most likely rendition is that white explorers probably found some old snowshoes discarded by Indians.

STARLIGHT: Wayne County. Around 1890, a post office was established here. Authorities in Washington sent a book of names from which the townspeople were to choose a moniker. "Starlight" was the one agreed upon.

SUGAR NOTCH: Luzerne County. For the abundance of sugar maple trees growing in the gap (notch) of a nearby mountain.

SUGAR RUN: Bradford County. For maple groves located at the mouth of Sugar Run Creek.

SUGARLOAF: Luzerne County. For a nearby conical-shaped hill.

TENMILE: Washington County. For the creek. The stream was so named because it empties into the Monongahela River ten miles southwest of Brownsville.

TOODLEYTOWN: Bradford County. A name derivation of the Tuteloe Indians, who had a small village here around 1767.

TORPEDO: Warren County. There is some doubt as to the validity of the origin of this community name, but it is the only explanation to surface. In 1883, a wagon carrying nitroglycerin, known colloquially as "torpedo," became deeply mired in mud across a stretch of railroad track. Apparently the mud covered enough of the wagon's cargo to prevent an explosion, because it was hit by a train traveling at full speed, yet with little damage to the train. The hamlet located near the site of the explosion took its name from the incident.

TRANSFER: Mercer County. For its location at the junction of three railroads, each with a different-size track. Because of this, freight had to be "transferred" between the various railroads at this point.

TUNA: McKean County. Village acquired its name by shortening Tunuanguant, the title of a nearby creek.

TURKEY CITY: Clarion County. For Turkey Creek, with the stream probably named for wild turkeys in the vicinity.

TURNIP HOLE: Clarion County. This hamlet is located near the Clarion River. In that stream, near here, is an eddy, or whirlpool, referred to locally as a "turn hole." It is from corruption of "turn hole" that the settlement received its handle.

UNION DEPOSIT: Dauphin County. Originally called Union, or Unionville. In the mid- or late 1800s, the site became a deposit for grain and produce, and the name Union Deposit eventually evolved.

UNITED: Westmoreland County. Remembers the United Coke Company.

UPPER BLACK EDDY: Bucks County. For an eddy (water current) in the Delaware River at this point. Apparently, the water was also dark.

VIRGINVILLE: Berks County. For Maiden Creek. Both the stream and the village derived their names from the Indian word *ontelaunee*, meaning "virgin" or "maiden."

WAMPUM: Lawrence County. When the first white settlers entered this area in 1796, they found it populated by Delaware Indians. The settlement name was most likely derived from the Indian medium of exchange, wampum.

WARRIORS MARK: Huntingdon County. From old "markings" on trees in the area thought to have been carved by Indian warriors.

WHITE DEER: Union County. Christened when a white deer was killed here.

WHITE HORSE: Chester County. For an early tavern.

WILLOW STREET: Lancaster County. For its location on the road (street) south of Lancaster, which is lined with willow trees.

YELLOW HOUSE: Berks County. For the Yellow House Tavern that was, true to its name, a house painted yellow. At last report, the house is still standing and is still painted yellow.

Rhode Island

Little Rhody

Nooseneck

Westerly

Watch Hill

Block Island

BLOCK ISLAND: Washington County. Honors Adrian Block, an explorer.

NOOSENECK: Kent County. From information available, it appears that the Big River runs through a valley here and is split at one point by a section of land. It is at the split that a "running noose" was situated, but why is unknown. Since this is one of the highest points of land in the state, the place eventually acquired the name Nooseneck Hill. One other thought is that "Nooseneck" was derived from an Algonquian word meaning "beaver place."

WATCH HILL: Washington County. Although the name of this village is said to have been derived from the time early colonists used the hill as a watch to signal for oncoming enemies, some believe the tag goes back even earlier, when Indians were said to use the hill for the same purpose. Other thoughts as to the origin of the moniker revolve around an old watchtower once located here, or that it was derived from an Algonquian word meaning "mountain country," which would also be appropriate.

WESTERLY: Washington County. Appropriately named, since it is situated in the extreme western portion of the state.

South Carolina

The Palmetto State

BOUNTY LAND: Oconee County. Christened for the bounty lands granted to Revolutionary War veterans.

CAESARS HEAD: Greenville County. This mountain resort community received its name from a large granite rock located nearby. It is generally believed the stone was so named because an early mountaineer, traveling through the area, stopped to rest at this spot. Glancing up at the prominent rock formation, he was surprised at how the shape resembled the head of his dog, Caesar; thus, the name. A mountain legend contributes another version and does so in an intriguing, beautiful, mythological story. When the great Roman, Julius Caesar, was slain by Brutus and his fellow conspirators, the gods were so angered that they decided to erect a monument to the gallant and wise Caesar. This they did, but to chastise the Romans, they placed the memorial in a far land, which would go unvisited for many centuries. To punish Brutus, the gods saw to it that he was defeated and slain in the Battle of Philippi. Furthermore, the ghost of Brutus was to guard the monument to the murdered Caesar. Brutus's tenure as sentinel was not to be endless, however. He was to stand watch until the great rock was discovered by a later generation. Fifteen hundred years afterward, a Spaniard by the name of Don Fernandez Cordoze landed on the shores of what is now South Carolina, and he and his soldiers were captured by Indians. All of the Spaniards were slain except Cordoze, who was to be put to death in a special ceremony. Winona, daughter of the Indian chief, fell in love with the Latin stranger and helped him escape. The lovers headed north, toward a large chain of mountains, where they felt they would be safe. As they reached the peak of one of the rises, it seemed that an unseen hand grabbed the reins of Cordoze's horse and held them fast. Thus, the mountain monument to Julius Caesar was discovered, and the ghost of Brutus was freed from its punishment as sentry. The legend goes on that Winona and the Spaniard spent the rest of their lives living happily in the mountains. To make matters ironic, it seems Don Fernandez Cordoze was descended from an ancient Roman lineage, thus fulfilling the decree of the gods.

CENTENARY: Marion County. Refers to a church that, in turn, was so named because it was founded on the 100th anniversary (centennial) of the birth of Methodism.

CHARITY CHURCH: Berkeley County. For an old church once located here.

COWARD: Florence County. Family name.

COWPENS: Spartanburg County. Name comes from the cow pens once owned and operated by a man by the name of Hanna. In earlier times, such pens were used by drovers moving cattle, who

could, for a small fee, herd their stock into the pens for safety and thus enjoy a peaceful night's rest without worrying about their animals.

CRACKER NECK: Anderson County. So named because the strip of land on which the town is situated is shaped like a neck and borders the river across from Georgia, residents of which are known as "Crackers."

CROSS ANCHOR/CROSS KEYS: Spartanburg/Union Counties. These two communities are adjacent, and their foundings are interwoven. Long ago, a ship docked in the port of Charleston, and the vessel's captain and purser decided to journey to South Carolina's interior. After a long trip they arrived at a crossroads at this spot. Liking what they saw, they "dropped anchor." The purser, who is traditionally the keeper of the ship's keys, traveled on farther for five miles and made his camp on a knoll. The two men made a pledge that when their sailing days were over, they would return and build homes on these spots. True to their word, they did return and did build homes. Large rock chimneys were part of the structures, and on his chimney the captain placed his symbol, "crossed anchors," and the purser personalized his chimney with "crossed keys." Only a year or so later, the two men returned to their ship and were lost at sea, never to return to their landed estates. When communities grew up in the area, they took the names of the symbols the two seafarers had proudly placed on the stone smokestacks, which were still standing at the time.

DEADFALL: Newberry County. Supposedly this town acquired its handle from early day hangings that took place here. The victims were said to have taken a deadfall when dropped from the gallows with ropes around their necks.

DOCHENO: Abbeville County. Some skepticism exists as to the origin of the name of this Southern Railway stop. Seems a woman once boarded a train without buying a ticket. Later, when the conductor made his rounds, she had to confess that she had no ticket. The trainman, in an irritated voice, bellowed, "Madam, don't you know that everyone has to have a ticket?" The comment supposedly took place about where the stop is now located, and through corruption of the conductor's ". . . don't you know . . ." came Docheno.

DUE WEST: Abbeville County. It would appear that this community moniker has nothing to do with direction. Around 1777, a man by the name of De Witt lived here. Various pronunciations were given to the name, including Du Ett and Du Wet. Apparently, by the time the town was organized, De Witt's name had been corrupted to Due West, which the townspeople adopted.

EARLY BRANCH: Hampton County. For the stream, which was so named because, during the Civil War, General Jubal Early and some of his soldiers camped near the creek (branch).

FAIR PLAY: Oconee County. This community name dates far back and is said to have come about when two men, going at it rough and dirty in a fight, were encouraged to use fair play in their brawl.

FIFTY SIX: Kershaw County. For its location fifty-six miles from the city of Kershaw.

FINGERVILLE: Spartanburg County. For its founder, Joseph Finger.

FLOP EYE: Fairfield County. For a resident who had a "drooping eyelid."

FOLLY BEACH: Charleston County. In early English, *folly* meant "a clump of trees." That is the basis for the town's name.

FOUR HOLES: Orangeburg County. For the swamp. Seems the swamp came up with its tag from early days when there were four fords used for crossing before a bridge was built.

FROGMORE: Beaufort County. For an early plantation.

GREENSEA: Horry County. A descriptive name given in 1858 by Joseph Derham because the green, grassy area reminded him of his native Ireland.

HARDSCRABBLE: Anderson County. A term used in early days to denote land that was worthless or marginal for farming. To make a living was a "hard scrabble." It is assumed the community took its label from that fact.

HELL HOLE: Berkeley County. This little village received its handle in early times, when residents were active moonshiners. The "white lightnin'" produced here was so powerful that anyone drinking it thought they "were in hell."

LICK SKILLET: Aiken County. At one time, local townspeople went through rough times and had to "lick the skillet" clean to survive.

LUCKNOW: Lee County. More than likely received its name when a logging company official found a promising stand of virgin timber and exclaimed, "We are in luck now."

LUGOFF: Kershaw County. Remembers Count Lugoff, a Russian engineer who helped build the Seaboard Air Line Railway through here in 1899.

NINETY SIX: Greenwood County. For its location ninety-six miles from the principal town of the Cherokee Nation.

OLD HOUSE: Jasper County. For the creek, which was probably named for an old house once situated nearby.

OLD JOE: Berkeley County. The community name probably relates to an old black man, maybe a former slave, who once lived here.

OLD VAT: Berkeley County. For an old cattle vat once located here.

PEEDEE: Marion County. One source claims the moniker came from the initials of Patrick Daly, found carved on a tree near here. Another version is that it came from the Indian word *piri*, meaning "something good," or *mosapede*, meaning "hurry do."

PIGEON POINT: Beaufort County. This was once a roosting spot for wild pigeons.

PROMISED LAND: Abbeville County. This black community, established in 1871, was begun following the Civil War as an aid to former slaves. The commission set up to help the recently liberated people was said to have promised each family forty acres and a mule. The elegant Cedar Grove Plantation was bought by the commission, surveyed into forty-acre plots, and sold to the freedmen. The settlement then became known as Promised Land.

PROSPERITY: Newberry County. Originally known as Frog Level; it took its present name from a church.

PUMPKINTOWN: Pickens County. Early settlers were known for the large amount of corn and pumpkins grown in the area. One day, during a "corn shucking," discussion was held as to a name for the community. One well-inebriated soul stood up, waved his arms over the fertile scene before him, and bellowed, "Men, jest quit arguin' 'bout the whole thing and jest call 'er Pumpkin Town!"

QUICKTOWN: Orangeburg County. Honors Reverend Quick, an early day black preacher.

RAZORVILLE: Colleton County. More than likely derived its name from that of an early doctor, Thomas Raysor.

ROUND O: Colleton County. A conference between whites and Indians was once held here. One of the Indian negotiators had a large white circle painted on his chest. The village took its name from the symbol.

SECESSIONVILLE: Charleston County. Way back, area planters moved their families from the plantations during the summer to avoid "country fever" (malaria). Their haven away from home was a place called Fort Johnson. The road used for the migration was long, hot, and rutted, making travel by horse and buggy extremely difficult and uncomfortable. Some of the travelers decided that another place, one more accessible, would be most desirable. The site selected was called Stent's Point. Several families built homes here and moved in. Those remaining faithful to Fort Johnson chided the Stent's Pointers, ridiculing them as "secessionists." The criticism was answered by the new developers when they

changed the name of their settlement from Stent's Point to
Secessionville.

SILVERSTREET: Newberry County. Assumably, the community was so
christened when the sun striking silver maple leaves caused someone to compare the scene to a "silver street."

SIX MILE: Pickens County. For the creek; the stream became so called
because it was located six miles from the town of Keowee, on the
old Cherokee Trading Path.

SLABTOWN: Anderson County. In early days, boards (slabs) were
used to build sheds, outhouses, and other buildings. A traveler
passing through noticed the widespread use of such boards and
referred to the place as Slabtown. The name stuck.

SOCIETY HILL: Darlington County. The St. David's Society was established on a hill here in December 1778. Later, when other settlers
moved into the hilly region and formed a community, they named
it Society Hill.

SOUTH OF THE BORDER: Dillon County. While this site is not really
a residential settlement, it is, nevertheless, a community in every
sense of the word. With its own fire and police departments, shopping center, motel, and so on, South of the Border (so named
because it is just south of the North Carolina–South Carolina line)
is a self-contained amusement center that beckons to anyone and
everyone traveling the area.

STARTEX: Spartanburg County. Relates to Startex Mills, a textile
plant.

SWANSEA: Lexington County. This is probably a corruption of the
German *zwanzig*. Early in the village's history, a German ran a
store here. When passersby stopped to ask how many miles it was
to Columbia, the storekeeper responded, *Zwanzig* ("twenty").

TEN MILE HILL: Berkeley County. For an early tavern.

THREE C'S: Kershaw County. This tiny hamlet acquired its moniker
from the Charleston, Cincinnati and Chicago Railroad, popularly
known as the Three C's.

TICKVILLE: Berkeley County. Took its name from the large number of
ticks found in nearby woods.

TRIO: Williamsburg County. The name is pronounced "Try-o."
Sources available, however, state it was named for a trio of men—
W. D., W. E., and James Bryan—who established the post office
here.

WHITE ROCK: Richland County. For a grouping of white-colored
rocks.

WHITE STONE: Spartanburg County. For the hue of native rock.

WIDEAWAKE: Charleston County. Around the turn of the century, a merchant opened a store in this small village. He informed his customers that he was always "wide awake" to business opportunities. Thus, the community name.

WILDHOG: Oconee County. Derived from the time when a number of traders stole some hogs. They were later caught, brought to trial, and freed, their defense being that the hogs belonged to no one, that they were "wild," thus could not be considered stolen property.

WOLF STAKE: Oconee County. Could have taken its handle from the fact that stakes were driven around large pits to confine trapped wolves, which once roamed freely in this region.

YELLOW HOUSE: Berkeley County. Received its title either from a yellow house situated on a nearby hill, or from a tavern once located here.

South Dakota

THE COYOTE STATE

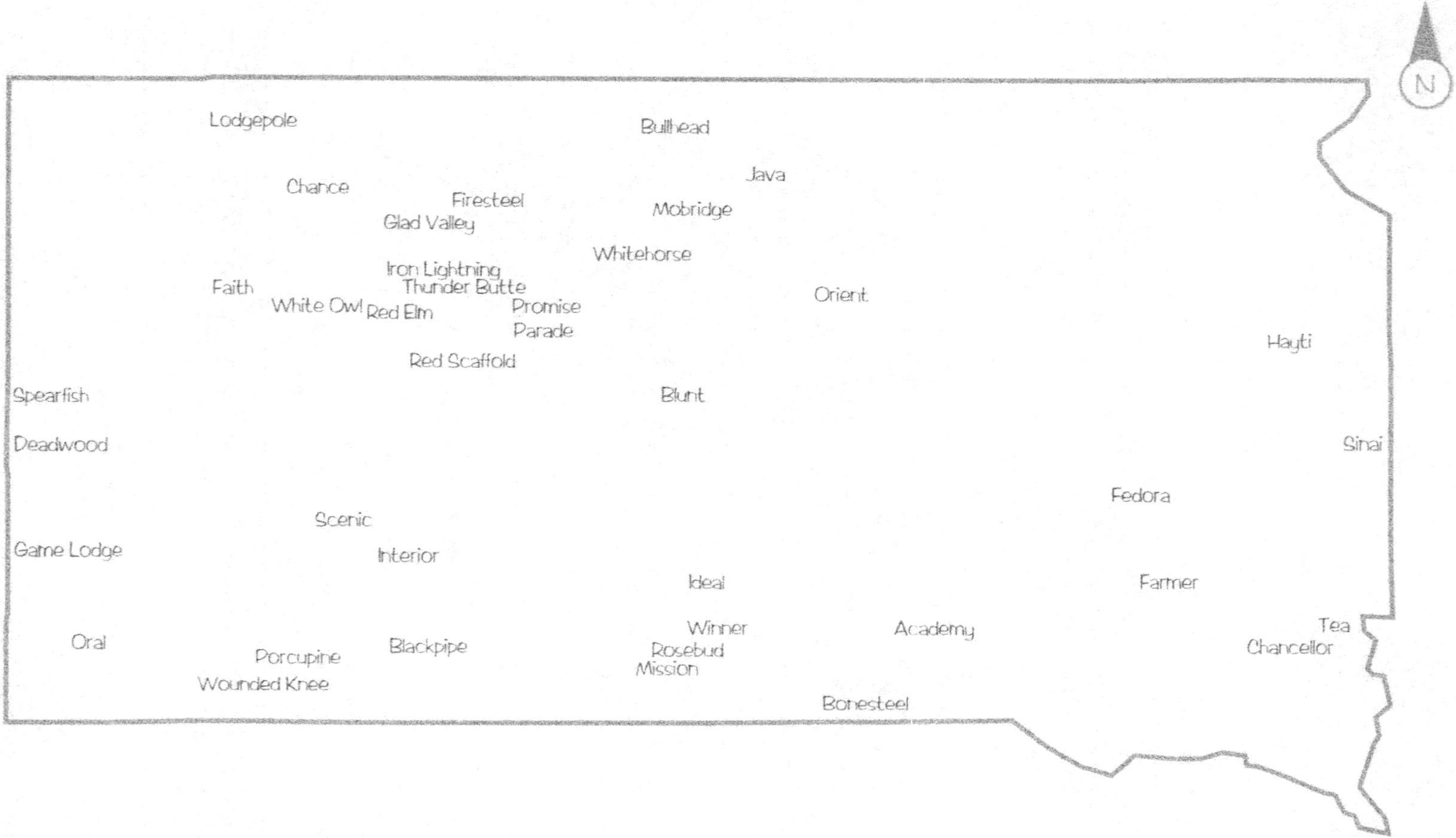

Lodgepole

Spearfish

Deadwood

Game Lodge

Oral

Porcupine
Wounded Knee

Chance

Faith
White Owl Red Elm

Glad Valley
Firesteel

Iron Lightning
Thunder Butte
Promise
Parade

Scenic

Interior

Red Scaffold

Blackpipe

Bullhead

Mobridge

Whitehorse

Java

Blunt

Ideal

Winner
Rosebud
Mission

Academy

Orient

Bonesteel

Farmer

Fedora

Hayti

Sinai

Tea
Chancellor

N

ACADEMY: Charles Mix County. Relates to a congregationalist school, Ward Academy, established here in 1893.

BLACKPIPE: Bennett County. For the Blackpipe Day School, which derived its moniker from a creek.

BLUNT: Hughes County. Remembers John E. Blunt, chief engineer for the North Western Railroad.

BONESTEEL: Gregory County. Honors H. E. Bonesteel, a settler.

BULLHEAD: Corson County. Salutes Seth Bullhead, a miner and marshal.

CHANCE: Perkins County. One belief on the origin of this community name is that it comes from the Chance Ranch. Tom Veal, owner, so named it because he figured it was his last chance to make a go of things. Another version is that the townspeople felt they had no chance of getting a post office (but they did).

CHANCELLOR: Turner County. Christened by German settlers for Prince Otto von Bismarck, the Iron Chancellor of Germany.

DEADWOOD: Lawrence County. A famous town out of the Old West, it was tagged for the dead and decayed wood found in a gulch. Western, or cowboy, advocates can readily recognize many familiar names associated with the town of Deadwood: Wild Bill Hickock, Jack McCall (the man who killed Wild Bill), and Calamity Jane, to mention just a few.

FAITH: Meade County. Moniker came about either because of the faith of early pioneers, or for Faith Rockefeller, daughter of one of the principal stockholders in the Milwaukee Railroad.

FARMER: Hanson County. Designated by Joseph Altenhofer because he viewed the settlement as a paradise for, and one that would be supported by, farmers.

FEDORA: Miner County. Some believe this hamlet name honors the wife of a railroad clerk. Another rendition is that when Christopher Wilson opened a store here, one of the most popular items in stock was the fedora hat. Citizens liked the name so well that they petitioned to have their town named Fedora.

FIRESTEEL: Dewey County. Took its title from the creek, which was named by Indians because they found flints along the stream that they used to strike against "steel" to make "fire."

GAME LODGE: Custer County. This resort, the summer home of President Calvin Coolidge in 1927, received its tag from the fact that the first building erected here was to be a hunting lodge and residence/headquarters for the state game warden.

GLAD VALLEY: Ziebach County. For the valley.

HAYTI: Hamlin County. While at first this community name might seem a corruption of the island of Haiti, there is no relation between the two. The moniker could have come about because of its originality; or it may have been taken from an early day "hay" dealer by the name of "Tie." A more logical explanation is that long ago, during heavy blizzards, settlers supplemented their heat by using a third stove with hay as fuel. A machine twisted the hay into a compact bale and fed it into the stove. The pioneers were partial to those old stoves, and when time came for them to christen their small community, they submitted the name Haytie, which is what they fondly called their "hay-burners." A Washington official, however, thought the citizens wanted to name their town for the Caribbean island, so he returned the recorded name as Hayti.

IDEAL: Tripp County. For its location in what is generally considered ideal farming territory.

INTERIOR: Jackson County. Originally called Black, cowhands objected to that name, and it was changed to reflect the town's geographic location.

IRON LIGHTNING: Ziebach County. Salutes a famous Indian chief who served under Sitting Bull at the Battle of Little Big Horn in 1876.

JAVA: Walworth County. This town was christened, according to at least one source, by officials of the Milwaukee Railroad, and is often called Coffee Town. Whether or not Java was designated because it is a slang expression for coffee is unknown. Another source, however, states that the community was named because a man put up a coffee shack near the railroad siding. Railroad workers began referring to the small place as Java, and the town later took the name.

LODGEPOLE: Perkins County. For the creek, which was tagged for some buttes.

MISSION: Todd County. For an Episcopal mission.

MOBRIDGE: Walworth County. In 1906, the Milwaukee Railroad laid track through here. A telegrapher was stationed at this site to send in daily reports of progress. Since the place had no name, the telegrapher signed the reports "Missouri Bridge." As days passed, and more reports were sent in, the operator began signing the wires "Mo. Bridge." From that time on, the site has been referred to by that name, with citizens later dropping the period and combining the words.

ORAL: Fall River County. Some think the spot was named for a son of the first postmaster. Others claim that with a name such as *Oral*, which means "spoken," people would no longer just point to the site, but would "speak" its name.

ORIENT: Faulk County. This was one of five names submitted for consideration as a community name.

PARADE: Dewey County. First called Paradis, for George Paradis. There was another town by the same name in South Dakota, so citizens simply changed the name of their settlement to Parade.

PORCUPINE: Shannon County. Either tagged for the number of porcupines found in the vicinity or for Porcupine Butte.

PROMISE: Dewey County. Named through error. An early settler was an Indian minister by the name of Wahoyapi. Translation of his name was "once called," but a mistake in translation by a Washington official resulted in Promise.

RED ELM: Ziebach County. For a variety of elm trees.

RED SCAFFOLD: Ziebach County. For the creek. The stream apparently acquired its name when two Indian women, quarreling over a man, killed each other near the stream and were laid side by side on a scaffold painted red.

ROSEBUD: Todd County. For a short time this site was called Spotted Tail Agency, having been named for an Indian chief. The name was changed to Rosebud for the abundance of wild roses in the vicinity.

SCENIC: Pennington County. For the panoramic view the community offers of the surrounding White River Badlands, a favorite visiting spot for tourists and natives alike.

SINAI: Brookings County. For its surroundings, which are claimed to resemble the Sinai region in Egypt.

SPEARFISH: Lawrence County. For the creek. The stream possibly received its name when two men were standing on the bank and one of them said, "This would be a good place to spear a fish." Maybe the stream name came about because Indians used to spear fish here.

TEA: Lincoln County. At a meeting called to select a name for the settlement, a suggestion was made to call it Beer, for the favorite beverage of the citizens. The name was turned down because they were afraid it would reflect negatively on the town. Tea was suggested and accepted as a compromise beverage name. Another rendition is that after much discussion for a name, and with no decision forthcoming, one attendee called out that it was "teatime."

THUNDER BUTTE: Ziebach County. For nearby Thunder Butte.

WHITE OWL: Meade County. For the creek, with the stream being named simply to distinguish it from Red Owl Creek, which it eventually joins.

WHITEHORSE: Dewey County. Honors an Indian chief.

WINNER: Tripp County. When the North Western Railroad began construction through the area, this community was the first to be established along the right of way; thus, it was the winner.

WOUNDED KNEE: Shannon County. This historical spot, once a trading post and made famous as the site of the last official battle between the Indians and the white men, was named for a creek. The stream acquired its name when, on the creek bank, an Oglala Sioux was wounded in the knee during a battle with a band of Crow Indians.

Tennessee

THE VOLUNTEER STATE

Potreck

Red Boiling Springs

Iron Valley
Indian Mound

Sugar Grove

Memorial

Gold Dust
Golden Grove
Friendship
Lickskillet
Leighton Corner Camp Creek
Big Hill
Gift

Old Hometown

Skullbone
Hollow Rock

Hurricane Mills

Frog Jump

Finger

Sugar Tree

Five Points
Harms
Minor Hill Iron City

Only
Spot

Mud Tavern

Theta Lickskillet Bell Buckle

Wartrace

Daylight

Readyville

Canyon

Defeated
Difficult

Nettle Corner

Silver Point Big Lick Purdy

Seven Springs

Petros

Cracker Neck
Ozone

Peaked Chestnut

Ten Mile

Sunbright

Pall Mall

Jellico Hell
Reliance
Ducktown
Turtletown

Mascot Alcoa
Greenback Brick Mill
Friendsville

Progeny Forge

Strawberry Plains

Bean Station Bulls Gap

Flag Pond

Pressmens Home
Devils Kitchen

Laurel Bloomery

ALCOA: Blount County. For the Aluminum Company of America, which has a plant here.

BEAN STATION: Grainger County. This community, located near the old Daniel Boone and Great Indian Warpath trails, was first settled by three brothers named Bean.

BELL BUCKLE: Bedford County. One idea on how the community acquired its unusual title is that a large cowbell with its buckle was found here by early settlers. Another is that a bell and buckle were found carved in a tree. Prior to settlement of this area, agents were sent into the region to classify the land. Ground suitable for farming was designated by carving a plow in the trees. Land better for grazing was denoted by carving a cowbell and buckle.

BELLS: Crockett County. For John and William Bell, landowners.

BIG LICK: Cumberland County. For a salt lick. Once called Deer Lick, with the passage of time the lick grew larger and residents changed the name to its present designation.

BRICK MILL: Blount County. For a large brick house, still standing, that once served as Union headquarters during the Civil War.

BUCKSNORT: Hickman County. The most reasonable explanation for the origin of this moniker is that it comes from the time when a particular male deer (buck) came into the area early in the morning, and would stomp and "snort." The more lyrical origin revolves around a man supposedly named Buck Duke, who settled on Sugar Creek to make his enticing brand of "snort." The waters from the stream, according to Buck, gave "him a head start on fermenting ground and corn" for his product. The settlement acquired its name from the fact that husbands often told their wives that they were going to "see Buck to get some snort."

BULLS GAP: Hawkins County. Takes its moniker from an opening (gap) in Clinch Mountain, which was named for John Bull. Bull was the early gunsmith who made the famous Tennessee long rifles.

CAMPAIGN: Warren County. Probably remembers Galvin Campaign, a resident.

CRACKER NECK: Cumberland County. Lore has it that this tag stems from the time a Tory spy was captured here during the Revolutionary War and hanged from a tree. The community name probably alludes to a "cracked neck."

CURVE: Lauderdale County. Relates to a wide curve in the Jeff Davis Highway.

DAYLIGHT: Warren County. When this place was only a hamlet, three men—Oliver Towles, Harvey Dodd, and U.S. Knight—were discussing a name for the settlement. Knight suggested it be named for him, but Dodd disagreed, saying he would rather call it "Daylight" than Knight. Another contention is that Daylight was one of three names submitted to postal officials, but why it was recommended no one knows.

DEFEATED: Smith County. For the creek. The stream was so named because a hunting party was once badly defeated in a battle with Indians in the area.

DEVILS KITCHEN: Johnson County. This village is located in a hollow, and the moniker is supposed to have originated when some men were cooking supper and later swore they saw the devil himself appear. Opinion is that the "devil" was brought on by an overconsumption of moonshine.

DIFFICULT: Smith County. Could have acquired this name from postal authorities because the first name submitted was too difficult to handle. Another thought is that it was named before roads were paved, and it was difficult to maneuver up the steep hill to reach the settlement.

DRY HILL: Lauderdale County. Village possibly acquired its designation from the fact that there was once a stagecoach rest stop here, but no water for either passengers or horses.

DUCKTOWN: Polk County. Possibly named for Cawoneh, a Cherokee Indian chief whose name, when translated into English, meant "duck."

FINGER: McNairy County. Around the turn of the century, a group met to decide on a name for their newly organized town. The meeting lasted several hours and became heated. One man rose and, trying to make a point, aimed his finger at the group. Another man stood and, after quieting the crowd, stated he had noticed the gesture made by the other man and recommended they call the place Finger. Everyone agreed. Finger is the birthplace of Buford Pusser, county sheriff of *Walking Tall* fame.

FIVE POINTS: Lawrence County. This wee spot was first known as Deer Crossing then, for a short time, by the unique name of Lizard Trot. In the 1920s, during road construction, a workman suggested the name Five Points for the five roads that intersected at this site.

FLAG POND: Unicoi County. So named because the area was once dotted with small ponds, bordered with flowers known as blue flags (irises).

FRIENDSHIP: Crockett County. This town was established in 1844. Prior to that date two stores opened about a mile apart. The Post Office Department decided to set up an office in the community, to be located in one of the stores. For the convenience and benefit of the residents, the owners moved their stores to the center of the settlement. For this display of amiability, postal officials named the new facility Friendship. At last acknowledgment, the town symbol was two hands clasped in friendship.

FRIENDSVILLE: Blount County. Settled by the Society of Friends (Quakers).

FROG JUMP: Gibson County. Settlers entered the area in the 1820s and came to the banks of the Forked Deer River. One bend in the stream was so sharp that not only was it not navigable, it was possible for a "frog to jump" from one part of the river to another without touching the ground. Although a canal has been dug to connect the two parts of the river, the village still goes by the name of Frog Jump.

GIFT: Tipton County. Refers to William R. Gift, a store owner.

GLIMP: Lauderdale County. Refers to John Glimp, postmaster.

GOLDDUST: Lauderdale County. Christened for a Mississippi River steamboat. As the story goes, the ship ran out of wood for fuel near here, and the captain, spying cabins on a coastal bluff, asked residents for wood. They complied, and he thereafter made this a regular refueling stop, thus bringing cash to the small hamlet.

GREENBACK: Loudon County. Relates to the Greenback political party, active in post–Civil War days, which advocated the printing of money as a way to reduce inflated farm prices.

HARMS: Lincoln County. Family name.

HOLLOW ROCK: Carroll County. Relates to a large, hollow rock. It is said the hollow space is big enough to hide a man.

HURRICANE MILLS: Humphreys County. For the creek. The stream was named by a Mr. Anderson because of the swiftness of the water. Anderson owned a farm and dammed the water to provide power for a grain grinding mill; thus, Hurricane Mills.

INDIAN MOUND: Stewart County. For Indian burial mounds.

IRON CITY: Lawrence County. For an iron ore mine in production here in the early 1900s.

IRON VALLEY: Stewart County. For iron ore found in the valley hills.

JEFFREYS HELL: Monroe County. In the long ago, this was an untamed region, hilly and heavily forested. One day a hunter named Jeffrey wandered from camp and became lost, not being found for two days. When his companions asked where he had been, his reply was, "I don't know, but I have been in hell!"

KEY CORNER: Lauderdale County. Settlement acquired its handle when early surveyors carved a "keystone" in a large sycamore tree and called it the key corner of their survey.

LAUREL BLOOMERY: Johnson County. Took its handle from coke ovens, called "bloomers," because they resembled blooming "roses."

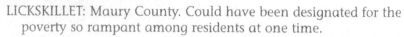

LICKSKILLET: Maury County. Could have been designated for the poverty so rampant among residents at one time.

LIGHTFOOT: Lauderdale County. Family name.

MASCOT: Knox County. Some claim the American Zinc Company of Tennessee christened this site by using a combination of letters from the company name: Am, Z, Co, T. Another thought is that the town was originally known as Meek. This was not appealing, in the minds of the townfolk, for a prosperous community. A Mrs. McMillan, wife of one of the original settlers, had lost a cat that she called her mascot. She suggested Mascot for the community name, and it was accepted.

MEMORIAL: Clay County. For the Austin Peay Memorial Highway.

MINOR HILL: Giles County. Relates to the Minor family.

MUD TAVERN: Davidson County. Remembers an old tavern that once stood here, built of logs filled with mud, and the inside smeared with mud to prevent the fireplace from catching fire. History tells us that Andrew Jackson spent a couple of nights in the tavern on his way to Kentucky for a duel with Charles Dickinson, who had insulted Jackson's beloved Rachael.

NETTLE CARRIER: Overton County. For the creek. Indian legend carries forth that in earlier days two braves were in love with the same maiden. The village chief was asked to select the right man for the woman. The chief decided to hold a contest to determine the winner. The braves were to throw a twig into the creek and the brave whose twig was carried the farthest could have the maiden's hand in marriage. One Indian threw a thorn into the water, while the other tossed in a nettle. The "nettle" was "carried" the farthest, so he won, and from that time forward the creek was known as Nettle Carrier.

OLD HOMETOWN: Shelby County. Remembers a filling station and restaurant situated here called Old Home Town, and operated by Jimmie Hurston.

ONLY: Hickman County. First known as Dreamer. One version contends that the name was changed because of duplication, and the new name so designated because it was the only one like it. Another claim is that the name was changed from Dreamer because residents feared people would think the community was asleep. Only came up because a storekeeper, when asked the price of merchandise, always replied, "It's only. . . ."

OZONE: Cumberland County. For its fresh, clean air.

PALL MALL: Fentress County. Relates to the famous street in London, England. John M. Clemens, father of Samuel Clemens (a.k.a. Mark Twain), opened the post office here in April 1832.

PEALED CHESTNUT: White County. For Pealed Chestnut Academy, established here around 1845.

PETROS: Morgan County. This is a form of the word *Petra*, the name of an ancient city, the ruins of which are in the Middle Eastern country of Jordan. This little coal mining hamlet is thought to have derived its label, however, from parts of the names of Governor Peter Turner and a man named Ross.

PIGEON FORGE: Sevier County. Refers to an iron foundry (forge) once situated on the Little Pigeon River.

POTNECK: Stewart County. As legend has it, this hamlet received its title from a sorceress who once lived here and had a large goiter (gland deformity) on her neck.

PRESSMENS HOME: Hawkins County. This small, private community was established by the International Printing Pressmen and Assistants Union. Its primary purpose was to educate and train people in the printing industry and provide care and comfort for retirees.

READYVILLE: Cannon County. Honors Charles Ready, the first postmaster.

RED BOILING SPRINGS: Macon County. Around 1840, Shepherd Kirby and his family arrived at a small settlement here. Kirby had long suffered from an eye infection, and one day, while working in the fields, he felt intense pain. Walking to a nearby spring, he bathed his eyes, and the pain disappeared almost immediately. Within a few days, and following more eye baths, the infection was completely healed. The wonders of the miraculous curative powers of the spring spread far and wide and led to a vast health spa being set up on the premises. The nearby community took the name Red Boiling Springs from the spa. The red coloring of the water, coming from underground hot spots, accounts for the name of the spring.

RELIANCE: Polk County. First known as Higdon Junction, for the Higdon family. It was then a railroad stop, and when the Higdons became involved in a feud with railroad officials, the latter asked Mrs. Sarah Vaughn, postmistress, to rename the village. She named it Reliance, for no particular reason other than seeing what had happened when a place carried a family name, and she didn't want the Vaughn name disgraced.

RUGBY: Morgan County. Thomas Hughes, author of *Tom Brown's School Days*, named this village, taking the tag from the school in his book.

SEVEN SPRINGS: DeKalb County. Christened for a health resort, the springs of which contained seven kinds of mineral water.

SILVER POINT: Putnam County. Originally known as Head of the Valley, for its location overlooking Buffalo Valley. A petition for a post office was denied because the name was too long to fit on a postage stamp. Citizens were advised they could resubmit the application if they provided a shorter name. One day, several men were sitting on the porch of a local store discussing possible names. A stranger rode up and, remaining on his horse, listened as the men talked. The rider looked off into the distance just as the sun was going down on the horizon. There happened to be a barn nearby with a new tin roof. The setting sun hit the roof brightly, causing the stranger to comment, "That looks like a silver point over there, doesn't it?"

SKULLBONE: Gibson County. This little community was founded in 1839 by Henry Dowland. From almost the beginning the village became the site of bare knuckle fights that continued as part of the social attraction until around 1900. The place name came from the strange rule of the fights that permitted opponents to strike each other only on the head. Any blows below the collar were fouls, and all fights were to the finish—no time limit was imposed.

SPOT: Hickman County. In earlier times, when this site was only a small, unnamed settlement, one of its residents traveled north. Having stopped at a hotel, the man was filling out the register when he came across a section of the form that asked for his home address. Pausing because the community didn't have a name, the ink pen in his hand leaked and dropped a blot on the paper. The innkeeper, seeing the blot, smiled and asked, "Where are you from? Spot?" The man signed that as his address, and when he returned home and informed other residents of what had transpired, they decided that name was as good as any other.

STRAWBERRY PLAINS: Jefferson County. For the abundance of wild strawberries in the area.

SUGAR GROVE: Sumner County. Took its label from a one-acre tract of sugar maple trees.

SUGAR TREE: Perry County. For the large number of sugar maple trees in the vicinity.

SUNBRIGHT: Morgan County. The generally accepted origin for this moniker is that one day a convict, who was working on the railroad, stood on a nearby hill and looked over the land spread out in front of him. In a loud voice he proclaimed, "Sun bright."

TEN MILE: Rhea County. For the creek. The stream was named for its location ten miles from its source to its demise, at Sewee Creek.

THETA: Maury County. Village named by John R. Ragsdale after the thirteenth letter of the Greek alphabet, for reasons unknown.

TURTLETOWN: Polk County. Honors a Cherokee chief.

WARTRACE: Bedford County. For an old war trail (trace) once used
by Indians that is situated near here.

Texas

THE LONE STAR STATE

ACE: Polk County. Remembers Ace Emanuel, the first postmaster.

AIR TERMINAL: Midland County. Originally known as Terminal. Once the site of an air base, it was sold to the city during World War II, and the barracks were converted to apartment houses.

ANDICE: Williamson County. The name submitted to postal authorities was Audice, for Audice Newton, son of an early settler. The word was misspelled somewhere along the line, and Andice was recorded as the town name.

ART: Mason County. Known as Plehweville when postal officials requested the name be changed for simplification, preferably to a three-letter word. "Art" was chosen by citizens, the general consensus being that there was no significance to the selection. Some believe, however, that the name was taken from the last three letters of the name of the postmaster at the time, a Mr. Dechart.

BABY HEAD: Llano County. For the mountain. The mountain received this very unusual name around 1850, when a Comanche raiding party kidnapped a white baby and later, after killing the infant, decapitated it and mounted the head on a pole and placed it on the mountain, where it was found by settlers.

BACHELOR: Kaufman County. Two bachelor brothers founded the settlement.

BALD PRAIRIE: Robertson County. A descriptive name, for its location on a treeless plain.

BANGS: Brown County. Remembers Samuel Bangs, who owned the land on which the town was built.

BANKERSMITH: Gillespie County. Temple D. Smith was founder of the first bank in the city of Fredericksburg. He was popularly known as Banker Smith.

BANQUETE: Nueces County. Spanish for "banquet." One belief for the name origin is that it came from a feast held to celebrate the completion of a road linking the Nueces River with the Rio Grande, and the city of San Patricio, Texas, with Matamoras, Mexico. Another tenet, however, contends that the name came about from a feast put on by Mexicans when they greeted Irish settlers to this area in 1832.

BEBE: Gonzales County. This community had no name prior to a post office being approved for the site. Needing a title, a store owner looked at one of the shelves in his store and saw a can of Bebee Baking Powder. With a slight alteration in spelling, the community name was born.

BEE CAVES: Travis County. Founded around 1870 by Will Johnson and appropriately named, for a large cave of wild bees discovered nearby.

BEE HOUSE: Coryell County. When the first settlers arrived here, they discovered cliffs and caves full of beehives. They erected a community house and named it Bee House Hall. Later, when application for a post office was sent to Washington, they suggested the name Bee House.

BELLS: Grayson County. Originally called Gospel Ridge, for the large number of churches located here. Each of the churches had a bell, so when application for a post office was made, the name Bells was sent in, and it was accepted.

BEN BOLT: Jim Wells County. On September 2, 1843, the *New York Mirror* published a four-line poem, "Ben Bolt," written by Dr. Thomas Dunn English. Later, the poem was expanded in length, put to music, and made the theme of a play presented in New York. It reached its height of popularity during the Civil War, then faded into obscurity. In 1894, it was revived with George du Maurier's novel *Trilby.* Ten years later, in 1904, a town was settled in Texas and named Alice, for Alice Kleberg, wife of the founder of the famous King Ranch. At about this time, L. B. Collins founded a small settlement near Alice. He had no name for it, but because Alice was nearby, and that was the name of Ben Bolt's loved one in the song, it was only appropriate that the song would be inspiration for the small hamlet's name.

BEND: San Saba County. For its location on a bend in the Colorado River.

BEST: Collin County. Honors Tom Best, a settler.

BIBLE: Smith County. Christened by early settlers as an expression of their religious convictions.

BIGFOOT: Frio County. Salutes William A. "Bigfoot" Wallace, an Indian fighter. It was the Indians who gave him the nickname.

BIRTHRIGHT: Hopkins County. For C. E. Birthright, a pioneer.

BLACK JACK: Kaufman County. For blackjack oak trees.

BLACK MONK: Fannin County. Has nothing to do with a religious member of the dark race, having been christened for two prominent families, Black and Monk.

BLANKET: Brown County. For the creek. The stream received its name in 1852 when a surveying party came across a band of Tonkawa Indians. The Indians had been caught in a heavy rain and had spread their blankets on bushes along the creek bank to dry. The sight of the blankets gave encouragement for the name.

BLESSING: Matagorda County. When the railroad established a town on the ranch of Jonathan and Shanghai Pierce, they wanted to name it Thank God. Postal officials weren't overly fond of the

name, but christened the community in a religious vein—
Blessing—anyway.

BLOOM: Lamar County. For the abundance of wildflowers in the area.

BLUE: Lee County. Christened for the "bluest water that anybody ever saw . . ." in a nearby stream.

BLUE GROVE: Clay County. For its location in a grove of trees, which, from a distance, had a bluish haze.

BLUEBERRY FLAT: Titus County. Descriptive, relating to berries grown in the vicinity, and to the terrain.

BOARD: Van Zandt County. For Jim Board, a settler.

BOARD HOUSE: Blanco County. Tagged for a board house built by an early settler. This was an unusual sight at the time because most residents lived in dugouts.

BONUS: Wharton County. Some claim the community was named by William Dunovant for his Bonus Plantation. Others believe the first settlers were so pleased with the fertile soil that they called the place Bono, derived from the Latin for "good," and that the name Bonus subsequently evolved.

BOX CHURCH: Limestone County. For a church established before the Civil War. The church took its name from the fact that it was constructed of "boxing plank" without framing. The community was originally known as Hog Range.

BRIGHT STAR: Rains County. For a Primitive Baptist church from earlier times. The church acquired its name, as the story goes, when settlers, resting on a hill, saw a bright star in the night sky.

BRIGHT STAR: Van Zandt County. Community also took its name from a church, which, in turn, was influenced by the biblical star so prominent at the time of the birth of Christ.

BROADWAY: Lamar County. F. E. Hutchings, first postmaster, christened the settlement for the broad prairie on which it is situated.

BRONCO: Yoakum County. Community named for its location in range country where many cowboys engage in the skill of "bustin'" broncos. On the other hand, a shoe salesman traveling through the area offered a cowboy five dollars to exhibit bronc riding. When the feat was completed, the salesman asked the storekeeper why the settlement didn't have a name. Upon being informed that postal officials had rejected all the suggested names, the salesman said, "How about Bronco?"

BUFFALO MOP: Limestone County. Hamlet once had a store that carried a line of brooms by the brand name of Buffalo.

BUG TUSSLE: Fannin County. The area in which this village is located was once a popular Sunday school picnic spot. The handle comes from either the time an ice cream social was held here and bugs came out in such force that they ruined the party, or because after the picnic festivities were over, there was little to do except sit around and watch the tumble bugs "tussle" (scuffle).

BURNING BUSH: Smith County. Settled by a Free Methodist sect. The handle was taken from the burning bush that the Bible relates as being the form God used to appear before Moses when He presented the Ten Commandments.

BYSPOT: San Jacinto County. Known as Teddy until 1913. Present name derived by reversing a portion of the name of Topsy Bennett.

CALL: Newton County. Remembers Dennis Call, a sawmill owner.

CARBON: Eastland County. An engineer platted the town and said the area was rich in mineral deposits; ergo, the name. The street names perpetuate the engineer's theory: Lignite, Coal, Anthracite, etc.

CASH: Hunt County. J. A. Money endeavored long and hard to have the Texas Midland Railroad extended to this point. When his efforts bore fruit, E. H. R. Green, railroad president, wanted to name the station in honor of the tireless worker. Not wanting a train station by the name of Money, Green substituted the word *Cash*. As an added note: Mr. Money was the first postmaster of Cash.

CAT SPRINGS: Austin County. An early settler killed a wildcat at a nearby spring.

CAYOTE: Bosque County. Misspelling of "coyote," for which the hamlet was supposed to be named, for the wolves that roamed nearby Bosque Prairie.

CEE VEE: Cottle County. For the C. V. Ranch.

CHALK: Cottle County. Honors James M. Chalk, the first postmaster.

CHARCO: Goliad County. Could have been christened for a petrified tree stump that served as a marker for early travelers.

CHEAPSIDE: Gonzales County. This name, which is also that of a prominent street in London, England, was suggested by J. Henry, an early settler.

CHEEK: Jefferson County. For J. R. Cheek, who laid out the town site in 1907.

CHOCOLATE BAYOU: Brazoria County. For the bayou, the inlet apparently being named for the color of the water.

CHOICE: Shelby County. Postal officials suggested three possible names for the settlement. The citizens, unable to decide, countered, "Pick your choice."

CIRCLE BACK: Bailey County. For the Circle Back Ranch. The ranch took its name from its stock brand, which was a circle on the animals' backs.

CLICK: Llano County. A tribute to G. W. Click.

COKE: Wood County. No relation to the popular soft drink, having been designated for Richard Coke, governor of Texas at the time of the community's christening.

COMBINE: Kaufman County. Received its label when a blacksmith shop, grocery store, and post office "combined" their operations into one building.

COMFORT: Kendall County. The town founder, Ernest Herman Algelt, believed this to be the place for everlasting comfort. An interesting fact about this town is that during the Civil War, Kendall County and several of its neighbors remained loyal to the North. Comfort is the only city in the South that has a monument dedicated to Union soldiers.

CONCAN: Uvalde County. Relates to a card game Mexicans used to play at an old gristmill.

CONCRETE: De Witt County. For the concrete houses that dotted the landscape when the area was settled around 1846.

CONE: Crosby County. Remembers S. J. Cone, an early day mailman.

COST: Gonzales County. Known as Oso when postal authorities requested the name be changed to one with four letters. Residents dropped one "o" and added "c" and "t." No apparent reason for doing so is given.

COTTON GIN: Freestone County. For a cotton gin built here in 1848.

COUNTRY CAMPUS: Walker County. This was once one of several World War II prisoner of war camps in the United States. After the war the site became a housing unit for students attending nearby Sam Houston State Teachers College. This latter fact probably accounts for the community title.

COWBOY: McCulloch County. Town site laid out on ranches owned by W. G. S. Hughes and J. W. Black.

COWSKIN: Collin County. In cattle driving days, drovers tried to force a herd across a swollen stream near here. Many animals were killed, and the drovers, determined to at least save the hides, skinned the cattle and hung their hides across bushes and in trees, intending to return for them later. They didn't get back, and for several years the stiff, dried-out skins made eerie noises in the wind and gave inspiration for the name of the hamlet that grew up here.

CROSS CUT: Brown County. In 1879, citizens applied for a post office. At the same time they suggested the name Cross Out, because the

community was "across country" and "out" of the way of the usually traveled lanes. Either by chance or by design, Washington
changed the second word to "Cut."

CROSS TIMBERS: Johnson County. This is a term used to describe a
stand of timber that lies "crosswise" to the normal flow of traffic.
The community took its name for its location near the Western
Cross Timbers region in east Texas.

CRUSH: Hopkins County. One source contends this town took its
name from the "crushing" process used to make bricks in a local
plant. A more official version tends to make the origin somewhat
gruesome. A publicity stunt took place at this spot in September
1896. Two steam locomotives from the Missouri, Kansas and Texas
(MKT) Railroad made a head-to-head run at each other at speeds
approaching ninety miles an hour. An estimated 50,000 people
witnessed the event. The ultimate crash resulted in the boilers
exploding and killing two and injuring many more. The settlement located at the site of the event didn't take its name from the
crash, but from the man who arranged the catastrophe, William
G. Crush.

CUT: Houston County. Christened when the railroad cut through
here around 1872, and this village was established as a watering
stop for trains.

CUT N SHOOT: Montgomery County. One thought proffered for con-
sumption is that the town moniker came from the time residents
had a physical disagreement about, of all things, plans for a new
church steeple! Just as ironic is another rendition, which states
that churchgoing husbands went for knives and guns when a
preacher was accused of being too friendly with their womenfolk.
Ray "Cut 'n' Shoot" Harris, who fought for the world boxing
championship in 1958, was once county clerk here.

CUTHAND: Red River County. For the creek, which acquired its name
when a Kickapoo Indian cut his hand while working in the
stream. Yet another version has it that the name came from Old
Cuthand, an Indian chief.

DAM B: Tyler County. Hamlet took its handle from the fact that two
reservoirs were planned for the area, but only one was built, and
designated Dam B.

DAWN: Deaf Smith County. In 1887, J. H. Parrish opened a store on
his ranch, which he referred to as the "Dawn of the Century."

DEPORT: Lamar County. Originally called Deeville, for Colonel Dee
Thompson. Citizens often associated the name with the devil in
pronunciation. Disgusted with it all, Thompson's family eventually changed the name to Deport (Dee-port).

DEPORT: Red River County. The "De" part of the name honors the same Dee Thompson mentioned above. The "port" was added by citizens as an expression of futuristic growth projected for the tiny village.

DESERT: Collin County. In 1846, Will Wardon was scouting the area, looking for land to settle. He brought with him a cook who, frightened by the Indians, "deserted." Local pronunciation no longer associates the name with the event, however, being pronounced as the noun *desert*, for a large sand mass, rather than as the verb.

DEWVILLE: Gonzales County. Salutes Frank Dew, the first postmaster.

DIAMOND: Scurry County. For the Diamond M Ranch.

DIES: Taylor County. Perpetuates Congressman Martin Dies.

DIME BOX: Lee County. Prior to the receipt of a post office, residents placed a mailbox on a spot on the road to San Antonio. Freighters making trips through the vicinity picked up and delivered mail. The service charge for each roundtrip was one dime. The settlement grew, and a petition for a post office was submitted. To preserve the memory of the community mailbox, Dr. R. H. Morgan, resident, suggested the name Dime Box.

DIMPLE: Red River County. Samuel R. Crockett, postmaster, suggested this name to honor a small girl in the community, apparently one with prominent dimples.

DINERO: Live Oak County. Spanish for "money," and the community name dates back to the era of the Mexican general Santa Anna. As legend goes, Santa Anna and his forces were traveling through this area escorting a forty-mule team hauling gold. Meeting obstacles at this point, Santa Anna was forced to bury the gold and flee back to Mexico. The legend persists to this date, and the buried treasure is still hunted by seekers of wealth. Since the supposed secret cache is somewhere in the area, this hamlet took its name from the Spanish treasure.

DING DONG: Bell County. Some believe the village received its name in jest, simply because it is located in Bell County. Others say it was christened for two cousins named Bell

DIRECT: Lamar County. By tradition, this community was designated when some Indians were holding a powwow in Indian Territory (now Oklahoma). They ran out of whiskey, and since Oklahoma at the time was dry, one Indian said he was going direct to Texas to a saloon.

DIVOT: Frio County. Another settlement name that came about by mistake. When first established, the hamlet was situated at a crossroads. Citizens opined that the logical name for the place was Pivot (to turn). Washington officials mistook the "P" for a "D."

340

DODGE: Walker County. When the railroad came through the area, citizens of Huntsville showed little interest. Because of their attitude, railroad officials decided to bypass that town and set a station at another point. Since they were "dodging" Huntsville, officials named their new site Dodge.

DOMINO: Cass County. First called Alamo Mills, confusion soon arose with the town of Alamo. The new tag came about because, at the time, it was customary for passengers to play dominoes while waiting for the train. Conductors often referred to the place as Domino, rather than Alamo Mills, so the new name was an appropriate one.

DOT: Falls County. Originally known as Liberty, the name was changed in 1894 to avoid duplication. Dot was selected by William B. Murphy, postmaster, and honored his daughter, Dorothy.

DOUBLE HORN: Burnet County. For the creek, so named when a hunter found two interlocked antlers lying by the stream. Apparently the deer had been fighting and gotten themselves so entangled they couldn't separate and died on the spot.

DRAW: Lynn County. For its location on Moar's Draw (ravine).

DREAMLAND: Starr County. Christened by E. Pirez, postmaster, because he thought the beauty of the place was like something out of a dream.

DRYBURG: Jasper County. Named because it was so dry, both in alcohol and in rainfall.

DUGOUT: Brewster County. The first residence was dug out in the side of a hill.

DUMP: Collin County. Gene Marchant wanted a post office for this site. A postal representative asked what the name of the community was to be. Marchant replied, "I don't care what they call this dump as long as we get a post office." The agent asked, "Why don't you call it Dump, then?" "Dump, it is," replied Marchant, going on to add, "You are now in Dump, Texas."

DUPLEX: Fannin County. Named for two of the original settlers. Rather than carry their names, residents chose this dual designation.

EARLY: Brown County. For Walter Early, who donated land for a school and Baptist church.

EARTH: Lamb County. Some think the site was named by O. H. Reeves because the terrain was treeless and "all that could be seen for miles around was earth." Another thought contends that the name Good Earth was submitted to postal authorities, because of the value residents placed on the soil. The post office dropped "Good."

EAST DIRECT: Lamar County. For its location east of the town of Direct.

EASTER: Castro County. For W. F. Easter, a settler.

EASTERLY: Robertson County. Remembers D. J. Easterly, a resident.

EBONY: Mills County. For ebony (hardwood) trees found here in earlier times.

EDGE: Brazos County. Honors John Edge, a settler.

ELECTRA: Wichita County. For Electra Waggoner, the daughter of a ranch owner.

EMBLEM: Hopkins County. Originally called Soon Over by residents because they didn't hold much hope for their town's survival. As time passed, however, they changed their minds and desired a more suitable name. In front of the local store owned by W. T. Peck hung a large sign on which was an eagle advertising a soft drink. The eagle gave inspiration for the name Emblem.

EMHOUSE: Navarro County. Salutes Colonel E. M. House, superintendent of the Bayou Valley Railroad.

ENERGY: Comanche County. For the "energetic" nature of the townspeople.

EQUALITY: Gregg County. Citizens liked what the word meant.

ERA: Cooke County. For Era Hargrove, the daughter of an early settler.

EULOGY: Bosque County. Charles W. Smith founded the town and opened a store in July 1884. The event was celebrated with a barbecue and square dancing, a "eulogy" to the event.

FAIR PLAY: Panola County. John Allison established a boarding house, blacksmith shop, and general store on this site. The place name is said to have come from a traveler who stated he was impressed by the fair costs in Allison's enterprises.

FAIRY: Hamilton County. For Fairy Fort, the daughter of a settler.

FAKER SWITCH: Camp County. Settlement grew up around a railroad switch, near property owned by the Faker family.

FASHING: Atascosa County. Citizens gathered at the general store to consider a name for their community. The storekeeper noticed a stock of Fashion Tobacco on a shelf and suggested that name. Apparently the handwriting was difficult to read because officials in Washington recorded the name as Fashing.

FATE: Rockwall County. Christened for either Lafayette "Fate" Brown, one-time county sheriff, or Lafayette "Fate" Peyton, gin owner.

FLAT: Coryell County. For its location on a flat strip of land.

FOOT: Collin County. Remembers Dr. Foote, the first physician in the county.

FORT SPUNKY: Hood County. Originally known as Barnardville. There was such rambunctious reaction among the citizens when awarded a post office that the community was tagged with this livelier name.

FORWARD: Lamar County. Early settlers thought this was the direction their community would move.

FRAME SWITCH: Williamson County. This town was once a "switching" site for the International–Great Northern Railroad, and was christened by combining "Switch" with the surname of David Frame, a cattleman.

FREE ONENESS: Bowie County. For a church.

FRIDAY: Trinity County. Honors Fred Friday, a settler.

FRIJOLES: Culberson County. Spanish for "beans," and was one of several names submitted to postal authorities for consideration.

FROGHOP: Lamar County. For the large number of frogs in the area.

FROGNOT: Collin County. A schoolteacher used to be plagued with boys bringing frogs to class. Whenever he discovered the owners of the reptiles, he would give the boys a lashing. Soon, the "frog not" policy of the teacher served as inspiration for the hamlet name. Another rendition is that when the area was first settled, there were so many frogs that residents had to go on a mass frog-hunting trek. Soon, because of the killings, there were "no more frogs"; ergo, Frognot. By the latest information available, the local water tower, which dominates the skyline, has painted on it a picture of a frog on a toadstool, which serves as the logo for the community.

FROST: Navarro County. Salutes Judge Sam M. Frost.

FRY: Brown County. Acknowledges M. E. Fry, a ranch owner.

GASOLINE: Briscoe County. One of the first gasoline gins (processors) in the state was located here.

GAY HILL: Washington County. For two early settlers, G. H. Gay and W. C. Hill.

GEM: Hemphill County. For Gem Hibbard, wife of the owner of the land on which the town site was built.

GINTOWN: Red River County. Town grew up around a cotton gin.

GIST: Jasper County. This is a word normally used when referring to the heart of an issue. The town was named, however, for J. P. Gist, a settler.

GLENFAWN: Rusk County. Did Ellis "Glen" kill a "fawn" here?

GLOBE: Lamar County. T. H. Wheeler asked his family for name suggestions, and one of his sons, eyeing a kerosene lamp, noticed the globe part of the lamp and recommended that as a name.

GLORY: Lamar County. In the 1880s, Nich Ratliff, store owner, suggested the name Richland, extolling the fertile earth that surrounded the settlement. An official in Washington, upon reading Ratliff's glorious description of the countryside, replied, "Only Glory would do your town justice," and that was the name recorded.

GOLDFINCH: Frio County. For the brightly colored bird.

GOLLY: De Witt County. For Anton Golly, a school board trustee.

GOODNIGHT: Armstrong County. For Colonel Charles Goodnight, a trailblazer.

GRAPEVINE: Tarrant County. For the spring, so named by Indians for the grapevines covering the banks.

GRASSHOPPER: Hunt County. For a grasshopper plague that once struck the area.

GRAYBACK: Wilbarger County. A cowboy camp was once located here. The site became overrun with lice, referred to locally as "graybacks," and later, when a town name was considered, Grayback was chosen.

GREATHOUSE: Ellis County. Remembers Archibald Greathouse, a settler.

GREEN STREET: Morris County. Took its label from a row of green houses that once lined a local street.

GRIT: Mason County. For the terrain, which is covered with gravel (grit).

GROOM: Carson County. Refers to B. B. Groom, a rancher.

GROW: King County. One of several names sent to postal officials.

GUM: Wise County. For "Gum" Thompson, a store owner.

GUN BARREL CITY: Henderson County. For an old cattle trail that was as "straight as a gun barrel."

GUNSIGHT: Stephens County. For a ridge, which is as "straight as a gun barrel," with a projecting peak for the sight.

GUY: Fort Bend County. Remembers Guy Rowland, the daughter of a settler.

HACIENDA: Uvalde County. Spanish for "large farm" or "ranch layout," the community was named for the many ranches in the area.

HAIL: Fannin County. For severe hailstorms that once hit the region.

HAPPY: Swisher County. Some believe the town was named for a creek, which is so called because travelers were so happy to find water. Another version, closely related to the first, is that an Indian, having journeyed a long distance, finally came upon water here and named the place "Happy Hunting Ground." Finally, there are those who believe the spot was named by J. B. Harper. A freighter, Harper and his brother were traveling through the region when they became lost in a snowstorm. For two days and nights they wandered, not knowing where they were. Then, just as they were about to give up hope, they spied a dim light in the distance. Making their way to the source, they found a cabin occupied by an elderly couple. The two weary, cold freighters were invited in, fed, and given hot coffee. In the course of conversation, Harper asked the name of the place. He was informed that it had no name and was invited to recommend one. Harper responded that he believed Happy would be a good name, because it would make anyone happy to see a light and fire on such a bad night.

HAPPY HOME: Rockwall County. Christened by early settlers because they all lived together as one big, happy family.

HAPPY UNION: Hale County. Basically the same as Happy Home, above.

HATCHETVILLE: Hopkins County. Honors the Hatchet family.

HIGH ISLAND: Galveston County. This is the highest point between Sabine Pass and Point Bolivar, at forty-seven feet above sea level.

HIGHWAY: Bowie County. For its location on both sides of Highway 5.

HOBBY: Fort Bend County. For W. P. Hobby, onetime governor of the state.

HOG EYE: Gregg County. Some men were standing in front of B. F. Chapman's store. Suddenly, one of them pointed down the hill and exclaimed, "Look." He was pointing at a man most people in the community considered a hog thief. Another man commented, "Yonder goes old Hog Eye!" Hence, the hamlet name.

HONEST: Delta County. A name for the site was being discussed when Saint Thompson, postmaster, walked into the store and spotted a tin of Honest Snuff; the rest is history.

HOOP N HOLLER: Liberty County. By tradition, the site was named for its location, deep in the Big Thicket of east Texas, where a person can make noise and not be heard. A comical incident occurred when the developers had a conflict with state and federal agencies, as well as local bird watchers, regarding the ivory-billed woodpecker. In the first election held by the community, a jackass was elected mayor by write-in votes, to "communicate with other jackasses in federal, state, and local governments." The jackass held office for two years.

HOOT INDEX: Bowie County. For "Hoot" White.

HOT WELLS: Hudspeth County. For area hot water wells.

HUMBLE: Harris County. Salutes P. S. Humbler, a settler.

IAGO: Wharton County. One version of the origin of this moniker is that it was suggested by a Dr. Reliford because of its shortness, and the fact that it contained three vowels. A more romantic rendition is that it was coined by Mrs. S. W. Cates for Iago, the villain in Shakespeare's *Othello*, who planted distrust in Othello toward his wife, Desdemona.

IBEX: Shackelford County. For the Ibex Oil Company, not the wild goat.

IMPACT: Taylor County. For the advertising firm of Impact, Inc.

INDEPENDENT HOPE: Camp County. For a church, established "independent" of the Baptist denominational association.

JOLLY: Clay County. For W. H. Jolly, a landowner.

JOT EM DOWN: Delta County. Dion McDonald built a store here in 1936. At the time, and for many years thereafter, one of the favorite radio shows to be broadcast was *Lum and Abner,* whose antics took place in their hometown of Jot 'Em Down, Arkansas. Residents started referring to McDonald's store as "Jot 'Em Down." The store owner considered the title undignified and refused to accept the name. Later, a Jot Em Down Gin Corporation was organized, and when state highway officials marked the area, they wrote the name Jot Em Down, and it became the community's official designation.

JOY: Cass County. For the granddaughter of Will Grogan, a lumberman.

JOY: Clay County. The first settlers were so "elated" over bountiful crops produced their first season.

JUMBO: Castro County. For a Mexican sheepherder known as Jumbo, for his size.

JUNO: Val Verde County. In 1885, Henry Stein had the only place of business here, and his main offerings were frijoles (beans) and a drink known as "near beer." When asked what he had to drink, his patient reply was, "You know." There was a large Mexican population here, and they pronounced Stein's response as "Ju-know." From that evolved Juno.

LARIAT: Parmer County. For the cowboy's rope.

LATCH: Upshur County. Relates to L. A. "Daddy" Latch, a lumberman.

LATEX: Panola County. This has nothing to do with paint, being a company town organized in 1924 by the Magnolia Gas Association. The site is named for the two states in which the company operates, and in which the town limits lie, Louisiana and Texas.

LAZBUDDIE: Parmer County. For the original settlers, D. Luther (Laz) Green and Andrew (Buddie) Sherby.

LEGION: Kerr County. The American Legion established a veterans hospital here in 1920.

LICK SKILLET: Collin County. By tradition, the community acquired its moniker when campers, after preparing supper and retiring for the night, were awakened by a noise. Looking outside their tents, they saw a bear and some cubs licking the dirty cooking utensils.

LITTLE FLOCK: Harrison County. A Baptist church opened here in 1884, and on the day of the first service, Parson Lancaster commented, "Indeed, this is a little flock," apparently referring to the small attendance. His comment served as inspiration for the community label.

LITTLE HOPE: Wood County. Early residents had little hope their community would survive.

LIVELY: Kaufman County. In early days, dances were held here, and people referred to it as a "lively little place."

LOCKER: San Saba County. Pays tribute to J. Monroe Locker, settler.

LOCO: Childress County. Spanish for "crazy," the village was christened for the locoweed, which, while not fatal, does make animals act crazy.

LONE CAMP: Palo Pinto County. In 1904 a ranch was divided up and sold to farmers. A Mr. Spencer was appointed to build and petition for a post office. At the time, his family had gone off to visit relatives, and he was living in a tent. There was no one else in the area, and he thought to himself how lonely the place was. Thus, the name.

LONE STAR: Delta County. In 1878 three men from Kentucky set up a school here. A lone star painted on a barn was inspiration for the school, and later the community, name.

LONE STAR: Wise County. From the state motto.

LONG TAW: Delta County. Early freighters, using animal-drawn wagons, referred to a haul as a "taw." There was an unnamed community here at the time, and freighters said that the drive from a bridge on the South Sulphur River to this spot was a long taw. Thus, the town's name.

LOOP: Gaines County. One belief for the origin of this place name is that it was taken from a ranch brand, a loop, or an "O." Another tenet is that a post office had been approved for the site, and Ted Beltcher, who was to be the first postmaster, was asked to suggest a name for the new facility. At the time he was performing a popular cowboy trick, that of whirling a rope into a loop, then jumping in and out of the loop as it spun. That gave him the idea for the office name, which was also taken by the community.

LOVING: Young County. For Oliver Loving, the son of an early merchant.

LOYAL VALLEY: Mason County. For residents who remained loyal to the North during the Civil War.

MAGIC CITY: Wheeler County. Christened following the discovery of oil (magic gold) in Wheeler County in 1926.

MAGNET: Wharton County. One contention is that the place was tagged by settlers because they believed the good soil would "attract" other settlers. Another belief is that the town was promoted by the Taylor-Fowler Land Company of Oklahoma, and by choosing this handle, they hoped to attract more settlers. Some opine that attractions other than growth opportunities drew people to the small village. The closest town of any size, Bay City, was dry; Magnet was not. Maybe the saloons in the latter were the big attraction. Regardless, none of the dreams materialized, and today the hamlet barely survives.

MARATHON: Brewster County. Christened by Albion E. Shepherd, a sea captain, because the terrain reminded him of Marathon, Greece.

MART: McLennan County. In earlier times this was the central place, or "market," for the region.

MATADOR: Motley County. The place name could have come from the Matador Land and Cattle Company. Or it might have been tagged for the Matador Ranch, which could have also been the cattle company name. Motley County was organized in 1891, at which time there was no town here. Certain legal requirements existed to qualify for incorporation as a town. To meet those requirements, twenty "businesses" were set up by ranch hands from the Matador Ranch for a period of one day only. The charter was granted, the businesses closed, and the cowboys dutifully returned to their jobs at the ranch.

MAVERICK: Runnels County. For Samuel Maverick, a landowner. It was from this individual that the term "maverick" was made popular and, like its namesake, a maverick seldom travels in anyone else's footsteps.

MEDICINE MOUND: Hardeman County. There are actually four mounds here, but only one is listed as the community name. The reason for this is that just one had a medicinal herb growing on it, which was once used to cure an Indian princess. It is from that incident that the town took its name.

MELON: Frio County. For the large quantity of watermelons grown in the vicinity.

MERCEDES: Hidalgo County. This has nothing to do with the luxurious automobile. The town was named for the wife of Porifio Diaz, president of Mexico at the time, as a sort of sycophantic gesture. It was hoped that through flattery Diaz would be influenced to exert his power to prevent Mexican banditry in the area. If the gesture worked at all it was short-lived, because border trouble continued well into the twentieth century.

MERIT: Hunt County. Community acquired its handle through compromise. Some residents wanted it named for Judge Merritt; others objected to having the place carry an individual's name. Merit was the compromise, apparently still derived from the judge's name.

MICKEY: Floyd County. Respects Floyd Mickey, the first postmaster.

MICO: Medina County. Christened by the Medina Irrigation Company.

MONKSTOWN: Fannin County. Carries James Monk's name.

MOON: Cottle County. For a ranch.

MOUNT CALM: Hill County. The original town, situated on a hill, was named for the peacefulness surrounding it. The present site is in a valley, but still retains the original title.

MUD CITY: Travis County. Little is left of this hamlet, whose claim to fame is that FBI agents once hid out here, waiting for the 1920s outlaws Bonnie Parker and Clyde Barrow (they didn't show). The hamlet acquired its designation because when Cottonwood Creek flooded, the roads became so muddy that walking on them was virtually impossible.

MUD DIG: Hunt County. The town was built on soil that became nothing but black, sticky mud every time it rained, and residents had to dig their way out.

MULESHOE: Bailey County. For the Muleshoe Ranch, on which the original town site was established.

MUSE: Wise County. For John Muse, a blacksmith.

MUTT AND JEFF: Wood County. This once-popular barbecue site is virtually deserted today. Like the cartoon characters for which it was named, there once lived here two men of varying heights.

NECESSITY: Stephens County. This community was born during extremely difficult times in America's history, the Civil War and Reconstruction. To make matters worse, area ranchers had to suffer through the severe drought of 1886. Apparently, citizens named the settlement by reflecting on the hard times they had experienced, when everything was a necessity just for bare living.

NEMO: Somervell County. No relation to Jules Verne's mythical "Captain Nemo." The community was labeled by W. H. Rinker, store owner, just so it would rhyme with such surrounding settlement names as Bono and Rainbow.

NEW DEAL: Lubbock County. Took its moniker from the New Deal Consolidated School District, which was built during the New Deal days of President Franklin Roosevelt.

NEWGULF: Wharton County. Coined by Texas Gulf Sulphur Company simply because there was already a town named Gulf in Matagorda County.

NEW HARP: Montague County. Remembers Nixon P. Harp, a store owner.

NEW HOME: Lynn County. Residents considered this their new home.

NINE: McCulloch County. For its location nine miles southwest of the town of Brady.

NOBILITY: Fannin County. Original settlers wanted the rather pretentious name of Gentry. This was rejected because of duplication, so they selected Nobility, which still maintained an air of supremacy.

NOCKENUT: Wilson County. This unusual name was designated by Henry Hastings, although he misinterpreted and misspelled the sources. Hastings took the name from two trees, "nockeway" and "hickernut." However, *nockeway* comes from an Indian tribe, the Anaqua. *Hickernut* was Hastings's misspelling of "hickory nut."

NOODLE: Jones County. For the creek, so named because it twists and turns like a noodle.

NOONDAY: Harrison County. Originally called Shortview, a meeting was called in 1876 to choose a new title. Since the meeting was set for high noon, this inspired residents with an appropriate tag for the community.

NOONDAY: Smith County. Named by Captain Edward S. Smith for the Noonday Baptist Church in his hometown in Georgia.

NOTREES: Ector County. Named by Charles J. Brown, first postmaster, because when he and his wife arrived here, there was only one native tree, and it was later cut down.

NOVICE: Coleman County. Christened by Joe and Will Fletcher, brothers who opened a store here, and considered themselves novices in the mercantile business.

NOVICE: Lamar County. Some believe this name was received when Hugh Jones donated land for a church and school in 1900 and residents had a "new" beginning. Others opine the name was derived from Navis, the moniker of a family that once lived here.

NURSERY: Victoria County. Gilbert Onderdank opened a nursery here in 1882. His business grew so fast that it was necessary to have a post office. The facility was given the name Nursery, which the village adopted.

350 OATMEAL: Burnet County. This breakfast food label was taken from that of an early settler. In August of each year the community holds an "Oatmeal Festival," with such events as Oatlympics, grasshopper parade, cow chip toss, oatmeal box stacking, and dozens of other highlights.

ODDS: Limestone County. When a name for the community couldn't be decided on, people were asked to write their suggestions on slips of paper and toss them in a hat. Still no agreement could be reached. Because of the secret ballot, though, one attendee remarked that that was an odd way to name a town. The word *odd* caught the attention of the people and by adding an "s," they came up with the place name.

OKLAUNION: Wilbarger County. Handle suggested by Joe "Buckskin Joe" Wright, who founded the town in 1889, and commemorates the union by rail between the town and Oklahoma.

OKRA: Eastland County. For the farm crop grown here.

OLD OCEAN: Brazoria County. For a nearby oil field, which geologists contend is the bed of an ancient ocean.

OLD GLORY: Stonewall County. Originally called Brandenberg by early German settlers, the name was changed during World War I in a show of patriotism.

OMEN: Smith County. Named by W. W. Orr because he thought it might bring the people good luck.

PAINT ROCK: Concho County. For Indian paintings found on a bluff near the Concho River.

PANCAKE: Coryell County. Another breakfast food, this one was named for J. R. Pancake, a rancher.

PANDALE: Val Verde County. Descriptive, the village being situated in a small valley (dale) shaped like a pan.

PANDORA: Wilson County. Community christened tongue-in-cheek. In earlier days, two prominent families lived here, the Montgomerys and the Sykeses. As is often the case in small towns, these families had their names on virtually every business and piece of property. When the railroad came through, bringing with it some prominence, the question arose as to whether to call the place Montgomeryville or Sykestown. Realizing what a bucket of worms had been uncapped, and thinking of how one of the families would react should its name not be selected, a railroad employee commented, "We've opened the box. We'll call it Pandora." This name refers to the mythical figure that opened a forbidden box and unleashed a horde of evils upon the world.

PANHANDLE: Carson County. For its geographical location in the panhandle part of the state.

PEACOCK: Stonewall County. Relates to J. M. Peacock, the first postmaster.

PEATOWN: Gregg County. First called Edwardsville, the tag was changed when, one year, the only successful farm crop was peas.

PEBBLE: Kerr County. For the large quantities of small stones (pebbles) found on the bank of the south fork of the Guadalupe River.

PEELTOWN: Kaufman County. For Monroe Peel, a landowner.

PEP: Hockley County. In 1923, the Yellow House Ranch put up 42,000 acres of land for sale for the establishment of a Catholic colony. The land sold quickly, and it wasn't long before the new settlers had built a school, new homes, and the land was plowed and fenced. Because of the things accomplished in such a short time, the town adopted the name Pep, as an expression of their energy. At least one source, however, believes the name might be a shortened form of "pepper."

PETROLEUM: Jim Hogg County. For its location in an oil field.

PILGRIM REST: Rains County. In earlier times, Marshall, Jefferson, and Shreveport were the trading centers of this area. A church, which later took the name Pilgrim Rest, was where travelers, known as pilgrims, moving between the three marketing centers, would stop to rest.

PILGRIMS REST: Fannin County. Early settlers from Tennessee considered this spot a place to rest after their tiresome travels.

PLACID: McCulloch County. Descriptive, for its quiet, serene location.

PLANK: Hardin County. For the many lumber operations in the vicinity.

PLASTERCO: Fisher County. Remembers a gypsum plant.

PLEDGER: Matagorda County. For William E. Pledger, a settler.

PLUCK: Polk County. Moniker suggested by George H. Deason because he felt it took pluck (stamina) to settle here.

POETRY: Kaufman County. One name origin revolves around a young man who once worked at a local newspaper and loved poetry so much that he always filled his columns with verse. Another rendition is that the handle came from the fact that at one time many amateur poets met here to read and talk about poetry. A third source is the least logical, yet the one most accepted. A drummer passing through noticed a small ragged boy followed by an equally scrawny dog. In those days, "tray" was a common term for a dog. The drummer commented, ". . . there's a poor tray if I ever saw one." Residents were, at the time, trying to decide on a name for the town and, hearing the drummer's words, changed "poor tray" to Poetry.

POINTBLANK: San Jacinto County. Christened by Florence Dissesway because all directions to this site were point blank (unobstructed).

POLAR: Kent County. For Polar Singletary, the daughter of a settler.

PONDER: Denton County. A personal name.

POSSUM TROT: Bowie County. Opossums once had a regular trail through here.

POST: Garza County. Honors C. W. Post, cereal magnate, who founded the town in 1907 and owned approximately 400,000 acres of land in the region.

POT RACK: Fannin County. At a campsite once located here, pot racks were hung in trees for the convenience of passersby.

POWDERLY: Lamar County. For T. V. Powderly, Commissioner of Immigration during the McKinley administration.

PUMPVILLE: Val Verde County. This was once a pump station for the Southern Pacific Railroad.

QUAIL: Collingsworth County. For the large number of quail in the area.

QUARTERWAY: Hale County. Christened by Rodney and Marjorie Heck, gin owners, for its location quarterway between the towns of Olton and Plainview.

RACE TRACK: Delta County. For a horserace track that existed here.

RADIANCE: Travis County. A communal development established for practitioners of Transcendental Meditation. The name Radiance comes from Super Radiance Effect, the theory that communal medication brings peace and understanding, and will ultimately serve to cure many social ills.

RAGTOWN: Garza County. So many early settlers lived in tents that it was soon dubbed Ragtown.

RAGTOWN: Lamar County. According to tradition, the folk who lived here were so clean that they washed their clothes until they were nothing more than rags.

RAISIN: Victoria County. Known as Lucy at the time, when a post office was approved the name had to be changed because of its similarity to other Texas town names. Several labels were submitted to postal officials, but all were rejected. One day, some men were gathered in a store owned by J. Riemenschneider when in walked J. K. Reeves from a nearby settlement. Reeves had a bunch of grapes, and one of the men said the grapes should make fine raisins. Another man made the tongue-in-cheek comment that maybe they ought to name their community Raisin—and they did.

RATTAN: Delta County. For C. V. Rattan, postmaster at nearby
Cooper, who played an important role in getting a post office for
this site.

RAZOR: Lamar County. When a name for the town site was being
considered, someone noticed a popular brand of tobacco by the
name of Razor, which was sold in a store owned by A. K. Haynes.

RED BARN: Pecos County. For a landmark, a red barn situated on the
Yates Ranch.

RED LAWN: Cherokee County. From early times, when residents did-
n't have grassy lawns in the front of their houses, only red clay.

RED ROCK: Bastrop County. For the red rock chimney attached to the
first house built here, which was owned by John Brewer.

REDWATER: Bowie County. First called Ingersoll, named by religious
nonbelievers for Bob Ingersoll, the agnostic and anti-Bible critic. E.
T. Page moved here from London, England, in 1889, when the settlement was undergoing a great religious revival. The time was
ripe for a name change so Page suggested Redwater, for the
nearby sulfurous springs that sprouted red-tinted water.

RETREAT: Navarro County. An old schoolhouse was moved several
times from one location to another. Consequently, citizens thought
Retreat would be an appropriate name for the settlement.

RISING STAR: Eastland County. One version of the origin of this handle has it that T. W. Anderson applied for a post office in 1882. He
submitted the name Rising Sun, but this was rejected because of
duplication. He then sent in Star, which also existed elsewhere.
Officials combined both suggestions and came up with Rising Star.
The second version is that the town was designated by D. D
McConnell, when he described the area as a rising star because of
the bountiful crops reaped from the farmland.

ROCK CRUSHER: Coleman County. Named for a railroad switch on
the Santa Fe, used to haul crushed rock for construction on the
railroad bed.

ROSEBUD: Falls County. Moniker inspired by an American Beauty
rosebush growing in the yard of Jennie Mullins.

ROUND TIMBER: Baylor County. Refers to the round clumps of oak
trees found in the area.

ROUND TOP: Fayette County. This is a misnomer. At last report this
is the smallest incorporated town in Texas and was named for a
tower that stood on top of a house owned by Alvin Soergel. The
tower was octagonal in shape, not round.

ROYALTY: Ward County. Oil was discovered in the vicinity in 1927,
and the town was named for the "royalties" received by landowners.

RUGBY: Red River County. For the brand of bicycle owned by T. J. Lemens.

RULE: Haskell County. A personal name.

RUNAWAY BAY: Wise County. This is a resort development built on the Hastings Ranch. The tag is from that of a similar development on the Caribbean island of Jamaica.

SALTY: Milam County. For the creek.

SAMPLE: Gonzales County. For A. H. and Jim Sample, settlers.

SANATORIUM: Tom Green County. For the local Tuberculosis Sanatorium.

SATIN: Falls County. A citizen once commented that the community was "as fine as split silk" (satin).

SECLUSION: Lavaca County. Originally known as Boxville, the name was changed to reflect its isolated location.

SECURITY: Montgomery County. Relates to the Security Land Company, which promoted settlement here.

SEMINARY HILL: Tarrant County. For the Baptist Seminary.

SEVEN SISTERS: Duval County. For the nearby Seven Sisters Oil Field.

SHALLOWATER: Lubbock County. In this section of the country, wells usually have to be sunk deep to find water. Here, however, it was found at very shallow depths.

SHAMROCK: Wheeler County. George Nickel, an Irishman, suggested this name because it symbolized luck and courage.

SHINER: Lavaca County. For H. B. Shiner, a settler.

SHOE STRING: Harrison County. Took its title from the fact that the first oil explorers in this region operated their business short of cash (on a shoestring).

SHORT PONE: Rusk County. Times were hard in the South during Reconstruction, and this little village was known for making very "short" corn bread (pone).

SISTERDALE: Kendall County. For its location between two streams known as Sister creeks.

SIX MILE: Calhoun County. For its location six miles north of Port Lavaca.

SIX MILE: Milam County. For its location six miles from Old Nashville-On-The-Brazos.

SLABTOWN: Lamar County. Received its title because a sawmill that cut timber into slabs once operated here. At times the roads were so muddy, they became passable only if slabs were laid out on the roads.

SLAY: Ellis County. A personal name.

SLIDE: Lubbock County. Originally known as Block Twenty, the community name was changed in 1903 when a new survey discovered that nearly two hundred sections of land were farther west than first thought. Because of this, all the settlers in the area, and one school, had to "slide" over.

SNAP: Panola County. Reveres Dr. "Snap" Cariker.

SODA: Polk County. Four names were sent to postal officials, who didn't particularly care for any of them. By using the first letters of each of the four names, however, they came up with Soda.

SOUR LAKE: Hardin County. For the mineral waters near here that feed into Sour Lake.

SPADE: Lamb County. For the stock brand of a local ranch.

SPEAKS: Lavaca County. A personal name.

SPRINKLE: Travis County. A personal name.

SPUR: Dickens County. For the stock brand of the Espula Land and Cattle Company. *Espula* is Spanish for "spur."

STAPLES: Guadalupe County. For a store owner.

STRANGER: Falls County. Known as Upper Blue Ridge, citizens were searching for a new name, not too happy with their present one. A stagecoach pulled into town, and a man debarked and introduced himself as Stranger. The county tax rolls of 1870 list a man named Strangere, so it is possible the two were one and the same. Whether this is the case or not has little bearing, because the townspeople liked the idea of their settlement being called Stranger.

STRIP: Hale County. Nothing erotically suggestive about this community, since it was named for its location on a strip of land one and a half miles wide and fifteen miles long.

STUDY BUTTE: Brewster County. For Will Study, a resident.

SUGAR LAND: Fort Bend County. Named by Samuel M. Williams for the sugar cane plantation he developed.

SUGAR LAND: Harris County. Relates to a large sugar refinery.

SUNDOWN: Hockley County. Originally called Slaughter, for Bob Slaughter, a landowner. He didn't want the community to bear his family name and suggested Sundown, because a movie by that name had once been made on his father's ranch in Mexico. Another version is that a meeting was held to decide on a name. The session had gone on all day and no agreement reached. Finally, in desperation, one citizen suggested, "Aw, just name it Sundown, because that's what it is now."

SUNNY SIDE: Waller County. For its location on the sunny side of a knoll.

SUNRAY: Moore County. Remembers the Sunray Oil Company.

SUNSET: Montague County. Name suggested by the postmaster general. In days when travel was difficult, distance meant much more than it does today. The postal chief must have had that in mind when he commented to local residents, "You are so far toward the setting sun, why not the name Sunset?"

SWAYBACK: Collin County. Now known more popularly as Walnut Ridge, this community received its original name from a large building erected here in early days. The building, which housed a Presbyterian church and a school, was constructed of green lumber. In time the lumber cured, and the long, center poles that supported the structure warped. From a distance people compared the roof to a swaybacked horse.

SWEET HOME: Lavaca County. Early settlers were well satisfied with this location for building homes.

TALCO: Titus County. Took its name from the Texas, Arkansas, Louisiana Candy Company.

TARZAN: Martin County. Said to have been named by Tant Lindsay, first postmaster, for the character in the popular comic strip.

TEACUP: Kimble County. For the mountain, so named because it resembles an upside-down teacup.

TELEGRAPH: Kimble County. The first telegraph and telephone poles used in the county were cut in a nearby canyon.

TELEPHONE: Fannin County. Poke Hindman, storekeeper, petitioned for a post office to be placed in his store. He submitted several names for consideration, but they were all rejected because of duplication. Trying to decide on a suitable title, the thought occurred that he was the only person in the community with a telephone.

TELL: Childress County. Long ago, this site was known as Tell Tale Flats, being so named because of the habit of residents appearing before grand juries and "telling everything they knew." Over time, "Tale" and "Flats" were dropped.

TERRAPIN NECK: Wood County. In 1876, a fish fry was held in this new community. Instead of fish, however, the only thing anglers were successful in catching were terrapins. This incident, plus the location of the settlement—on a neck of land—accounts for the name.

TESNUS: Brewster County. This is "sunset" spelled backward, and was probably chosen because Sunset might have been a duplication.

THREE LEAGUES: Martin County. So designated because three leagues (numbers 251, 253, 254) made up the district.

THREE P: Fannin County. Took its moniker from the Three P School. The school tag came about when three schools, all beginning with the letter *P* (Prairie Hill, Portland, and Philadelphia), were combined.

THRIFT: Wichita County. Refers to Thrift Wagonner Bank, which opened here during oil boom days.

THRIFTY: Brown County. For the "frugality" of the residents.

TICKY VALLEY: Collin County. So called because it was once subjected to a tick plague.

TIGERTOWN: Lamar County. A saloon owner hung a picture of a tiger over the bar, and cowboys soon acquired the habit of saying, "Let's go over and take a shot at the tiger." Another source of the town's name says that some drunks riding through town saw buildings covered with advertisements for a circus. Most of the posters depicted a tiger, and the drunks rode down the main street shouting, "Tigertown! Tigertown!" A third rendition is that at a dance one night local boys bested a group of boys from nearby Bonham. The out-of-towners slipped back into the community later that night and painted a large tiger on a wall to symbolize the fierceness of the fight.

TINRAG: Hopkins County. This is the family name of Garnit spelled backward.

TIP TOP: Rusk County. Christened years ago when it was thought the community was situated on the highest point in the then Henderson County area.

TOMBALL: Harris County. For Tom Ball, a lawyer.

TOURS: McLennan County. For the French city.

TOW: Llano County. Remembers Billy and Wilson Tow, brothers who settled here.

TRICKHAM: Coleman County. Emory Peters, store owner, often played tricks on cowboys, such as putting pepper in snuff, etc. The name for the store was originally Trick 'Em, but was changed when residents petitioned for a post office.

TRUCE: Jack County. Family name.

TURKEY: Hall County. For the creek, so named for wild turkeys in the area.

TURPENTINE: Jasper County. Harks back to the days of the Western Naval Stores Company, a turpentine camp and distillery located here in 1907–1918.

TWIN SISTERS: Blanco County. For two mountains identical in size and form.

TWO MILE: Milam County. For its location two miles from Old Nashville-On-The-Brazos.

UNCERTAIN: Harrison County. Several possibilities exist for the origin of this community name. In the times of steamboat travel on Caddo Lake, one spot near here was extremely difficult for docking, thus earning the name Uncertain Landing. Maybe the name came from a comment made by fishermen. One day, W. J. Sedberry and some friends were angling in the area and stated they weren't certain they would ever be able to find their way out. Another rendition is that the community was incorporated solely for the purpose of voting approval for the sale of alcoholic beverages. The state attorney general looked upon the incident with a jaundiced eye and said he would never let state incorporation laws be so flagrantly violated. Therefore, the community of Uncertain was uncertain of its legal status as a town. Along this same line, the town may have been so named from the fact that it was the only "wet" town in the area, and people coming here from nearby cities were often uncertain they would be able to get home.

VALENTINE: Jeff Davis County. It is thought this place name came from a Longfellow poem; others feel it honors the president of the Wells Fargo Company. There are also those who believe it was christened because the first train to run through here did so on Saint Valentine's Day.

VERIBEST: Tom Green County. Relates to a packing company's trademark.

VICTORY CITY: Bowie County. This patriotic title was given to the community, established at the entrance to the Lone Star Defense Plant, during World War II.

WEALTHY: Leon County. Originally known as Poor, citizens didn't like the name and changed it to the opposite sometime between 1894 and 1896.

WEEPING MARY: Cherokee County. More than likely settled by former slaves following the Civil War. Probably took its name from the religious image of Mary Magdalene weeping at the tomb of Jesus.

WELCOME: Austin County. Either version of the name origin is a reflection of local hospitality. As one story goes, a traveler spent the night at a citizen's home and the next morning attempted to pay for the accommodations. Surprised at his host's generosity in refusing money, the man gushed with words of appreciation, to which the host replied, "You're welcome." Another rendition is that J. F. Schmidt named the town for the friendly welcome given newly arrived settlers by the forest, flowers, and meadows.

WELFARE: Kendall County. Originally called Bon Ton, the name change was probably a spur-of-the-moment, whimsical choice of a few residents. There is thought, however, that the name comes from the German *wohlfahrt*, meaning "pleasant trip."

WELLBORN: Brazos County. A personal name.

WHITE DEER: Carson County. For a creek, which was so named because a white deer was once spotted nearby.

WHITE SETTLEMENT: Tarrant County. The site was settled by Caucasians from Kentucky and Tennessee.

WHITE STAR: Motley County. During buffalo days a small beetle, or bug, favored the thick hide and hair of buffalo as home. The bugs were grayish-black, with a white star on their backs. Buffalo hunters, naturally associated with the bugs, often camped here, and the site acquired the label White Star.

WHITEFACE: Cochran County. For the Whiteface Pasture. Colonel C. C. Slaughter brought the first Hereford (white-faced) cattle to this section and grazed them in this special pasture.

WHITEFLAT: Motley County. For its location in flat country, covered with white grass.

WHO'D THOUGHT IT: Collin County. Little of this hamlet remains; it received its unusual handle from the remark an individual made when he first saw the place.

WILDCAT: Harrison County. Until the 1860s this area was known as the Shepherd School District. It was during this period that while students were enjoying class recess, a wildcat ran across the schoolyard.

WILDHORSE: Culberson County. In the 1800s, Indians attacked a wagon train. A young white girl was tied to a wild horse and dragged to death. From this incident came the community name.

WINK: Winkler County. Derived its tag from the county designation.

WIZARD WELLS: Jack County. For wells that dispense mineral water with "curative" powers.

XRAY: Erath County. For its location at a road intersection.

YARD: Anderson County. Bruce Gray, store owner, was making a list of community names to send to postal authorities. Someone entered the store and asked for a yard of cloth. Gray wrote "Yard" on the list, and it was selected by the Post Office Department.

YELLOW HOUSE: Lamb County. This community moniker came from either the color of clay found in nearby Yellow House Canyon, or the limestone bluff nearby (probably in the canyon), which gives the appearance of a grouping of yellow houses.

ZIGZAG: Medina County. For the winding road leading to the village.

ZIP CITY: Dallas County. According to folklore, the community acquired its moniker from the time an elderly lady sat on her porch and watched automobiles "zip" through town.

Utah

THE BEEHIVE STATE

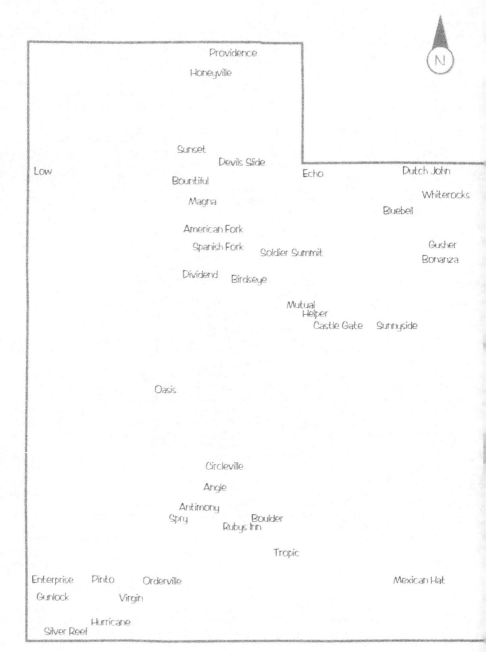

AMERICAN FORK: Utah County. For the creek. The stream achieved
its name simply as opposed to Spanish Fork Creek, which also
runs in this area.

ANGLE: Piute County. Selected by postal officials from a list of six
names sent in by residents, and has no apparent significance.

ANTIMONY: Garfield County. Once known as Coyote, the community was renamed for the ore found nearby.

BIRDSEYE: Utah County. For deposits of bird's-eye marble.

BLUEBELL: Duchesne County. For the flower.

BONANZA: Uintah County. This company town, owned by American
Gilsonite, is the site of the only commercial Gilsonite (black
asphalt) deposits in the world. "Bonanza" is often used to denote a
rich ore deposit, as in this case.

BOULDER: Garfield County. For the abundance of lava boulders in the
region.

BOUNTIFUL: Davis County. Originally called Sessions Settlement for
its founder; renamed for a city cited in the Book of Mormon.

CASTLE GATE: Carbon County. A rock formation resembled a castle
gate that seemed to open and close as one traveled the approaching winding road. Part of the "gate" was blasted away some years
ago to widen the road.

CIRCLEVILLE: Piute County. The community is almost completely
"encircled" by mountains.

DEVILS SLIDE: Morgan County. For a rock formation.

DIVIDEND: Utah County. Christened by E. J. Raddatz for the divi-
dends and profit received from a nearby mine.

DUTCH JOHN: Daggett County. Remembers John Honselena, settler,
because he was German and when he spoke his accent made it
difficult for listeners to understand him.

ECHO: Summit County. For the canyon. The canyon, route of the
Donner-Reed wagon train in 1846, and then the Mormons in later
years, presented a very distinct echo to early travelers.

ENTERPRISE: Washington County. A reservoir was built here to provide water for farming and for the town. The community moniker
came from the fact that citizens were very enterprising in con-
structing the reservoir with few people and no money.

GUNLOCK: Washington County. For William Hamblin, settler and
hunter known as "Gunlock Will."

GUSHER: Uintah County. The handle expressed optimism when oil
was discovered in the Uintah Basin.

HELPER: Carbon County. This site is elevated at a steep angle, and in early days, additional locomotives were needed to assist (help) trains over the Soldier Summit Divide.

HONEYVILLE: Box Elder County. Probably evolved from the family name Hunsaker.

HURRICANE: Washington County. For a nearby fault, which was so named by Erastus Snow because he was once caught in a storm hereabout.

LOW: Tooele County. For its location on a low pass near three mountain ranges.

MAGNA: Salt Lake County. For a local mine.

MEXICAN HAT: San Juan County. For a rock formation that resembles a Mexican hat and weighs almost five million pounds.

MUTUAL: Carbon County. Relates to the Mutual Coal Company.

OASIS: Millard County. The site is an oasis in the surrounding desert country.

ORDERVILLE: Kane County. Town was organized by Mormons of the United Order; thus, inspiration for the name.

PINTO: Washington County. Spanish for "painted," and the community was tagged for variegated geological formations.

PROVIDENCE: Cache County. First known as Spring Creek, the name was changed in 1859 by Elder Ezra Taft Benson because he thought the location as ". . . appearing to us somewhat a providential place . . ."

RUBYS INN: Garfield County. Christened for an inn built at the entrance to Bryce Canyon and owned and operated by Rueben "Ruby" and Minnie Syrett.

SILVER REEF: Washington County. Named by Hyrum Jacobs, store owner, apparently for its elevated location in silver mining territory.

SOLDIER SUMMIT: Wasatch County. At the onset of the Civil War, Camp Floyd, located in the Provo area, was closed. Soldiers stationed there were ordered east to fight for the North. Some of the soldiers were Southerners and deserted. They took a southern route in an attempt to reach Confederate territory, but were caught in a snowstorm at the summit of Spanish Fork Canyon. Two of the soldiers died and were buried there.

SPANISH FORK: Utah County. For the creek, so labeled because the Old Spanish Trail of the 1700s ran parallel to the stream.

SPRY: Garfield County. Honors William Spry, Utah's governor from 1909 to 1917.

SUNNYSIDE: Carbon County. This section was called the "sunny side of the mountain" by early prospectors and miners in lieu of claim markers.

SUNSET: Davis County. For the view the town site displays of the sunset over Great Salt Lake.

TROPIC: Garfield County. For its warm (tropical) climate.

VIRGIN: Washington County. Originally known as Pocketville, the name was changed, taking its new designation from the nearby Virgin River.

WHITEROCKS: Uintah County. This Indian town, once frequented by Kit Carson and John Fremont, is thought to be the oldest settlement in Utah, certainly in the Uintah Basin. It was named for rocks in the valley that looked white when the sun struck them.

Vermont

THE GREEN MOUNTAIN STATE

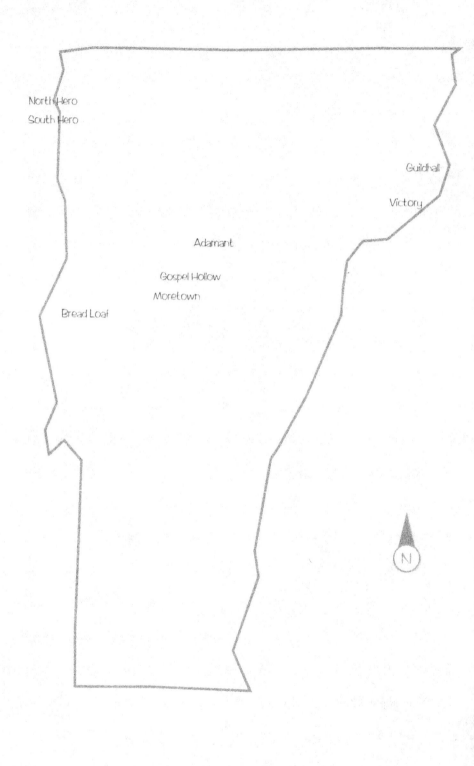

ADAMANT: Washington County. First known as Sodom, the name
was changed when townspeople finally objected to the wicked biblical name. Adamant was chosen because it reflected the hardness   369
of granite taken from a nearby quarry.

BREAD LOAF: Addison County. For the mountain, which was coined
for its shape, like a loaf of old-fashioned home-baked bread.

GOSPEL HOLLOW: Washington County. Christened for an early
church later used as the town hall.

GUILDHALL: Essex County. Named for the Guildhall, a building in
London, England, that housed trade unions.

MORETOWN: Washington County. It has been stated that the town
received its name because, when the site was first being platted,
surveyors discovered a chunk of land that had not been included
in the first survey. One of the surveyors supposedly exclaimed,
"My God, more town!" This origin is rebuked by historians, however, claiming it was on the original grant and referred to either
an early grantee named Moore, or possibly to a place in England
known as Moreton.

NORTH HERO/SOUTH HERO: Grand Isle County. These were once
united and known as Two Heroes; probably named for Ethan
Allen and his brother, Ira.

VICTORY: Essex County. As was common with most New England
colonies, New Hampshire (of which Vermont was then a part) was
greatly concerned about the course of the Revolutionary War. This
hamlet was named in a patriotic gesture, the people deeply yearn-
ing for a victory when defeat seemed so imminent.

Virginia

THE OLD DOMINION

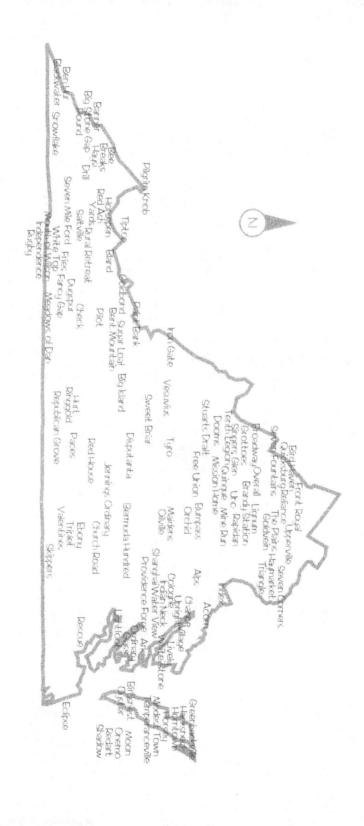

ACORN: Westmoreland County. The first post office was situated near an "oak" tree.

ALPS: Caroline County. For its location in "hilly" terrain.

ARK: Gloucester County. Relates to the Old Ark Farm.

BANNER: Wise County. Refers to a type of coal.

BEE: Dickenson County. Shortened form of Beatrice, the daughter of a settler.

BEN HUR: Lee County. Could have been named by a friend of Lew Wallace, author of the novel *Ben Hur*. Or, maybe it recognizes Ben Snead. Seems Snead owned the land where the town is now located. Ben always referred to his wife as "Her," and when the community was organized, citizens christened the place for "Ben" and his wife, "Her," with loose spelling of the latter.

BENT MOUNTAIN: Roanoke County. For the mountain. The rise received its moniker either because of its horseshoe (bent) shape, or for the Bent brothers, surveyors.

BERMUDA HUNDRED: Chesterfield County. In early days a shipload of settlers destined for Virginia crashed near the island of Bermuda. One hundred people supposedly perished in the disaster. This community was christened in memory of those unfortunates.

BIG ISLAND: Bedford County. Thought to have been labeled for a large island in the James River.

BIG STONE GAP: Wise County. For its location in a gap (opening) in Stone Mountain.

BIRD HAVEN: Shenandoah County. When a factory was built here in earlier times, a large number of birds were in the area. Consequently, the factory owner named the settlement Bird Haven.

BIRDSNEST: Northampton County. Could have taken its handle from a tract of land known as Birdsnest. Possibly, the name was inspired by a tall, three-story building on the site, the lower floor of which was a nesting place for birds.

BLACKWATER: Lee County. Sawdust from sawmills used to flow into a nearby stream, turning the water black.

BLAND: Bland County. Family name.

BRANDY STATION: Culpepper County. This was an active battle site during the Civil War, but received its name much earlier. At one time there was a tavern here that sold an excellent quality of brandy. During the War of 1812, soldiers were stationed in the area, and the tavern owner was unable to stock enough brandy to meet the demand. Unhappy soldiers hung a large sign reading "Brandy" on a tavern wall, and the place became known as Brandy Station.

BREAKS: Dickenson County. For a ravine known as The Breaks, which runs through the Cumberland Mountains.

BROADWAY: Rockingham County. Acquired its handle when a bunch of ruffians prowled the streets of the community, on their "broad way" to destruction.

BUMPASS: Louisa County. Family name.

CHANCE: Essex County. Christened by the Post Office Department.

CHECK: Floyd County. As tradition has it, a general store was a favorite gathering place for checkers players; thus evolved the hamlet's name.

CHURCH ROAD: Dinwiddie County. For an old country road that once led to a church.

COLOGNE: King and Queen County. When a name was needed for the village, a store owner noticed a battle of Hoyt's cologne on a shelf and proposed that name.

DISPUTANTA: Prince George County. Tag came about due to a disagreement among residents on a name for the settlement. In resignation, or disgust, someone suggested Disputanta (a reflective of dispute), and it was accepted.

DOOMS: Augusta County. For John Dooms, a settler. The Shenandoah Valley Railroad ran its line through here, but came face-to-face with stiff opposition in the form of John Dooms. He bitterly opposed the line because it would cut his farm down the middle. The railroad, experienced in these matters, offered to name the depot for him, and he relented.

DRILL: Russell County. For an old drilled well.

DUGSPUR: Carroll County. For a railroad spur dug here, leading to the main road.

EBONY: Brunswick County. Either for ebony trees, or for a black racehorse.

ECLIPSE: Nanesmond County. Labeled around 1900 for a solar eclipse.

FANCY GAP: Carroll County. Named for the description given by Colonel Ira Coltrane of a gap (opening) in the Blue Ridge Mountains.

FREE UNION: Albermarle County. First called Nicksville, for a blacksmith, the name was changed to recognize a local church.

FRIES: Grayson County. Family name.

FRONT ROYAL: Warren County. Prior to the American Revolution, this site was known as Helltown, for the shenanigans of the young men living here. The name Front Royal is an old and historic one. Following the Revolution, the mainstay of America's military force was the local militia. Civilian officers and noncommissioned officers trained the local gentry as best they could in military maneuvers. In an event that took place here in the 1780s, such training was going on in the public square. Prominent in the square was a large oak tree known as the "royal" tree of England. The drillmaster, disgusted with the ineptitude of his motley militia, barked, "Front the royal oak." Amused onlookers took up the command and kept repeating it. In time the town changed its name to Front Royal.

GLASS: Gloucester County. Remembers Henry Glass, a merchant.

GOLDBOND: Giles County. For the trademark of the National Gypsum Company, which was located here.

GOLDVEIN: Fauquier County. For the gold rush fever that once prevailed in the region.

GREENBACKVILLE: Accomack County. Christened for an early land deal, whereby land was bought for greenbacks, the name for the money issued by the federal government in 1862.

GROTTOES: Rockingham County. For nearby caves.

HACKSNECK: Accomack County. For Dr. George Hack, settler. A large neck of land was on his property, stretching to the Chesapeake Bay.

HAYMARKET: Prince William County. For a famous racetrack in London, England.

HAYSI: Dickenson County. Hamlet remembers two partners in a store, Hayter and Sypher.

HORNTOWN: Accomack County. The community name is believed to have come from either the fact that two branches of Savage Creek resemble a pair of horns, or from the early day practice of peddlers blowing horns to announce their arrival in the village.

HORSEPEN: Tazewell County. For an animal corral (pen) once located here.

HORSEY: Accomack County. Recognizes two early postmasters.

HURT: Pittsylvania County. For John L. Hurt, who planned the town site.

INDEPENDENCE: Grayson County. In 1849, a contest existed between the communities of Old Town and Elk Creek to see which would be designated the county seat. A third settlement was asked for an opinion and the reply received was, "We're independent, we're not taking sides." To settle the dispute, the county seat was awarded to the "independents" and the community took that as its name.

INDEX: King George County. When the postmaster was trying to decide on a moniker for the village, he flipped through a book of names and happened to notice the word *Index* at the top of a page.

INDIAN NECK: King and Queen County. For Indian Neck Woods.

IRON GATE: Alleghany County. Took its title from the Iron Gate water gap cut through White Mountain by the Jackson River.

JENNINGS ORDINARY: Nottoway County. In the 1700s, an *ordinary* was a tavern or inn. Apparently a man named Jennings once owned an ordinary on this site.

LIGHTFOOT: James City County. Salutes Philip Lightfoot, a lawyer and merchant.

LIGNUM: Culpepper County. Named by Rev. Frank P. Robertson. The word is Latin and means "wood" or "stick." The vicinity was a very wooded area at one time.

LIVELY: Lancaster County. Originally known as Lively Oak, for the large number of oak trees in the area. The village later dropped "Oak," possibly because the trees died or were dying.

MAIDENS: Goochland County. Formerly known as Maiden's Adventure, having been so named from the legend that told of a young girl crossing the James River to save her lover from Indian raiders. In time, "Adventure" was dropped, and the remaining word assumed the plural form.

MEADOWS OF DAN: Patrick County. For the meadows located along the Dan River.

MINE RUN: Orange County. For a stream that runs past an old gold mine.

MISSION HOME: Greene County. Christened for a mission erected here among the mountains. It consisted of a church, living quarters, stables, and a school.

MODEST TOWN: Accomack County. Supposedly tagged for two proper and prim (modest) ladies who ran a boarding house that also served as a stagecoach stop and post office.

MOON: Mathews County. This moniker was inspired when, after all previous ones had been rejected, the postmaster, while taking his nightly constitutional, happened to notice a bright moon.

MOUTH OF WILSON: Grayson County. For its location where Wilson Creek unites with the New River.

OILVILLE: Goochland County. Harks back to a sassafras oil processing plant located here in the late 1800s.

ONEMO: Mathews County. Hamlet name arose simply because, while there were already ninety-nine post offices in the county, citizens saw plenty of reason for at least "one more." When a name was needed for the facility and community, a play on words came up with Onemo.

ORCHID: Louisa County. A wild orchid was spotted here at the time a community name was being debated.

ORDINARY: Gloucester County. For Long Bridge Ordinary, built here before 1730.

OVERALL: Page County. Family name.

OYSTER: Northampton County. The town is a big supplier of oysters and is the site of several packing houses.

PACES: Halifax County. For the man (Pace) who donated two acres of land for the railroad station. An official in Washington added the "s."

PAINT BANK: Craig County. For the paint ore found nearby, which was mined on a small scale during World War II.

PILGRIM KNOB: Buchanan County. Supposedly christened for Pilgrim Knob Coffee, which was sold in a local store.

PILOT: Montgomery County. Personal name.

POUND: Wise County. At one time a horse-driven grinder was situated at the bend of the river. People for miles around brought grain to the site to have it ground (pounded) into meal. They referred to the place as "The Pounds"; thus the name.

PROVIDENCE FORGE: New Kent County. In 1769, Charles J. Smith, a Presbyterian minister, bought land here and, in anticipation of building a church, named it Providence Plantation. He died before his plans came to fruition. Francis Jerdone bought the land and in partnership with a Mr. Bold, erected a forge on the property; ergo, the name.

QUICKSBURG: Shenandoah County. Honors William A. Quick, a landowner.

QUINQUE: Greene County. Latin for "five." So tagged because this was once the "fifth" stage stop on the road from Richmond to Harrisonburg.

RAPIDAN: Culpepper County. Village was designated for England's Queen Anne, often referred to as "rapid Anne."

RED ASH: Tazewell County. Took its name from the color of the ash left after burning locally mined coal.

RED HOUSE: Charlotte County. Supposedly, all the houses here were at one time painted red.

REDART: Mathews County. Relates to a settler by the name of Trader. For some reason, citizens honored him by spelling his name backward.

RELIANCE: Warren County. This handle was recommended because of the "reliability" of the townspeople.

REPUBLICAN GROVE: Halifax County. This community name could have come from the Republican Church. In reverse consideration, the town may have been so named from an early incident. Apparently political feelings were strong at one time because, as the story goes, a Republican was hanged in a grove of trees near here.

RESCUE: Isle of Wight County. William T. Carter, first postmaster, was asked to choose a name for the community's post office. Thinking about the man who had been riding a mule for a long time, bringing mail to the little settlement, Carter said, "The mail has been rescued from the mule's back." Rescue was extracted as a place name. Another source states that a Methodist church was organized here with the main purpose being to rescue the residents from sin.

RINGGOLD: Pittsylvania County. Although gold was discovered and mined here in early days, only enough of the precious metal was brought out to make a "ring of gold."

RUGBY: Grayson County. For the surrounding "rugged" scenery.

RURAL RETREAT: Wythe County. Harks back to an early tavern.

SALTVILLE: Smyth County. Refers to the local production of salt.

SEVEN CORNERS: Fairfax County. For the number of roads that intersect at this point.

SEVEN FOUNTAINS: Shenandoah County. Christened for seven separate springs that emit seven different kinds of mineral water, all located in less than one acre.

SEVEN MILE FORD: Smyth County. For a ford (crossing) once located seven miles from the early Royal Oak Settlement.

SHADOW: Mathews County. This was one of the monikers submitted to Washington by the community's first postmaster.

SHANGHAI: King and Queen County. Probably one of several names coming from postal officials, and was selected by local residents.

SINGERS GLEN: Rockingham County. Originally known as Mountain Valley, there lived here a man by the name of Joseph Funk. Funk was a writer and music teacher and wrote "Harmoni Sacra," of which there have been at least twenty editions published. Funk was such a good teacher that his pupils left the valley and followed musical careers, often using his material. Because of the musical ability of the residents, and the choral sounds that echoed throughout the valley, the people decided in 1860 to change the name of the settlement to Singers Glen.

SKIPPERS: Greensville County. Some people believe the community handle is a corruption of Mrs. Skipwith, a resident. Others think a railroad signalman by the nickname of Skippers had the community christened in his honor.

SNOWFLAKE: Scott County. This place name came about when the post office at Big Branch was moved here. During the relocation, a snowstorm hit the area, and someone suggested the town site be named Snowflake.

STUARTS DRAFT: Augusta County. For the Stuart family, who owned a small valley (draft) near here.

SUGAR LOAF: Roanoke County. For the mountain, which acquired its name from its shape.

SWEET BRIAR: Amherst County. For a variety of wild rose.

TEMPERANCEVILLE: Accomack County. First known as Crossroads, but in 1824 the four landowners sold off some of their holdings, stipulating in the deeds that no whiskey could be sold on the land. This resulted in the name Temperanceville.

TENTH LEGION: Rockingham County. It is believed that Thomas Jefferson labeled this village, for the reason that the Tenth Legion Artillery Company was started here. The military unit was, in turn, named for the Tenth Legion that fought under Julius Caesar.

THE PLAINS: Fauquier County. First called White Plains, for the outcropping of white rocks. The area is situated on a level tract of approximately forty square miles, in comparison to the surrounding hilly terrain. When the white rocks were gone, having been used for building houses and fences, the people changed the name to the geographically descriptive The Plains.

TIPTOP: Tazewell County. For its location on top of a hill.

TRIANGLE: Prince William County. For the triangle of highways that junction at this point.

TRIPLET: Brunswick County. As the story goes, at the time consideration was being given to a name for the community, a local couple became parents of triplets.

TYRO: Nelson County. From the Latin, meaning "novice" or "beginning." Tyro was the name of a home owned by William E. Morris, and was probably so tagged because it was the "original" homestead in the area.

UNO: Madison County. First known as Kingdom, the name was supposedly changed to Uno for the fact that a bar was once located here, and people, when asked where they were going, would answer, "You know . . ."

UPPERVILLE: Fauquier County. Believed to have been so labeled because this was the last, or uppermost, stop on a stage line between Alexandria and Winchester.

UPRIGHT: Essex County. Community handle either came from the vertical (upright) boarding used on the first store here, or it was meant to describe the moral character of the residents.

VALENTINES: Brunswick County. Salutes William N. Valentine.

VESUVIUS: Rockbridge County. Harks back to an early iron smelting furnace and foundry located here that were named for the volcano in Italy.

VILLAGE: Richmond County. First called Union Village, because two county lines met nearby. Some confusion arose with the name, and "Union" was eventually dropped.

WATER VIEW: King and Queen County. Descriptive, since the village sits on the Rappanhannock River and has a good view of the water.

WHITE STONE: Lancaster County. For White Stone Beach.

WHITETOP: Grayson County. For the mountain. Indians christened the mountain because even in summer snow remains on the very top, which is barren of trees. The Indians said the mountaintop reminded them of the head of an old squaw.

YARDS: Tazewell County. Refers to nearby railroad yards.

Washington
THE EVERGREEN STATE

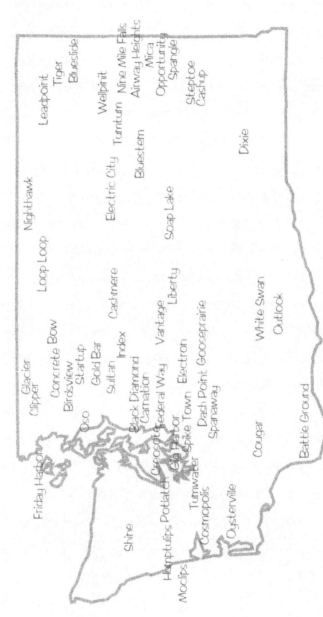

AIRWAY HEIGHTS: Spokane County. For its location near two airfields outside the city of Spokane.

BATTLE GROUND: Clark County. Refers to the battle between soldiers from Fort Vancouver and Indians that took place here in the mid-1800s.

BIRDSVIEW: Skagit County. A play on the name of the community's first postmaster, Birdsey D. Minkler.

BLACK DIAMOND: King County. For the Black Diamond Coal Company.

BLUESLIDE: Pend Oreille County. Tagged for the bluish-colored clay hill that was subject to landslides when it rained.

BLUESTEM: Lincoln County. For a variety of wheat.

BOW: Skagit County. For a district in London, England.

CARNATION: King County. Originally known as Tolt, the name was changed in 1917 by the state legislature for the Carnation Milk Products Company, which established a research farm here.

CASHMERE: Chelan County. First called Mission, the name was changed in 1903 to reflect the town's beauty and productivity, as compared to the Kashmir region of India.

CASHUP: Whitman County. Reflects on James H. Davis, merchant, known as "Cashup" Davis, because he granted credit to no one.

CLIPPER: Whatcom County. Relates to the Clipper Shingle Company.

CONCRETE: Skagit County. For the Portland Cement Company.

COSMOPOLIS: Gray Harbor County. Apparently a commendatory name, combining the Greek forms of *cos,* meaning "world," with *polis,* meaning "city."

COUGAR: Cowlitz County. Residents sent in the names of several wild animals to postal officials, and this is the one that was chosen.

CREOSOTE: Kitsap County. For a creosoting plant that was, at the time, the community's main industry.

DASH POINT: Pierce County. Could have derived its handle from a survey "point" shown on early maps.

DIXIE: Walla Walla County. For a musical trio, the Kershaw Brothers, whose favorite tune was "Dixie."

ELECTRIC CITY: Grant County. Planners hoped to make the hamlet an all-electric model city, but their plans fell through.

ELECTRON: Pierce County. For its location near an electric power plant on the Puyallup River.

FEDERAL WAY: King County. For Federal Way School. The school was christened for its location near the Pacific Highway, which, having

been built with government funds, was referred to as "Federal Highway."

384 FRIDAY HARBOR: San Juan County. Tribute to Friday, a Kanaka sheepherder brought here in early times by the Hudson's Bay Company to tend its flock.

GIG HARBOR: Pierce County. The town was named for the harbor, which was so designated because early travelers found the water deep enough for a small boat (gig).

GLACIER: Whatcom County. For the creek, which derived its label from the Coleman Glacier on nearby Mount Baker.

GOLD BAR: Snohomish County. Although referred to as Gold Bar by early prospectors, the community was not formally designated until 1900, when the Gold Bar Improvement Company platted and named the town.

GOOSEPRAIRIE: Yakima County. Christened by John and Tom Fite when a goose made its nesting place on their homestead.

HUMPTULIPS: Grays Harbor County. Community name is thought to have come from an Indian word meaning "chilly region," an appropriate designation.

INDEX: Snohomish County. For a mountain, which was so named because a sharp pinnacle on top resembled an index finger.

LEADPOINT: Stevens County. For the Electric Point Lead Mine.

LIBERTY: Kittitas County. Designated in 1892 for a word in postmaster Gus Nelson's open invitation to "feel at liberty to do what you want; this is really your place."

LOOP LOOP: Okanogan County. Title derived from the French *loup*, meaning "wolf," and so named because of the abundance of furs garnered in the area by early trappers.

MICA: Spokane County. For mica deposits found in the vicinity.

MOCLIPS: Grays Harbor County. This is from the Quinault Indian language, and refers to a place where young Indian maidens were sent for puberty rituals.

NIGHTHAWK: Okanogan County. For a mine, which was labeled for a species of whippoorwill found in the region.

NINE MILE FALLS: Spokane County. For its location at a hydroelectric dam nine miles downstream from the city of Spokane.

OPPORTUNITY: Spokane County. When a contest was held to choose a name for this site, Laura Kelsey submitted Opportunity. Her prize was ten dollars (in 1905).

OSO: Snohomish County. Spanish for "bear," and was named for a town in Texas.

OUTLOOK: Yakima County. Refers to the widespread view (outlook) offered by E. W. Dooley's cattle ranch. It was on this ranch that a telephone toll station was installed to connect the ranch with Dooley's home in Yakima. "Outlook" was the call word used by Dooley.

OYSTERVILLE: Pacific County. A natural name, for the number of oysters harvested annually nearby. This is a nationally recognized landmark, and the town has, as far as possible, remained as it looked during the mid-1800s.

POTLATCH: Mason County. This is a Chinook Indian word meaning "to give," and relates to the feasts various chiefs put on as demonstrations of friendship. The community took its title from the fact that it is situated on the site of a former Indian potlatch house.

SHINE: Jefferson County. Townspeople submitted Sunshine as the name for their village, but the Post Office Department rejected it. They did accept Shine, the abbreviated form.

SOAP LAKE: Grant County. For the lake, which was named by early travelers for the soapy feel of the water, and the suds that gathered along the lake's bank, especially during cool weather.

SPANAWAY: Pierce County. Probably Indian in origin, meaning "beautiful waters."

SPANGLE: Spokane County. No glittering objects here, the village having been named for William Spangle, who platted the town site in 1886.

SPIKE TOWN: Pierce County. Honors William D. C. Spike, a mine owner.

STARTUP: Snohomish County. For George G. Startup, manager of Wallace Lumber Company.

STEPTOE: Whitman County. Salutes Lt. Colonel Edward J. Steptoe, who, along with 150 soldiers, was defeated by some one thousand Palous Indians in the Battle of Te-Hots-Nim-Me on May 17, 1857.

SULTAN: Snohomish County. For the river, which honors Tseultud, an Indian chief.

TIGER: Pend Orielle County. Remembers George Tiger.

TUMTUM: Stevens County. Took its name from the Chinook word meaning "heard," which the Indians pronounced "thum(p), thum(p)."

TUMWATER: Thurston County. This town's moniker closely relates to Tumtum, in that *thum-thum* was the word used by Chinooks when describing the sound of falling water.

VANTAGE: Kittitas County. A takeoff on the name of Van Slack, a ferryboat operator here until the Columbia River Bridge was opened in the 1930s, putting him out of business.

WELLPINIT: Stevens County. From the Nez Perce, meaning "meadow stream that disappears."

386 WHITE SWAN: Yakima County. For an Indian chief.

West Virginia

THE MOUNTAIN STATE

ADVENT: Jackson County. For the Advent Christian Church.

ALLOY: Fayette County. A company town owned by the Electro Metallurgical Company, and named for the ferro-alloys manufactured by the firm.

AUTO: Greenbrier County. The first horseless carriage that appeared in this area so impressed the citizens that they named their settlement Auto, short for automobile.

BALD KNOB: Boone County. For a treeless hill that rises above the town.

BIG CHIMNEY: Kanawha County. The community took its handle from the remains of a chimney foundation that was part of a saltworks located here in the 1700s.

BIM: Boone County. For Bim Gump, a character in "The Gumps" comic strip.

BLACK BETSY: Putnam County. Relates to the Black Betsy Coal and Mining Company.

BLOOMINGROSE: Boone County. For the abundance of roses in the vicinity.

BLUE JAY: Raleigh County. Relates to the Blue Jay Lumber Company.

BLUE PENNANT: Boone County. Also known as Red Dragon, the village carries the name of a brand of coal.

BOB WHITE: Boone County. For the bird.

BOLT: Raleigh County. Remembers George Bolt, the postmaster.

BOOMER: Fayette County. Salutes Boomer Huddleston, a settler.

BURNING SPRINGS: Wirt County. Christened for a hole discovered near here that emitted gas. When ignited, the gas would burn; thus, "burning springs."

BURNT HOUSE: Ritchie County. For a three-story tavern once located here that burned to the ground.

BURNWELL: Kanawha County. For the burning quality of coal mined locally.

CABIN CREEK: Kanawha County. Christened for a cabin once situated on a stream. The story goes that Indians kidnapped two of the children living in the cabin, killed the other members of the family, and burned the building.

CANVAS: Nicholas County. According to legend, this community was originally called Earle. Residents didn't care for the name and looked around for a new one. As it so happened, Bill Bryant owned a store, and one of the newest items carried was canvas gloves.

CASHMERE: Monroe County. Descriptive, for its valley location, which some say resembles the beautiful Vale of Kashmir in India.

CENTURY: Barbour County. So tagged because the coal deposit discovered here was expected to last for a century.

CHARMCO: Greenbrier County. Took its moniker from the Charleston Milling Company.

CINCO: Kanawha County. Refers to a brand of cigar.

CLEARCO: Greenbrier County. Took its name from the Clear Coal Company.

CLOTHIER: Logan County. A term normally applied to someone who makes or sells clothing. This town, however, was named for William J. Clothier, coal operator.

CLOVER LICK: Pocahontas County. For Clover Lick Farm. The farm name came about when the area was first visited by white men and they saw a deer lick near a field of clover.

COOL RIDGE: Raleigh County. This village handle came about through mistake. When a post office came into being in 1915, Leona Lilly was postmistress and was asked to provide a name for the settlement. She suggested Coolidge, for Calvin Coolidge, who was the president at the time, but it was officially recorded as Cool Ridge.

CORE: Monongalia County. Once called Pedlar Run, the name was changed in 1898 to recognize a local family.

CORK: Tyler County. For Cork, Ireland.

CORNSTALK: Greenbrier County. Honors a Shawnee chief.

CROW: Raleigh County. The earlier suggested name of Pine Flats was rejected. Douglas Scott, the first postmaster, was mulling over another name when a black crow flew overhead. The rest, as they say, is history.

CRUMPS BOTTOM: Summers County. Took its name from a nearby bottom (valley or river bed) once occupied by the Crump family.

CUCUMBER: McDowell County. For the creek. The stream name could have come from the cucumber tree, a species of magnolia that bears a cucumber-like fruit.

CUMBO: Berkeley County. Takes its name from the Cumberland Valley Railroad and the initials of the B & O Railroad.

CYCLONE: Wyoming County. Remembers a cyclone that struck here in the early 1800s. The windstorm is reported to have cleared a strip of land three hundred yards wide and fifty-six hundred yards long.

CZAR: Randolph County. This is a word denoting "ruler," and was one of several names submitted to postal officials by the local postmaster.

DROOP: Pocahontas County. The hamlet is located on the Droop Mountains, so named because they slope (droop) toward the east.

DUCK: Clay County. For the creek. The stream acquired its name from early times when settlers came to the railroad depot to ship or pick up packages, and there was usually a flock of ducks around the creek.

EXCHANGE: Braxton County. So designated because places of business "changed" owners so often.

FANROCK: Wyoming County. From sources available, in early days, when transportation was by four-legged animal, there were two post offices in the area, one named Fanny, the other Ox. As transportation modes improved, the offices were eliminated, and one was established halfway between the two former facilities. The name for the new outlet was Fanrock, with the first syllable coming from the name of the old Fanny office, and the second from the fact that there were many rocks in the vicinity of the new office.

FOUR STATES: Marion County. Christened by John H. Jones, mine owner, because he had four mines in four different states.

FRIENDLY: Tyler County. Honors Friend Cochran Williamson, a settler.

FROST: Pocahontas County. Community acquired its label either for its location on high ground, which lends itself to chilling winds, or from early settlers who were not used to the late spring and early autumn frosts common to the area.

FROZEN: Calhoun County. For the creek, which received its name when two hunters killed and skinned a buffalo near the creek bank. That night, when they went to bed, one of the men wrapped up in the untanned hide. During the night the temperature dropped steadily, and the following morning the man found himself inside a frozen buffalo skin. His partner had to thaw the hide to get him out.

GIP: Braxton County. Received its moniker through mispronunciation of the first syllable of the surname of the postmaster, Frank Gibson.

GREYEAGLE: Mingo County. Remembers the Grey Eagle Coal Company.

GUARDIAN: Webster County. Once known as Removal, because the post office was moved so often. The hamlet was renamed in 1937, for the Guardian Coal and Oil Company.

GYPSY: Harrison County. Gypsies once camped here.

HEATERS: Braxton County. Family name.

HIGH COAL: Boone County. So labeled because the first coal mined here was located in seams eight to nine feet high.

HORSE SHOE RUN: Preston County. For the stream.

HUNDRED: Wetzel County. Originally known as Old Hundred, having been named for Henry Church, who died in 1860 at the age of 109, and was affectionately called "Old Hundred." In time, "Old" was dropped.

HURRICANE: Putnam County. Official sources state that the town was named for a creek, which was designated around 1774 when surveyors came to the stream and saw evidence that a hurricane had been through the area. Local color, however, says the name came about when someone called "Hurry, Cain," to a man by that name during a rainstorm.

INSTITUTE: Kanawha County. Christened for the Colored Institute, founded in the 1890s. A most interesting story lies behind this town. Institute is predominantly a black community and acquired its start when Samuel I. Cabell, a white slaveholder, moved to the site before the Civil War. Cabell was an individualist, a man rare for the times. One of his slaves was a black woman named Mary Barnes, whom Cabell took as his mate. This was not an uncommon occurrence in the days of the "peculiar institution," but Cabell was an unusual man. He fathered thirteen children with Mary, had no other bedmate all the time he was with her, and took legal, ironclad steps to assure that Mary and their children were not only freed from the chains of slavery in the event of his death, but recorded a will stating that all his wealth was to be divided equally among the mother and the children. Cabell was allegedly murdered in July 1865 by white Union loyalists. The defendants were eventually acquitted due to lack of evidence, and to this day the exact circumstances of Samuel Cabell's death are unknown. While he was alive, though, this exceptional gentleman saw to it that his offspring were well educated. Since there were no black schools in West Virginia, he sent them to a private college in Ohio. Some of them became doctors, some teachers. The community of Institute came about in the government drive to educate Negroes. In 1890, Congress passed a law that, in essence, required states to educate blacks. Thereupon, the state legislature established the West Virginia Colored Institute. No community would accept the idea of having a colored school, but Cabell's daughter, Marina, sold thirty acres on which to build the school. Once the town was organized, Marina became its postmistress and is believed to have been the first black woman to hold such a position. The Colored Institute later became West Virginia State College.

JENKINJONES: McDowell County. Recognizes two early settlers, Jenkins and Jones.

JUMPING BRANCH: Summers County. For the creek. The stream was so named because in early days, before bridges were built, travelers had to jump the creek (branch) on horseback to get from one side to the other.

JUNIOR: Barbour County. Refers to the son of Henry Gassaway Davis.

JUSTICE: Mingo County. Family name.

LEFT HAND: Roane County. For its location on the left-hand branch of Sandy Creek.

LOOKOUT: Fayette County. Close by is a formation known as Spy Rock. This point was used in the past as a lookout by Indians, then later by Union soldiers.

LOST CITY: Hardy County. First called Cover, the name was changed around 1895, for a creek. One version of the stream name is that an exploring party became lost in the area, and a member of the party was separated from the group. The following spring the remainder of the party discovered what was left of the man—a skeleton—and named the stream Lost Creek. Another rendition is that early explorers found several trees in the area with the initials "T. G." carved into them. They deduced that the individual had gotten lost near the creek; ergo, the name.

MAIDSVILLE: Monongalia County. As the story goes, two unmarried women (old maids) once lived here.

MAMMOTH: Kanawha County. More than likely christened for the "large" deposits of coal, oil, and gas found in the vicinity.

MAN: Logan County. As the story goes, this village received its handle from the last syllable of Ulysses Hinchman, a member of the House of Delegates, 1866–1869.

MEDLEY: Grant County. Family name.

MONTANA: Marion County. Could be that a mine was opened here in 1889, the year Montana was admitted to the Union.

MOUNT HOPE: Fayette County. For Mount Hope School.

MOUNT STORM: Grant County. Village named for the mountain, which received its tag for the many storms raging through the hills.

MOUTH OF SENECA: Pendleton County. For its location at the mouth of Seneca Creek.

MUD: Lincoln County. For the river, which was probably named for the appearance of the water.

NITRO: Kanawha County. Hamlet started as a wartime city in 1918, being planned as a site for extensive federal manufacturing, and was appropriately named, since it was to be the site of explosives production.

ODD: Raleigh County. Citizens wanted a community with an odd name.

OMPS: Morgan County. Family name.

ORGAS: Boone County. For the Orange Gas and Coal Company.

PANSY: Grant County. For the flower.

PANTHER: McDowell County. For the creek. The stream received its name prior to the Civil War, when Tommie Lester came face-to-face with a panther. His gun failed to fire, and he survived only because of his hunting dogs and a bowie knife.

PAW PAW: Morgan County. For the tree.

PAX: Fayette County. Latin for "peace." As far as the village name is concerned, however, "Pax" is a misspelling of "Packs," and was supposed to have been christened for Packs Branch, a stream that saluted Samuel Pack, a settler.

PICKAWAY: Monroe County. The original spelling of this hamlet's name was Pique, and came from a branch of the Shawnee Indians of the same name. In earlier times, the Battle of Point Pleasant took place in nearby Ohio. Men from Monroe County were involved in the battle, and after a treaty was signed in the Pickaway Plains region of Ohio, the West Virginians returned home and brought the name Pickaway with them.

PIE: Mingo County. A resident was overly fond of any kind of pie.

PIGEON: Roane County. For the creek, which was so named because it was once the roosting place for wild pigeons.

PINCH: Kanawha County. For Pinch Gut Creek, with "Gut" being dropped with the passage of time. The stream received its name from an early incident, when a party of hunters was besieged by Indians. They were trapped near the creek so long they nearly starved; thus, the stream name came from their condition of hunger.

PIPESTEM: Summers County. For the creek. There once grew along its bank a small brush, the stalk of which was hollow and used for making pipe stems.

POVERTY HOLLOW: Ritchie County. For the poverty so rampant in the vicinity.

PREMIER: McDowell County. For an area coal mine.

PROSPERITY: Raleigh County. For a mine.

PURSGLOVE: Monongalia County. At first glance, this town name would appear to be a combination of two articles of women's apparel (purse and glove). The town was christened, however, for Samuel Pursglove, of the Pursglove Coal Company.

QUIET DELL: Harrison County. A commendatory name.

RED DRAGON: Boone County. Also called Blue Pennant, this village was named for a brand of coal.

RED HOUSE: Putnam County. For a large rock that was red in color. There is a second version, that the village was christened for a red house built here in 1840 by Joseph Ruffner.

RED JACKET: Mingo County. For the Seneca Indian chief. The chief received his handle from a red jacket presented to him by British soldiers during the Revolutionary War. Red Jacket didn't support the British cause, but followed the course his people wanted, and displayed brilliant military tactics on the battlefield.

RED STAR: Fayette County. In the beginning, this hamlet was named Star; "Red" was added later to avoid confusion with Star, Virginia.

RIG: Hardy County. Salutes Elmer L. Riggleman, the first postmaster.

ROCKBOTTOM: Boone County. For the Rock Bottom Coal Company.

ROMANCE: Jackson County. Remembers Mr. Romance Parsons, a new arrival in the community, whose first name attracted the attention of residents.

ROUGH RUN: Grant County. Named for a rough run (a stream that flows downward) from a nearby mountain.

RUMBLE: Boone County. Pays tribute to Walter J. Rumble.

SAWPIT: Boone County. Remembers a pit for whipsawing.

SHANGHAI: Berkeley County. Refers to the Shanghai Manufacturing Association, a lumber enterprise.

SHANKS: Hampshire County. This has nothing to do with legs, being tagged for Abraham Shank, first postmaster.

SHOCK: Gilmer County. Family name.

SISTERVILLE: Tyler County. This Ohio River town was named for two sisters, Delilah and Sarah Wells.

SKYGUSTA: McDowell County. Sometimes referred to as Skygusty. The moniker is an Indian word meaning "terrible at war." This nickname was given to Henry Harman, an early resident, who was fierce in battle and had several unfriendly encounters with Indians. Despite the many wounds suffered by Skygusta, he lived to the ripe old age of ninety-five, and only nature could defeat him in battle.

SLAB FORK: Raleigh County. As sources reveal, this wee village received its name when settlers moved into the area and felled trees, cut them into slabs, and built houses on the fork of a creek.

SMOKELESS: Mercer County. For the Smokeless Coal Company.

SOD: Lincoln County. Derived its label from the first postmaster, Samuel Odell Dunlop.

SPANISHBURG: Mercer County. For Spanish Brown, a settler.

STRANGE CREEK: Braxton County. Hamlet was christened for William Strange. He became lost in a heavily wooded area and carved on a birch tree: "Strange is my name/and I'm on strange ground/and strange it is/that I cannot be found." His skeleton, and the inscription, were discovered after a long period of time.

SUN: Fayette County. Derived from the Sunset Mining Company.

SUNDIAL: Raleigh County. Took its name from a brand of shoes sold in a local store.

SURVEYOR: Raleigh County. For a creek.

TAD: Kanawha County. Designation taken from the nickname of Talmadge Dunlop, first postmaster.

TANGO: Lincoln County. Some residents claim that the name came about when a man was lost in nearby woods and carved the word *tango* on a tree.

TENMILE: Upshur County. For the creek; the stream was believed to be ten miles long.

THREE CHURCHES: Hampshire County. Christened for three churches located here when the hamlet was first organized.

TOLL GATE: Ritchie County. Relates to an old tollgate on the Northwestern Turnpike, the construction of which was a favorite project of George Washington. The tollgate opened in 1838, but is no longer in existence.

TOMAHAWK: Berkeley County. Moniker comes from either the time there were three springs here in the shape of a tomahawk, or there was only one spring and a tomahawk was found in the water by settlers.

TRIADELPHIA: Ohio County. From the Greek, meaning "three brothers." The community label was either for three brothers, or for three men who were very close friends.

TRUE: Summers County. Early citizens petitioned authorities for a post office, listing all the reasons for such a facility, and ending their request with the statement, "All these facts are TRUE." They not only received the facility, but "true" was written so boldly it attracted the attention of postal officials and they recorded the village name as such.

TWILIGHT: Boone County. Selected by postal authorities from several names submitted by residents.

UNEEDA: Boone County. From the trademark of a brand of crackers sold locally.

UPPER TRACT: Pendleton County. Named for an early division of property, one section (tract) being described as Upper Tract, the other as Lower Tract.

VICARS: Roane County. No religious connotation intended, the community having been christened for W. L. Vicars, first postmaster.

WALLBACK: Clay County. Family name.

WAR: McDowell County. For the creek. The stream acquired its name during early days when it was either the scene of several Indian battles, or the trail used by Indian raiding parties.

WAR EAGLE: Mingo County. For a coal company.

WARRIOR MINE: McDowell County. Apparently named for the aforementioned War Creek, plus the fact that a mine entrance was discovered near here.

WIDEMOUTH: Mercer County. For the creek. The stream was so tagged because it is wider where it flows into the Bluestem River than at any other point from its mouth.

WIDEN: Clay County. Respects L. G. Widen, a railroad engineer.

WILDCAT: Lewis County. Remembers the once-prominent animal.

WOLF SUMMIT: Harrison County. Community acquired its name from two sources: Because it is located on the highest point on the B & O Railroad between Parkersburg and Grafton and, in part, for Peter Wolfe, the area's first settler.

Wisconsin

THE BADGER STATE

AGENDA: Ashland County. At the time this township was organized, a meeting was held to discuss various items on the agenda, one of which was a community name. To save time, citizens felt Agenda was as good a name as any other.

AVALANCHE: Vernon County. For a rock formation resembling a landslide.

BEAR TRAP: Ashland County. Christened for a trap used to catch a black bear even before a town existed.

BEETOWN: Grant County. In early 1827, Cyrus Alexander moved a large bee tree on this site and discovered a nugget of lead weighing 425 pounds. The discovery was called the Bee Lead, and from that evolved the name of the town.

BIG PATCH: Grant County. Named by Welsh miners for a large area of lead ore found in the vicinity. In Wales, people often refer to areas as "patches," so it was only natural they would call their find a "big patch."

BLACK EARTH: Dane County. For the creek.

BLOOMER: Chippewa County. Family name.

BLUE MOUNDS: Dane County. Christened by early French missionaries for three mounds that have a bluish tint, caused by copper ore.

BLUEBERRY: Douglas County. Named for the berry.

BROWN DEER: Milwaukee County. Originally called White Deer, because an albino deer was once spotted in the vicinity. Since brown deer were more common, however, the name was later changed.

BUTTERNUT: Ashland County. For a grove of butternut trees.

CALAMINE: Lafayette County. For the zinc oxide mineral mined locally.

CALVARY: Fond du Lac County. More than likely named for a convent.

CHILI: Clark County. This little hamlet received its name through a play on words. About 1880, the Northwestern Railroad built a line through here for local sawmills. The following year, officials traveled to the site to christen it with a name. The weather was cold and bitter, and none of the officials wanted to venture from the warmth of the railroad car. This prompted one man to propose: "Let's call this stop Chili, because it is really chilly here."

COMBINED LOCKS: Outagamie County. For the Fox River canal locks.

COMMONWEALTH: Florence County. For the Commonwealth Iron Mining Company.

COON VALLEY: Vernon County. For the creek, which took its name from the large number of raccoons that once frequented the area.

CORNUCOPIA: Bayfield County. Christened by F. J. Stevenson for the abundance of fruit growing here.

EGG HARBOR: Door County. Took its name from the harbor. One version of the place name is that a man by the name of Increase Claflin, the county's first settler, so named it because he found a nest of duck eggs in the harbor. Another version is comical. In early days, two ships were vying to be the first to dock. The sailors, caught up in the friendly competition of the moment, began throwing eggs at each other.

ELEVA: Trempealeau County. A man started painting a sign on a grain elevator, but bad weather set in before he could finish. The letters he had painted (Eleva) served as inspiration for the community name.

EMBARRASS: Waupaca County. For the river. The stream was tagged for one of two reasons. It is from the French *embarrase*, meaning "to obstruct" or "to entangle." When French lumbermen were in the area, they had difficulty sending logs downriver because of the many snags in the stream; thus, the name. A more whimsical version is that when early pioneers reached the shallow stream, they named it Embarrass because "they could see its bottom."

EMERALD: Saint Croix County. Designated by early Irish settlers for their former home, the Emerald Isle.

ENDEAVOR: Marquette County. Relates to the Christian Endeavor Academy.

EXELAND: Sawyer County. The Arpin Lumber Company and the Wisconsin Railroad built lines through here to reach the rich timber in the region. Where the two lines crossed an X was formed, and the village that grew up here named itself Exeland.

FAIR PLAY: Grant County. Originally called Hard Town, because of the brawling miners. Around 1841, some honest landowners discovered a lead mine that proved rich in deposits. Claim jumpers had their eyes on the mine and were determined to take it over, by foul deed if necessary. They hadn't reckoned with the landowners, who were not only honest but also brave enough to join forces to protect their property. Cooler heads prevailed, though, and a meeting was called, whereby "fair play" was encouraged. A rightful decision was rendered in favor of the landowners, who then named their mine Fair Play, as did the local community their town.

FELLOWS: Rock County. Family name.

FENCE: Florence County. Takes its handle from a method of hunting used by Indians. They would build a large brush fence, and behind the fence drive sharp stakes into the ground. They then forced deer toward the brush, and when the animals jumped the fence, they were impaled on the stakes.

FOOTVILLE: Rock County. For Ezra A. Foot, a settler.

FREEDOM: Outagamie County. Seems an old escaped slave by the name of Andrew Jackson once lived here. Jackson was well liked and was a familiar figure on the streets of what was known as Appleton. He was often seen and heard playing his flute and selling peanuts and popcorn to the children. When the township was organized, the proposal was to name it Jackson. Hearing of the plan, the old man would have none of it. He reportedly settled the issue by saying, "No, gentlemen. Don't call it Jackson, no sir! Call it Freedom, because here's where I got my freedom!"

FUSSVILLE: Waukesha County. Remembers an early settler.

GREENBUSH: Sheboygan County. Named by Sylvanus Wade, town founder, for his former home, Greenbush, Massachusetts.

HAPPY CORNERS: Grant County. Christened by Barbara Richards for the many happy times residents had at dances and other social gatherings held here.

HIGH BRIDGE: Ashland County. Probably named for a high railroad bridge constructed across Silver Creek.

HUMBIRD: Clark County. Refers to a well-known settler.

HUSTLER: Juneau County. Some question exists as to the exact origin of this place name. When the village was platted, one of the street names was Hustler, intended, as the story goes, that the "hustlers" would live there. It could have also originated when *hustler* meant "farmer," and the hustlers pestered the Omaha Railroad for a freight loading dock. Regardless of which rendition is correct, Hustler was the only name on a long list submitted to postal officials that was not a duplicate of some other place name.

INCH: Columbia County. This moniker might have derived from the old Gaelic *inis* or *innis,* meaning "island." *Inches* means "meadow" or "meadowland." Another possibility is that a creek was so narrow in spots that it was called Inch Creek.

IRON BELT: Iron County. Relates to the iron industry, once prominent here.

JERUSALEM CORNERS: Pierce County. Christened for a black family that entertained residents by singing spirituals.

LITTLE BLACK: Outagamie County. For the river.

LITTLE CHUTE: Outagamie County. From the French *La Petite Chute,* which was what they called the falls in the Fox River.

LOYAL: Clark County. Town named to honor its male population. It is reported that during the Civil War every eligible male in the community volunteered for military service.

LUCK: Polk County. This was at one time a stopover for settlers traveling from the Cumberland, Wisconsin, area to Taylor Falls, Minnesota. The trip was a long and uncomfortable one, and travelers felt they were in luck if they made it this far by dark. Possibly Daniel F. Smith founded the town and named it because "I propose to be in luck the rest of my life."

MAIDEN ROCK: Pierce County. Took its name from a rock, which Indian legend relates to some rejected romance.

NEW DIGGINGS: Lafayette County. Christened by miners who moved into the region around 1824.

PHLOX: Langlade County. For the flower.

POLAR: Langlade County. Honors Hi B. Polar, early English prospector and Indian trader.

PORCUPINE: Pepin County. Community was named either by early surveyors who saw a porcupine while surveying, or by Eli Place, a pioneer who shot a large porcupine and nailed it to a tree.

PORT WING: Bayfield County. For Isaac Wing, a colonel in the Civil War, and later organizer of Wing's Guards, a unit in the Spanish-American War.

POUND: Marinette County. Salutes Thaddeus C. Pound, who, although he never lived here, was a prominent lumberman, member of Congress, and later lieutenant governor of Wisconsin.

REDVILLE: Taylor County. Many early settlers painted their houses red.

RIB LAKE: Taylor County. For the lake, which acquired its name for its shape.

RISING SUN: Crawford County. Named by T. H. Wilder. When he first settled here, it had been raining steadily for two weeks. The following day, the sun came out.

ROMANCE: Vernon County. For its location among hills of beautiful forests, which lends itself to romanticizing.

SAXON: Iron County. Originally known as Dogwood, the name was changed in 1892. The present moniker has nothing to do with race or ethnic grouping. Rather, it comes from the time a man by the name of Grey, a longtime railroad employee, put mail on trains, afterward calling out, "Sacks on." After a period of time the nickname Sacks-on became more popular than Dogwood, and citizens decided to change the name, and altered the spelling at the same time.

SIREN: Burnett County. The first post office here was located in the home of its postmaster, a Swede by the name of Charles F. Segerstrom. His house was surrounded by lilacs, so Segerstrom rec- ommended the name Syren, Swedish for lilacs. The Post Office Department approved the name but changed the spelling.

SLINGER: Washington County. Refers to B. Schleisinger Weil, a store owner. The middle name was changed in spelling for convenience.

SOLDIERS GROVE: Crawford County. Army troops pursuing Black Hawk and his braves camped in a pine grove here.

STRUM: Trempealeau County. For Louis Strum, a state senator from this district.

SUGAR BUSH: Brown County. For a grove of sugar maple trees.

SUN PRAIRIE: Dane County. The prairie was named two years before a settlement was established. In 1837, a surveying party en route to a site designated as the future capital of the state (Madison) was besieged by cold, dark, rainy weather. Finally, as they reached the crest of a hill they looked down on a long stretch of prairie, on which the sun shone with all its glory. The town boasts of having the largest Sweet Corn Festival in the nation, held annually on the third weekend of August. Also, it carries on a tradition born at least thirty years ago, that of holding a groundhog ceremony each February second. Officials even issue a "Groundhog Birth Certificate" to people born on that day.

TOMAHAWK: Lincoln County. For the river. The stream was so named when a tomahawk was buried on the riverbank, symboliz- ing peace between the Sioux and the Chippewa.

UNION: Burnett County. Honors Union soldiers of the Civil War.

VESPER: Wood County. Hamlet was christened for the many vesper sparrows in the vicinity.

VETERAN: Burnett County. Also honors veterans of the Civil War.

VICTORY: Vernon County. Commemorates the Battle of Bad Ax, which was fought near here and ended the Black Hawk War.

WILD ROSE: Waushara County. The first settlers here came from Rose, New York, and wanted to name their new home the same. A woman in the group bent over and picked a wild rose growing in the ground. Since it wasn't the season for roses, the people mused if the flower was a portent of the future. The woman then sug- gested they call the settlement Wild Rose.

Wyoming
THE EQUALITY STATE

N

Big Horn
Pitchfork   Kleenburn   Recluse   Colony
                   Story   Ucross
Emblem   Aladdin
                                                        Sundance

                   Greybull
Nowood   Ten Sleep Saddle String   Four Corners
                          Ono
                   Kaycee
Thermopolis   Redman

Crowheart   Midwest   Verse   Bright
         Lost Cabin   Dull Center   Dogie
     Lysite   Badwater   Lost Springs
Sand Draw   Teapot
Freedom   Goose Egg   Node

                                                    Jay Em

                                                    Sunrise

                                                    Chugwate
Border Diamondville   Medicine Bow
     Nugget   Reliance   Vete
         Little America   Difficulty
         Red Desert   Centennial   Fede
Lonetree   Burntfork   Encampment   Tie Siding

ALADDIN: Crook County. For the character in the novel *Arabian Nights*, and intended to signify good luck and wealth.

BADWATER: Natrona County. For the creek, which was named by Indians because the stream often flooded.

BIG HORN: Sheridan County. For the river; which took its tag from bighorn sheep.

BORDER: Lincoln County. Sits on the Wyoming-Utah state line.

BRIGHT: Niobrara County. Personal name.

BURNTFORK: Sweetwater County. For the creek, which acquired its name from the burned timbers found along the water's edge.

CENTENNIAL: Albany County. Christened by S. W. Downey in 1876 because it was the nation's centennial year.

CHUGWATER: Platte County. For the creek, which derived its moniker from Chug Springs. The Indian legend surrounding the spring relates that in earlier times an Indian chief known as The Dreamer lived here. Too lazy to hunt buffalo the ordinary way (with bow and arrow or spear), he hit upon the idea of running the animals over a crumbly chalk cliff. At the foot of the drop was a stream, and the sound of falling water brought on the Indian name, "water at the place where the buffalo chug."

COLONY: Crook County. This settlement was intended to attract retired schoolteachers from the East who, it was hoped, would form a colony. The plan failed.

CROWHEART: Fremont County. For the butte. The hill probably took its name from the time a Shoshoni killed a crow on the site and ate its heart, a ritual to either gain strength or show strength.

DIAMONDVILLE: Lincoln County. For a type of coal.

DIFFICULTY: Carbon County. For the creek. The stream was so tagged when settlers were chasing Indians who had stolen their horses. The settlers attempted to cross the stream but became mired in the soft bottom. Only with great difficulty were they able to pull themselves free.

DOGIE: Niobrara County. Mrs. Reta A. Butler initially suggested Eureka as a community name, but it was rejected by postal officials. She then submitted Dogie, for a motherless calf she happened to see.

DULL CENTER: Converse County. Remembers Walter B. Dull, the first postmaster.

EMBLEM: Big Horn County. Originally called Germania by early German settlers; the name was changed during World War I, probably as a patriotic gesture, to honor America's emblem of freedom, the flag.

ENCAMPMENT: Carbon County. For the creek. The stream was so named because it was beside the water that Indians held their annual encampment. It was also at this spot that such famous mountain men as Jim Bridger, Kit Carson, and Bill Sublette traded with the Indians.

FEDERAL: Laramie County. Relates to the Federal Land and Securities Company, donor of the land for a town site.

FOUR CORNERS: Weston County. So labeled because the post office was situated where two highways crossed, thus making four corners.

FREEDOM: Lincoln County. Community handle came about during early Mormon settlement. In 1879, Arthur Clark led a group to this spot, located near the Idaho-Wyoming state line, and set up a colony. He named it Freedom because he believed, "Here we shall find freedom." His statement was to prove more profound than even Clark visualized. Idaho at the time was attempting to ban polygamy within the state. Wyoming, on the other hand, was encouraging settlement, so left the Mormons alone. When the Mormons became pressured in Idaho, they simply stepped across the state line to "Freedom." Later, after the issue had passed, a reverse crossing over took place when Wyoming residents walked across the state line to take advantage of lower liquor prices in Idaho.

GOOSE EGG: Natrona County. For the Goose Egg Ranch. The ranch name came about when the Searight brothers brought 27,000 head of cattle from Texas and established a ranch near here in 1877. Cowhands found a nest of wild goose eggs near Poison Spider Creek and took them to the cook. This gave inspiration for both the ranch name and stock brand, and eventually the community name.

GREYBULL: Big Horn County. For the river. Indians christened the stream after spotting an "albino" bull in the area, which, from that time on, they held sacred.

JAY EM: Goshen County. For the stock brand of Jim Moore, a rancher.

KAYCEE: Johnson County. For a stock brand.

KLEENBURN: Sheridan County. In 1920, a Chicago syndicate bought coal camps in this area and offered a prize for a name for the new operation. Kleenburn was the winning entry, and the town adopted that name.

LITTLE AMERICA: Sweetwater County. In the 1890s, S. M. Covey, a young sheepherder, became lost in a severe Wyoming blizzard. The temperature dropped to forty below zero and Covey vowed that if he ever again found a warm fire, he would one day build a shelter in this area so other travelers would not have to suffer as he had. Covey did survive, and true to his promise erected the first building here in 1932. Inspired by Admiral Byrd's colony in Antarctica, Covey likewise named his new settlement Little America. His venture gradually grew to include a thriving community of service stations, motels, restaurants, and shops and was visited annually by tourists totaling almost twice the population of the entire state of Wyoming.

LONETREE: Uinta County. A river stop long ago had a "single" cottonwood tree growing on its bank.

LOST CABIN: Fremont County. This community moniker came from the endeavors of John B. Okie, a self-made millionaire. Okie built a mansion here, which Indians called "Big Tepee." He then erected an entire village around his house and named it Lost Cabin, for the Lost Cabin Mine. Since this mine has never been found, speculation is rampant regarding both its existence and its location. One version is that prior to the Civil War, some Swedes discovered gold somewhere in the Big Horn Mountains. They built a cabin there but later were attacked by Indians, and all but two of the Swedes were killed. The survivors made their way to Fort Laramie, where they asked the sutler (storekeeper) to store some baking powder cans for them. It is rumored the cans contained about $7,000 in gold. The following spring the Swedes left the fort with the gold and were never heard of again. Another rendition is that only one Swede survived the Indian attack; he made his way to the fort, but died before he could revel the location of the mine. Still another opinion is that around 1849 Albert Hulburt discovered a rich vein of gold. He erected a cabin nearby, was attacked by Indians, and fled without leaving a landmark. Later, he and some men returned to the vicinity but were unable to locate the mine. The other men, thinking Hulburt had fooled them, wanted to kill him, but again he escaped. A final story is that Indians showed a man from Kentucky where the mine was located. He later built a cabin, but never revealed their secret.

LOST SPRINGS: Converse County. For a spring that appears then disappears into the ground several places during its run.

LYSITE: Fremont County. For a mountain, which was tagged for Jim Lysaght, with a variation on the spelling. Lysaght was a miner, killed by Indians in the 1870s.

MEDICINE BOW: Carbon County. For the mountain, which was named by Indians because it was here they gathered ash wood used in making bows and arrows. During the ritual of gathering wood, they held ceremonial medicine dances to cure illnesses.

MIDWEST: Natrona County. This is the main station of the Midwest Oil Company; thus, the name. It is reported that the first football game ever played under electric lights took place here in 1925.

NODE: Niobrara County. For a stock brand.

NOWOOD: Washakie County. For a creek. A cavalry unit once camped here and could find no wood with which to build a fire.

NUGGET: Lincoln County. Prospectors supposedly found some gold nuggets here.

ONO: Johnson County. A meeting was held to decide on a name for the community. Following each suggestion there would be a loud, "Oh, no!" Finally, in jest as well as desperation, residents decided on Ono.

PITCHFORK: Park County. For the creek; the stream took its title from the stock brand of rancher Otto Franc.

RECLUSE: Campbell County. For the community's "remote" location.

RED DESERT: Sweetwater County. For Red Desert, reportedly the world's largest body of shifting sand. It is red in color and covers some seven hundred square miles.

REDMAN: Johnson County. For the Indians (redmen) who once considered this their favorite hunting ground.

RELIANCE: Sweetwater County. For Reliance Coal Mines. Mines were christened by officials of the Union Pacific Railroad for the fine burning quality of the coal.

SADDLE STRING: Johnson County. For the strings cowboys used to tie extra clothing to their saddles.

SAND DRAW: Fremont County. For a sand draw (ravine).

STORY: Sheridan County. Honors Charles Story, a U.S. congressman.

SUNDANCE: Crook County. For the mountain, which was a religious spot for the Sioux, who held an annual sun worship here.

SUNRISE: Platte County. For the excellent view of the sunrise.

TEAPOT: Natrona County. For a large, almost completely eroded rock that once had a teapot spout and handle.

TEN SLEEP: Washakie County. A method used by Indians to compute time is the origin of this hamlet's name. They said this spot was "ten sleeps" from Fort Laramie.

THERMOPOLIS: Hot Springs County. From the Greek, meaning "hot city"; the town was labeled for local hot springs.

TIE SIDING: Albany County. This sparsely populated community was the terminal for the Union Pacific Railway in the late 1860s. Located in a heavily wooded area, the site was important for railroad ties, and as rail construction moved westward, the terminal retained its importance. In 1874, J. S. McCoole opened a general

store here, thus establishing an official community. Once upon a time, the place was an important origin point not only for railroad ties but also for telephone poles, fence posts, and many other products requiring the use of trees.

413

UCROSS: Sheridan County. For the stock brand of an area ranch, which was a "U" with a "+" underneath.

VERSE: Converse County. Some think the village moniker is from a family that once lived here; others feel it came about by deleting "Con" from the county name.

VETERAN: Goshen County. Received its designation because the community was formed in 1920 almost entirely by veterans of World War I.

Sources

ALABAMA

Alabama Department of Archives and History, Montgomery.
Birmingham News, 2 May 1962, 9 March 1972.
Chambless, Ann B., of Scottsboro.
Days, W. F., Postmaster, Magazine.
Escambia County Commission, Brewton.
Etowah County Courthouse, Gadsden.
Jefferson County Courthouse, Birmingham.
Mobile Register, 25 March 1956.
Pickens County Courthouse, Carrollton.
Quimby, Myron J. *Scratch Ankle, U.S.A.—American Place Names and Their Derivations*. NY: A. S. Barnes & Co., 1969.
Reform City Hall.
Smith, L. B., postmaster of Wing.
University of Alabama Library.
Washington & Greenville Advertiser, 7 December 1950.
Wolk, Allan. *The Naming of America*. Nashville: Thomas Nelson, Inc., 1977.

ALASKA

Alaska Historical Library, Juneau.
Alaska Planning and Management. Alaska Community Survey, 1972.
Orth. *Dictionary of Alaska Place Names*. 1967.
Phillips, James W. *Alaska—Yukon Place Names*. 1973.

ARIZONA

Ajo District Chamber of Commerce.
Apache County Superior Court, St. Johns.
Arizona Daily Republic, 18 March 1979.
Arizona Daily Star, 13 December 1976.
Arizona Historical Society, Tucson.
Barnes, Hill C. *Arizona Place Names*.
Coconino County Board of Supervisors, Flagstaff.
Hall, Sharlot, Historical Society, Prescott.
Leverton, John D., Scottsdale.
Mohave County Voluntary Action Commission, Kingman.
Palmer, K. T. *For Land's Sake*.
Roll, J. H., Jr., Postmaster, Roll.
Surprise Town Hall.

ARKANSAS

Albright, Eula, Harrison.
Arkansas Historical Association, University of Arkansas, Fayetteville.
Arkansas History Commission. *The Empire That Missouri Pacific Serves*. Little Rock.
Atkinson, J. H., ed. *The Pulaski County Historical Review*. 3 (September 1960): 39–40.
Baxter County Library, Mountain Home.
Benton County Historical Society, Siloam Springs.
Bishop, Duane E., Postmaster, Dogpatch.
Board Camp Postmaster.
Carroll County Historical Society and Heritage Center, Berryville.
Camden Public Library.
Cawhorn, Mrs. C. W., Morrilton.
Cheatham, John H., Blytheville.
Columbia County Courthouse, Magnolia.
Cragle, Larry, Postmaster, Forty Four.
Crawford County Courthouse, Van Buren.
Cross County Historical Society, Wynne.
Crowley Ridge Regional Library, Jonesboro.
Cupp, Jackie, Light.
Dalton, Glen, Pocahontas.
Deane, E. C., Fayetteville.

416

Democrat City Hall.
Desha, Drew, and Lincoln Counties Regional Library, Monticello.
Faulkner-Van Buren Regional Library, Conway.
Fayette Public Library, Fayetteville.
Fordyce News Advocate.
Fulton County Courthouse, Salem.
Fulton County Library, Salem.
Garland County Historical Society, Hot Springs.
Gaten, Novella W., Colt.
Gist, Mrs. Thomas H., Sr., Marianna.
Goodner, Norman, Waldron.
Hardy Public Library.
Harris, Mamie, Van Buren.
Hempstead Regional Library, Evening Shade.
Hurst, Mrs. H. R., Lewisville.
Independence County Chronicle, The.
Izard County Library, Calico Rock.
Jackson County Library, Newport.
Lancaster, Mrs. J. W., Harrisburg.
Lawrence, Mrs. J. R., Leola.
Lewis, Joe, Mayor, Success.
McInturff, Orville J., Marshall.
Marion County Courthouse, Yellville.
Meyer, Norman C., Busch.
Michel, Lillian, Clarksville.
Miller, E. John Wilson. "The Naming of the Land in the Arkansas Ozarks: A Study in Culture Process."
Mississippi County Courthouse, Osceola.
Monroe County Library, Clarendon.
Moore, Mrs. Caruth S., Evening Shade.
Mueller, Myrl R., Paragould.
Nevada County Courthouse, Prescott.
Newton County Library, Jasper.
Owens, Magora Wingfield, Murfeesboro.
Phillips, Jewell, Story.
Pinkerton, Pauline A., Postmistress, Umpire.
Pocahontas City Hall.
Poinsett County Courthouse, Harrisburg.
Pope County Library, Russellville.
Randolph County Courthouse, Pocahontas.
Scott-Sebastian Regional Library, Greenwood.

Sevier County Historical Society, DeQueen.
Sharp County Record, 8 August 1963.
Smith, Quinby, Mountain Home.
Stone County Courthouse, Mountain Home.
Stone County Library, Mountain Home.
Texarkana Public Library.
Union County Courthouse, El Dorado.
University of Arkansas Library, Fayetteville.
Van Buren County Library, Clinton.
White County Library, Searcy.
Williams, Harry Lee. *History of Craighead County.*
Wolf, John Quincy. *Life in the Leatherwoods.*
Woodruff County Historical Society. *Rivers and Roads and Points in Between.* 3 (Summer 1978).
Woodruff County Library, Augusta.
Wright, Betty, Postmistress, Rosebud.
Young, Betty H., Associate Professor of English, University of Central Arkansas, Conway.

CALIFORNIA

Bailey, Richard C. *Explorations in Kern.* Kern County Historical Society, 1962.
_____. *Kern County Place Names.* Kern County Historical Society, 1967.
Barnes, Jane, Nice.
California State Archives, Sacramento.
Coarsegold postmaster.
Eastern Madera County Chamber of Commerce, Oakhurst.
Fresno County Courthouse, Fresno.
Gudde, Erwin G. *California Place Names.* Berkeley: University of California Press, 1969.
Heritage Association of El Dorado, Placerville.
Johnson, Bettye, Postmistress, Diablo.
Joshua Tree Chamber of Commerce.
Kern County Library System, Bakersfield.
Kern County Museum, Bakersfield.
Nut Tree Restaurant, Nut Tree.
Polen, Gertrude, Postmistress, Shingletown.
Schindler, Val, Red Top.
Toulumne County Courthouse, Sonora.

COLORADO

Arapahoe County Courthouse, Denver.
Brush postmaster.
City of Fort Collins, Public Library.
Colorado Archives and Public Records, Denver.
Colorado Prospector, The. June 1972; August 1972.
Danson, Frank. *Place Names in Colorado.*
East Yuma County Historical Society and Wray Museum, Wray.
Eichler, George R. *Colorado Place Names.* Boulder: Johnson Publishing Co., 1977.
Golden postmaster.
Owen, Mrs. J. R., Hugo.

CONNECTICUT

Connecticut State Library, Hartford.
Edwards, Avis R., Postmaster, Tariffville.
Hughes, Arthur H. and Morse S. Allen, *Connecticut Place Names.* Hartford: Connecticut Historical Society, 1976.

DELAWARE

Hindes, Ruthana. *Place Names of the State of Delaware.* The Archaeological Society of Delaware, 1950.
Historical Society of Delaware, Wilmington.
U.S. Department of the Interior Geological Survey. *Delaware Place Names.* Geological Survey Bulletin No. 1245.
University of Delaware Library, Newark.

FLORIDA

Bland, Gladys S., Postmistress, Pinetta.
Bradbury, Alford G. and Hallock E. Story. *A Chronology of Florida Post Offices.* The Florida Federation of Stamp Clubs, 1962.
Captiva Memorial Library, Captiva Island.
Clay County Historical Commission, Jacksonville.
Collier County Circuit Court, Naples.
Florida Historical Society, Tampa.
Florida State Archives, History and Records Management, Tallahassee.
Franklin County Circuit Court, Apalachicola.

Gadsden Chamber of Commerce, Quincy.
Historical Society Museum of Valparaiso, Valparaiso.
Jackson County Public Library, Marianna.
Kidder, Virginia, Postmistress, Goldenrod.
Lake County Chamber of Commerce, Eustis.
Longboat Key City Hall.
Marathon Branch Library.
Marathon Chamber of Commerce.
Monroe County Public Library, Key West.
Monroe County 16th Judicial Circuit Court, Key West.
Morris, Allen. *Florida Place Names.* Coral Gables: University of Miami Press, 1974.
Mutter, Gaynelle H., Postmaster, Intercession City.
Santa Rosa County Courthouse, Milton.
State Library of Florida, Tallahassee.
Sweat, Elizabeth A., Postmistress, Balm.
Washington County Circuit Court, Chipley.

GEORGIA

Arabi City Hall.
Brinkley, Hal E. *How Georgia Got Her Names.* Lakemont: CSA Printing and Bindery, 1973.
Bryant, Susie D., Postmistress, Calvary.
Charlton Public Library, Folkston.
Echols County Superior Court, Statenville.
Elbert County Superior Court, Elberton.
Georgia Historical Society, Savannah.
Goff, John H. *Place Names of Georgia.* Edited by Francis Lee Utley and Marin R. Hemperley. Athens: University of Georgia Press, 1975.
Irwin County Superior Court, Ocilla.
Krakow, Kenneth K. *Georgia Place Names.* Macon: Winship Press, 1975.
Randolph Superior Court, Cuthbert.
San Marcos (Texas) Daily Record, 8 September 1985.
Southwest Georgia Regional Library, Bainbridge.
Statesboro Public Library.

Wilcox County Commissioners,
Abbeville.

IDAHO

Adams County District Court, Council.
Clark County District Court, Dubois.
Felt postmaster.
Idaho State Historical Department,
Twenty-Third Biennial Report of
(1951–1952).
Idaho State Historical Society, Boise.
Keele, Ruby, Darlington.
Owyhee County Historical Complex,
Murphy.
Shoshone County Courthouse, Wallace.
Turner, Joyce, Postmistress, Greenleaf.

ILLINOIS

Abel, W. M., Postmaster, Lowpoint.
Barge, William D. and Norman W.
Caldwell, "Illinois Place Names."
*Journal of the Illinois State Historical
Society.* 3 (October 1936): 189–304.
Bible Grove postmaster.
Brinkley, O. E., Postmaster, Timewell.
Brown, Mrs. Marion L., Aledo.
Bureau County Courthouse, Princeton.
Bureau County Historical Society,
Princeton.
Bussard, Mrs. Iris, Robinson.
Cairo Public Library.
Carloc, Don, Glen Ellyn.
Carmi Public Library.
Carnegie Public Library, Lewiston.
Carroll County Genealogical Society, Mt.
Carroll.
*Combined History of Edwards, Lawrence
and Wabash Counties, Illinois.*
Philadelphia: J. L. McDonough &
Company.
Fairfield Public Library.
Hagen, W. G., Jr., Postmaster, Golden
Eagle.
Henderson County District Library,
Biggsville.
Hoffman, Muriel M., Fairbury.
Hubbs, Barbara Burr. *Pioneer Folks and
Places: An Historical Gazetteer of
Williamson County, Illinois.* 1939.
Illinois State Historical Library,
Springfield.
Joy postmaster.

Loyal Order of the Moose, Mooseheart.
Marion Carnegie Library.
Matthes, Helen, Effingham Library.
Matthew, Melvin R., Blue Mound.
Normal Town Hall.
Ogle County Courthouse, Oregon.
Perrin, William Henry, ed. *History of
Effingham County, Illinois.* Chicago:
O. L. Baskin & Co., 1883.
Platt County Courthouse, Monticello.
Pontiac Public Library.
Quincy Public Library.
Sandwich City Hall.
Shawneetown Public Library.
Simkins, Patty, London Mills.
Totten, James E., Postmaster, Bone Gap.
Ulrich, E. J., Grand Chain.
University of Illinois Library, Urbana.

INDIANA

Baker, Ronald L. and Marvin Carmony.
Indiana Place Names. Bloomington:
Indiana University Press, 1975.
Barrett Memorial Library, Petersburg.
Bloomfield Carnegie Public Library,
Bloomfield.
Carnegie Public Library, Wabash.
Gray, A. M., Punkin Center.
Greensburg Public Library.
Hartford City Public Library.
Huntington Public Library.
Indiana Historical Society Library,
Indianapolis.
Indiana State Library, Indianapolis.
Jay County Library, Portland.
Johns, La Donna, Postmistress, French
Lick.
McClellan, Ruth M. *Price County History.*
Evansville: Unigraphics, Inc., Printers,
1976.
Mayfield Earl, Postmaster, French Lick.
Morgan County Public Library,
Martinsville.
Ripley County Historical Society,
Versailles.
Schultz, George F., Columbia City.
Twelve Points Merchants Association,
Terre Haute.
Whitley County Courthouse, Columbia.
Windfall postmaster.

IOWA

Corning Public Library.
Dilts, Harold E., Kathleen Ann Dilts, and Linda Jo Dilts. *From Ackley to Zwingle: A Collection of the Origins of Iowa Place Names.* Ames: Carter Press, 1975.
Gangestad, Leon M., Postmaster, Bode.
Greene, Barbara, Sergeant Bluff.
Iowa Department of Archives and History, Des Moines.
Iowa State Historical Society, Iowa City.
Lone Rock postmaster.
Remmer, Robert, Postmaster, Charter Oak.
Shelby County District Court, Harlan.
Winnebago County District Court, Forest City.

KANSAS

Friend postmaster.
Girard Public Library.
Grant County Museum, Ulysses.
Grogg, William, Howard.
Kansas Department of Archives and History, Topeka.
Kansas State Historical Society, Topeka.
Medicine Lodge Chamber of Commerce.
Morrill Public Library, Hiawatha.
Rydjord, John. *Kansas Place Names.* Norman: University of Oklahoma Press, 1972.
Smith, Mrs. Stanley C., Garden City.

KENTUCKY

Aflex postmaster.
Alice Lloyd College, Pippa Passes.
Allen County Public Library, Scottsville.
Allen, George B., Bandana.
Amburgey, Geraldine, Postmistress, Means.
Anderson Public Library, Lawrenceburg.
Arnet, Maralea. *Annals and Scandals of Henderson County, Kentucky.* 1976.
Ballard County Courthouse, Wickliffe.
Bandana City Hall.
Bath County Courthouse, Owingsville.
Beach, Mrs. James, Sr., Franklin.
Bevins, Ann B., Georgetown.
Biggs, Nina. *History of Greenup County, Kentucky.* 1951.
Blankenship, Betty L., Postmistress, Stopover.
Bow postmaster.
Bowling Green Public Library.
Boyd County Historical Society, Ashland.
Breathitt County Library, Jackson.
Brewer, Mary T., Wooton.
Brown, Opal, Morehead.
Bullitt County Courthouse, Sheperdsville.
Butler County Public Library, Morgantown.
Cadiz Public Library.
Calloway County Courthouse, Murray.
Campbell, Flossie H., Postmistress, Fall Rock.
Chaney, F. M., Postmaster, Wolf Coal.
Citizens Voice and Times. (Ravenna).
Clark County Public Library, Winchester.
Climax postmaster.
Combs, Edward, Postmaster, Quicksand.
Conley, Mrs. O. M., Postmistress, Burning Fork.
Conrad, William, Florence.
Cox, Mrs. Edgar L., Utica.
Crittenden County Historical Society, Marion.
Cythiana Public Library.
Dowden, J. C., Postmaster, Pleasureville.
Dowdy, L. F., Postmaster, Soldier.
Dwarf postmaster.
Dunn, Mrs. W. H., Stanford.
Eighty Eight postmaster.
Ellison, Mrs. M. W., Victory.
Ermine postmaster.
Estill County Public Library, Irvine.
Filson Club, The, Louisville.
Fox, John, Jr. *Christmas Eve on Lonesome and Other Stories.* NY: Charles Scribner's Sons, 1910.
Frye, Peter M., Postmaster, Yellow Rock.
Goody postmaster.
Graves County Courthouse, Mayfield.
Grayson County Public Library, Leitchfield.
Green County Public Library, Greensburg.
Greenup County Historical Society, Oldtown.
Greenup County Public Library District, Greenup.

420

Hackney, Bernice, Feds Creek.

Halo postmaster.

Hancock County Public Library District, Hawesville.

Harbin Memorial Library, Greenville.

Harding, George M., Bardstown.

Harlan County Public Library, Harlan.

Hart County Historical Society, Munfordville.

Hazard postmaster.

Henderson County Public Library District, Henderson.

Hendrickson, Virginia, Four Mile.

Henry, J. Milton. *Land Between the Rivers.* 1976.

Hiatt, W. L., Wildie.

Hicks, Dolores D., Postmistress, Tram.

Hodge, Laura, Symbol.

Hopkins County Historical Society, Madisonville.

Howell, Otis, Hodgenville.

Jessamine County Courthouse, Nicolasville.

Johnson, Arthur C. *Early Morgan County.* Ashland: Economy Printers, 1974.

Johnson, Eunice, comp. *Perry County History.* Daughters of the American Revolution, 1953.

Jones, Edna, Tyner.

Jones, Harry C., Lexington.

Jones, Mrs. J. A., Elizabethtown.

Keller, Dora, Postmistress, Lone.

Kenton County Public Library, Covington.

Kentucky Historical Society, Frankfort.

Kentucky Place Names Survey.

Kidd, R. Jewell, Postmistress, Co-Operative.

Kirby, Dixie, Irvine.

Klein, Theodore R., Crestwood.

Knox County Historical Society, Barbourville.

Krypton postmaster.

Kyle, Mrs. E. Arawana, Dawson Springs.

Laurel County Public Library, London.

Lewis County Historical Society, Vanceburg.

Lewis, Verlin, Stephensport.

Linn's Stamp News. 22 January 1979.

Logan County Public Library, Russellville.

Louisville Times. 21 October 1936.

Lovely postmaster.

Lynn, Mrs. Ralph D., Elkton.

Lyon County Public Library, Eddyville.

Madison County Historical Society, Richmond.

Marion County Public Library, Lebanon.

Marshall County Public Library, Benton.

Marshall, Phyliss, Postmistress, Gypsy.

Martin County Board of Education, Inez.

Martin, Mrs. Ruth, Postmistress, Democrat.

Mash Fork postmaster.

Meade County Public Library, Brandenburg.

Menifee County Public Library, Frenchburg.

Metcalfe County Public Library, Edmonton.

Milliken, Rena, Russellville.

Montgomery County Courthouse, Mount Sterling.

Moore, George L., Olive Hill.

Moore, R., Postmaster, Beauty.

Mount Sterling Library, Mount Sterling.

Mudd, Mrs. Raymond, Ready.

Nelson County Courthouse, Bardstown.

Nelson County Public Library, Bardstown.

Nicholas County Public Library, Carlisle.

Northern Kentucky Historical Society, Fort Thomas.

Ohio County Historical Society, Hartford.

Old Landing postmaster.

Overlook postmaster.

Owen County Historical Society, Owenton.

Owen County Public Library, Owenton.

Owensboro Public Library, Owensboro.

Pendleton County Library, Falmouth.

Pennyroyal Area Museum, Hopkinsville.

Pippa Passes postmaster.

Plank postmaster.

Printer postmaster.

Pulaski County Public Library, Somerset.

Quillen, Sam W., Neon.

Record-Herald. (Greensburg). 23 October 1975.

Reed, Rufus, Lovely.

Rennick, Robert M. "Place Names of Kentucky."

Rice, Edith, Postmistress, Eastern.

Rogers, L. A., Postmaster, Cobhill.

Roller, Carl D., Gravel Switch.

Rowan County Historical Society, Morehead.

Sarver, Amon R., Postmaster, Falls of Rough.

Shelby County Historical Society, Shelbyville.

Skaggs, Brownsville.

Smith, J. C., Postmaster, Marrowbone.

Sparrow, Ezra, Lawrenceburg.

Spoon, Amon R., Postmaster, Fairplay.

Stamper, Martha, Frankfort.

Talley, William M., McGill University, Quebec, Canada.

Tarter, James L.

Taylor County Historical Society, Campbellsville.

Thompson, Lawrence C. *Kentucky Tradition.* Hamden, CT: Shoestring Press, 1956.

Trimble County Library, Bedford.

Turner, Grace, Bakerton.

Tutor Key postmaster.

University of Kentucky Library, Lexington.

Vanover, Anna M., Postmistress, Closplint.

Warfield, Mrs. C. A. "Pewee Valley."

Watkins, W. M., Liberty.

Wayne County Historical Society, Monticello.

Western Kentucky University Library, Bowling Green.

Wheelwright City Hall.

White, Mrs. Bert L., Sandy Hook.

Whitley County Public Library, Williamsburg.

Williams, J. D., Hudson.

Willingham, Mrs. K., Fulton.

Willis, Mrs. Louise S., Rumsey.

Wilson, Jess D., McKee.

Wireman, Connie A., Fredville.

"175th Anniversary of Harrison County, August 11–16, 1969." Cynthiana Publishing Co.

LOUISIANA

Ascension Parish Library, Donaldsville.

Assumption Parish Judicial District Court, Napoleonville.

Audubon Regional Library, Clinton.

Bagley, Barbara Allen. "Tensas Can Be Proud." *Tensas Gazette.* (12 July 1957–6 June 1958).

Caldwell Parish Library, Columbia.

Creative Solid-Medics Corporation, Vienna, VA.

Douglas, Lillian. "Place-Names of East Feliciana Parish." (Type manuscript), Baton Rouge, 1932.

Evangeline Parish Library, Ville Platte.

Fortier. *Louisiana.* 1914.

Franklin Parish Development Board. "Franklin Parish Resources and Facilities."

Franklin Parish Library, Winnsboro.

Franklin Sun. Centennial Issue, 1956.

Hadnot, Jack, Leesville.

Iberville Parish Library, Plaquemine.

Jackson Independent. 17 December 1959.

Jackson Parish Library, Jonesboro.

Lamkin, Marjorie E. Tensas Parish. 1963.

LaSalle Parish Development Board, Jena.

Leeper, Clare D'Artois. *Louisiana Places.* Baton Rouge: Legacy Publishing Co., 1976.

Louisiana Archives and Records Service, Baton Rouge.

Modeste postmaster.

Moreland, Mrs. Julius, Monterey.

Mulhern, Rowena E., Rayville.

Oil City Town Hall.

Plaquemine Parish Library, Buras.

Pointe Coupe Parish Library, New Roads.

Robinson, M. A., Postmaster, Oil City.

St. John The Baptist Parish Library, La Place.

St. Tammany Parish Courthouse, Covington.

"Tangiapahoa Parish, Louisiana Centennial, March 23–29, 1969."

Times-Picayune. 24 December 1950; 14 September 1960.

Trees postmaster.

"Uncle Sam Sez Welcome." Pamphlet prepared by Freeport Chemical Co., Uncle Sam.

MAINE

McInnes, Postmaster, Old Town.

422 Maine Archives, Augusta.

Rutherford, Phillip R. *The Dictionary of Maine Place-Names.* Freeport: The Bond Wheelwright Co., 1970.

Snow, Roy M. Postmaster, Blue Hill.

Soldier Pond postmaster.

Stadig, Rita, Belfast.

Tucker, Payson W., Post Office, Merepoint.

MARYLAND

Allegany County Courthouse, Cumberland.

Allegany County Library System, Cumberland.

Allen, Irvin G. "History of Oldtown."

Artes, Dorothy Beecher. "The Legend of Indian Head."

Austin American-Statesman (Texas). 3 August 1982.

Calvert County Historical Society, Prince Frederick.

Cecil County Courthouse, Elkton.

"Chatauqua '76 Bicentennial in Cabin John, June 5, 1976, Souvenir Program." Cabin John Citizens Association, 1976.

Cresap, Michael, Museum, Oldtown.

Dorchester County Public Library, Cambridge.

Evening Capital. (Annapolis). 23 September 1964; 27 September 1971.

Flowers, Thomas A., ed. "Souvenir Book—Dorchester Tercentenary—Bay County Festival, 1669-1969."

Footner, Delbert. *Rivers of the Eastern Shore.*

Hall, Marion. *The History of Oriole and Its Satellites.*

Harper, J. S., Royal Oak.

Historical Society of Carroll County, Westminster.

Howard County Library, Columbia.

Jackson, N. A., Postmaster, Issue.

Long, Myra Thomas. *The Deal Island Story.*

Mitchell, Clara, Preston.

Montgomery County Historical Society, Rockville.

Papenfuss, Edward C., G. A. Stiverson, S. A. Collins, L. G. Carr, eds. *Maryland: A Guide to the Old Line State.* Baltimore: John Hopkins University Press, 1976.

Perry, Mrs. Robert H., Point of Rocks.

Public Library of Annapolis and Anne Arundel County, Annapolis.

Rockville Library.

Somerset County Library System, Princess Anne.

Talbot County Free Library, Easton.

Washington County Free Library, Hagerstown.

Washington County Historical Society, Hagerstown.

Wicomico County Free Library, Salisbury.

Windhaus, Darrell J., Postmaster, Boring.

Worcester County Library, Snow Hill.

MASSACHUSETTS

Barnstable Clerk of the Courts.

Bourne Chamber of Commerce, Buzzards Bay.

Freeman. *The History of Cape Cod. 2.* 1852.

Greenbush postmaster.

Plymouth Public Library, Plymouth.

Scituate city clerk.

Stenbeck, Hilda M., Archivist, Scituate.

Town of Norwell.

University of Massachusetts, Amherst, Library.

Works Progress Administration. *The Origin of Massachusetts Place Names.* NY: Harlan Publications, 1941.

MICHIGAN

Allegan Public Library.

Antrim County Courthouse, Bellaire.

Bayliss Public Library, Sault Ste. Marie.

Bellaire Public Library.

Benzie County Courthouse, Beulah.

Burdett, Harriet E., Post Office, Cement City.

Case, Leonard. "Benzie County: A Bicentennial Reader."

Descendants of Jacob Wiltse, Linus Frost, Henry and Francis Dice. Rockford: d. Unltse, 1975.

Devol, Robert P., Old Mission.

Dodge, Roy L. *Michigan Ghost Towns*. vol 3. Tawas City: Glendon Publishing, 1973.

Eldredge, Robert F. *Past and Present of Macomb County*. Chicago: S. J. Clarke Publishing Co., 1905.

Ellis, J. Dee, Lapeer.

Erickson, Wilfred, Atlantic Mine.

German, Robert W., Portland.

Hall-Fowler Memorial Library, Ionia.

Hamilton, Charlotte. "Chippewa County Place Names." *Michigan History Magazine*. 27 (1943): 641.

History of Bay and Tuscola Counties. 1883.

Joseph County Historical Society, Centreville.

Leedel, E., Post Office, Maybee.

Lough, Linda, Remus.

Macomb County Library, Mount Clemens.

Manistee County Historical Museum, Manistee.

Manistee County Library, Manistee.

Michigan Library Services, Lansing.

North Star postmaster.

Petoskey Public Library.

Public Libraries of Saginaw, Saginaw.

Romig, Walter. *Michigan Place Names*. Grosse Point: Walter Romig, Publisher, 1973.

Sandusky Public Library.

Traverse City Record. 22 January 1976.

Tuscola County Courthouse, Caro.

Watrousville-Caro Area Historical Society, Caro.

Wayne Historical Commission.

MINNESOTA

Anderson, Roxanne M., Post Office, Fifty Lakes.

Ceylon postmaster.

Northeast Minnesota Historical Center, Duluth.

Otter Tail County Historical Society, Fergus Falls.

Stewart, George R. *American Place-Names*. NY: Oxford University Press, 1970.

Togo town clerk.

Trail postmaster.

Upham, Warren. *Minnesota Geographic Names: Their Origins and Historic Significance*. St. Paul: Minnesota Historical Society, 1969.

MISSISSIPPI

Biographical and Historical Memoirs of Mississippi.

Blue Mountain postmaster.

Brieger, James F., comp. *Home Town Mississippi*.

Campbell, David E., Meadville.

Coahoma County clerk, Clarksdale.

Covington County court clerk, Collins.

Greenwood-Leflore County Chamber of Commerce, Greenwood.

Hudson, Marjorie L., Postmistress, Friars Point.

Jackson-George Regional Library System, Pascagoula.

Jayess postmaster.

Madison County-Canton Public Library, Canton.

Marion County Historical Society, Columbia.

Mississippi Department of Archives, Jackson.

New Site postmaster.

Pontotoc Public Library.

Smith, Maggie, Postmistress, Learned.

Stewart, George R. *American Place-Names*. NY: Oxford University Press, 1970.

MISSOURI

Anderson, Kim, Powersite.

Andrew County Historical Society, Savannah.

Audrain County Historical Society, Mexico.

Bollinger County Library, Marble Hill.

Boss postmaster.

Brown, Joe, Bell City.

Carnegie Public Library, Shelbina.

Christian County Library, Ozark.

City of Chamois.

Clarkson, Edna M., Postmistress, Blue Eye.

Cook, Albert W., Peace Valley.

Dallas County Historical Society, Buffalo.

Defiance postmaster.

Dobbs, Lyman, Rocky Comfort.

Fann, Linda K., Postmistress, Diggins.

Forsyth Public Library.

Green Castle postmaster.

Howes, Gladys, Dawn.

424 Kinderhook Regional Library, Lebanon.

Knox County Historical Society, Novelty.

Linns Stamp News. 24 September 1979.

Livingston County Memorial Library, Chillicothe.

Mason, R. K., Post Office, Noel.

Missouri Historical Review.

Missouri Historical Society, St. Louis.

Missouri Office of Archives, Jefferson City.

Moser, Arthur Paul, comp. *A Directory of Towns, Villages and Hamlets Past and Present of Laclede County, Missouri.*

Newkirk, Lula E., Maysville.

Owens, Mary, Humansville.

Polmateer, Esther R., Post Office, Kingdom City.

Quimby, Myron J. *Scratch Ankle U.S.A.— American Place Names & Their Derivation.* NY: A. S. Barnes & Co., 1969.

Ramsey, Robert L. *Our Storehouse of Missouri Place Names.* Columbia: University of Missouri, 1973.

Roberts, Mary A., Doniphan.

Schowengerdt, M., Warrenton.

Scott, Lois, Post Office, Neck City.

Scotland County Historical Society, Memphis.

Scotland County Public Library, Memphis.

Shaw, Lonee C., Greentop.

Skaggs, Tom, Clinton.

State of Missouri Historical Society, Columbia.

Stewart, George R. *American Place-Names.* NY: Oxford University Press, 1970.

Success postmaster.

Wayne County court clerk, Greenville.

West Plains Library.

MONTANA

Big Timber Public Library.

Cascade County Historical Society, Great Falls.

Carnegie Public Library, Lewiston.

Carter County District Court, Ekalaka.

Cheney, Roberta Carkeek. *Names on the Face of Montana.* Missoula: University of Montana, 1971.

Compton, Henry, Malta.

Dawson County District Court, Glendive.

Erny, Mrs. R. H., Port Angeles, WA.

Flathead County Library, Kalispell.

Glacier County Courthouse, Cut Bank.

Great Falls Public Library.

Haughian, Mary, Terry.

Hill, Mrs. Pete, Powderville.

Historical Society of Sidney.

McCormick, John R., Postmaster, Kremlin.

Martinsdale postmaster.

Meagher County Library, White Sulphur Springs.

Montana Historical Society, Helena.

Phillips County Courthouse, Malta.

Phillips County Library, Malta.

Powder River County Courthouse, Broadus.

Prairie County District Court, Terry.

Stillwater County Library, Columbus.

Thompson Falls Library, Thompson Falls.

Whitefish Chamber of Commerce.

Whithorn, Bill and Doris, Livingston.

NEBRASKA

Buffalo County Historical Society, Kearney.

Cherry County Genealogical Society, Valentine.

Cherry County Historical Society, Valentine.

Custer County Historical Society, Broken Bow.

Fitzpatrick, Lilian L. *Nebraska Place Names.* Omaha: University of Nebraska Press, 1960.

Grattan Township Public Library, O'Neill.

Harlan County Courthouse, Alma.

Link, John T. "Nebraska Place Names." Lincoln: Nebraska State Historical Society (collection of notes).

Nebraska State Historical Society, Lincoln.

Neligh Public Library.
Saunders County Courthouse, Wahoo.
Saunders County Historical Society, Wahoo.
Sheridan County Historical Society, Rushville.
Tomlinson, R. E. Bob, O'Neill.
Wahoo Public Library.
Wirka, Anton, Prague.

NEVADA

Carlson, Helen S. *Nevada Name Places: A Geographical Dictionary.* Reno: University of Nevada Press, 1974.
Churchill County Courthouse, Fallon.
Greater Reno Chamber of Commerce, Reno.
Humboldt County Courthouse, Winnemucca.
Nevada Department of Highways, Carson City.
Nevada Historical Society, Reno.
Northeastern Nevada Museum, Elko.
Pershing County Library, Lovelock.
Tonopah Public Library.
Urrutia, E., Postmaster, Battle Mountain.
Works Progress Administration. *Origin of Place Names.* Nevada State Writers' Project, Reno, 1941.

NEW HAMPSHIRE

Chaput, Arthur R., Postmaster, Suncook.
Fowler, William P., North Hampton.
Merrimack County Superior Court, Concord.
New Hampshire Records Management and Archives, Concord.
State of New Hampshire Manual for the General Court, 1977, American Guide Series, *A Guide to the Granite State.*

NEW JERSEY

Bisbee, Henry H. *Sign Posts: Place Names in History of Burlington County, New Jersey.* Willingboro: Alexia Press.
Ellis, Franklin. *History of Monmouth County, New Jersey.* Philadelphia: R. T. Peck & Co., 1885.
Emmons, L. H., Sergeantsville.
Genealogical Magazine of New Jersey, The. 1 (July 1932): 29.

Hoffman, Joseph E., High Bridge.
Liberty Corner postmaster.
Metuchen Borough Offices.
Monmouth County Library, Freehold.
Mowder, Harvey S., Washington.
New Jersey State Library, Trenton.
Ocean County Courthouse, Toms River.
Origin of New Jersey Place Names, The. Reissued by New Jersey Public Library Commission, Trenton.
Palmer, F. Allen. *Where On Earth Is Deerfield Street?* Cumberland County Historical Society.
"Place Names Bibliography." Gloucester County Historical Society, 1964.
"Place Names of Salem County, N. J." Salem County Historical Society Publications. 4:3.
Schmidt, Hubert G. *Some Hunterdon Place Names.* Flemington: D. H. Moreau, Publisher.
Scotch Plains Town Hall.
Van Horn, J. H. *Historic Society.* Historic Societies of Somerset County, 1965.
Zinkin, Vivian. *Place Names of Ocean County, New Jersey, 1609–1849.* Toms River: Ocean County Historical Society, 1976.

NEW MEXICO

Albuquerque Public Library.
Alamogordo Public Library.
Branigan, Thomas, Memorial Library, Las Cruces.
Church Rock postmaster.
Gallagher, Laurelle R., Angel Fire.
Hinshaw, Gil. *Lea, New Mexico's Last Frontier.*
Lovington Public Library.
Mountainair Civic Library.
New Mexico Records Center and Archives, Santa Fe.
Padillo, Mrs. C. B., Postmistress, Tome.
Pearce, T. M., ed. *New Mexico Place Names: A Geographic Dictionary.* Albuquerque: University of New Mexico, 1965.
Tucumcari Public Library.
Wier, Charles, Postmaster, Loco Hills.
Yeso postmaster.

NEW YORK

Albany Institute of History and Art.

Albany Knickerbocker News. 30 November 1973.

Albany Public Library.

Allegany County Museum, Belmont.

Association of Suffolk County Historical Societies, Brightwaters.

Barackman, Floyd H., Bible School Park.

Barnes, Joseph W., Rochester.

Bear, Jeanne, Greenville.

Beetle, David H. *Up Old Forge Way.* Utica: Observer-Dispatch, 1948.

Bell, Barbara H., Watkins Glen.

Big Flats Historical Society.

Bird, Carlton., Town (Triangle) Historian, Whitney Point.

"Brookhaven Villages of 1874." Brookhaven Town Bicentennial Commission, 1976.

Buffalo and Erie County Public Library, Buffalo.

Candor Free Library.

Candor postmaster.

Cannon Free Library, Delhi.

Carey, Dick, Huguenot.

Carnes, Ethel K., Cattaraugus County Historian, Great Valley.

Cayuga County Historical and Genealogical Referral Center, Auburn.

Cooperstown Village Library.

Delaware County Historical Association, Delhi.

Di Carlo, Marion. "Western."

Erbin, Mrs. Thelma M., Town Historian, Lowville.

Essex County Historical Society, Elizabethtown.

Finckenor, George A., Village Historian, Sag Harbor.

Fiori, James V., Town Historian, Endwell.

Frank, Maude E., Town Historian, Penfield.

French's Gazetteer of the State of New York.

Greene County Historical Society, Coxsackie.

"Guide and History—Town of Red Hook, N. Y." Bicentennial Edition, 1975–76, Red Hook Chamber of Commerce.

Herkimer County Historical Society, Herkimer.

History Center of Canton.

History of Oneida County: Commemorating the Bicentennial of Our National Independence. Utica: Oneida County Government, 1977.

Horseheads Historical Society.

Kahule, George, Victory Mills.

Kilts, Harlan D. Town (Lincoln) Historian, Clockville.

Kingston Area Library.

Larsen, Nancy, Painted Post.

Lewiston Town Office.

McAllister, Arden. R., Orleans County Historian, Albion.

MacDonald, Ray, Postmaster, Rock Tavern.

Meneilly, JoAnn, Inlet.

New York State A&I School for Boys, Industry.

New York State Historical Association, Cooperstown.

Oneida Historical Society, Utica.

Overton, David A., Patchogue.

Parrow, Rose T., Post Office, Sundown.

Peterson, Alice V., Town Historian, French Creek.

Polley, Cecil E., Margaretville.

Preston, Wendell, Sheds.

Purcell, Barbara, Town (Neversink) Historian, Grahamsville.

Purchase postmaster.

Red Hook Town Office.

Reymore, Eva, Central Square.

Roberts, John, Post Office, Salt Point.

Saratoga County Courthouse, Ballston Spa.

Smallman, C. Walter, Franklin County Historian, Dickinson Center.

Southern Tier Library System, Corning.

Speculator Public Library.

Starace, Carl A., Town Historian, West Islip.

Sullivan County Historical Society, Hurleyville.

Swatling, Muriel K., Ballston.

Thomas, Robin, Post Office, Fishs Eddy.

Town of Crawford Free Library, Pine Bush.

Town of Webb Historical Association, Old Forge (notes from file of Paul Reynolds).

Truesdale, L. T., Town and Lake George Historian, Diamond Point.

Ulster County Historical Society, Kingston.

Warren County Municipal Center, Lake George.

Wayne County Public Information Office, Lyons.

Wilson, John G., Wyoming County Historian, Warsaw.

Wood, Mabel. *Introduction to Big Flats, New York.*

Yeier, Brenda S., Candor.

NORTH CAROLINA

Allegany County Superior Court, Sparta.

Anson County Superior Court, Wadesboro.

Bemis Memorial Library, Robbinsville.

Beshears, W. F., Postmaster, Deep Gap.

Brown, George H. and Laura E., Washington.

Carter, Betsy M., Postmistress, Ingold.

Carteret County Public Library, Beaufort.

Caswell County Historical Association, Yanceyville.

Chatham County Courthouse, Pittsboro.

Columbus County Public Library, Whiteville.

Cook, Nellie, Pine Level.

Craven-Pamlico-Carteret Regional Library, New Bern.

Currituck County Library, Coinjock.

Dare County Superior Court, Manteo.

Davidson County Superior Court, Lexington.

Dixon, Wyatt T., Durham.

Durham County Library, Durham.

Eden Chamber of Commerce.

Flowers, John B. III and Margurite Schumann, *Bull Durham Beyond.* 1976.

Gaston County Art and History Museum, Dallas.

Gibbs, Douglas A., Swan Quarter.

Gibson, Gerald B., Postmaster, Pine Hall.

Grawley, Jackie, Brevard.

Greater Winston-Salem Chamber of Commerce.

Greensboro Public Library.

Halifax County Superior Court, Halifax.

Harmony postmaster.

Harnett County Superior Court, Lillington.

Haywood County Public Library, Waynesville.

Head, Susan M., Postmistress, Scaly Mountain.

Henderson County Public Library, Hendersonville.

Herring, Dallas, Rose Hill.

Hertford County Courthouse, Winton.

Hillsborough Historical Society.

Hurst, K. B., Jacksonville.

Hyconeechee Regional Library, Yanceyville.

Iredell County Library, Statesville.

Iredell County Superior Court, Statesville.

Keever, Homer M., United Methodist Church, Charlotte.

Kinston Daily Free Press. 24 April 1977.

Lee County Library, Sanford.

Lee, Mrs. Denton F., Smithfield.

Lincoln County Superior Court, Lincolnton.

Macon County Public Library, Franklin.

Madison County Public Library, Marshall.

Moore County Library, Carthage.

Moore, Elizabeth, New Bern.

Morganton-Burke Library, Morganton.

Morrison Library, Newland.

Neuse Regional Library, Kinston.

News and Observer, The. 7 January 1974.

Newsome, Mrs. Lloyd I., Ahoskie.

North Carolina Department of Cultural Resources, Raleigh.

North Carolina State Division of Archives and History, Raleigh.

Oakley, J. L., Postmaster, Providence.

Pack Memorial Public Library, Asheville.

Pathfinders, Past and Present: Davidson County, North Carolina. 1972.

Pender County Historical Society, Burgen.

Peterson, B. R., Clinton.

Polk County Public Library, Columbus.

Postmarks, A History of Henderson County, North Carolina, 1787–1968. Lenoir: Ray Adams Press, 1970.

Powell, William S. *The North Carolina Gazetteer.* Chapel Hill: University of North Carolina Press, 1968.

Pyatte, Martha A., Newland.

Robeson County Courthouse, Lumberton.

Rowan Museum, Salisbury.

Rutherford County Courthouse, Rutherford.

Rutherford County Library, Rutherford.

Sandhills Area Chamber of Commerce, Southern Pines.

Sharpe, Bill. *A New Geography of North Carolina.* vol 4. Raleigh: Sharpe Publishing Co.

Sheppard Memorial Library, Greenville.

Simmons, Abe, Marion.

Smith, Sam J., Lexington.

Smith, Culver H., Chattanooga, TN.

Stanly County Public Library, Albermarle.

Stumpy Point postmaster.

Suit postmaster.

Surry County Historical Society, Dobson.

Surry County Historical Society, Mount Airy.

Thomas, Walter, Spruce Pine.

Transylvania County Library, Brevard.

Tyrrell County Public Library, Columbia.

Union County Public Library, Monroe.

Vance, Ivor C., Postmaster, Plumtree.

Wake County Public Libraries, Raleigh.

Warren County Memorial Library, Warrenton.

Watauga County Library, Boone.

Whitaker, M. G., Postmaster, Horse Shoe.

Whitfield, Ann B., Roxboro.

Wilkes Genealogical Society, North Wilkesboro.

Wilson County Historical Society, Wilson.

Worthington, Sam W., Jr., Windsor.

Yadkin County Historical Society, Yadkinville.

Yadkin County Public Library, Yadkinville.

NORTH DAKOTA

Bottineau County District Court, Bottineau.

Divide County District Court, Crosby.

Forthun, T. A., Columbus.

LaMoure County Courthouse, LaMoure.

North Dakota Historical Society, Coleharbor.

State Historical Society of North Dakota, Bismarck.

Williams, Mary Ann Barnes. *Origins of North Dakota Place Names.* 1966.

OHIO

A Brief History of Riley Township and Pandora. 1932.

A History of Adams County. 1900.

Adams County Probate Court, West Union.

Alliance City Hall.

Belmont County Genealogical Society, Barnesville.

"Bicentennial Gourd Festival, Felicity, Ohio, September 5, 6, 7, 1975." (Newsletter)

Black, Paul R., Lore City.

Bowers, Brian F., Postmaster, Shadyside.

Bucyrus Historical Society, Bucyrus.

Cable City Hall.

"Cable, Ohio: Railroad Frontier Town— 125th Birthday, 1852–1977."

Carpenter, Eimer E., Firebrick.

Carroll, Audrey S., Ottawa.

Champaign County Library, Urbana.

Clark, Phyllis J., Postmistress, White Cottage.

Compton, Ethel A., Blacklick.

Defiance City Hall.

Dute, Georgia F., Postmistress, Shinrock.

Dwyer-Mercer County Library, Celina.

Eddy, L. D., Postmaster, Dart.

Empire City Hall.

Engle, Donna, Postmistress, Broadway.

Fisher, Joanne M., Union City, IN.

Forbes, Shirley C., Postmistress, Carbon Hill.

Fox, Mary M., Postmistress, Blue Rock.

Friedly, Julia, Convoy.

Gallipolis Area Chamber of Commerce.

Geirer, Merrel D., Postmaster, Pandora.

428

Gratis Town Hall.
Guernsey County District Public Library, Cambridge.
"Guide to Tuscarawa County." Federal Writer's Project, New Philadelphia, 1939.
Hardin County Archaeological and Historical Society, Kenton.
History of Cincinnati and Hamilton County, Ohio: Their Past and Present. Cincinnati: S. B. Nelson & Co., 1894.
History of Marion County. Chicago: Leggett, Conaway and Co., 1883.
Holmes County Public Library, Millersburg.
Krausser, John W., Felicity.
Licking County Historical Society, Newark.
Marion County Historical Society, Marion.
Marion Public Library.
Medina County Information and Referral Service, Medina.
Middleton, Judge Evan P., ed. *History of Champaign County, Ohio: Its People, Industries and Institutions.* vol 1. Indianapolis: B. F. Bowen & Co., 1917.
Morris, Naomi, Constitution.
Mount Healthy City Hall.
Myles, Jerome Paul, Liberty Center.
Newark Public Library.
Ohio Historical Society, Columbus.
Pandora City Hall.
Pomeroy-Middleport Public Libraries, Pomeroy.
Portage County Historical Society, Ravenna.
Public Library of Cincinnati and Hamilton County, Cincinnati.
Public Library of Steubenville and Jefferson County, Steubenville.
Rising Sun Village Council.
Rootstown postmaster.
Rupp, Ida, Public Library, Port Clinton.
Ryall, Lydia J. *Sketches and Stories of the Lake Erie Islands.* Norwalk: American Publishers Co., 1913.
Schmid, Betty J., Postmistress, Big Prairie.
Scipio-Republic Area Historical Society, Republic.

Seiler, Mrs. E. Jim, Greenville.
Shade postmaster.
Stout, Reba, Postmistress, Feesburg.
Tiffin-Seneca Public Library, Tiffin.
Torch postmaster.
Tuscarawa County Library, New Philadelphia.
Union Furnace postmaster.
Williams, Albert B., ed. *Past and Present of Knox County, Ohio.* vol. 1. B. F. Bowen & Co., 1912.
Witzleb, John H., Mayor, Seven Mile.

OKLAHOMA

Bowring postmaster.
Carnegie Public Library, Shawnee.
Carter County Courthouse, Ardmore.
Fox, Myrtle R., Post Office, Shady Point.
Gould, Charles N. *Oklahoma Place Names.* Norman: University of Oklahoma Press, 1933.
Idabel Public Library.
Oklahoma Historical Society, Oklahoma City.
Sallisaw Chamber of Commerce.
Seminole Public Library.
Sherrer, Leonard F., Postmaster, Snow.
Shirk, George H. *Oklahoma Place Names.* Norman: University of Oklahoma Press, 1974.
Stillwater Public Library.
Woodward Carnegie Library.

OREGON

Christmas Valley postmaster.
Clackamas County Historical Society, Oregon City.
Douglas County Museum, Roseburg.
Ironside postmaster.
McArthur, Lewis A. *Oregon Geographic Names.* Portland: Oregon Historical Society, 1974.
Oregon Historical Society, Portland.
Port Orford City Hall.
Salem City Hall.
Stubblefield, Cora M., Monument.
Sweet Home Chamber of Commerce.
Tanget City Hall.
Washington County Museum, Hillsboro.

PENNSYLVANIA

Adams County Courthouse, Gettysburg.

430 Annesi, Jacquelynee D., Postmistress, Presto.

Antoine, Sister Marie, I.H.M., Immaculata College, Immanencelata.

Arnez, Ralph M., Postmaster, Center Hall.

Ball, Catherine, Postmistress, Coupon.

Bean, Theodore W., ed. *History of Montgomery County, Pennsylvania.* Vol. 2. Philadelphia: Everts & Peaks, 1884.

Bedford Heritage Commission.

Biles, D. M., Skytop.

Brown, James V., Library, Williamsport.

Bucks County Free Library, Doylestown.

Carnegie Library of Pittsburgh.

Chest Springs postmaster.

Christian, Mrs. John J., Starlight.

Colt Industries/Crucible, Inc., Pittsburgh.

Delaware County Historical Society, Chester.

Diller, Mrs. D. L., Postmaster, Intercourse.

"Discover the Oil City Area." Oil City Chamber of Commerce, 1979.

Drifting postmaster.

Ellis, Franklin and Samuel Evans, *History of Lancaster County, Pennsylvania.* Philadelphia: Everts & Peck, 1883.

Espeshade, A. Howry. *Pennsylvania Place Names.* Baltimore: Genealogical Publishing Co., 1970.

Franklin Public Library

Gilland, Raymond C., Postmaster, Greenstone.

Goode, Mrs. Virginia, Washington.

Hahn, J. W., Postmaster, Crown.

Hall, R. C., Postmaster, Coal Center.

Heller, Bernard J., Postmaster, Mary D.

Heverly. *History and Geography of Bradford County, Pennsylvania, 1615–1924.*

Hill, Verla J., Postmaster, Needmore.

History of Butler County, Pennsylvania. Vol 1. R. C. Brown & Co., Publishers, 1895.

"History of Mt. Wolf, Pennsylvania as of 1886." History of York County, Pennsylvania. Library of Congress.

(Contributed by Congressman George A. Goodling).

Johnson, Mrs. Eugene, Lewisburg.

Johnstown City Hall.

Kreamer, Joanne, Lewisburg.

Lancaster County Historical Society, Lancaster.

Large postmaster.

Lefever, Jacob F., Smoketown.

Lowry, Thomas P., Postmaster, Blue Bell.

McAllbough, Stewart, Postmaster, Oil City.

McKean County Historical Society, Smethport.

McNamara, Dolores V., Postmistress, Ringtown.

MacReynolds, George. *Place Names in Bucks County, Pennsylvania.* Doylestown: Bucks County Historical Society, 1955.

Meginness, John F. *History of Lycoming County, Pennsylvania.* Chicago: 1892.

Miles, Bob, Postmaster, Distant.

Monroe County Public Library, Stroudsburg.

Montgomery County-Norristown Public Library, Norristown.

Morrison, Alice E., Titusville.

New Bethlehem Area Free Library.

New Castle Public Library.

Nu Mine postmaster.

Pilgrim Gardens postmaster.

Pillow postmaster.

Plasterer, Jerry, Post Office, Walnut Bottom.

Plum Borough, Office of the Secretary, Pittsburgh.

Pymatuning Township Office, Transfer.

Richards, Bart. *Lawrence County.* New Castle: New Castle Area School District, 1968.

Robeson, R., Postmaster, Smokerun.

Roth, Merl T., Butler.

San Marcos Daily Record. (Texas). 2 September 1979.

Scranton Public Library.

Seltzer postmaster.

Shaft postmaster.

Slickville postmaster.

Standard-Sentinel. (Hazleton). 22 October 1960.

Sugar Run Township Office.

Thomas, E., Postmaster, Railroad.

Tondorich, Katherine J., Postmistress, Mammoth.

Towanda Public Library.

Union County Historical Society, Lewisburg.

United postmaster.

Vajk, Mrs. Raul, Uniontown.

Walker, B. J., Post Office, Airville.

Wayne County Public Library Association, Honesdale.

Westmoreland County Historical Society, Greensburg.

RHODE ISLAND

Peck, Reginald E. *Early Land Holders of Watch Hill.* 1936.

Rhode Island State Archives, Providence.

West Greenwich Town Office.

Westerly Public Library, Westerly.

SOUTH CAROLINA:

Bishop, Joan H., Postmistress, Early Branch.

Charlotte Observer, The. 16 April 1978.

Cross, J. Russell, Cross.

Darlington County Historical Commission, Darlington.

Doyle, Mary Chevy. *Historic Oconee in South Carolina.*

Greenwood County Library, Greenwood.

Index-Journal, The. (Greenwood). 24 June 1978.

Lowell, Hollie B., Postmistress, Trio.

Names in South Carolina. Department of English, University of South Carolina, Columbia (Winter 1972): 48, and (Winter 1978): 5.

Neuffer, Claude Henry, ed. *Names in South Carolina.* Vols. 1–12. Columbia: University of South Carolina, 1972.

Oconee County Library, Walhalla.

Perry, Grace Fox. *Moving Fingers of Jasper.* Columbia: R. L. Bryan Publishing Co.

Rhame, L. Richard, Orangeburg.

Seyle, Mary A., G.R.S., Greenville.

Spartanburg County Public Library, Spartanburg.

Startex postmaster.

Watson, Margaret. *Greenwood County Sketches—Old Roads and Early Families.* Greenwood: Attica Press, Inc.

Works Progress Administration. *South Carolina: A Guide to the Palmetto State.* Workers of the Writers' Program, NY: Oxford University Press, 1941.

SOUTH DAKOTA

Dewey County Library, Timber Lake.

Faulk County Courthouse, Faulkton.

Historical Resources Center of Pierre.

Kennebec Public Library.

Marshall County Courthouse, Britton.

Mission postmaster.

Rapid City Public Library.

Sneve, Virginia Driving Hawk. *South Dakota Geographic Names.* Sioux Falls: Brevet Press, 1973.

South Dakota State Game Lodge, Custer.

Sturgis Public Library.

Tripp County Library.

Works Progress Administration. *South Dakota Place Names.* Vermillion: University of South Dakota, 1940.

Ziebach County Courthouse, Dupree.

TENNESSEE

Adams Memorial Library, Woodburg.

Aiken, Leona Taylor. *Donelson, Tennessee: Its History and Landmarks.*

Alderman, Pat. *Wonder of the Unakas— Unicoi County.*

Austin American-Statesman. (Texas). 17 October 1982.

Barker, D. M., Postmaster, Readyville.

Bell Buckle Town Office.

Blunt County Library, Maryville.

Carr, John. *Early Times in Middle Tennessee.* Nashville: Parthenon Press.

Carter, Mrs. Claude A. Marymaud, G.R.S., Lawrenceburg.

Cash, Marie, Postmistress, Reverie.

Chattanooga-Hamilton County Bicentennial Library, Chattanooga.

Chattanooga Times. 4 June 1916.

Cherry, Lex, Red Boiling Springs.

Chestnut Mound postmaster.

Clay County Public Library, Celina.

Crockett County Historical Society, Alamo.

Decatur County Courthouse, Sugar Tree.

Durrett, Mrs. Charles, Springfield.

432 Fentress County Historical Society, Pall
Mall.

Ford, Jerry R., Lauderdale County
Historian, Ripley.

Frytag, Ethel and Glena Kreis Ott, *A
History of Morgan County, Tennessee*.
Specialty Printing Co., 1971.

Gift, Robert, Memphis.

Giles County Historical Society, Pulaski.

Haney, Charles H., Jr., Postmaster, Minor
Hill.

Harris, Lloyd, Mayor, Finger.

Hickman County Public Library,
Centerville.

History of Tennessee. Part 2. Nashville:
Goodspeed Publishing Co., 1887.

Hollow Rock City Hall.

Horne, David J., Mountain City.

Humphreys County Historical Society,
Waverly.

Hyder, Sandra Webb, Postmistress,
Reliance.

Jones, Sue, Postmistress, Campaign.

Knoxville–Knox County Public Library,
Knoxville.

Lincoln County Public Library,
Fayetteville.

Looney, Faylah D., Postmistress, Iron
City.

McClain, Iris Hopkins. *A History of
Stewart County, Tennessee*. 1965.

McMinnville at a Milestone.

Mangrum, Bonita, McMinnville.

Murray County Public Library,
Columbia.

Memphis-Shelby County Public Library
and Information Center, Memphis.

Peacher, Ruby Tippit, Indian Mound.

Peeler, Tom, Mayor, Greenback.

Peters, Kate Johnson. *Lauderdale County:
From the Earliest Times*. Ripley: Sugar
Hill-Lauderdale County Library,
1957.

Public Library of Nashville and
Davidson County, Nashville.

Red Boiling Springs City Hall.

San Marco Daily Record. (Texas) 9 May
1979; 23 August 1979.

Smith, W. T., Postmaster, Silver Point.

Stewart County Public Library, Dover.

Tennessee State Library and Archives,
Nashville.

Tindell, Ted. Blount County Communities.

Unicoi County Public Library, Erwin.

Van Norstran, Clem E., Wartburg.

Webster, Thomas G., DeKalb County
Historian, Smithville.

Works Progress Administration.
Tennessee: A Guide to the State. Federal
Writers' Project. NY: The Viking Press,
1939.

TEXAS

Austin American-Statesman. 1 November
1980; 21 March 1982; 5 August 1982;
4 October 1983; 11 December 1983.

Abilene Public Library System.

Alice Public Library.

Baylor County Free Library, Seymour.

Bexar County Courthouse, San Antonio.

Bennett, Carmen Taylor. *Our Roots Grow
Deep: A History of Cottle County*.
Floydada: Blanco Offset Printing Co.,
1970.

Burnet Free Library.

Carson County Square House Museum,
Panhandle.

Carthage Circulating Book Club. *History
of Panola County*. Carthage: 1935.

Carthage Service League Library.

Cass County Courthouse, Linden.

Castro County Courthouse, Dimmitt.

Centennial Memorial Library of
Eastland.

Cherokee County Heritage Association,
Alto.

Clark, Pat B. *The History of Clarksville and
Old Red River County*. Dallas: Mathis,
Van Nort & Co., 1937.

Corpus Christi Caller-Times. 1 May 1960.

Crofford, Lena H. *Pioneers on the Nueces*.
San Antonio: Naylor Co., 1963.

Dawson County Public Library, Lamesa.

DeWitt County Historical Museum,
Cuero.

"Diamond Jubilee—75th Anniversary of
Castro County, Texas, August 11–20,
1966."

Early City Hall.

Evans, Grace (Moran). *Swisher County History.* Wichita Falls: Nortex Press, 1977.

"Eyes of Texas." Channel 12 (Television), San Antonio, 18 August 1979.

Falls County Historical Survey Committee, Marlin.

Biggs, Mrs. Clane R. "Candle Lights of Oatmeal Community."

Gonzales County Historical Commission.

Gray, Mrs. Elmer, Llano.

Hale County Historical Commission, Plainview.

Hall, Mrs. Roy F., McKinney.

Havins, T. R. *Something Brown (A History of Brown County).* Brownwood: Banner Printing Co., 1958.

Houston County Historical Commission, Crockett.

Hutchison County Library, Borger.

Junction City Hall.

Kaufman County Library, Kaufman.

Kelley, Dayton, ed. *Handbook of Waco, McLennan County, Texas.* 1972.

Kendall County District Court, Boerne.

Kunkel, Grace M., Bastrop.

Laine, Tanner. *What's In a Name?* Hereford: Pioneer Book Publishers, 1971.

Leon County Courthouse, Centerville.

Limestone County Historical Museum, Groesbeck.

Llano County Historical Association, Llano.

Llano News, The. 14 December 1978.

Love, Annie Carpenter. *History of Navarro County.* Dallas: Southwest Press, 1933.

Lubbock City-County Library, Lubbock.

Madison, Virginia and Stillwell, Hallie. *How Come It's Called That?* Albuquerque: University of New Mexico Press, 1958.

Martin County Courthouse, Stanton.

Massengill, Fred I. *Texas Towns.* 1936.

Montgomery County Courthouse, Conroe.

Motley County Courthouse, Matador.

Neal, Bill. *The Last Frontier: The Story of Hardeman County.* Quanah, TX.

Nueces County Historical Society. *The History of Nueces County.* Austin: Jenkins Publishing Co., 1972.

Parker County Courthouse, Weatherford.

Parmer County Historical Society. *A History of Parmer County.* Vol 1. Quanah, TX: Nortex Press, 1974.

Polk County Courthouse, Livingston.

Polk County Historical Commission, Livingston.

Pool, William C. *Bosque Territory: A History of an Agrarian Community.* Clifton: Chaparral Press, 1964.

Quillan, Garrison, Angleton.

Ramsey, Allan, E., Santo.

Richardson, Rupert, Dr., Hardin-Simmons University, Abilene.

Rusk County Courthouse, Henderson.

South Texas Drummer, The. 18 January 1979.

Spikes, Nellie Witt and Temple Ann Ellis, *Through the Years: A History of Crosby County, Texas.* San Antonio: Naylor Co., 1952.

Tarpley, Fred. *Place Names of Northeast Texas.* Commerce: East Texas State University, 1969.

Texas Monthly Magazine. April 1982.

Tyler, Ron et al., ed. *The New Handbook of Texas.* 6 vols. Austin: The Texas State Historical Association, 1996.

Tyrrell Historical Library, Beaumont.

Van Horn City-County Library, Van Horn.

Victoria Public Library.

Waco-McLennan County Library, Waco.

Webb, Walter Prescott et al. *The Handbook of Texas.* 3 vols. Austin: The Texas State Historical Commission, 1952.

Weyland, Leonie Rummel and Houston Wade, *An Early History of Fayette County.* LaGrange Journal Plant, 1936.

White Settlement City Hall.

Williams, Annie Lee. *A History of Wharton County: 1846–1961.* Austin: Von Boeckmann-Jones Co., 1964.

Williamson County Historical Commission, Liberty Hill.

Wilson County Historical Commission, Floresville.

Winfrey, Dorman H. *A History of Rusk County, Texas.* Waco: Texian Press, 1961.

Wise County Historical Survey Committee. Rosalie Gregg, ed. *Wise County History: A Link with the Past.* Northex Press, 1975.

UTAH

Baker, Mary, Postmistress, Snowbird.

Division of Utah State History, Salt Lake City.

Flaming Gorge National History Association, Dutch John.

Muir, Karleen, Rubys Inn.

Piute County Courthouse, Junction.

Porter, Myrl H., Tooele.

Utah Archives and Records Service, Salt Lake City.

Van Cott, John, Brigham Young University, Provo.

White Rocks postmaster.

Works Progress Administration. *Origins of Utah Place Names.* Utah Writers' Project. Utah State Department of Public Instruction, 1941.

VERMONT

DeLong, Alice, Moretown.

Essex County Herald, The. 11 August 1950.

Essex County Superior Court, Guildhall.

Hagerman, Robert L., Assistant Editor of State Papers, Montpelier.

Swift, Ether Munroe. *Vermont Place Names.* Battleboro: Stephen Greene Press, 1977.

VIRGINIA

Baird, L. W., Postmaster, Ebony.

Big Island postmaster.

Big Stone Gap Chamber of Commerce.

Clougherty, Hugh E., Postmaster, Broadway.

Fairfax County Public Library, Fairfax.

Glocester Historical Committee.

Hanson, Raus McDill. *Virginia Place Names.* Verona: McClure Press, 1969.

Hensley, Pearl Dinkins, Whitetop.

Hohnan, H. S., Lawrenceville.

Israel, Walter C., Honaker.

Ivy postmaster.

Jefferson-Madison Regional Library, Charlottesville.

Kenny, Welby R., Postmaster, Upperville.

Kent, William B. *A History of Saltville.* Radford: Commonwealth Press, Inc., 1955.

Kimball, Louise, Postmistress, Cardinal.

Lockerman, Alex, Postmaster, Gasburg.

Mathews Memorial Library.

Mission Home postmaster.

Owen, W. L., Postmaster, Paces.

Providence Forge postmaster.

Robbins, Mrs. Ernest, Banner.

Russell County Courthouse, Lebanon.

Tanner, Douglas W. "Madison County Place Names." Occasional Publication No. 21, Virginia Place Names Society.

Turpin, Gene, Postmaster, Saltville.

University of Virginia Library, Charlottesville.

Willis, A. G., Postmaster, Lignum.

Wiltshire, Maud P., Post Office, Mine Run.

Works Progress Administration. *History of the Town of "Drill," Virginia.* Russell County, 1937.

WASHINGTON

Clough, Jean, Glacier.

Hull, Carol, Postmistress, White Swan.

Jarvis, Barbara, Oysterville.

Meany, Edmond S. *Origin of Washington Geographic Names.* Seattle: University of Washington Press, 1923.

Phillips, James W. *Washington State Place Names.* Seattle: University of Washington Press, 1971.

Pierce County Library, Tacoma.

Soap Lake Chamber of Commerce.

Spokane County Library, Spokane.

Stevens County Historical Society, Addy.

WEST VIRGINIA

Boone-Madison Public Library, Madison.

Bryant, Rosalea, Postmistress, Canvas.

Chambers, Arlene, Postmistress, Bolt.

Comstock, Jim. *The West Virginia Heritage Encyclopedia.* 1976.

Elkins-Randolph Public Library, Elkins.

Fayette County Public Library, Fayetteville.

Frame postmaster.

Haught, James A. "Institute: It Springs From Epic Love Story." *West Virginia History.* 2 (January 1971): 101–107.

Hedrick, Charles B. *Official Blue Book of Mercer County, West Virginia.* Mercer County Blue Book Association, 1931.

Kenny, Hamil. *West Virginia Place Names.* Piedmont: Place Names Press.

Kith and Kin of Boone County, West Virginia. Madison: Boone County Genealogical Society, 1977.

Krebs, Charles E. *West Virginia Geological Survey.* 1916.

Left Hand postmaster.

Long, Betty, Postmistress, Sundial.

McCallister, Wanda, Postmistress, Sod.

McClure, J. F., Hamlin.

McDowell County History. Fort Worth, TX: University Supply and Equipment Co., 1959.

Martin, M. M., Postmaster, Slab Fork.

Nottingham, J. B., Postmaster, Duck.

Parker, Georgia M., Postmistress, Maidsville.

Puchy, Alfred E., Coalwood.

Raleigh County Historical Society, Beckley.

Rib postmaster.

Roberts, Evelyn, Postmistress, Cool Ridge.

Rowe, Frances D., Postmistress, Wolf Summit.

Sexton, Syvella D., Postmistress, Auto.

Shamblen, Howard E., Postmaster, Mammoth.

Sharp, Jane P., *The Pocahontas Times.*

Spears, Barbara, Postmistress, Saltpetre.

Thomas, Nona M., Postmistress, Fanrock.

Thrash, Marguerite, Petroleum.

West Virginia Division of Archives and History, Charleston.

West Virginia State Gazetteer and Business Directory. Detroit: R. L. Polk & Co., 1904–1905.

WISCONSIN

Ashland Town Clerk, High Bridge.

Austin American-Statesman. (Texas). 12 July 1982.

Bayfield County Historical Society, Port Wing.

Demby, Mrs. Robert, Arena.

Gard, Robert E. and L. G. Sorden, *The Romance of Wisconsin Place Names.* NY: October House Inn, 1968.

Gilbertson, Lester, Postmaster, Coon Valley.

Greenbush Town Hall.

Humbird postmaster.

Lafayette County Courthouse, Darlington.

Lee, Willard, Postmaster, Star Prairie.

Malone, C. E., Pound.

Phlox postmaster.

Pound postmaster.

St. Croix County Library System, New Richmond.

Sun Prairie Chamber of Commerce.

Volm, Denice, Postmistress, Bryant.

WYOMING

Carlisle, Charlotte, Diamondville.

Converse County Courthouse, Douglas.

Converse County Library, Douglas.

Hinton, Nancy. *The Douglas Budget.* Douglas.

Lonetree postmaster.

Natrona County Public Library, Casper.

Sweetwater County Historical Museum, Green River.

Urbanek, Mae. *Wyoming Place Names.* Boulder, CO: Johnson Publishing Co., 1974.

GENERAL

Caldwell, Erskine, ed. *Corn Country.* NY: Duell, Sloan & Pearce, 1947.

King, Mrs. Seminara, Interlibrary Loan Department, Southwest Texas State University, San Marcos.

Quimby, Myron J. *Scratch Ankle, U.S.A.— American Place Names and Their Derivation.* NY: A. S. Barnes & Co., 1969.

Stewart, George R. *American Place-Names.* NY: Oxford University Press, 1970.

About the Author

Don Blevins is a freelance writer and researcher. His work has been published in more than forty journals and magazines, including *True West, Carolina Country, American History Illustrated, Minnesota Monthly,* and the *Old Farmer's Almanac.* A native of Johnson City, Tennessee, he is a member of the Texas State Historical Association and lives with his wife, Esther, in San Marcos, Texas.

Printed in the USA
CPSIA information can be obtained
at www.ICGtesting.com
JSHW012018140824
68134JS00033B/2756